101

ANNA BUCCIARELLI

Watercolor
Secrets

ESSENTIAL INSIGHTS AND TECHNIQUES FOR PAINTERS

101 Watercolor Secrets

ANNA BUCCIARELLI (annabucciarelli.com)

Editor: Jocelyn Howell
Project manager: Lisa Brazieal
Marketing coordinator: Koryn Olage
Layout and type: Anthony Paular Design
Front cover design: Frances Baca
Cover production: Anthony Paular Design

ISBN: 979-8-88814-253-0
1st Edition (4th printing)
© 2025 Anna Bucciarelli

Rocky Nook Inc.
1010 B Street, Suite 350
San Rafael, CA 94901
USA
www.rockynook.com
info@rockynook.com
(415) 747-8756

Represented in the E.U. by:
Rheinwerk Verlag GmbH
Rheinwerkallee 4
53227 Bonn
Germany
service@rheinwerk-verlag.de

Distributed in the UK and Europe by Publishers Group UK
Distributed in the U.S. and all other territories by Publishers Group West

Library of Congress Control Number: 2024937198

Dedication

To my Mom, my greatest inspiration.

Table of Contents

Introduction

There's a unique thrill—a sense of delight and fascination—that accompanies your first steps into the world of watercolor. Maybe it started when you experimented with blending colors using the wet-on-wet technique, only to find that the mesmerizing results were wildly unpredictable. Perhaps you were enchanted by the rich textures created by granulating pigments, soon realizing that each tube of paint holds a powerful combination of traits, including varying levels of transparency, vibrancy, and texture, ready to complement an endless array of styles. Or, like me, you were captivated by how effortlessly the thinnest washes of paint can capture the luminous essence of sunlight, unmatched by any other medium.

This feeling of surprise and childlike wonder as you pick up the brush is a reminder that creativity is a precious gift. Unraveling the mysteries and navigating the creative challenges presented by this beautiful medium is at the heart of the human experience. It is during these moments of exploration and growth that we connect with our true selves, turning obstacles into opportunities for self-discovery and artistic expression.

As I grew more enamored with watercolor painting, I became driven to delve deeply into every enigmatic aspect of this unique medium. With each piece, I approached a new question that intrigued me, conducting research and experimenting with different techniques, uncovering new materials and pigment properties to solve my creative puzzles:

- Why do some colors blend seamlessly while others result in a muddy mix?
- How many transparent layers of paint are needed to achieve a three-dimensional effect on paper?
- Why is white traditionally avoided in watercolor, and what alternative techniques can I use?
- What pigments and layering techniques can create a glowing effect on rose petals?
- Which shades of green best capture the vibrant texture of tropical leaves?
- Where can I find the best references to create vivid, beautiful worlds on paper?

The book you're holding is the culmination of a decade's worth of thoughtful exploration, focusing on the most common challenges and stumbling blocks encountered in the watercolor journey. This isn't a step-by-step guide to painting specific subjects (though I do share some of my favorite techniques for rendering realistic animals, flowers, and birds). Instead, it reveals and explores the myriad "secrets" of watercolor, unlocking the mysteries of this medium and its unpredictable nature one by one. Along the way, you'll discover valuable tips to help you better understand and appreciate your tools, including different types of brushes and paper surfaces. I'll also introduce you to my favorite brushstrokes, composition strategies, and some lesser-known pigments—the hidden jewels that will be a welcome addition to your palette.

The next time you feel inspired to pick up your brush, or perhaps anxious about starting a new and complex composition, I invite you to open this book—on any page you choose. Regardless of your style or skill level, I hope you'll find a wealth of new information, techniques, and strategies to help you grow and refine your skills. Most importantly, I hope this book instills in you a renewed sense of wonder and encourages you to embrace the journey of growth and self-discovery through the watercolor medium.

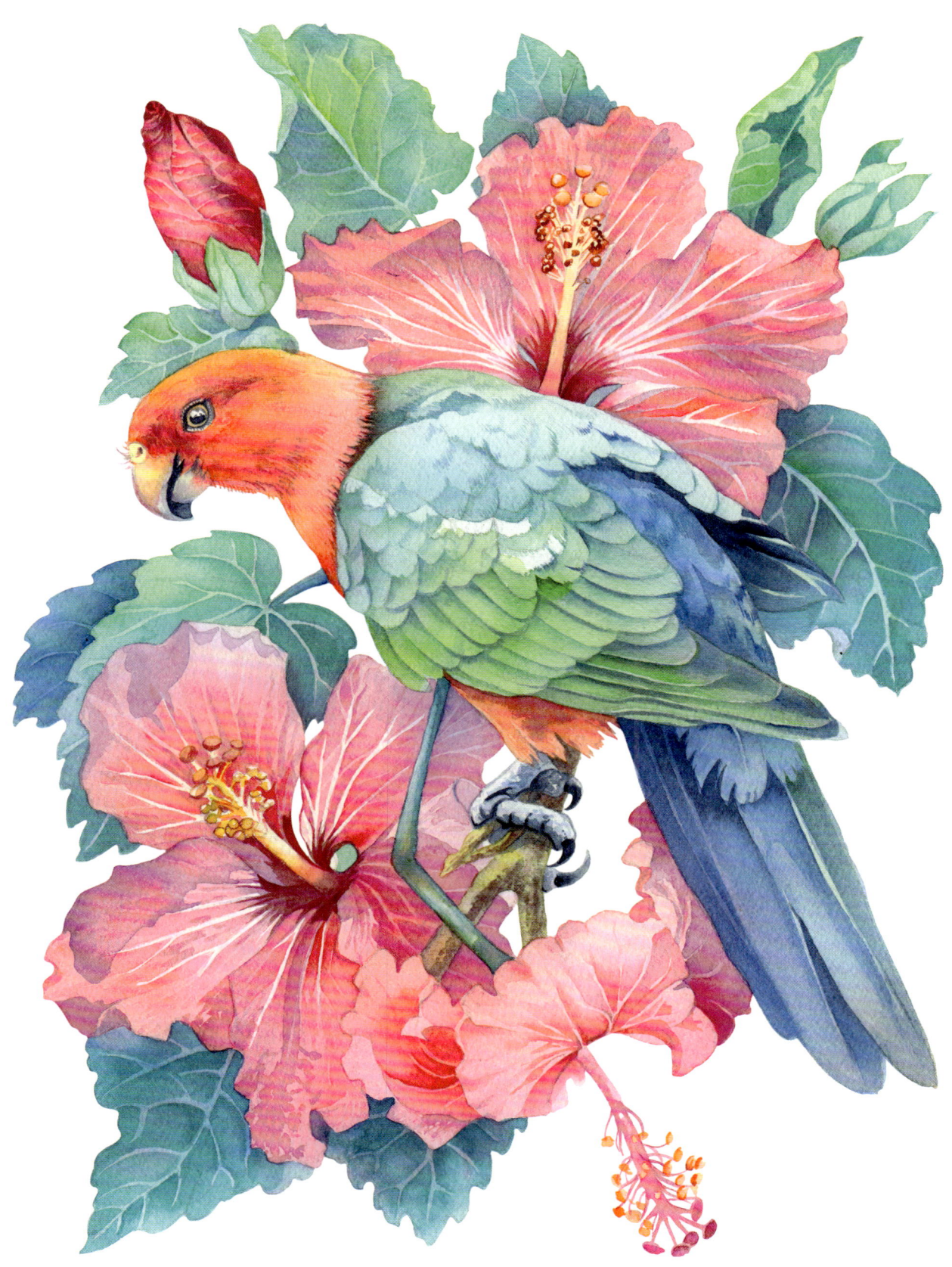

1

Decoding Pigment Labels

1.1 Introduction

Have you ever looked up close at your watercolor tube? It's full of labels—numbers, shapes, and letters—that may look confusing at first. Understanding and using these codes is like having a treasure map guiding you to unlock a world of artistic possibilities. They help us predict how each watercolor will behave so we can create magical worlds on paper!

Before you dip your brush into the paint, let's unravel the mystery behind those intriguing codes. There are five important characteristics that I want you to look for:

- Pigment number / Color Index (CI)
- Granulation property
- Transparency rating
- Lightfastness rating
- Staining property

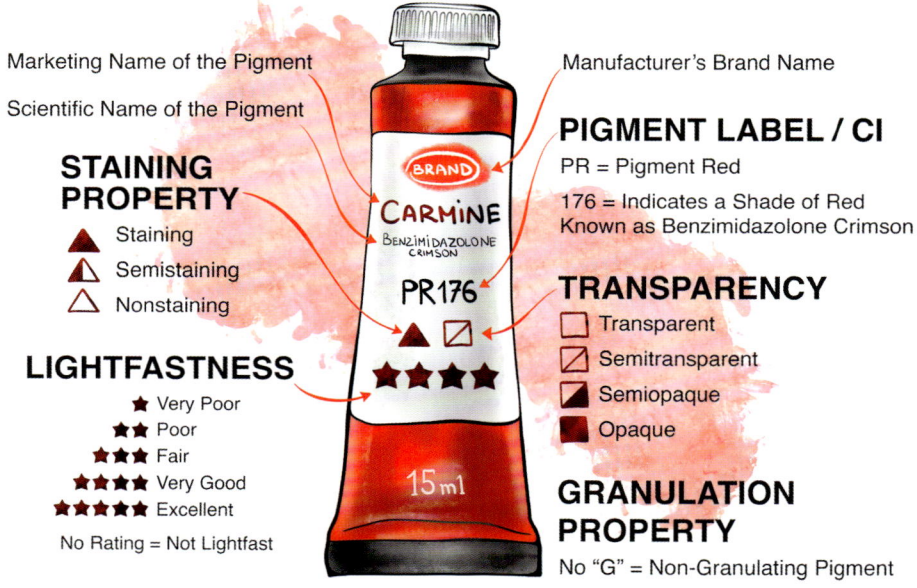

Throughout this chapter, we'll explore the significance of these labels in uncovering pigment properties and leveraging this knowledge to craft your ideal palette.

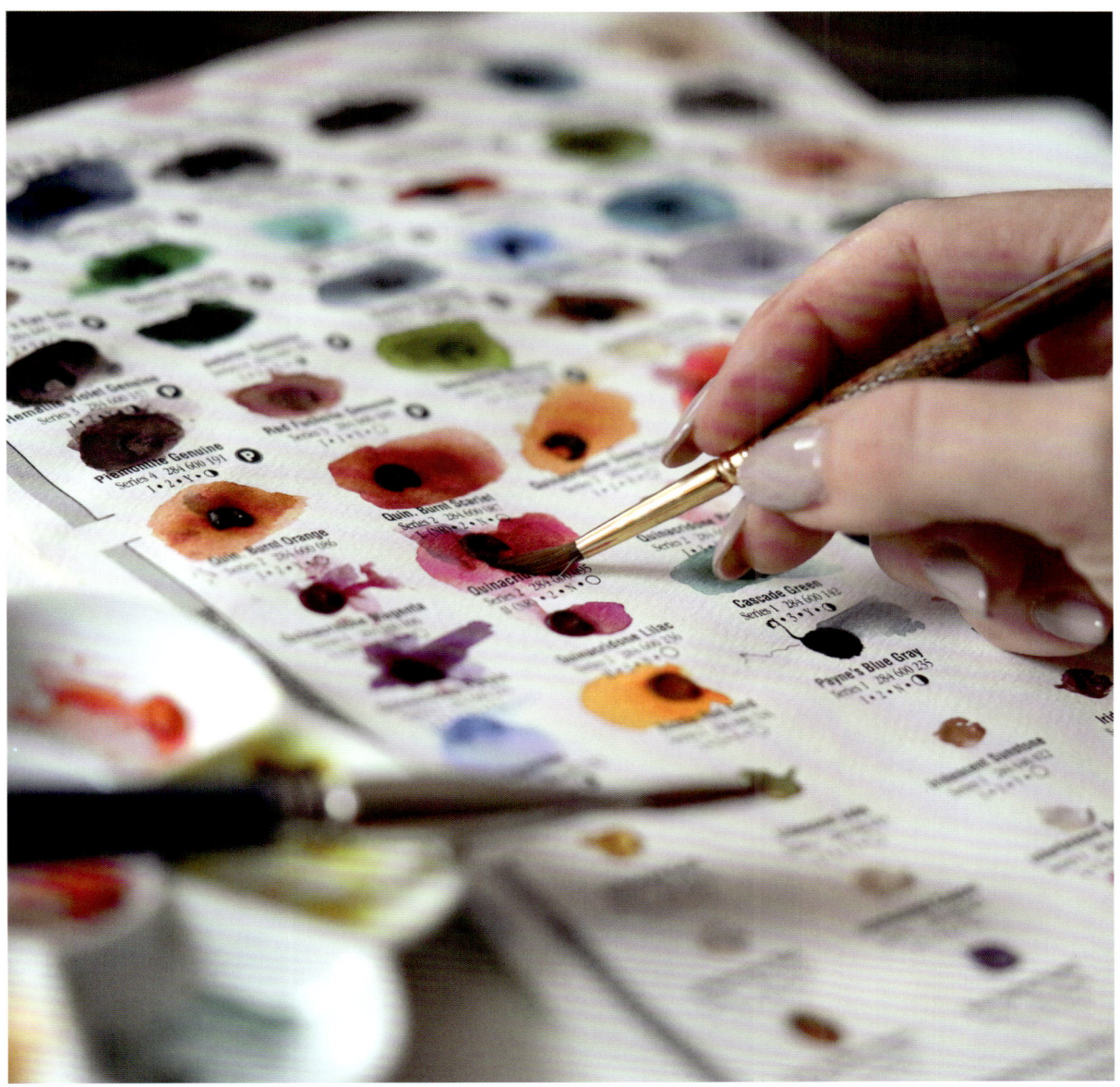

Dot Card from Winsor & Newton in Use

HELPFUL TIP

Watercolor pans and tubes often contain incomplete information, which is why it is better to refer to paint charts. Most manufacturers include these charts with their products, along with a helpful legend that explains all the markings and color properties you need to be aware of. You can also find a digital copy on the manufacturer's website, or purchase a dot card that will allow you to sample the colors before investing in a full tube of paint.

1.2 Pigment Codes: Unveiling Secret Recipes

Let's start with the most common and frequently overlooked label: the Pigment Code. The cryptic codes that make up this label are based on the internationally recognized Color Index™ published by the Society of Dyers and Colorists (SDC) and American Association of Textile Chemists and Colorists (AATCC). This label is your key to understanding what's actually inside the paint tube.

The letter usually indicates a basic color category: Y is for yellow, R is for red, and so on.

PW	**= Pigment White**	**PB**	**= Pigment Blue**
PY	**= Pigment Yellow**	**PG**	**= Pigment Green**
PO	**= Pigment Orange**	**PBr**	**= Pigment Brown**
PR	**= Pigment Red**	**PBk**	**= Pigment Black**

Standard Pigment Codes

The numbers indicate which specific pigment from the Color Index was used. For example, the PG prefix in PG7 means Pigment Green, and 7 means it's Phthalo Green—that gorgeous, cool green with blue undertones that we often use to paint seascapes or tropical leaves. PB27 is just a fancy code for Prussian Blue, sometimes known as Berlin Blue, perfect for moody landscapes and abstract backgrounds.

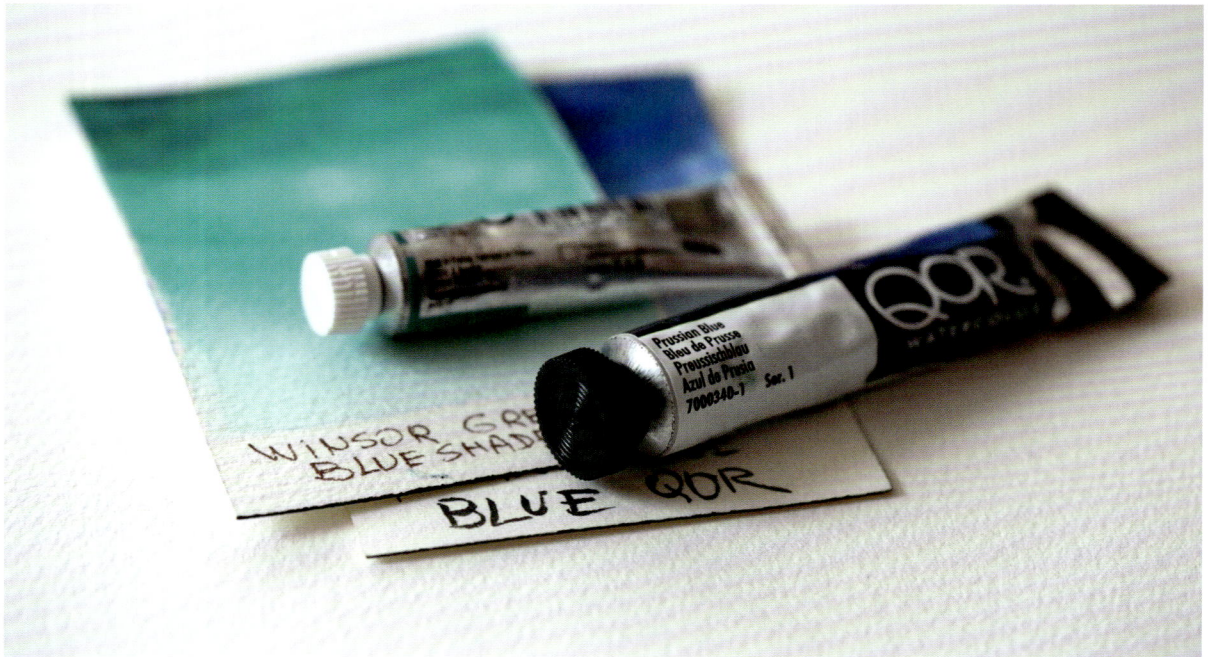

Tubes of Phthalo Green Blue Shade (PG7) and Prussian Blue (PB27)

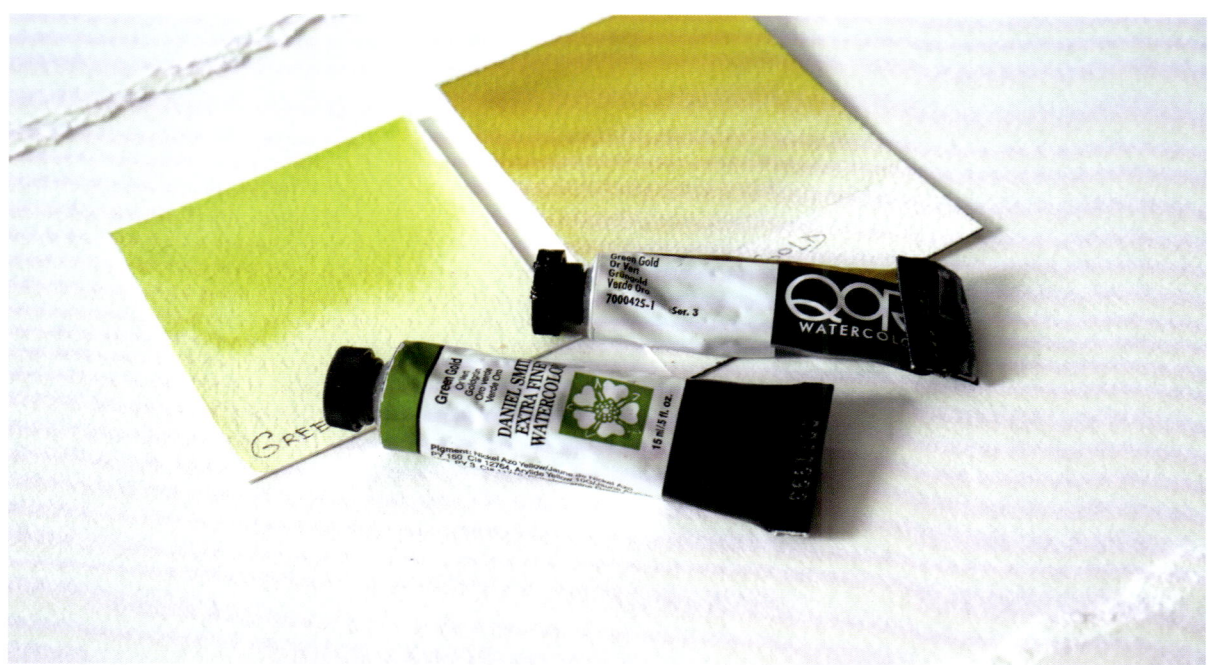

Swatches of Green Gold from QoR Watercolors (PY129) versus Daniel Smith (PY150, PY3, PG36)

HELPFUL TIP

Remember that paint manufacturers can choose to call their products whatever they want. The marketing name of the paint tube—like Aqua Green or Sleeping Beauty—is a lot less important than the pigment code. It's usually just something the brands come up with to entice you to buy their paint, so understanding the code is the only way to truly know what color you are getting and how it will look on paper. For example, Green Gold from QoR Watercolors contains a single transparent, semistaining PY129. When saturated, it displays more olive-green tone on paper compared to the similarly named Green Gold from Daniel Smith. The Daniel Smith version is actually a combination of three pigments—PY150, PY3, and PG36—and will give your washes a more yellow tone.

1.3 Convenience Mixes: Your Artistic Shortcut

Have you ever dreamt of effortless color consistency across your artworks? Convenience mixes serve as handy tools in our palette, offering accessibility to specific colors without the need for extensive mixing. They are a time-saving option for artists seeking immediate access to certain hues or those aiming for consistency in their artworks.

How Pigment Codes Relate

Convenience mixes refer to premixed or ready-made colors created by combining two or more pigments in precise ratios to produce a new color. They often have names like Sap Green or Green Gold, indicating a blend tailored for a particular hue. Instead of using individual pigments to mix a specific color, convenience mixes offer us a shortcut, ensuring that every stroke delivers the same vibrant, enchanting hue.

Most manufacturers transparently label convenience mixes with the individual **pigment codes** used in the mix. This helps us understand the colors that make up the mix and allows for better predictability in mixing or adjusting colors. It also allows us to create our own version when a particular mix is unavailable.

One of my favorite convenience mixes is a warm, natural green called Hooker's Green from Daniel Smith. It has the following code: PG36, PY3, PY150, PO48, indicating a mix of Phthalo Green, Hansa Yellow Light, Nickel Azo Yellow, and Quinacridone Orange.

Convenience Meets Consistency

There are both benefits and drawbacks to using convenience mixes, including the following:

- **Unique Properties:** Convenience mixes are crafted to possess unique characteristics that might not be easily achievable by blending primary colors. Some might granulate beautifully, creating captivating textures, while others boast a luminous quality that lights up your artwork.
- **Time-Saver:** These pigments save us time and effort by providing immediate access to a desired color and eliminating the need for trial-and-error mixing of various pigments.
- **Palette Continuity:** Convenience mixes offer consistency in color, ensuring that the same shade can be reproduced easily from painting to painting.
- **Limitations:** While convenient, these mixes might limit artistic experimentation to some degree. Instead of relying solely on convenience mixes, don't forget to find joy in the unpredictability of mixing and discovering unique shades on your own.

My Favorite Convenience Mixes

Some of my favorite convenience mixes include Cadmium Yellow Medium Hue (PY53, PY151, PY83), Green Gold (PY150, PY3, PG36), Hooker's Green (PG36, PY3, PY150, PO48), and Indigo (PB60, PBk6) from Daniel Smith.

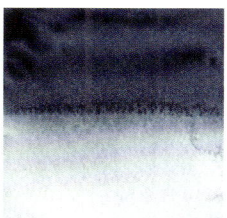

Cadmium Yellow Medium Hue from Daniel Smith (PY53, PY151, PY83)

Green Gold from Daniel Smith (PY150, PY3, PG36)

Hooker's Green from Daniel Smith (PG36, PY3, PY150, PO48)

Indigo from Daniel Smith (PB60, PBk6)

HELPFUL TIP

Experiment by blending convenience mixes with other pigments to create unique shades or modify the intensity of the premade color. My favorite approach in botanical painting is to use a warm green convenience mix called Hooker's Greens from Daniel Smith (PG36, PY3, PY150, PO48) as my base green, glazing or mixing additional pigments to modify the color temperature.

> *Glazing* involves applying thin layers of transparent color over previously dried layers of pigment. For more detail on the glazing technique, see page 112.

Case Study: Cockatoo and Stargazer Lilies

In this composition, I used Hooker's Green as a convenient starting point for the green leaves of the lily flower. In the first layer, I also added varying amounts of yellow and blue into this green mix to accentuate the warmer and cooler spots, respectively. The addition of yellow helped to highlight areas catching more light, giving a sense of warmth and vibrancy, while the blue provided depth and shadow, enhancing the cooler areas. As I glazed additional colors on top of my base green, I was able to achieve a full range of realistic green hues. For instance, I introduced touches of Green Gold (PY150, PY3, PG36) to bring out the sunlit portions of the leaves. I also added a hint of Aqua Green (Phthalo) and Dioxazine Purple (PV23) to deepen the shadows. This layering technique allowed me to build up the complexity of the leaves, creating a more lifelike and three-dimensional effect.

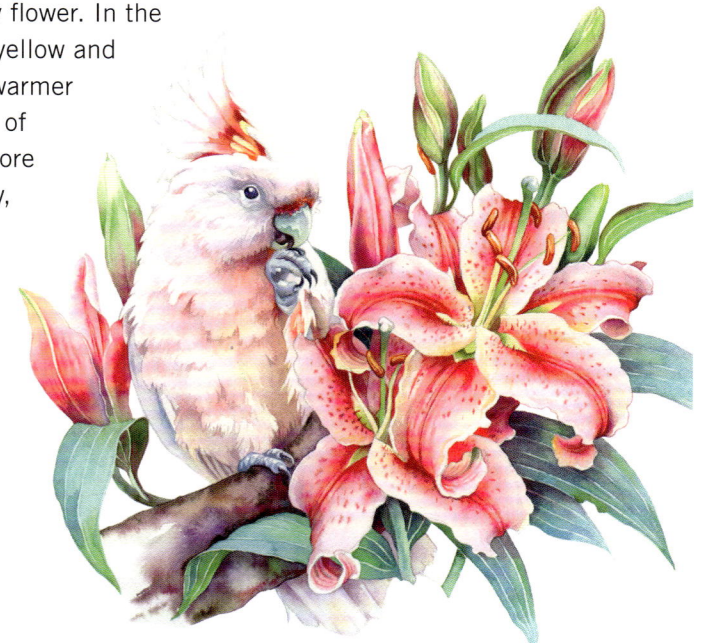

Cockatoo and Stargazer Lilies

Video Available ▶ rockynook.com/watercolor-secrets

1.4 Granulation Property: The Secret Language of Texture

The terms *granulating* and *non-granulating* refer to how watercolor pigments behave when we mix them with water and apply them to cotton paper. Understanding these differences will help you enhance your artwork by achieving unique visual effects.

Understanding Granulation Rating

Most paint manufacturers mention granulation properties on the paint tube or packaging. Look for labels like "G" or "GRANULATION" in the paint description, which implies the paint's tendency to create textured effects.

"G" = Granulating   **No "G" = Non-Granulating**

Cobalt Turquoise (PB36)   *Phthalo Turquoise (PB15:3/PG7)*

Granulation Rating: Cobalt Turquoise (PB36) versus Phthalo Turquoise (PB15:3/PG7)

Granulating watercolor pigments (typically marked "G" or "GRANULATING") contain larger and heavier particles of paint. When you apply granulating pigments to paper, these larger particles tend to settle into the texture of the paper, creating a grainy appearance.

- **Textural Effects:** Granulating pigments are excellent for creating texture in your watercolor paintings. Use them to depict rough surfaces like stones, tree bark, or rich greenery.
- **Visual Depth:** Granulating pigments provide more obvious variations in color and tone. By using them, you can easily create an illusion of extra depth without the need to apply multiple layers.
- **Subdued Colors:** The granulated particles can scatter and diffuse light, leading to slightly muted or softer colors compared to non-granulating pigments. I often use them to create muted abstract backgrounds.

Non-granulating watercolor pigments contain smaller and finer particles of paint. They disperse more evenly when applied to paper, resulting in a smoother and more uniform appearance with minimal or no visible texture.

- **Smooth Transitions:** Non-granulating pigments are ideal for achieving smooth, even washes and transitions of color in backgrounds, skies, and areas where a flat, consistent color is desired.
- **Clean Edges:** These pigments are great for producing clean and crisp edges in your watercolor paintings, especially in areas where you want sharp boundaries between color segments.
- **Vibrant Colors:** Non-granulating pigments tend to appear more vibrant and intense because their particles do not settle into the paper's texture. This is why I always use them for flower petals.

My Favorite Granulating Pigments

My favorite granulating colors include single-pigment Green Apatite Genuine (mineral) from Daniel Smith, as well as convenience mixes like Tundra Violet (PB29, PBr6) from Schmincke, and Cascade Green (PBr7, PB15) and Cobalt Blue Violet (PB28, PV19) from Daniel Smith.

 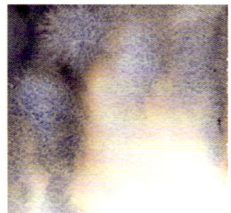 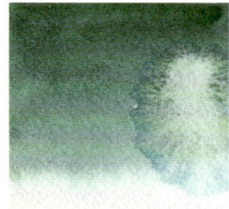 

Green Apatite Genuine from Daniel Smith (mineral)

Tundra Violet from Schmincke (PB29, PBr6)

Cascade Green from Daniel Smith (PBr7, PB15)

Cobalt Blue Violet from Daniel Smith (PB28, PV19)

HELPFUL TIP

Experimenting with different pigments and their granulation characteristics can be an exciting aspect of watercolor painting. Introducing intentional contrast between granulating and non-granulating pigments can create a captivating interplay of textures, enriching the overall visual experience of the painting.

Case Study: Partridge in a Pear Tree

In this composition, I used a combination of highly granulating and less-granulating greens to create texture and depth on the pear tree leaves. For the foreground greenery, I applied Green Apatite Genuine (mineral) and Cascade Green (PBr7, PB15) from Daniel Smith, enhancing the texture by using varying degrees of saturation. These granulating pigments added a rich, textured appearance to the leaves, making them appear more lifelike and detailed.

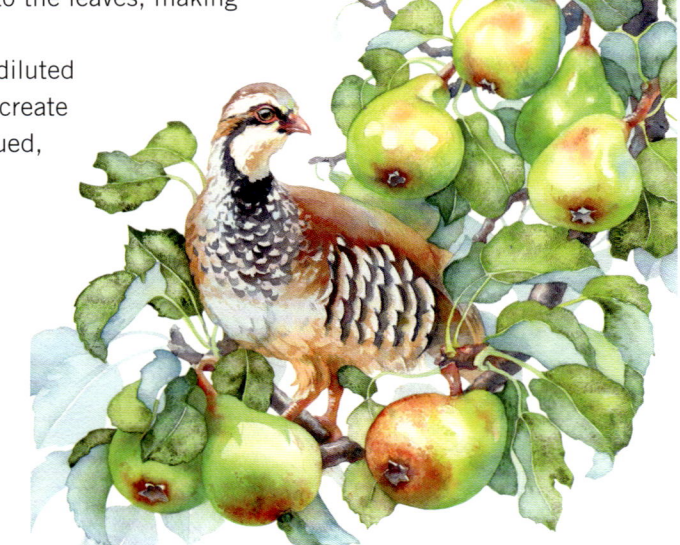

For the background greenery, I used very diluted and less-granulating Aqua Green (Phthalo) to create smooth, translucent washes and a more subdued, less visually striking texture. This contrast between the foreground and background not only helps to create a sense of depth, but also ensures that the main focus remains on the detailed, textured leaves in the foreground. The smoother, softer background washes provide a subtle backdrop that complements the more textured areas without competing for attention.

Video Available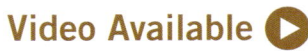

rockynook.com/watercolor-secrets

Partridge in a Pear Tree

1.5 Transparency Rating: From Opaque to See-Through

Transparency rating will help you predict exactly how much light can pass through the pigment layer on paper. Picture this: Some watercolors are like transparent magic windows that allow the underlying colors to show through. These are called **transparent** pigments, and they will help add depth and dimension to your artwork. **Opaque** pigments, on the other hand, tend to mask the underlying layers, offering more solid coverage.

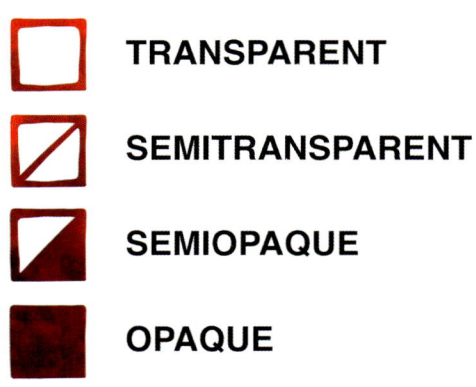

Transparency Rating

Understanding Transparency Ratings

Watercolor tube transparency ratings are commonly represented by geometric shapes (usually a circle). A solid, filled shape signals a fully opaque pigment. When the shape is filled halfway, it denotes a semiopaque pigment. An empty, outlined shape indicates a fully transparent pigment.

The manufacturer's watercolor charts typically contain a more comprehensive description indicating varying degrees of transparency: transparent, semitransparent, semiopaque, or opaque.

Transparent Watercolors

- **Slow glazing:** These pigments excel in glazing techniques, where each layer intensifies the color and adds depth, culminating in a radiant finish that seems to glow from within.
- **Atmospheric depth:** Transparent pigments never fully obscure the underlying layers, allowing you to build vibrant and complex compositions full of atmospheric depth.
- **Luminous effects:** Transparent colors allow for depth and complexity without losing luminosity in your artwork. When mixed together with lots of water, they dance and mingle on paper, creating captivating gradients and subtle transitions.

Opaque Watercolors

- **"Flat" color:** Opaque pigments are best suited for creating solid sections of color that appear dense and devoid of light.
- **Imperfections:** You can mask flaws by covering them with opaque strokes of darker color.

HELPFUL TIP

Experimenting with glazing very diluted transparent pigments in a series of thin washes can yield stunning luminous effects in your watercolor paintings. As mentioned in section 1.3, glazing involves applying thin layers of transparent color over previously dried layers. For example, glazing transparent greens over foliage can add richness and depth to your landscapes. Glazing can also be used to enhance the vibrancy of transparent reds in your botanical artwork paintings. My favorite method includes glazing successive layers of transparent blue to gradually build up depth, richness, and complexity in my backgrounds.

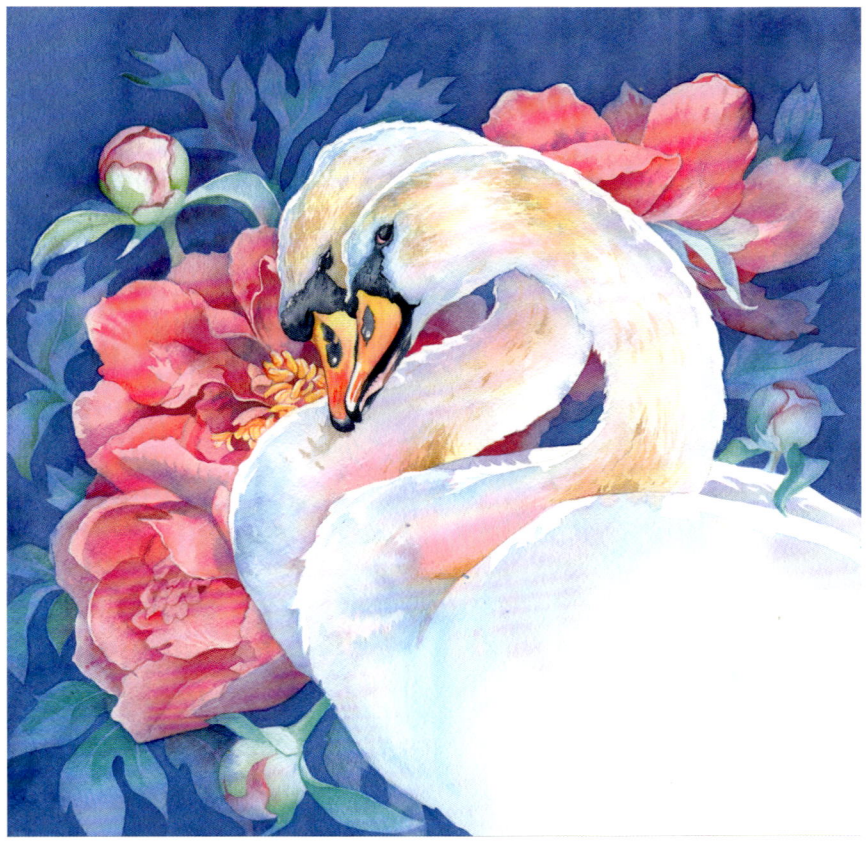

Swans and Peony Flowers

Case Study: Swans and Peony Flowers

In this painting, I employed one of my favorite transparent blues known as Phthalo Blue Red Shade (PB15:6). I applied several layers of this vibrant hue to the backdrop, gradually intensifying its color. This technique allowed glimpses of the underlying greens and reds to peek through, adding depth and creating a subtle interplay of background shapes. Additionally, I used a very diluted Phthalo Blue on the swans, applying it sparingly to achieve an airy, ethereal glow effect on their feathers. By strategically layering transparent pigments in this manner, I was able to enhance the luminosity of the painting while preserving its delicate nuances.

Video Available 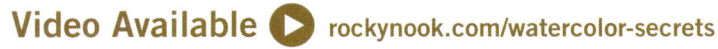 rockynook.com/watercolor-secrets

1.6 Lightfastness: The Color Story That Lasts

Ever wondered why some watercolors remain brilliant while others fade over time? It turns out that not all pigments are created equal in this respect. Lightfastness rating is your key to understanding whether your creations will retain vibrancy and brilliance when exposed to sunlight. As you dip your brushes into a world of vibrant colors, remember, the color story that lasts is the one painted with lightfastness in mind!

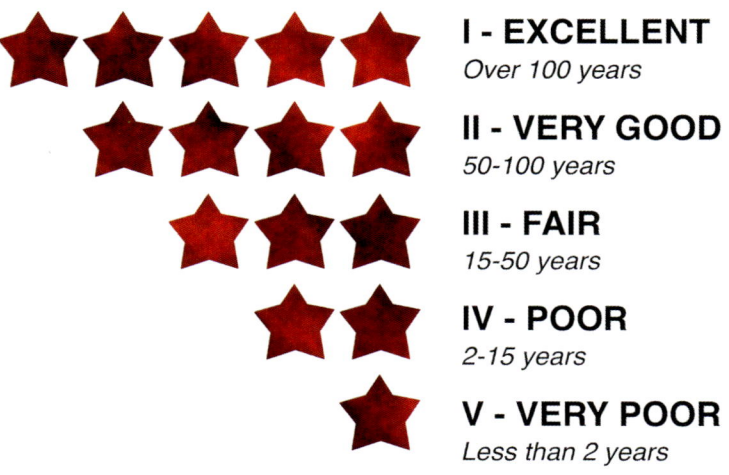

I - EXCELLENT
Over 100 years

II - VERY GOOD
50-100 years

III - FAIR
15-50 years

IV - POOR
2-15 years

V - VERY POOR
Less than 2 years

Lightfastness Rating and Expected Longevity Under Normal Conditions of Display*

*Normal conditions of display include no exposure to direct sunlight and framing behind a UV protective glass.
Source: www.astm.org

Understanding Lightfastness

Lightfastness refers to how long a color will maintain its vibrancy without fading or deteriorating. It is often graded on a scale from I to III, with a star rating, or with terms like "Excellent," "Good," or "Poor." A higher rating indicates better resistance to fading, while pigments with the lowest rating are often called "fugitive," meaning they lack permanence.

The American Society for Testing and Materials (ASTM) sets global technical standards for testing across various industries, including art materials. Their "Standard Test Methods for Lightfastness of Colorants Used in Artists' Materials" is the most widely accepted procedure for evaluating and reporting lightfastness. To be included on the ASTM list, a color must undergo rigorous testing, including prolonged outdoor and accelerated indoor exposure, a process that can take several years.

If you don't see any lightfastness information on the packaging or the manufacturer's website, it's likely that the pigment may fade quickly. However, high-quality brands typically provide lightfastness information, ensuring you can make informed choices about the materials you use.

Coping Strategies

Dealing with watercolor pigments with low lightfastness involves careful consideration, strategic use, and protective measures to ensure the longevity and preservation of your artistic creations. Here are some of my favorite coping strategies:

- **Layering:** Utilize low lightfast colors in underpainting or base layers where they'll be less exposed to light. Overlay them with more lightfast colors to protect the sensitive pigments.
- **Mixing:** When mixing colors, consider the lightfastness of each pigment involved. Try to blend low lightfast colors with more lightfast colors to mitigate the overall impact of the less-stable pigments.
- **Selective Use:** Consider reserving colors with low lightfastness for personal creative explorations and commercial projects where digitization can mitigate the effects of fading.
- **Framing:** Frame artworks behind UV-protective glass or acrylic to minimize exposure to harmful UV rays, extending the lifespan of colors with low lightfastness.

Modern Alternatives

Look for updated formulations of colors that historically had low lightfastness. For example, Daniel Smith now offers a permanent version of the beloved classic fugitive Alizarin Crimson. This convenience mix is called Permanent Alizarin Crimson (PR177, PV19, PR149).

Importance of Disclosure

When selling watercolor artworks, it's crucial to inform potential customers about the lightfastness of the pigments you use. Transparency about materials allows collectors or buyers to make informed decisions about the care and longevity of the artwork.

HELPFUL TIP

When creating artwork for sale, prioritize pigments with high lightfastness ratings and avoid fugitive colors that are prone to fading.

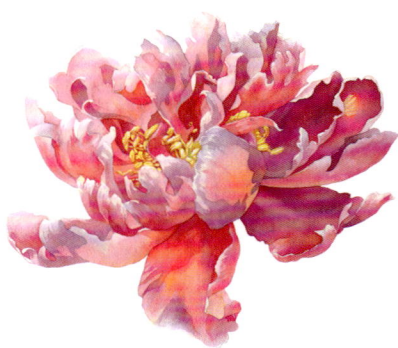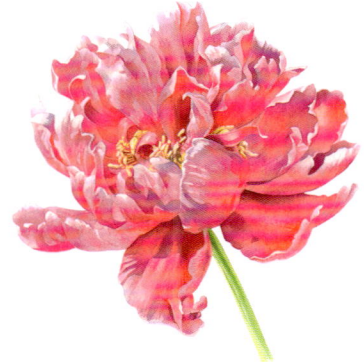

Pink Peony Painted with Lightfast
Quinacridone Magenta PR122

Pink Peony Painted with Fugitive Opera
Pink PR 122

Case Study: Pink Peony with Lightfast versus Non-Lightfast Colors

I painted two versions of this pink peony: one using lightfast Quinacridone Magenta (intended for sale), and another using fugitive Opera Pink PR122 (for commercial use). Despite sharing the same pigment code PR122, Opera Pink PR122 and Quinacridone Magenta PR122 differ significantly in their lightfastness ratings. The peony painted with Opera Pink appears more vivid, but without appropriate UV protection, it is likely to fade over time. In contrast, the peony painted with Quinacridone Magenta has a darker and less vivid hue. This version will maintain the original vibrancy, making it more suitable for display or sale.

1.7 Staining Property

The Staining Property refers to a pigment's ability to adhere to the paper's surface, creating a lasting and bold mark. This characteristic determines how easily the color can be manipulated—*lifted*, blotted or scrubbed—after the paper is dry. Balancing staining and nonstaining watercolors in a painting enables us to fix mistakes, create a variety of textures, and plan multiple layers effectively.

> *Lifting* can be accomplished by blotting with tissue or scrubbing gently with a clean, damp brush. It doesn't remove the color completely, but rather to a degree, depending on how staining the pigment is. For more information on the lifting technique, see page 109.

Understanding Staining Property Rating

Staining Property is often graded using a scale from I to IV, or using terms like Excellent, Good, or Poor. A lower rating of I or II indicates a very light discoloring of paper, while a higher rating of III or IV indicates a strongly anchoring pigment that won't easily lift after your paper is dry.

Note that Staining Property rating is not a judgement on quality, but rather an indication of specific pigment properties that may or may not be suitable for your particular subject and techniques. For example, a higher degree of staining is desirable for your background layers, where colors are painted over and rewetted multiple times.

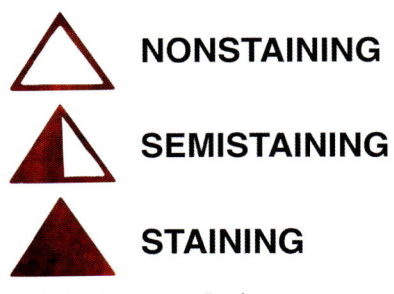

NONSTAINING

SEMISTAINING

STAINING

Staining Property Rating

Nonstaining and Low-Staining Pigments retain a degree of mobility on the paper surface, allowing for easier manipulation and even lifting. These pigments tend to offer more transparent and softer hues, with delicate transitions and subtle tonal variation. They work very well for creating gentle cloudy skies, atmospheric landscapes, and any other subjects where soft edges are essential.

Nonstaining pigments are excellent for wet-on-wet techniques, where you want your colors to blend softly and seamlessly. You can lift nonstaining pigments to create highlights and to rework or correct minor mistakes. For more information on wet-on-wet, lifting, and soft edge techniques, see chapter 5, "Essential Techniques."

Staining Pigments penetrate the paper fibers, creating intense, long-lasting marks that are challenging to lift once dry. These pigments tend to create vivid colors, suitable for vibrant subjects like tropical birds, bold florals, and striking architectural illustrations. They are excellent for creating deep, rich tones in landscapes, or any other subjects that require minimal lifting or corrections.

Staining pigments are ideal for color-charging and layering techniques where depth, permanence, and intensity are desired. For more information on these techniques, refer to chapter 5, "Essential Techniques."

> **Charging** is a technique in which several colors are applied consecutively onto the wet surface, with varying degrees of saturation. For more information on charging, see page 103.

HELPFUL TIP

Knowing the pigment family can help you to predict the staining properties. For example, most red Quinacridones and blue Phthalos tend to stain the paper and are hardly detachable when rewetted. On the other hand, Cobalts and Earth pigments don't anchor to paper as much, allowing for easy lifting and manipulation even after the paper is dry. For more information on pigment families, see chapter 2, "Exploring Color Families."

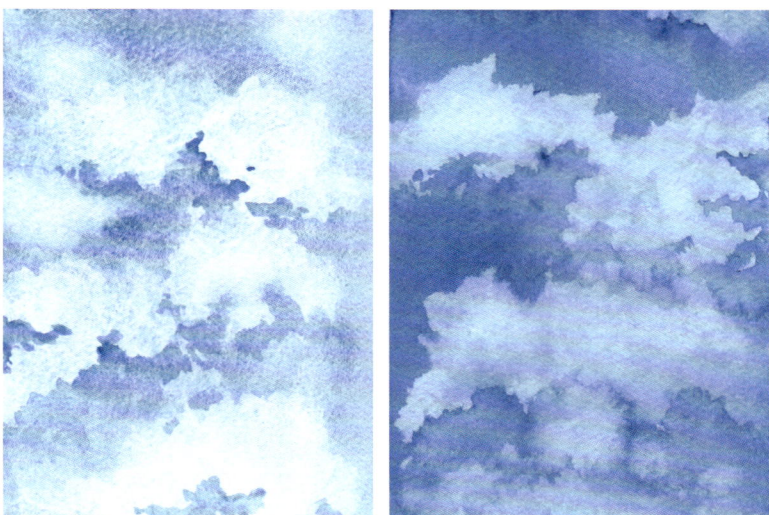

Clouds Painted with Low-Staining Cobalt Blue PB28 from Winsor & Newton versus Clouds Painted with Staining Winsor Blue Red Shade a.k.a. Phthalo Blue Red Shade PB15:6 from Winsor & Newton.

Case Study: Clouds with Staining versus Nonstaining Watercolors

I painted the clouds on the left by applying a thin layer of Cobalt Blue from Winsor & Newton (PB28), then lifting some segments with a dry tissue paper. Notice how the subtle granulation further accentuates the delicate and nuanced effects of the sky. Cobalt Blue, while vibrant and intense, has lower staining properties compared to Phthalo Blue on the right. It can be manipulated long after the paper is dry, allowing for greater flexibility and control.

The clouds on the right were painted using a highly staining, non-granulating blue called Phthalo Blue Red Shade (PB15:6). This pigment is quite intense, leaving vivid and long-lasting marks on the paper surface. Although it allowed for some limited lifting while the paper was still wet, after only ten minutes very little manipulation or lifting was possible.

2

Exploring
Color Families

2.1 Introduction

Watercolor pigments can be grouped into distinct categories, or families, ranging from intense and vibrant Quinacridones to soft and delicate Cobalts. Each family of colors holds a unique historical legacy and unlocks a spectrum of artistic possibilities based on their chemical composition. Understanding unique properties within each category will help you choose the right colors for your favorite subjects and give you the confidence to experiment boldly and build a signature palette that fits your style.

The existence of various types of watercolor pigments arises from a combination of factors involving chemistry, historical development, and the evolution of artistic needs.

Historical Significance

Among the earliest watercolor pigments were earth-derived hues like ochres, siennas, and umbers, prized for their rich tones and abundance in nature. These pigments were sourced from minerals and clays found in various regions worldwide, carrying distinct color profiles shaped by local geological compositions.

For example, **Ochres** originally came from iron oxide deposits, manifesting in shades ranging from yellow to deep red. Similarly, **Siennas** and **Umbers**, which contain varying levels of manganese and iron oxides, produced warm brown tones. The legacy of non-synthetic pigments remains, serving as a testament to the enduring relationship between art and the natural world, inspiring artists across generations to explore the depths of color embedded in the earth itself.

Advancements in Chemistry and Pigment Development

As artistic techniques evolved, so did the demand for pigments that suited specific styles or applications. Over time, the advancements in synthetic chemistry led to the development of new pigments aimed to replicate the qualities of natural pigments, while offering improved lightfastness, transparency, and color intensity. This evolution also led to advances in mixing capabilities, offering us a wider range of color options.

For example, Ultramarine derives its name from its historical sourcing from "beyond the sea," where it was initially acquired through a laborious process of grinding the precious gemstone lapis lazuli into a fine powder. Due to its costly nature, Ultramarine was reserved for esteemed patrons and iconic religious commissions in classical and Renaissance art. With advancements in pigment production, synthetic Ultramarine emerged in the nineteenth century, replicating the exquisite hue of natural ultramarine at a fraction of the cost. New and exciting varieties of synthetic blues were developed later in the twentieth century, including vivid Phthalos that offer green, red, and even turquoise hues.

In this chapter, I will explore some of my favorite color families, focusing on their unique properties and specific applications in watercolor. Note that each category brings a unique set of possibilities to our palette, enabling us to delve into a myriad of techniques and styles that we will cover in the later chapters.

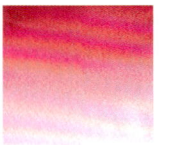   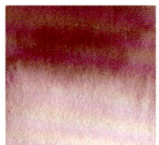 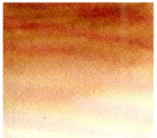  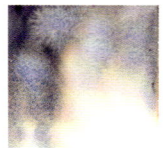

QUINA-
CRIDONE:
Quinacridone
Magenta
(PR122)

PHTHALO:
Phthalo Blue
Green Shade
(PB15:3)

COBALT:
Cobalt Teal
(PG50)

PERYLENE:
Perylene
Violet (PV29)

EARTH:
Burnt Sienna
(PR101)

PYRROL:
Pyrrol Orange
(PO71)

OTHER:
Tundra Violet
(PB29, PBr6)

- **Quinacridones** are known for their intense, vibrant colors that exhibit excellent lightfastness. They maintain their brilliance even when diluted, making them my favorite choice for botanical art.
- **Phthalo** pigments, short for Phthalocyanine pigments, lean toward blue or green shades. They tend to be very transparent and highly staining.
- **Cobalt** pigments are softer, exhibiting a more delicate and subtle range of hues. They offer gentler tonal variations, ideal for capturing serene and nuanced scenes. Cobalt pigments tend to be opaque and lift easily.
- **Perylenes** offer deep and rich hues with excellent lightfastness. They are prized for their ability to create dark, velvety tones, particularly useful for shadows and depth in landscape and floral paintings.
- **Earth** pigments (Siennas, Ochers, Umbers) include a range of warm colors that often possess granulating properties. They offer natural tones perfect for landscapes and portraits.
- **Pyrrol** pigments offer us a vivid spectrum of reds and oranges, known for their impeccable lightfastness.
- The **Other/Specialty** category in watercolor pigments encompasses a range of specialty pigments with distinctive characteristics and hues. These pigments give artists the ability to explore nuanced colors, unique textures, and diverse effects in their artworks, allowing for a broader spectrum of creative expression.

While this book highlights some of the more popular and widely used color families, it's important to acknowledge that the world of watercolor pigments is vast and diverse. Covering every color family in detail would be an enormous task, and perhaps an impossible one within the confines of a single book chapter. However, this limitation should not deter you from exploring the rich tapestry of watercolor pigments on your own. For instance, beyond the color families discussed here, the Cadmium pigments are renowned for their bright, warm colors, adding a range of vibrant oranges, reds, and yellows to your palette. These colors are particularly favored for their intensity, though some artists may choose to avoid them due to concerns about toxicity. As an alternative, the Hansa family of colors provides brilliant and versatile yellows. These pigments are less toxic and offer an excellent range of hues for artists seeking safer options without sacrificing vibrancy.

I encourage you to experiment with these and other pigment families to discover your own favorites and expand your palette according to your artistic needs and preferences. The joy of watercolor painting lies in its versatility and the endless possibilities it offers. By exploring various pigment families, you can uncover unique combinations that resonate with your personal style and artistic vision.

2.2 Quinacridones: A Symphony of Vibrant Hues

Quinacridone pigments are a group of synthetic organic pigments used in watercolor and other artistic mediums. They are highly regarded for their vibrancy, transparency, and lightfastness. In the realm of watercolors, Quinacridones aren't just pigments; they're the superheroes of your palette, ready to help you create mesmerizing masterpieces that dance with color, depth, and lasting brilliance!

Origins and Characteristics

- **Synthetic Origin:** Quinacridone pigments are synthetic organic compounds first developed in the early twentieth century to mimic and improve upon natural pigments.
- **Vibrancy:** Quinacridones come in a range of vibrant hues, including reds, pinks, violets, oranges, and golds. They're known for their high chroma and tinting strength, making them a favorite choice for botanical artists and commercial decorative illustrators.
- **Transparency:** Generally, these pigments are highly transparent, allowing for beautiful layering and glazing techniques in watercolor painting.
- **Lightfastness:** Quinacridones are prized for their excellent lightfastness, meaning they resist fading or changing when exposed to light over time, ensuring the longevity of your artwork.

Applications in Watercolor

- **Mixing:** Quinacridone pigments mix seamlessly with other colors, allowing you to create a broad spectrum of secondary and tertiary hues. Explore how these pigments interact with each other to create a wide range of rich purples, luscious pinks, and fiery oranges.
- **Layering:** Their transparency makes Quinacridones ideal for glazing techniques, allowing you to build up layers of color to achieve depth and luminosity.
- **Lifting:** Quinacridone pigments are quite staining, making them difficult to "lift."

HELPFUL TIP

Due to their high color concentration, Quinacridone pigments can look quite vivid, overwhelming other colors on your palette. A little goes a long way, especially when working with natural subjects. Dilute them to control the color intensity and prevent overpowering mixtures. I usually start with a mixture of 10% Quinacridone and 90% water and build saturation slowly. This can be achieved either by adding more concentrated Quinacridone using a wet-on-wet technique or glazing darker layers to manage color intensity in a more controlled way.

Worth a Try (My Favorites)

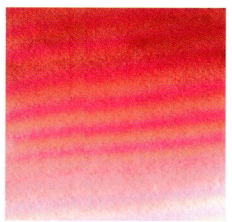
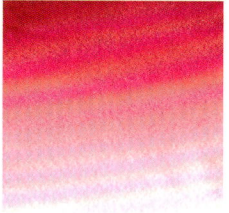

PV19 Quinacridone Red from QoR Watercolors

PR122 Quinacridone Magenta from QoR Watercolors

PY150, PO48 Quinacridone Gold from QoR Watercolors

Quinacridone Red (PV19): This pigment produces a vivid red hue and is often used as a primary color to mix a variety of secondary hues in combination with blue and yellow. I often use it as a starting wash for my botanical studies featuring red flowers, mixing in a variety of blues and oranges to capture color variations on the petals.

Quinacridone Magenta (PR122): Known for its intensity, this cool, deep pink has a slight purple bias and is another favorite among botanical artists. It mixes well with blues to create a gorgeous range of purples and violets. PR122 is an excellent choice for mixing skin tones as well (see page 150 for more information).

Quinacridone Gold (PY150, PO48): This gorgeous warm yellow is particularly useful for landscapes, sunsets, and generally for adding warmth to various subjects. Try mixing it with blues to create a range of natural greenery, or glaze on top of browns for a dazzling sun-kissed effect in autumn landscapes. Note that the genuine PO49 version was discontinued around 2018. Quinacridone Gold hues are widely available these days, most frequently as a convenience mix of Nickel Azo Yellow (PY150) and Quinacridone Orange (PO48).

Case Study: Geranium Flower

In this geranium study, I used two Quinacridones to infuse the composition with warmth and luminosity. Starting with a base layer of warm Quinacridone Coral, I established the foundation of the petals, building upon it with successive glazes of cooler Quinacridone Red to add complexity and richness to the color palette. By varying the intensity and concentration of each pigment, I was able to achieve a sense of transparency within the petals, allowing light to pass through and infuse them with a radiant glow.

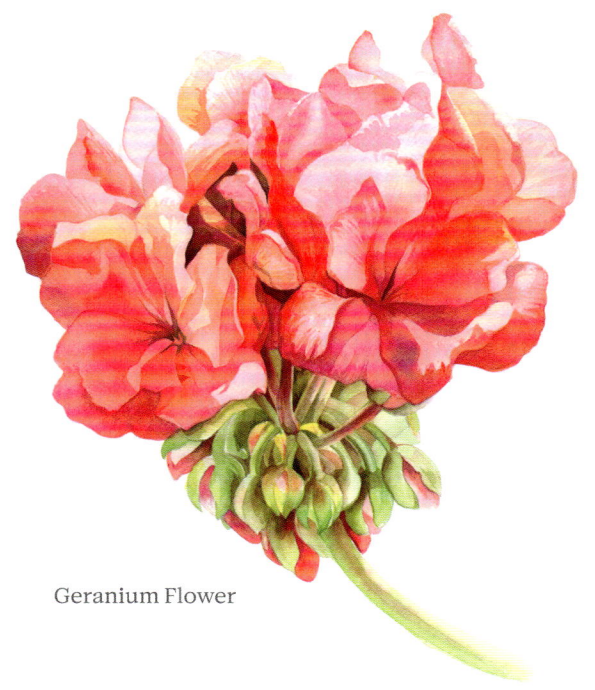

Geranium Flower

2.3 Phthalos: Transparency Powerplay

The Phthalo family of pigments is a group of synthetic organic pigments primarily leaning toward shades of blue or green. In watercolor art, the Phthalo pigments' intense hues, excellent transparency, and ability to mix well with other colors make them ideal for bold and intricately layered compositions.

Origins and Characteristics

- **Synthetic Origins:** Phthalo pigments, short for Phthalocyanine pigments, were developed in the mid-twentieth century as synthetic organic compounds. They were created to replicate and enhance the qualities of natural pigments.
- **Vividness and Brightness:** Phthalo pigments are known for their intense, vivid colors. They have unparalleled brightness and purity, making them stand out on the palette.
- **Transparency and Staining:** Most Phthalo pigments are highly transparent and have strong staining properties, meaning they adhere tenaciously to paper.

Applications in Watercolor

- **Mixing Possibilities:** Phthalo pigments are incredibly potent and mix well with other colors, allowing us to create a vast array of secondary and tertiary hues while maintaining their vibrancy and intensity. Experiment with mixing Phthalo pigments with other colors to create an extensive range of shades, from subtle tints to bold, deep tones.
- **Layering:** Their see-through nature makes Phthalo pigments masters of depth and complexity in your artworks, creating bold and beautiful layers.
- **Lifting:** Due to their strong staining properties, Phthalo pigments are not ideal for lifting techniques.

HELPFUL TIP

Due to its intensity, pure Phthalo Green may not align well with a palette favoring neutral and earthy tones. However, it is extremely versatile for mixing purposes and is therefore highly recommended as a compliment to your primary colors. For example:

- Blending earthy pigments like Raw Umber or Burnt Sienna with Phthalo Green neutralizes its vivid undertones, resulting in a spectrum of rich, pine-like green shades.
- Combining warm yellow with Phthalo Green yields a vibrant, natural hue reminiscent of the popular Sap Green convenience mix.
- When paired with its complementary red counterparts, Phthalo Green becomes instrumental in producing a deep black. Experiment with mixing it with Pyrrol Red or Pyrrol Crimson to craft a visually appealing alternative to the stark single-pigment blacks commonly found in beginner sets.

Worth a Try (My Favorites)

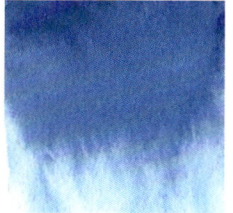 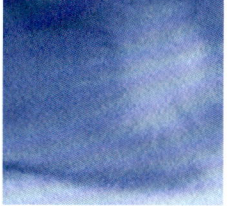   

PB15:3 Phthalo Blue Green Shade from QoR Watercolors

PB15:6 Phthalo Blue Red Shade from Daniel Smith

PB15:3/PG7 Phthalo Turquoise from QoR Watercolors

PG7 Winsor Green Blue Shade from Winsor & Newton

PG36 Winsor Green Yellow Shade from Winsor & Newton

Phthalo Blue (PB15:3 and PB15:6): This pigment offers a stunning bright hue, ranging from deep ocean blues to electrifying cyan skies. It's versatile, allowing us to mix beautiful greens when combined with yellow. A cooler PB15:3 Green Shade variety is perfect for flower petals, while a warmer PB15:6 Red Shade version is my go-to for deep and warm atmospheric backgrounds. (*See page 42 for more information on PB15.*)

Phthalo Turquoise (PB15:3/PG7): This particular Phthalo variation is renowned for its infusion of exotic, tropical tones. Its allure lies in its application within marine watercolors, unlocking a spectrum of artistic possibilities. It lends itself well to crafting natural, rhythmic ocean waves, deepening the shadows and capturing the elusive dance of reflections upon sea waters.

Phthalo Green (PG7 and PG36): Known for its intense green hues, this color is a welcome addition to any landscape or botanical palette. Think lush forests or tropical leaves that practically pop off your sketchbook page! Similar to Phthalo Blue, Phthalo Green is also available in two variations: Blue Shade (PG7) and Yellow Shade (PG36). My favorite variations come from Winsor & Newton and are called Winsor Green Blue Shade and Winsor Green Yellow Shade, respectively.

Case Study: Bird and Pomegranates

In a captivating scene featuring a blue bird perched amid the branches of a pomegranate tree, I introduced various Phthalo hues to infuse the composition with depth and vibrancy. Utilizing the intense pigmentation of Phthalo Blue and Phthalo Turquoise, I carefully layered multiple washes to create tonal variations on the bird's feathers. To add dimension to the background and frame the bird, I incorporated Aqua Green, another favorite Phthalo pigment from Winsor & Newton. The translucent quality of Aqua Green allowed the background to recede, creating a sense of atmospheric perspective so the vibrant fruit and the bird's feathers could truly shine.

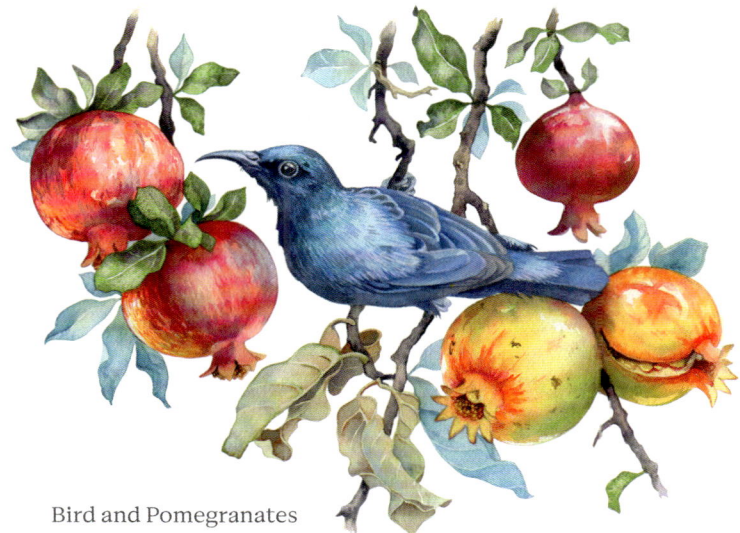

Bird and Pomegranates

2.4 Perylenes: Richness and Depth

Perylene colors are a fascinating family of pigments known for their richness, deep hues, and excellent lightfastness. Derived from the synthetic organic compound Perylene, these pigments offer us a range of colors with unique properties.

Origins and Characteristics

- **Synthetic Origin:** Perylenes are relatively new synthetic pigments, developed in the mid-twentieth century.
- **Rich, Deep Colors:** Perylenes come in deep and intense shades, often leaning toward dark reds. These colors have a robust, earthy quality that adds depth and complexity to landscapes and botanicals.
- **Lightfastness:** One of their most remarkable qualities is their exceptional lightfastness. Perylene pigments are known for their ability to withstand exposure to light over time without fading, ensuring the longevity of artworks.

Applications in Watercolor

- **Color Depth:** Perylene pigments excel in providing depth and richness to artworks, especially in shadows, earth tones, and darker color schemes.
- **Experimenting with Portraits:** Red and violet Perylenes are useful for glazing darker skin tones and creating rich and realistic hair texture.
- **Lifting:** Due to their strong staining properties, Perylene pigments are not ideal for lifting techniques.
- **Mixing Possibilities:** These pigments mix beautifully with other colors, including even the most vibrant greens and magentas. Try charging additional colors into wet Perylenes to brighten them up or create high-contrast mixes directly on paper. (*For more information on the charging technique, see page 103.*)

HELPFUL TIP

Don't be afraid to introduce Perylene pigments into your botanical art. Although they may look flat and heavy at first glance, they offer a beautiful balance that can easily ground your transparent Quinacridone washes. For example, Perylene Red can be used to add intricate accents and strong natural shadows on cold autumn florals (e.g., dahlias and chrysanthemums). Perylene Violet is my favorite choice for exotic chocolate orchids. Because of its relative neutrality, it mixes well with complementary greens, making it my go-to choice for delicate floral branches.

Worth a Try (My Favorites)

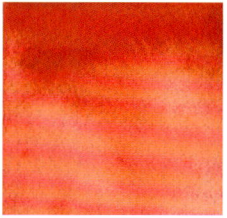

PR178 Perylene Red from Daniel Smith

PBk31 Perylene Green from Daniel Smith

PV29 Perylene Violet from Daniel Smith

Perylene Red (PR178): This pigment offers a dark red hue with excellent lightfastness. It's prized for its ability to create vibrant reds with a touch of depth and darkness. Use it on top of light Quinacridone washes to add intricate details and complexity to your still-life compositions featuring fruits and flowers.

Perylene Green (PBk31): This pigment provides extremely deep green hues, often leaning toward olive or even black. It's valued for its richness and depth in landscape paintings. I often use it in my botanical studies to add moody dark shadows in background greenery.

Perylene Violet (PV29): A intense and luscious reddish-violet, perfect for painting natural shadows and adding depth to watercolor backgrounds. Try using it in your portraits to create a range of rich, natural flesh tones. (*See page 48 for an in-depth exploration of PV29.*)

Case Study: Bluejay and Rowan Berries

In a winter composition featuring a striking bluejay amid a backdrop of snow-dusted branches, I employed Perylene Violet to capture the exquisite shades of rowan berry leaves. The deep, rich hues of PV29 proved instrumental in depicting the subtle variations in color within the leaves. The juxtaposition of the blue jay against the lush foliage created a striking contrast, further accentuating the beauty of both the bird and its surroundings.

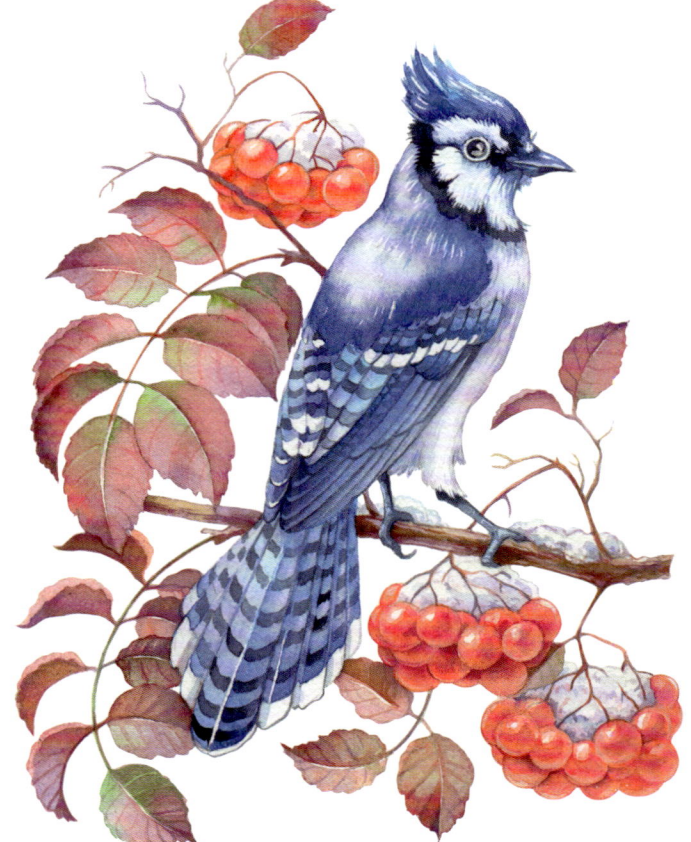

Bluejay and Rowan Berries

2.5 Earth Pigments: Nature's Gift

Earth pigments, derived from minerals found in the Earth's crust, offer us a rich spectrum of warm, muted hues. They bring a timeless, organic look to our watercolor palette, full of subtlety and nuance that can only be found in nature.

Origins and Characteristics

- Originating from the Italian city of Siena, **Sienna** pigments encompass warm, reddish-brown hues obtained from natural iron oxide deposits. Variations include Raw Sienna and Burnt Sienna. Also derived from hydrated iron oxide deposits from various locations globally, **Ochres** present a range of golden, yellow, and reddish tones. Named after the Italian word for shadow, *ombra*, **Umbres** encompass darker, cooler brown colors and are derived from natural clay deposits.
- **Lightfastness:** Earth pigments commonly exhibit good to excellent lightfastness, enabling us to create nuanced artworks that stand the test of time.
- **Transparency:** These pigments usually fall in the transparent to semitransparent range, allowing for beautiful glazing and layering effects without overwhelming the underlying colors.
- **Granulation:** Known for their moderate granulation, earth pigments exhibit subtle texture when applied, enhancing the natural feel of landscapes and organic subjects.
- **Staining Properties:** Earth pigments have a low staining quality, allowing for easier lifting or reworking of layers, making them versatile for creating soft washes and detailed textures.

Applications in Watercolor

- **Landscapes:** Ideal for portraying natural textures, Earth pigments add depth and realism to terrains, rocks, and soil.
- **Human and Animal Subjects:** Earth pigments provide a subtle and authentic touch to any organic subject, allowing us to depict various skin textures and fur details realistically.
- **Still Life and Architecture:** These pigments enhance the atmosphere in still-life compositions and architectural details, capturing the essence of nature's colors.
- **Mixing Potential:** Earth pigments mix harmoniously with other colors, offering a range of muted hues, natural greens when mixed with blues, and subdued violets when combined with reds.

HELPFUL TIP

You may enjoy the subtle granulation and tonal variations of Earth pigments, but prefer more vibrant hues with a stronger tint. In this case, you can explore convenience mixes with modern pigment alternatives. For example, Daniel Smith offers several exclusive blends of Earth and Quinacridone pigments. Most notably, a rich burgundy-brown called Raw Umber Violet, which combines PBr7 (found in traditional Umbers) and PV19 (also known as Quinacridone Red).

Worth a Try (My Favorites)

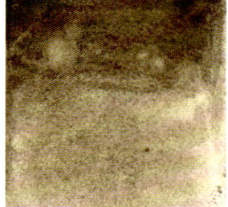

PY42 Gold Ochre from Winsor & Newton

PBr7 Raw Umber from QoR Water-colors

PR101 Burnt Sienna from Winsor & Newton

Gold Ochre (PY42): Gold Ochre, reminiscent of sunlit fields and golden hour, embodies the essence of sunlight captured in pigment form. Its granulation properties are very subtle, lending a delicate texture that enhances the luminosity of skin tones, sandy terrains, and architectural details. My favorite version from Winsor & Newton is more staining than a typical Ochre, and I often use it as a subtle underpainting on animal fur or as a base pigment for warm color mixtures.

Raw Umber (PBr7): Although it exists in different variations ranging from warm to cool brown, my favorite version from QoR Watercolors offers a blueish darker tone that is difficult to mix on my own. It is made with natural iron oxide containing manganese and is semi-opaque. It displays stronger granulating effects compared to other versions I tested, making it ideal for painting rocky textures and tree trunks.

Burnt Sienna (PR101): Derived from natural iron oxide deposits, Siennas offer deeper, reddish-brown hues compared to Ochres. My favorite transparent version from Winsor & Newton mixes very well with other colors and is incredibly useful for darker skin tones, rich soils, and autumnal foliage. (*For more information, see page 56.*)

Case Study: Mandarin Duck and Lotus Flowers

In this complex composition featuring a Mandarin duck perched upon a rock amid a lush array of lotus flowers and leaves, I used several Earth pigments to bring depth and richness to the scene. A wash of Yellow Ochre was applied to the intricate lotus leaves, imbuing them with a soft, luminous quality that echoed the gentle sunlight filtering through the foliage. To add texture and dimension to the duck feathers, I turned to the warm, earthy tones of Burnt Sienna and Umber. Layering these pigments allowed me to capture the intricate patterns and subtle nuances of the duck's plumage, from the fiery oranges to the subtle browns.

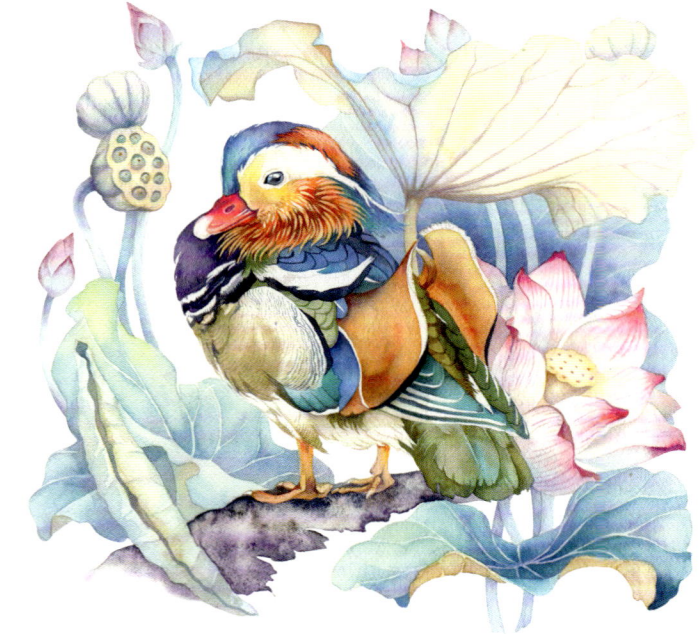

Mandarin Duck and Lotus Flowers

2.6 Cobalts: Delicate Serenity

The Cobalt family, with its refined hues and understated elegance, will bring a touch of sophistication and tranquility to your palette. These pigments hold the power to evoke feelings of serenity and elegance in watercolor compositions, from ethereal skies to delicate floral accents.

Origins and Characteristics

- Cobalt pigments first gained widespread popularity with the rise of French impressionism, exemplified by Claude Monet's serene water scenes and Auguste Renoir's dreamy figurative paintings. They continued to be used in the early twentieth century by artists interested in using colors to convey emotion. For example, Cobalt Teal is one of the prominent colors used in the Post-Impressionist masterpiece *The Starry Night* by Vincent van Gogh. Unique qualities of Cobalt pigments make them a popular choice in modern textiles, ceramics, and enameling.
- **Lightfastness:** Cobalt pigments, especially Cobalt Blue, exhibit excellent lightfastness, retaining their color intensity and stability over time.
- **Transparency:** Cobalt colors generally demonstrate semitransparency, allowing for limited layering and glazing techniques when well-diluted.
- **Granulation:** Most watercolor Cobalts exhibit a subtle granulating effect, creating textural interest in washes or layered applications. This characteristic adds depth and visual intrigue to artworks.
- **Staining:** Cobalts are generally nonstaining and can be easily lifted and manipulated long after the paint is dry.

Applications in Watercolor

- **Landscape Serenity:** Cobalt hues excel in portraying serene skies, peaceful waters, and distant horizons, adding depth and tranquility to landscapes.
- **Botanical Elegance:** Perfect for conveying subtlety and elegance in floral studies, Cobalt colors will help you create natural petal tones with soft edges and muted shadows.
- **Mixing Potential:** These pigments blend gracefully with other colors, allowing you to create a wide range of secondary and tertiary shades, including soft purples, calming greens, and various shades of blue.

HELPFUL TIP

Cobalt Blue (CB28) is an excellent choice for budding artists stepping into the world of color mixing and exploration. It is a key player in forming your essential triad palette, offering a reliable go-to blue without the complexities of green or red undertones. While Ultramarine is commonly suggested, I personally favor Cobalt for its gentle nature—it's less intense, making it incredibly forgiving and approachable, especially when you're experimenting with primary triad mixes. When mixed generously with water and a touch of your primary yellow and red, Cobalt Blue becomes an invaluable tool for creating delicate, nearly invisible cast shadows on extremely light or white subjects.

Worth a Try (My Favorites)

PB28 Cobalt Blue from Winsor & Newton

PB36 Cobalt Turquoise from Daniel Smith

PG50 Cobalt Teal from QoR Watercolors

Cobalt Blue (PB28): The most prominent member of the Cobalt family, Cobalt Blue presents a refined and balanced hue with excellent lightfastness and subtle granulation. Its understated yet vivid tones, reminiscent of twilight skies, make it a preferred choice among watercolor artists seeking depth and sophistication in their artwork.

Cobalt Turquoise (PB36): A delicate member of the Cobalt family with a strong hint of green, Cobalt Turquoise is ideal for portraying serene waters and adding a touch of mystery to foggy landscapes. Due to its subtle granulation, it can be used in multiple layers to paint snow-covered pine trees. When fully diluted, it acts as a wonderful base for wet-on-wet landscape explorations, offering a perfect hue for moody autumnal skies.

Cobalt Teal (PG50): An intriguing mix of blue and green, Cobalt Teal is perfect for capturing the vibrancy of tropical waters or adding an exotic touch to bird feathers. Sometimes called Cobalt Turquoise (Schmincke) or Cobalt Turquoise Light (Winsor & Newton), it exhibits a very smooth application, allowing for almost-transparent subtle glazes when fully diluted. At full saturation, it appears almost opaque and can be used to create beautiful accents next to rusty browns and earthy ochres in urban landscapes. For decorative and abstract applications, it pairs very well with complementary reds and orange.

Case Study: Blue Peacock

In this bird study, I applied a thin layer of Cobalt Blue and Cobalt Teal to create a vibrant underpainting on the peacock feathers. I followed with layers of rich Ultramarine to add depth and accentuate texture.

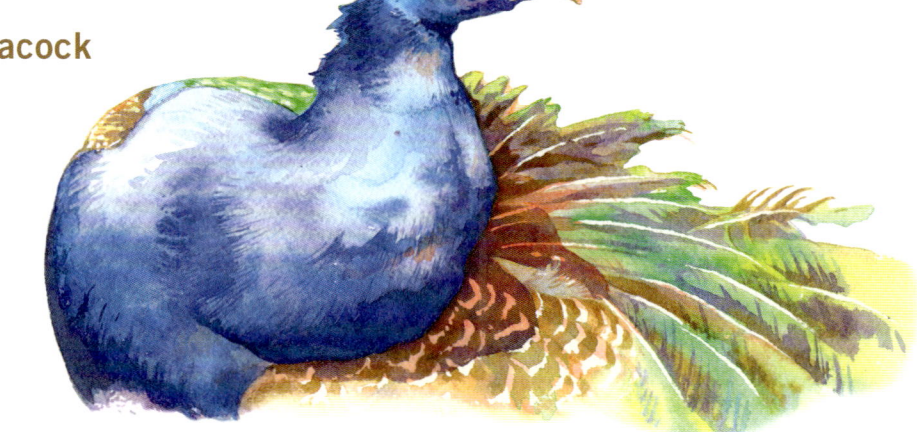

Blue Peacock

2.7 Pyrrol Pigments: A Splash of Energy

The Pyrrol family of watercolor pigments stands as a testament to modern pigment innovation, offering us a vivid spectrum of reds and oranges known for their impeccable lightfastness. These pigments blend seamlessly with other colors, producing pristine mixes and clean washes suitable for a plethora of popular watercolor techniques. Their versatility makes them suitable for an extensive range of watercolor styles, from bold florals to striking abstract compositions. Whether mixed with other colors or used boldly as standalone shades, Pyrrol pigments empower us to bring our creative visions to life with unparalleled vividness and depth.

Characteristics

- **Vividness and Versatility:** Pyrrol pigments are bright and radiant, offering exceptional saturation and purity. They bring to life the warmth of sunsets, the richness of flowers, and the vibrancy of autumn landscapes.
- **Lightfastness:** Renowned for their superb lightfast properties, Pyrrol pigments maintain their brilliance over time.
- **Mixing Capabilities:** These pigments mix well with other colors, allowing us to create nuanced shades and tones.
- **Staining:** Pyrrols are highly staining, allowing us to build up layers of color while retaining their vibrancy.

Applications in Watercolor

- **Vibrant Compositions:** Pyrrol pigments are ideal for creating bold, eye-catching compositions. Their intense colors add dynamism and energy to paintings, making them perfect for creating focal points or adding accents.
- **Mixing Possibilities:** Due to their compatibility with other pigments, Pyrrol colors can be mixed to produce a wide range of secondary and tertiary colors, adding vibrancy and rich midtones.
- **Layering and Depth:** These pigments excel in layering techniques, allowing us to build depth and dimension in our artworks. Whether used in washes or applied more densely, Pyrrol pigments offer versatility in achieving various effects.

HELPFUL TIP

Experiment by blending Pyrrol oranges with your preferred blues in varying ratios. Oranges and blues are complementary hues, positioned opposite each other on the color wheel. This relationship allows them to mingle harmoniously, neutralizing each other to craft an array of browns, subtle grays, and, when less diluted, deep blacks. Combining the non-granulating Phthalo Blue Red Shade with Transparent Pyrrol Orange will yield a refined spectrum of secondary browns, ensuring a smooth and clean outcome. Conversely, introducing a granulating blue such as Ultramarine will result in visually captivating, textured effects.

Color Mixing: Phthalo Blue Red Shade and Transparent Pyrrol Orange

Worth a Try (My Favorites)

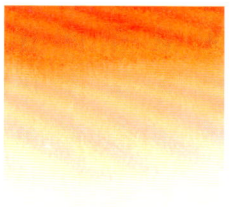
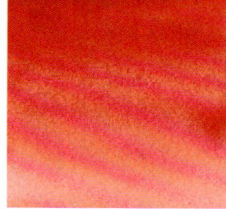

PO71 Transparent Pyrrol Orange from QoR Watercolors

PR264 Winsor Red Deep from Winsor & Newton

PR254 Pyrrol Red Medium QoR Watercolors

Transparent Pyrrol Orange (PO71): One of my favorite oranges, this bright, intense pigment offers excellent transparency and lightfastness, retaining its brilliance over time. It mixes beautifully with yellows to create vibrant, warm hues ideal for sunsets, florals, and autumnal scenes. (*See page 52 for a more in-depth exploration, where we'll delve into specific techniques and applications of PO71.*)

Pyrrol Crimson (PR264): This deep, semitransparent crimson with good tinting strength is a favorite among botanical and landscape artists. It's ideal for creating rich shadows on rose petals, or for mixing intense dark purples when combined with blue. My favorite version of this pigment is called Winsor Red Deep from Winsor & Newton.

Pyrrol Red Medium (PR254): Another excellent choice for botanical and also decorative artists, this warm fire-engine red offers versatility in mixing, providing a range of vivid oranges when mixed with yellow.

Case Study: Poinsettia Flower

In a holiday card project featuring a vibrant poinsettia flower, I used Pyrrol Crimson to capture the rich, deep red of the poinsettia's petals with striking intensity. I also applied delicate washes of Dioxazine Purple to add depth and realistic shadows, bringing a three-dimensional quality to the flower. Complementing the vivid reds, Phthalo Greens were used to paint the poinsettia's lush leaves, their bright, lively hues creating a perfect contrast.

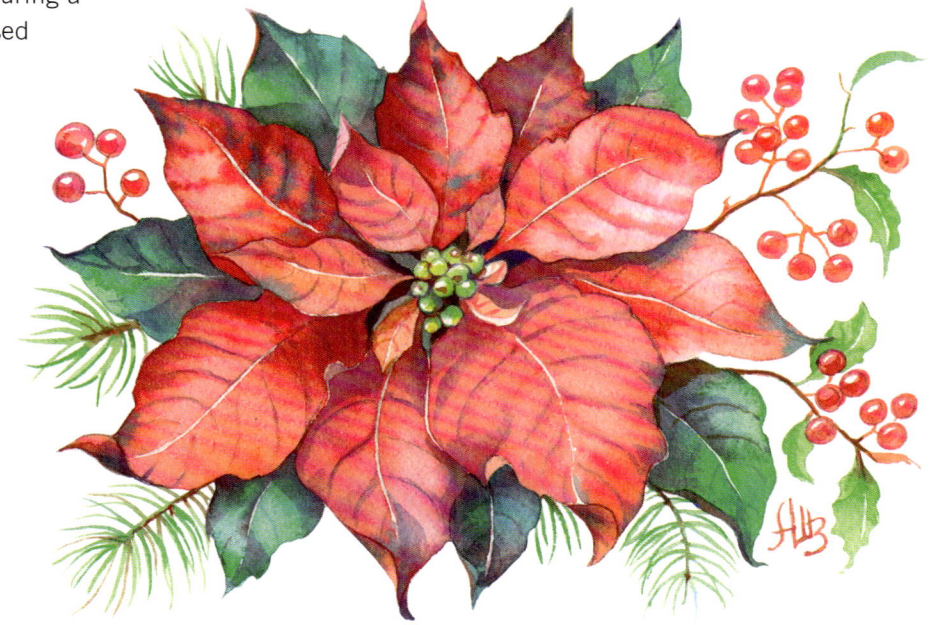

Poinsettia Flower

2.8 Other / Specialty Pigments

In addition to the traditional pigment families, the world of watercolor offers a fascinating array of specialty pigments that can add unique qualities and stunning effects to your artwork. These colors provide us with the opportunity to explore textures and effects that go beyond the conventional. Some of my favorite varieties include super-granulating mineral pigments and iridescent pigments, among many others.

Many reputable watercolor brands have developed special ranges of these unique pigments, and I encourage you to explore these to discover which ones resonate with your artistic style.

For Those Who Enjoy Extra Texture

- **Daniel Smith PrimaTek™ Watercolors:** Daniel Smith offers an impressive PrimaTek range of mineral pigments. These pigments are made from authentic mineral sources, ground into a fine pigment, and often provide very pronounced granulation that mimics the texture of the minerals themselves.
- **Schmincke Horadam Aquarell Super-Granulating Range:** Another exciting development in the world of specialty pigments is the range of super-granulating pigments from Schmincke. They combine multiple colors from different families, offering both granulation effects and beautiful color shifts within a single tube. You can explore a range of beautifully curated sets, offering pigments grouped by theme, such as Deep Sea or Galaxy.

For Those Who Love Shimmer and Sparkle

- **Daniel Smith Luminescent™ Watercolors:** These include Iridescent, Interference, Duochrome, and Pearlescent pigments. They have special reflective properties that make them shimmer and even shift in color depending on the angle of the light. They work well both on white and colored paper surfaces. However, a note of caution is warranted: It is hard, if not impossible, to preserve the unique qualities in a screen or surface design—a lot of the iridescent effects are lost in digital reproductions. Therefore, I primarily use these watercolors for fun, personal work and rarely for commercial applications.

Whether you are drawn to the natural textures of mineral pigments or the shimmering effects of luminescent colors, these unique materials can enhance your artwork in ways that traditional pigments cannot. Dive into these special ranges, experiment with different combinations, and let these extraordinary pigments inspire new directions in your art.

Worth a Try (My Favorites)

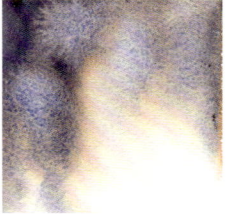

PB29 Tundra Violet
from Schmincke

PR108/PG26
Desert Green from
Schmincke

Green Apatite Gen-
uine (Mineral) from
Daniel Smith

Tundra Violet: One of my recent discoveries, Tundra Violet from Schmincke combines Ultramarine (PB29) and Mars Brown (PBr6), resulting in a complex multilayered violet with blue-violet and yellow-brown particles.

Desert Green: Another favorite from Schmincke's super-granulating range, Desert Green stands out both individually and when blended with other pigments, offering versatile possibilities particularly in landscape work. When diluted, this dark, opaque color separates into a surprising fusion of cool green and cool red hues.

Green Apatite Genuine: Green Apatite Genuine has been a staple in my botanical palette for years. Initially appearing as a dark, nearly brown, olive green in its concentrated form, this sedimentary color undergoes a captivating transformation when applied in washes, ranging from vibrant green to rich olive. (*See page 54 for a more in-depth exploration of this pigment.*)

Case Study: Summer Vegetables

In this painting, I used super-granulating Tundra Violet from Schmincke to create a textured background behind the vibrant vegetables. The particles of paint settled unevenly across the paper, creating a visually captivating backdrop that evoked the rough, earthy quality of soil. Additionally, the textured background provided an ideal setting for the delicate butterflies that adorned the garden scene.

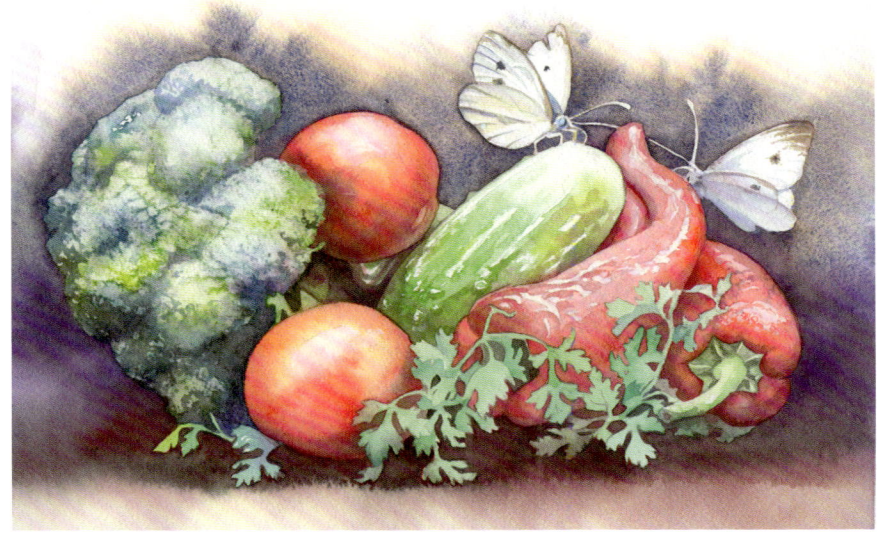

Summer Vegetables

3

Building Your
Signature Palette

3.1 Introduction

Selecting your watercolor palette can feel like stepping into a candy store—there's an abundance of pigment types and color properties to consider, as we explored in the previous chapter. With such a rainbow of options, where does one even begin?

In this chapter, we'll delve into a four-step approach to crafting and expanding your signature palette. I'll also unveil my personal selection of favorite watercolor pigments—the ones I reach for most frequently. From vibrant single-pigment "superstars" to subtle, nuanced convenience mixes, this collection spans a spectrum of possibilities. Additionally, I've included a few specialty pigments prized for their unique applications, particularly in experimental and commercial contexts.

It's important to remember that these examples are meant to ignite your creativity, not impose rules. There's no such thing as a "perfect" palette, so choose pigments that resonate with your unique watercolor style and the stories you wish to tell through color!

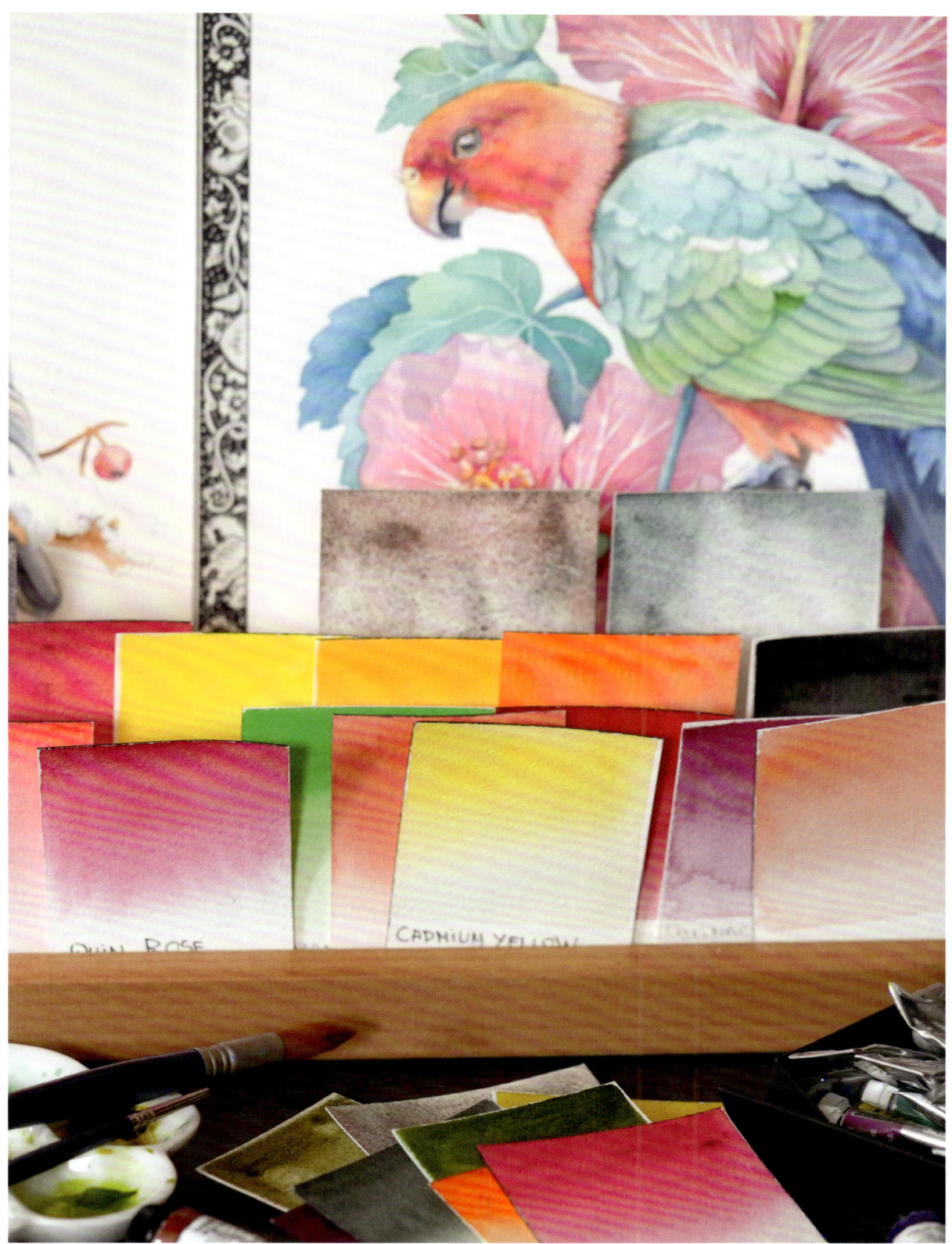

My favorite color swatches & palettes

3.2 A Four-Step Journey in Color Selection

Developing a signature palette is a journey as unique and personal as each brushstroke on a canvas. It's the process of selecting and refining a collection of colors that not only resonate with your artistic vision, but also serve as the foundation for your creative expression. Let's navigate this vivid maze together with a simple four-step approach that I've been using to set up and update my palette over the years.

1. Start with a Primary Triad

First, you will want to choose a basic set of single-pigment primary colors that will allow you to easily mix a variety of shades. Red, blue, and yellow will allow you to build a variety of hues. My favorite primary combination is Phthalo Blue, Quinacridone Magenta, and Cadmium Yellow. A more comprehensive approach involves choosing six primaries—one cool and one warm variation for each primary color. This would allow you even more flexibility and a broader range of hues in various mixing scenarios.

2. Add Subject-Based Staples

In addition to primary colors, you will want to include a few pigments that fit your unique style. This is a very personal choice and will largely depend on your favorite subjects and technique preferences. For example, I mainly focus on bold florals and tropical birds. Therefore, I often reach for vibrant Quinacridones, Phthalos, and Perylenes as a shortcut for matching my reference colors. I rarely use Cobalts because they tend to look more opaque and muted. If you are a landscape painter, you will likely want a variety of earthy hues or even green convenience mixes. Portrait artists, on the other hand, may look for pigments that most closely resemble various skin tones.

3. Include Favorites That Inspire

Don't forget to include pigments and mixes that spark your creativity! For example, I love Dioxazine Purple for its intensity and tonal variations, and I include it as a strong accent or a subtle glaze in most of my work. I also love Opera Pink. Although it is known to have limited lightfastness, I find it to be an inspiring (albeit temporary) compliment to my magentas.

4. Build Gradually & Experiment

Continue to refine your palette to suit your artistic needs and evolving sense of style. Experimentation is key! My latest obsession is super-granulating pigments from Schmincke. They're nudging me toward a more abstract and free-spirited style, something I used to shy away from when I first started experimenting with watercolors.

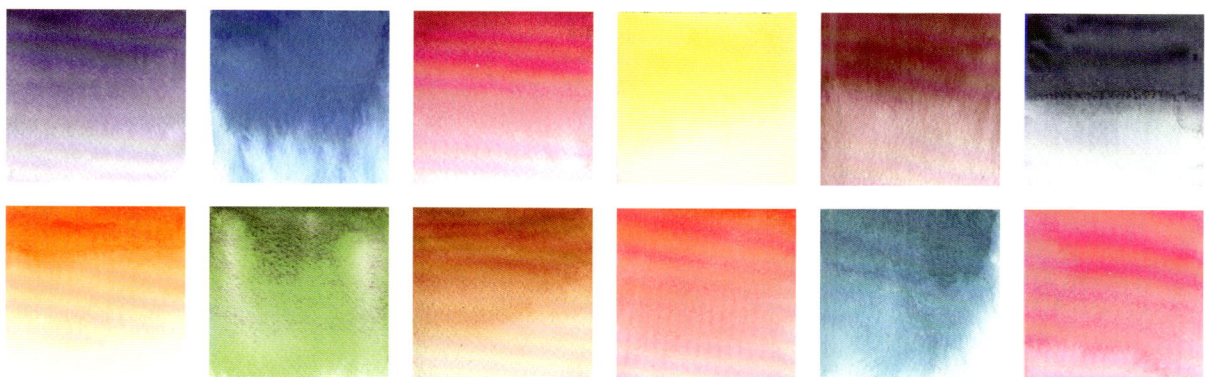

Twelve of my favorite pigments

Twelve of My Favorite Pigments

- Dioxazine Purple: PV23
- Phthalo Blue Green Shade: PB15:3
- Quinacridone Magenta: PR122
- Cadmium Yellow Medium Hue: PY53, PY151, PY83
- Perylene Violet: PV29
- Indigo: PB60, PBk6
- Transparent Pyrrole Orange: PO71
- Green Apatite Genuine: Mineral
- Burnt Sienna: PR101
- Quinacridone Coral: PR209
- Aqua Green: Phthalo (exact formulation is unlisted)
- Opera Pink: PR122

HELPFUL TIP

At the beginning of your watercolor journey, it's helpful to explore palette recommendations from well-established experts in the field. You can find high-quality and well-curated palette sets from reputable brands like Daniel Smith, Schmincke, and Winsor & Newton. Alternatively, you can refer to experienced artists, like Jane Blundell, to gradually build your own palette by purchasing individual tubes. Remember, quality should always prevail over quantity. To establish a strong foundation for your palette, prioritize a narrower selection of superior paints over student-grade sets.

3.3 Dioxazine Purple: My Signature Hue

If you explore my portfolio, you'll notice a recurring theme: various shades of purple ranging from pure and bold splashes to subtle glazes. It's no secret, PV23 reigns as my "signature" color, gracing nearly every painting I make. This pigment holds a special place as the first professional-quality color I ever acquired, marking the beginning of my enduring fascination with the watercolor medium.

Dioxazine
Purple

Pigment: PV23
Lightfastness: I – Excellent
Transparency: Semitransparent
Staining: 3 – Medium Staining
Granulation: Non-granulating
Brand: My favorite version of PV23 is from QoR Watercolors. You can find many alternatives, including Winsor Violet from Winsor & Newton and a red-leaning Carbazole Violet version from Daniel Smith that offers slight granulation.

Origins and Characteristics

- This transparent coal tar pigment (chemical name: Carbazole Dioxazine) was introduced into watercolor palettes in the twentieth century.
- **Unparalleled Intensity:** Dioxazine Purple stands out for its deep, vivid hue that typically leans toward a cooler blue tone. It boasts a vibrancy that ignites the canvas with an unmistakable presence, adding drama and depth to compositions.
- **Consistent Brilliance:** Every stroke of Dioxazine Purple bursts forth with bold, expressive color. It has a very dark and intense masstone, appearing close to black at full saturation. On the other hand, a diluted version reveals clear, softer shades of violet.

> **Masstone** refers to the color of the paint as it appears in its most concentrated, undiluted form—straight out of the tube.

Applications in Watercolor

- **Layering Dynamics:** The transparent nature of Dioxazine Purple invites layering, empowering you to build depth gradually while preserving unparalleled vibrancy, stroke after stroke.
- **Mixing Potential:** Experimenting with Dioxazine Purple in mixtures expands its potential. Combining it with warm reds or cool blues alters its appearance, providing an extensive palette particularly suited for botanical art.
- **Florals:** This color breathes life into floral compositions, allowing you to portray a mesmerizing array of flowers, each with its unique shade and depth. For example, in its pure form, it can be used to depict intensely rich Iris petals; more diluted PV23 is a great choice for purple pansies and columbines; fully diluted, it provides an excellent option for natural shadows on red roses, yellow daffodils, and pink hibiscus.
- **Portraits:** I often apply thin glazes of Dioxazine Purple to accentuate darker skin tones in my portrait work. PV23 is also useful as an underpainting for darker hair textures.

HELPFUL TIP

Experimentation is the key! Combine Dioxazine Purple with warm or cool tones, discovering a treasure trove of hues and muted shades waiting to adorn your canvas. I like to blend it with Quinacridone Magenta and Phthalo Blue to create an entire spectrum of purples, from deep, soulful violets to delicate, pastel lavenders.

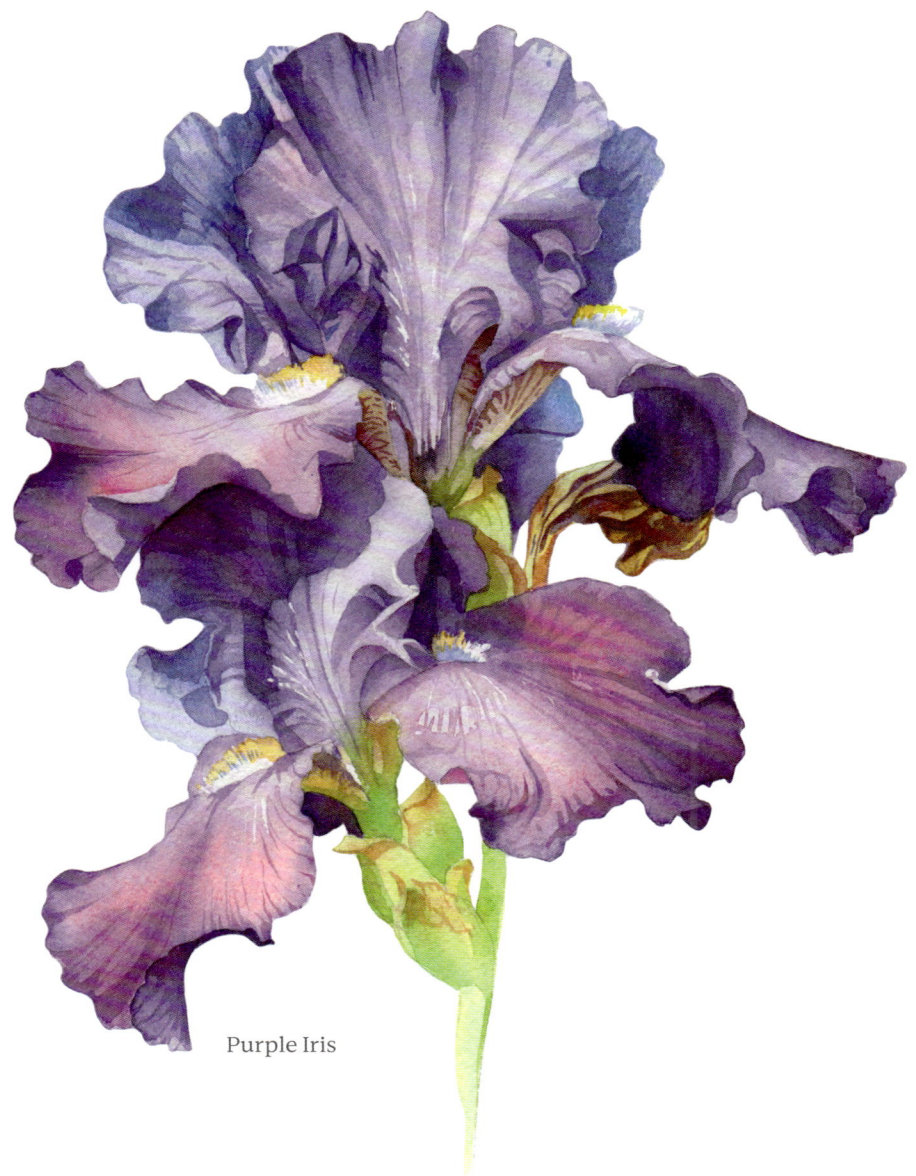

Purple Iris

Case Study: Purple Iris

I used Dioxazine Purple as the base color in this painting of an iris flower, applying several washes to gradually build depth and texture on the petals. I also introduced splashes of fluorescent Opera Pink to capture enigmatic sunlit petals at the bottom of the flower. For the background shadows, I mixed in Phthalo Blue Green Shade—another one of my favorite pigments that I describe in depth in this section.

3.4 Phthalo Blue Green Shade: Blue Primary

Pigment: PB15:3
Lightfastness: II – Good
Transparency: Transparent
Staining: 4 – High Staining
Granulation: Non-granulating
Brand: My favorite variation of Phthalo Blue Green Shade is from QoR Watercolors.

Phthalo Blue
Green Shade

Origins and Characteristics

- Phthalo Blue Green Shade, derived from the phthalocyanine family of synthetic pigments, emerged in the mid-twentieth century as a vibrant alternative to traditional blue pigments.
- **Intense Color:** Its intense color and lightfastness quickly made it a favorite among artists seeking to capture the luminous depths of the natural world.
- **Transparency:** Known for its transparent nature and high tinting strength, Phthalo Blue Green Shade is ideal for layering to create depth and complexity in paintings. It also mixes well with other colors, yielding a wide range of nuanced hues and tones.

Applications in Watercolor

- **Limited Palette / Primary Triad Studies:** Phthalo Blue Green Shade is an excellent choice of primary blue for limited palette explorations. Try mixing PB15:3 with Quinacridone reds to enjoy a range of gorgeous violets, or with yellows to get a variety of greens.
- **Botanical Art:** In botanical art, Phthalo Blue Green Shade adds a touch of vibrancy and depth to floral subjects. For example, you can use it to capture the lush hydrangea petals or the delicate blossoms of forget-me-nots, layering it with touches of purple to create the illusion of depth and volume.
- **Tropical Waters:** In seascapes, Phthalo Blue Green Shade will help you capture the brilliance of sunlit ocean waves and the mesmerizing beauty of tropical lagoons. Try glazing multiple layers of PB15:3 to convey a sense of depth and mystery in immersive underwater scenes.
- **Abstract Backgrounds:** Phthalo Blue Green Shade offers endless possibilities for creating dynamic and expressive backgrounds. I often use it in combination with Indigo and Perylene Violet to evoke mood and atmosphere in portrait backgrounds.

When embarking on botanical studies, consider swapping out traditional Ultramarine for non-granulating Phthalo Blue. I find that Phthalo Blue's smooth, non-granulating nature provides more seamless blending, facilitating the depiction of delicate textures and organic patterns with greater accuracy and control.

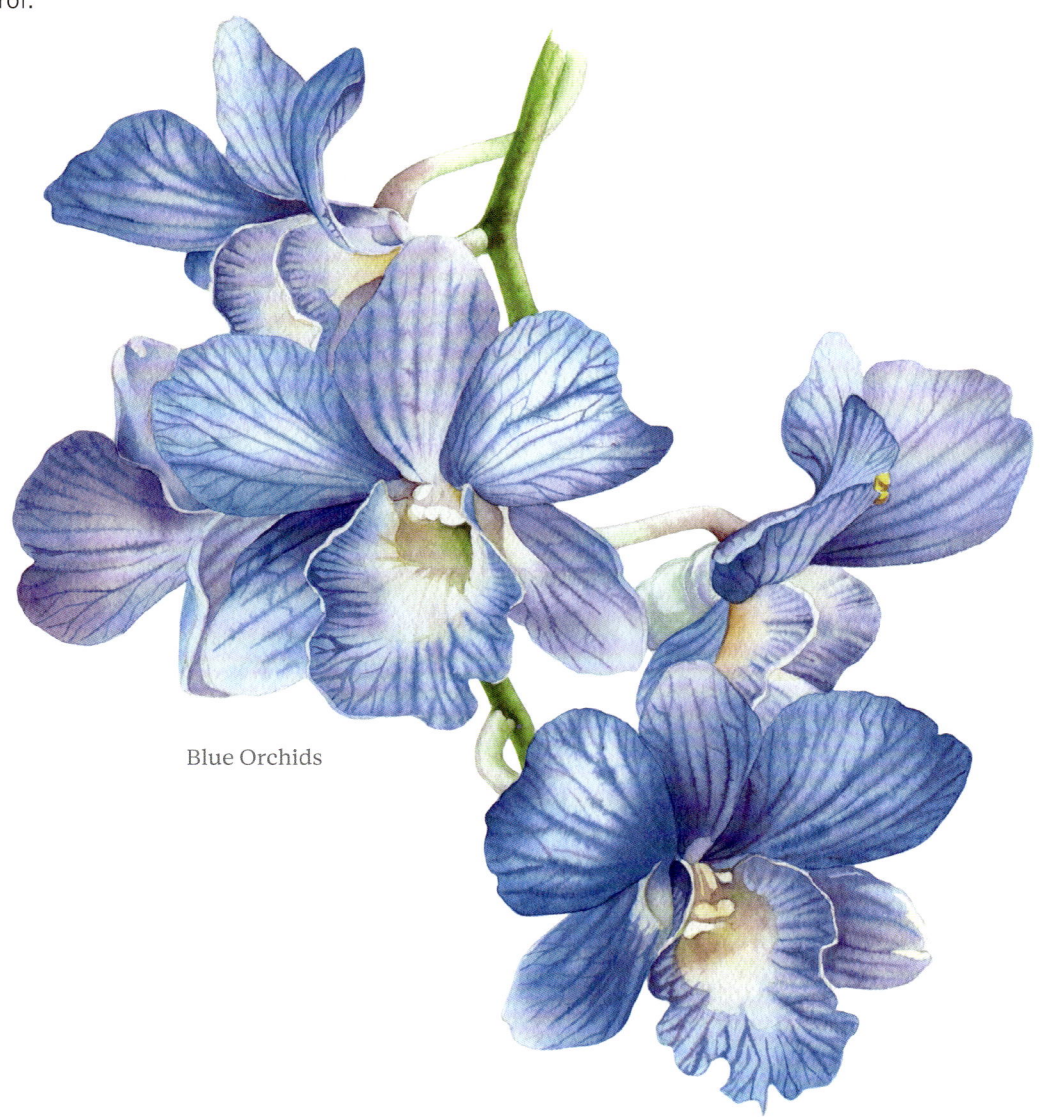

Blue Orchids

Case Study: Blue Orchid

In this study, Phthalo Blue Green Shade offers several advantages over Ultramarine, particularly in achieving soft petal veins, essential in capturing the intricate beauty of the orchid. First, I applied a light wash of PB15:3 to establish the base color of the orchid petals. Unlike granulating Ultramarine, Phthalo Blue ensured a smooth and even application, providing a perfect foundation for building up layers and details. With its high tinting strength and transparency, Phthalo Blue also allowed for more precise control over the intensity of color in my subsequent washes. I used wet-on-damp technique to create the illusion of organic veins on the orchid petals. By applying saturated Phthalo Blue to damp paper, I was able to achieve soft, diffused lines without the interference of granules.

3.5 Quinacridone Magenta: Red Primary

Quinacridone
Magenta

Pigment: PR122
Lightfastness: II – Good to I – Excellent
Transparency: Transparent
Staining: 4 – High Staining
Granulation: Non-granulating
Brand: My favorite version of PR122 from QoR Watercolors contains a unique formulation, accentuating the luminosity and brilliance of the pigment by using a binder called Aquazol®. Note the pigment's properties may vary depending on the brand, with some manufacturers offering different transparency and lightfastness ratings.

Origins and Characteristics

- Quinacridone Magenta comes from a family of aniline dyes, originally derived by distilling the colorant of the organic indigo. It was first produced in the 1850s and named in honor of the Italian-French victory in the Battle of Magenta.
- **Mixing Range:** One of my favorite Quinacridones, Magenta is a powerful blue-leaning red with good transparency and staining properties. It's mixing range will allow you to create a variety of secondary and tertiary colors, making it an invaluable asset in any limited palette studies.

Applications in Watercolor

- **Limited Palette / Primary Triad Studies:** Quinacridone Magenta can serve as an essential red in your primary triad. If you are building a more extended version of the limited palette using cool and warm variations of each primary, PR122 would be an excellent choice for your cool red.
- **Captivating Florals:** In botanical art, Quinacridone Magenta serves as a versatile tool for portraying a wide range of florals, from the bold and vibrant to the delicate and ethereal. For example, I often rely on saturated PR122 to capture the lush, layered petals of peonies, infusing them with a rich, pink hue that exudes elegance and charm. On the other hand, a more diluted version of PR122 can be used to depict the delicate blossoms of cherry trees, evoking feelings of renewal and beauty.
- **Mixing Skin Tones:** Quinacridone Magenta can be used as a cool pink hue to add depth and dimension to a range of skin tones. Whether painting fair-skinned subjects or capturing the rosy undertones of darker complexions, Quinacridone Magenta lends a natural warmth and vibrancy to the skin, enhancing the overall realism of the portrait.

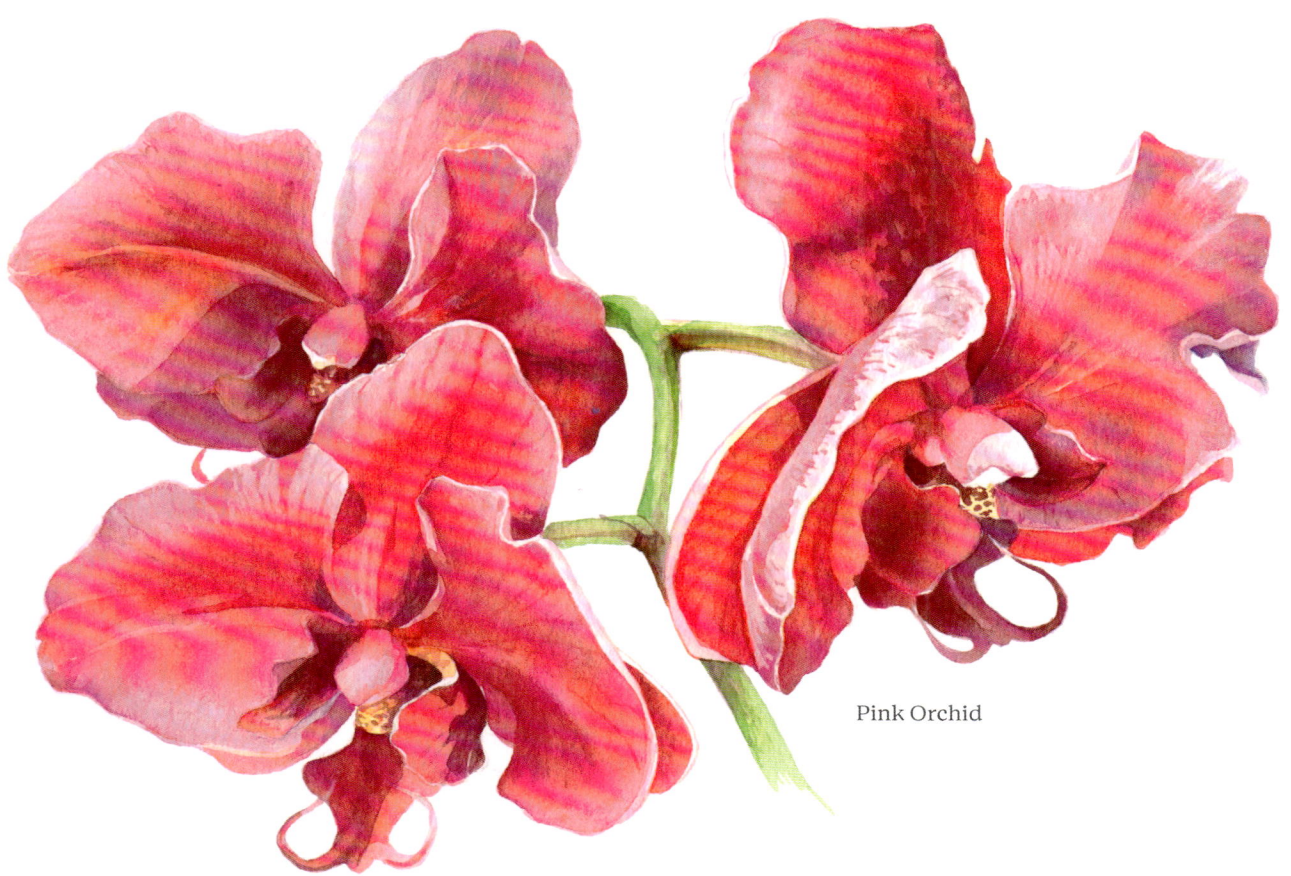

Pink Orchid

Case Study: Pink Orchid

In this study, I used non-fugitive Quinacridone Magenta to establish the base color of the Phalaenopsis orchid petals, gradually adding translucent glazes to build up the illusion of volume and achieve a rich and velvety texture. To enhance the depth and dimension of the petals, I painted darker shadows using Bordeaux and Quinacridone Violet. For an extra pop of vibrancy, I also introduced splashes of Opera Pink from Daniel Smith using wet-on-wet technique. This fluorescent version of PR122 adds a luminous quality to the petals, enhancing their natural beauty and allure. Use this fugitive pigment sparingly to highlight specific areas, as it tends to fade over time, especially when placed in direct sunlight. (*For more information on the fugitive fluorescent version of PR122, see page 62.*)

3.6 Cadmium Yellow: Yellow Primary

Cadmium
Yellow

Pigment: PY53, PY151, PY83
Lightfastness: I – Excellent
Transparency: Semitransparent
Staining: 2 – Low Staining
Granulation: Non-granulating
Brand: My favorite alternative to nontoxic Cadmium is from Daniel Smith. You can find similar hues in other brands. For example, Winsor & Newton offers a lovely Cadmium-Free Yellow Pale, as well as a brighter yellow called Winsor Yellow—a variation of the Hansa pigment.

Origins and Characteristics

- Cadmium Yellow Medium Hue from Daniel Smith is a versatile pigment crafted through a careful blend of PY53 (commonly known as lemon yellow), PY151 (Benzimidazolone yellow), and PY83 (Diarylide yellow). This combination results in a beautiful semitransparent non-granulating yellow.
- **Lightfast and Mixable:** As a safe alternative to low-soluble Cadmium, this hue offers similar properties, including excellent lightfastness and mixing potential.

Applications in Watercolor

- **Limited Palette / Primary Triad Studies:** Cadmium Yellow Medium Hue is an excellent primary yellow in limited palette studies, offering a vibrant base for exploring color relationships and harmonies. For example, a mix with Ultramarine Blue will produce slightly granulating greens, ideal for painting foliage and landscapes. Adjust the ratio of yellow to blue to achieve different shades of green, from bright and sunny to more subdued and earthy. Mixing it with Quinacridone reds yields a range of oranges and corals, perfect for painting vibrant floral compositions.
- **Botanical Art:** Included in the classic Daniel Smith watercolor set called "Floral: Cottage Gardens to Botanicals," it's no surprise that Cadmium Yellow Medium Hue is a staple in my botanical palette. It's particularly well-suited for painting daffodils, yellow roses, tulips, and peonies.
- **Fruits & Vegetables:** Use Cadmium Yellow Medium Hue to depict the bright, sunny colors of ripe fruits and vegetables. It's perfect for painting lemons, bananas, squash, and other yellow produce, adding a pop of color and freshness to your still-life compositions.
- **Landscapes:** Cadmium Yellow Medium Hue will add a touch of radiant sunshine to your landscapes, infusing them with warmth, vibrancy, and visual impact. Glaze it onto the areas of foliage, grass, or fields that are illuminated by sunlight to capture the golden tones.

Case Study: "Paeonia Bartzella" Yellow Peony

Peonies, with their lush petals and vibrant colors, are one of my favorite subjects. I used Cadmium Yellow Medium Hue to paint this gorgeous "Bartzella" peony, accentuating with complementary blues and greens to add shadows and depth.

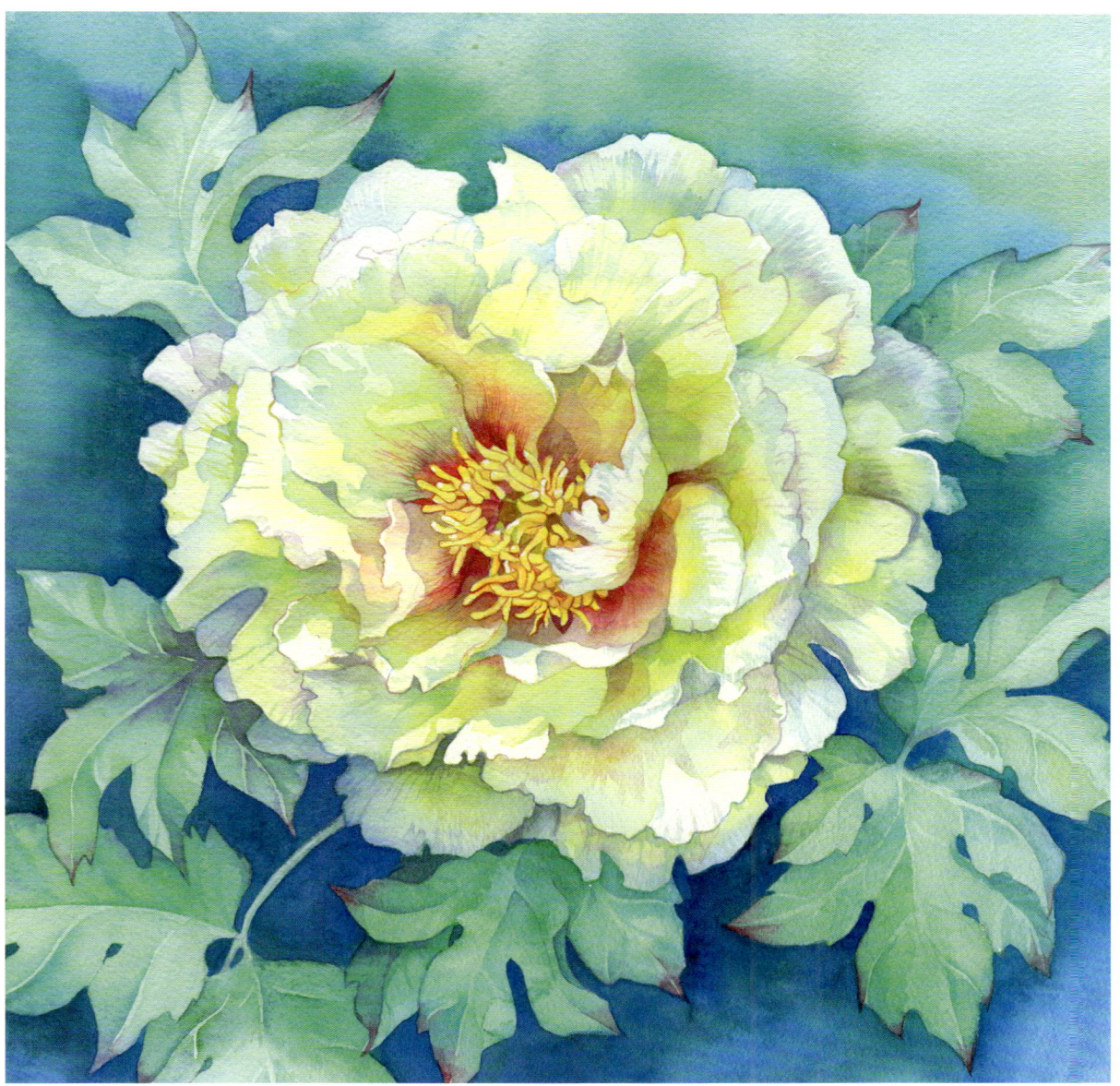

"Paeonia Bartzella" Yellow Peony

First, I used a medium-sized round brush to apply light washes of Cadmium Yellow Medium Hue as my base color on the peony petals. I built up the layers gradually, allowing each wash to dry before adding the next, to achieve the richness in the color I desired.

To create dimension in the petals, I introduced complementary blues and violets using wet-on-dry method to avoid accidentally creating a green mixture. I used very diluted Phthalo Blue Green Shade and Dioxazine Purple, applying transparent washes to the areas of the petals where shadows would naturally fall. A few touches of saturated Bordeaux and Quinacridone Red were used to accentuate the petals and the leaves.

For the background, I mixed variations of Phthalo greens with Indanthrone Blue to create a vibrant backdrop, allowing the colors to mingle and blend organically.

3.7 Perylene Violet: A Hidden Gem for Botanicals

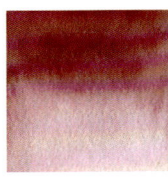

Perylene Violet

Pigment: PV29
Lightfastness: I – Excellent
Transparency: Transparent
Staining: 3 – Medium Staining
Granulation: Non-granulating
Brand: Perylene Violet from Daniel Smith quickly earned its place as a jewel in my palette, frequently making appearances in botanicals, portraits, and even decorative illustrations. I also like the version of PV29 from Winsor & Newton.

Origins and Characteristics

- Perylene Violet traces its roots back to the mid-twentieth century. Its emergence represents a stride forward in pigment technology, offering a reliable and stable option for achieving rich purple tones without compromising on lightfastness. Being relatively new compared to traditional pigments, Perylene Violet is gaining popularity among contemporary watercolorists looking to add depth and a touch of opulence to their artwork.
- **Tonal Range:** When fully saturated, this pigment looks closer to dark brown, with a hint of luscious purple undertones. When diluted, it resembles a juicy grape or ripe plum. Its rich tonal range allows for both subtle transitions and bold statements.
- **Exceptional Lightfastness:** One of its remarkable qualities is its outstanding lightfastness, ensuring that artworks retain their vibrant colors over time.

Applications in Watercolor

- **Expressive Depth:** Perylene Violet excels in creating depth and shadows in paintings, infusing scenes with a sense of mystery or drama.
- **Mixing Marvels:** Perylene Violet's versatility shines when it's mixed with other colors. It can create an array of purples, violets, and deep shadows when combined with blues, reds, or even earth tones.
- **Versatility:** Ideal for landscapes, floral compositions, or portraits, it adds richness and enduring beauty to your paintings. Embrace its regal hue when looking for an exciting alternative to your regular browns in botanical work. It also works well for mature and dark skin tones, adding an alluring depth to cast shadows and subtle wrinkles.

HELPFUL TIP

Watercolor charging technique works particularly well with Perylene Violet. Try adding vibrant oranges or magentas wet-on-wet to add visual interest to the petals like I did in this painting of a chocolate orchid. When mixed with warm greens, it adds a very natural effect to flower stems. You can also charge your favorite blues and purples for extra texture and depth in the background washes. (*For more information on the charging technique, see page 103.*)

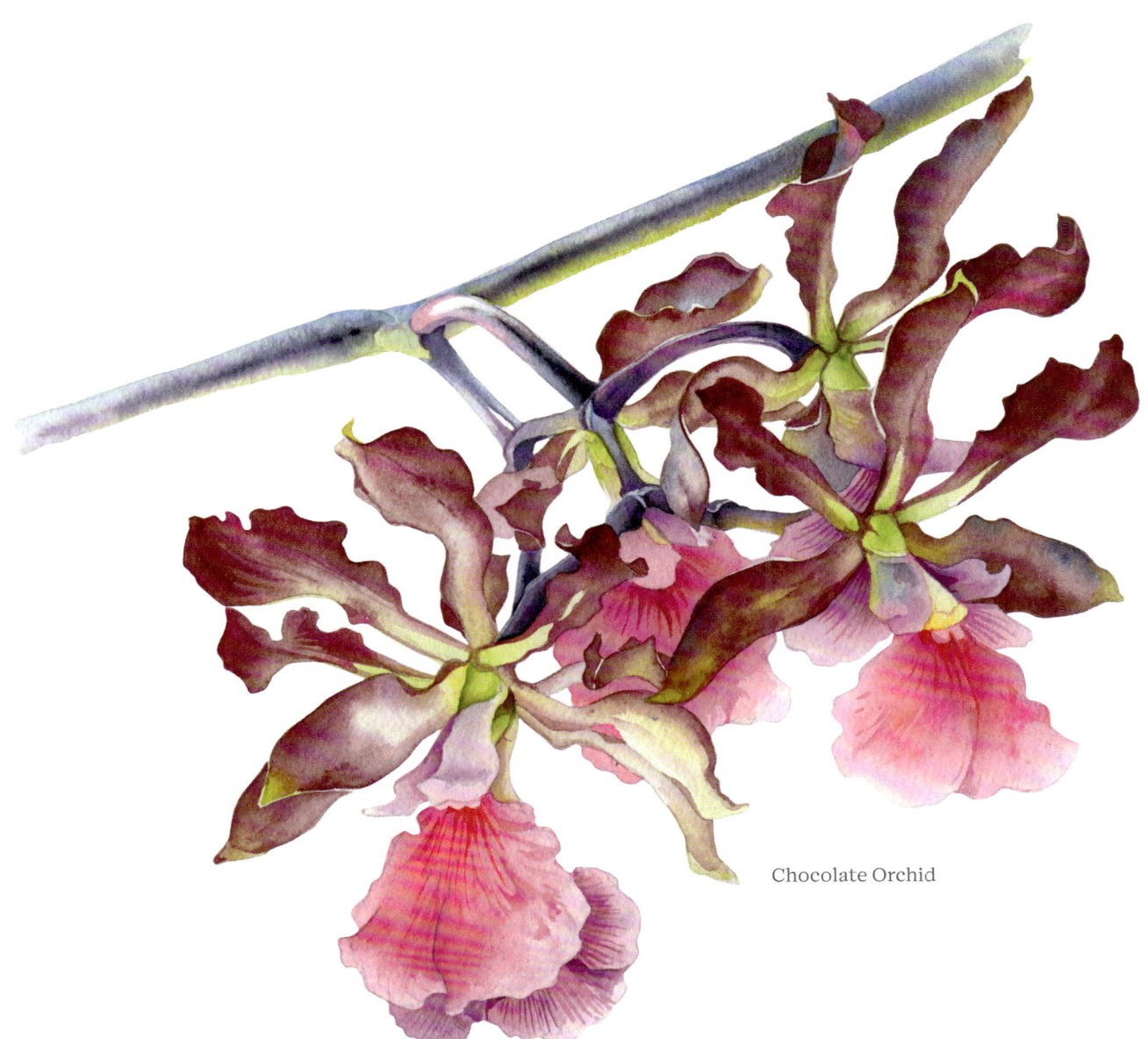

Chocolate Orchid

Case Study: Chocolate Orchid

In this orchid study, I used Perylene Violet both on the flower and on the stems, adding splashes of vibrant magenta, green, and even blue to enhance dimension. Applying multiple layers of PV29 allowed me to achieve the distinct deep coloring on the petals.

Video Available ▶ rockynook.com/watercolor-secrets

3.8 Indigo: Embracing Depth without Black

Indigo

Pigment: PB60, PBk6
Lightfastness: I – Excellent
Transparency: Transparent
Staining: 3 – Medium Staining
Granulation: Non-granulating
Brand: My favorite convenience mix from Daniel Smith uses a combination of Indanthrone Blue and Lamp Black to create a mesmerizing blue shade that closely resembles the original, organically derived color.

Origins and Characteristics

- Originally extracted from the sprigs of the Indigofera plant, Indigo boasts an ancient legacy. The original version of the pigment was created through a meticulous process involving fermentation and oxidation to produce the iconic blue hue. Revered in civilizations like ancient India and Egypt, Indigo was a symbol of prestige and spirituality, often associated with mysticism.
- **Rich and Lightfast:** By combining the timeless allure of Indigo with modern advancements in pigment technology, contemporary watercolors offer artists the best of both worlds: the rich hue of the original pigment with the added assurance of longevity and lightfastness.
- **Variety:** While I personally favor the Daniel Smith version of Indigo for its quality and consistency, it's worth noting that various manufacturers offer their own interpretations of this pigment. Some versions are formulated without the use of black, resulting in a different take on this beloved hue. You can find both warm and cool variations, and even granulating formulations, allowing you to tailor your blue palette to specific subjects or moods.

Applications in Watercolor

- **Value Studies:** Indigo is a perfect choice when it comes to creating monochromatic value studies. Its deep, rich hue lends itself beautifully to exploring the nuances of light and shadow in a single color spectrum. (*For more information on value studies, see page 236.*)
- **Moody Landscapes:** Indigo evokes a feeling of atmospheric depth used for expressive, moody skies. It possesses a wide range of values, from the darkest midnight blues to softer, lighter shades. This range will allow you to capture a full spectrum of tones within your work, making it perfect for depicting the subtle gradations of light and shadow in moody landscapes.
- **Mixing & Glazing:** Indigo is incredibly versatile and can be easily manipulated when mixed with other colors or diluted with water. By adjusting the concentration of pigment, you can achieve a wide variety of effects, from bold, opaque washes to delicate, translucent glazes. Indigo blueberries, blackberries, and plums are a few subjects to play with when using this technique.

HELPFUL TIP

Indigo isn't just another dark-blue color—it's one of your best alternatives to using pure black straight from the tube! Its depth and richness make it a powerful substitute, adding shadows, definition, and depth without the starkness of black pigments. For example, I often use Indigo when creating shadows in my botanical, bird, and animal studies. It offers a softer touch, allowing for more nuanced and natural-looking shadows that won't overpower or take attention away from my colorful subjects.

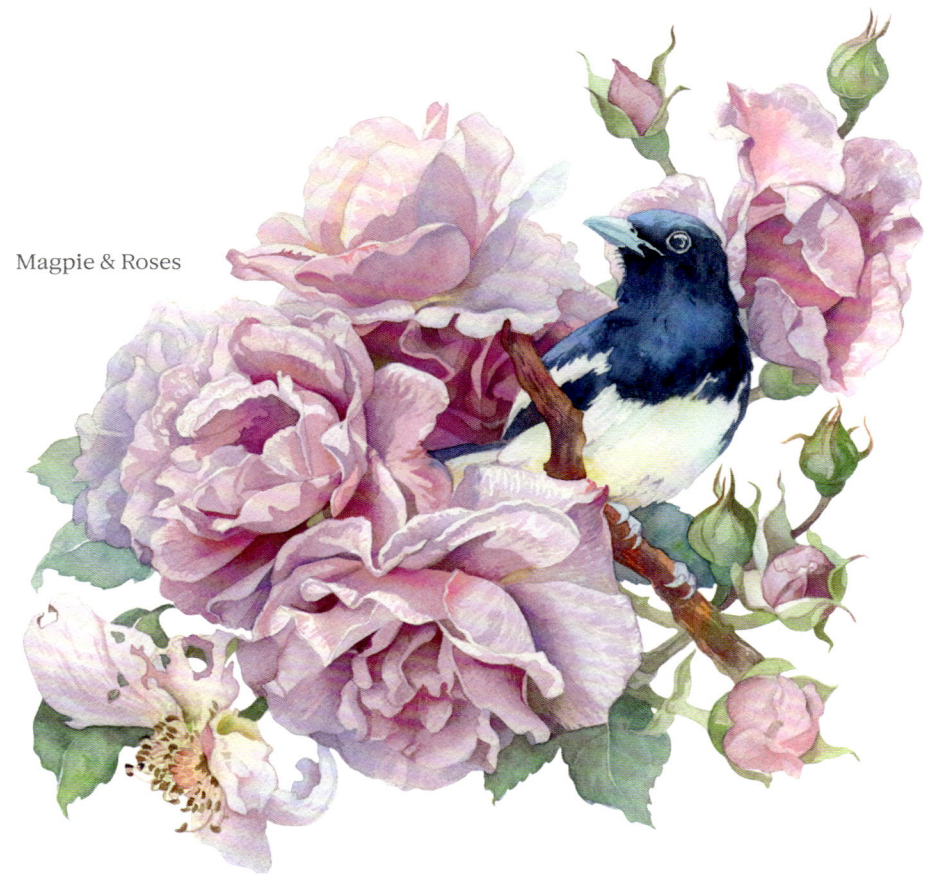

Magpie & Roses

Case Study: Magpie & Roses

In this composition featuring a magpie bird perched amid purple roses, the use of Indigo in watercolor can truly shine. I started with a combination of diluted Indigo and Phthalo Blue Green Shade to create subtle reflections dancing across the feathers of the magpie. This initial layer sets the foundation for depth and dimension, hinting at the bird's glossy plumage catching traces of light.

Next, I transitioned to the fully saturated Indigo to render the darkest areas of the magpie's feathers. Rather than appearing harsh or artificial, the Indigo adds a sense of realism and richness to the bird's appearance. Importantly, it doesn't overpower the delicate roses blooming nearby. Instead, it complements them, echoing the bluish tones found in the violet shadows cast by the petals. This subtle interplay of color ties the elements of the composition together harmoniously, creating a cohesive and visually compelling scene.

Video Available ▶ rockynook.com/watercolor-secrets

3.9 Transparent Pyrrole: An Orange Like No Other

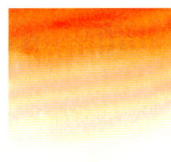

Transparent
Pyrrole Orange

Pigment: PO71
Lightfastness: I – Excellent
Transparency: Transparent
Staining: 2 – Low Staining
Granulation: Non-granulating
Brand: QoR Watercolors offers the boldest high-chroma version
of PO71 I could find.

Origins and Characteristics

- Pyrrole Orange is a synthetic pigment developed in the late-twentieth century as an alternative to more-toxic Cadmium oranges. It was originally used in the automotive industry and even in the production of some synthetic gemstones.
- **Vibrancy:** Transparent Pyrrole Orange is much bolder than a typical orange, adding extra depth and electric radiance to your work.
- **Lightfastness:** Like many Pyrrole pigments, Transparent Pyrrole Orange offers excellent lightfastness, ensuring your artworks will retain their brilliance through time.

Applications in Watercolor

- **Layering and Glazing:** Due to its transparent quality, Transparent Pyrrole Orange is excellent for layering techniques in watercolor. Applying multiple thin glazes will help you achieve depth and richness without sacrificing luminosity.
- **Mixing Possibilities:** When mixed with other colors, Transparent Pyrrole Orange produces a variety of bright and vibrant shades. It blends well with yellows to create warmer tones and with reds to create a subtle shift in hue and enhance the intensity. It is also excellent for neutralizing the most vivid blues, giving you a wide range of browns, grays, and blacks as a result. Try it with greens as well to create exquisite earthy hues that are both textural and warm.

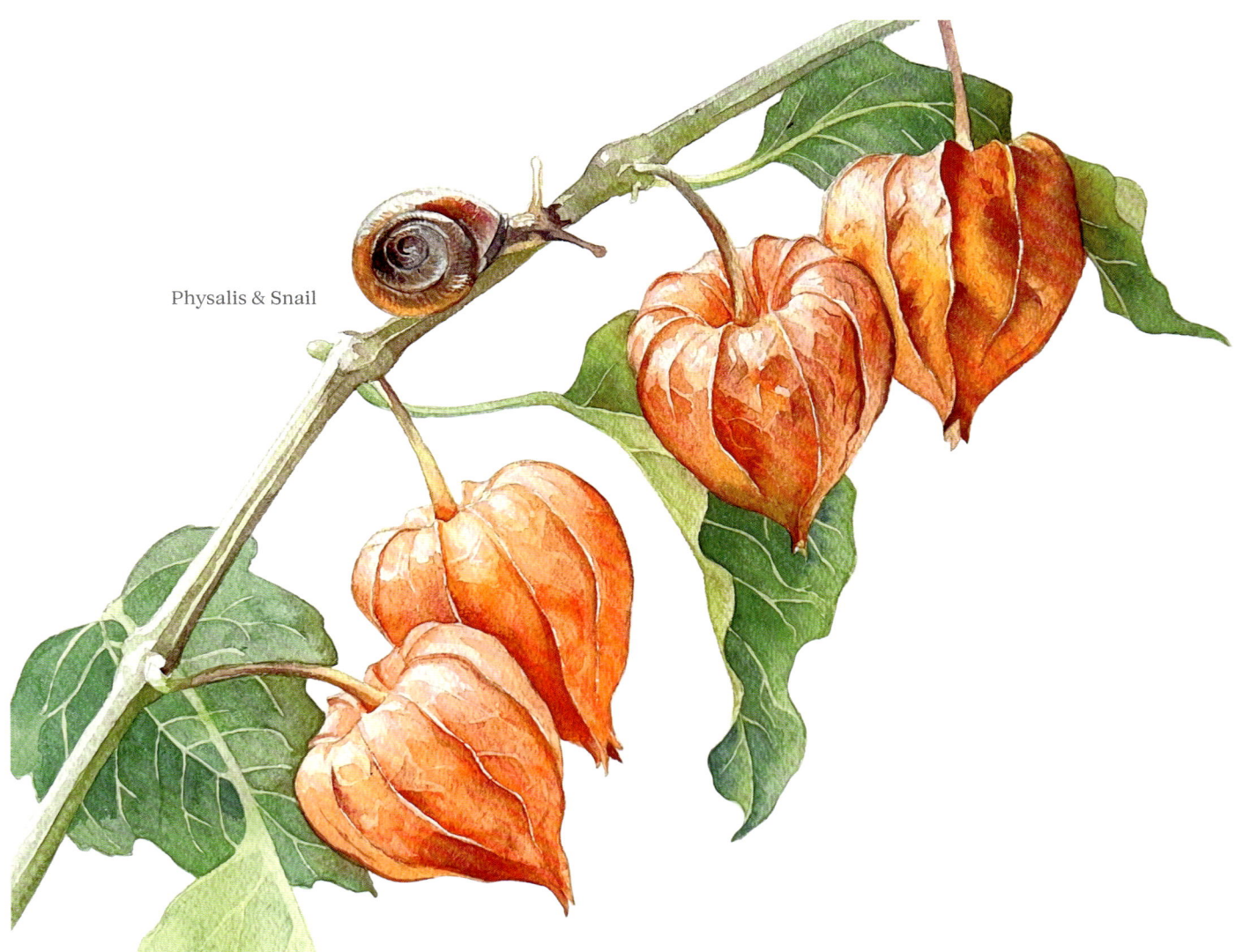

Physalis & Snail

Case Study: Chinese Lanterns (Physalis & Snail)

In this painting of a Physalis plant, I glazed several layers of PO71, building depth and intensity with each stroke. In the first layer, I mixed Pyrrole Orange with Hansa Yellow to create warm highlights. In the last layer, I added a splash of Quinacridone Burnt Orange to accentuate the shadows. In addition to the lanterns, I used PO71 on the leaves, glazing it as a thin layer on top of Hooker's Green. As you can see, PO71 is very smooth and evenly dispersed, which allowed me to build crisp edges around the thin white veins even on slightly textured cold-pressed paper.

Video Available ▶ rockynook.com/watercolor-secrets

3.10 Green Apatite Genuine: Granulating Wonder

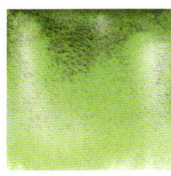

Green Apatite
Genuine

Pigment: Mineral

Lightfastness: I – Excellent

Transparency: Semitransparent

Staining: 2 – Low Staining

Granulation: Granulating

Brand: The Green Apatite Genuine pigment I use can be found in the PrimaTek™ line of mineral pigments under the Daniel Smith brand.

Origins and Characteristics

- All colors in the PrimaTek™ line from Daniel Smith are derived from minerals. Some even come from semiprecious stones.
- **Granulating Pigment:** Due to its sedimentary nature, Green Apatite Genuine exhibits strong granulation properties, while offering good lightfastness. The pigment particles "separate" beautifully on paper, creating intriguing washes featuring two distinct colors: a rich golden brown and a fresh, lively green.

Applications in Watercolor

- **Botanical Art:** In the realm of botanical art, Green Apatite Genuine offers a unique opportunity to breathe life into lush greenery. Its strong granulation properties infuse foliage with a captivating texture, reminiscent of the intricate details found in nature. Imagine painting a vibrant botanical scene where the leaves of a plant come alive with rich, warm greens that exhibit dynamic granulation.
- **Landscapes:** Green Apatite Genuine opens up a world of possibilities for creating atmospheric scenes brimming with depth and texture. Picture a sweeping landscape where distant hills fade into misty horizons and lush foliage dances in the breeze. One of my favorite techniques for harnessing the granulation of Green Apatite Genuine in landscapes is to embrace the fluidity of watercolor by spraying clear water onto the fresh wash and gently tilting the page. This action encourages the movement of pigment particles, accentuating the granulation effect and adding an extra layer of dynamism to the painting. The result is a landscape that feels alive with movement and texture, inviting viewers to immerse themselves in its beauty.

HELPFUL TIP

One of my favorite ways of using Green Apatite Genuine is to pair it strategically with non-granulating or lightly granulating colors, such as Phthalo Turquoise or Hooker's Green. By juxtaposing the textured greenery against smooth washes, you can create a visually striking contrast that enhances the overall depth and interest of the composition.

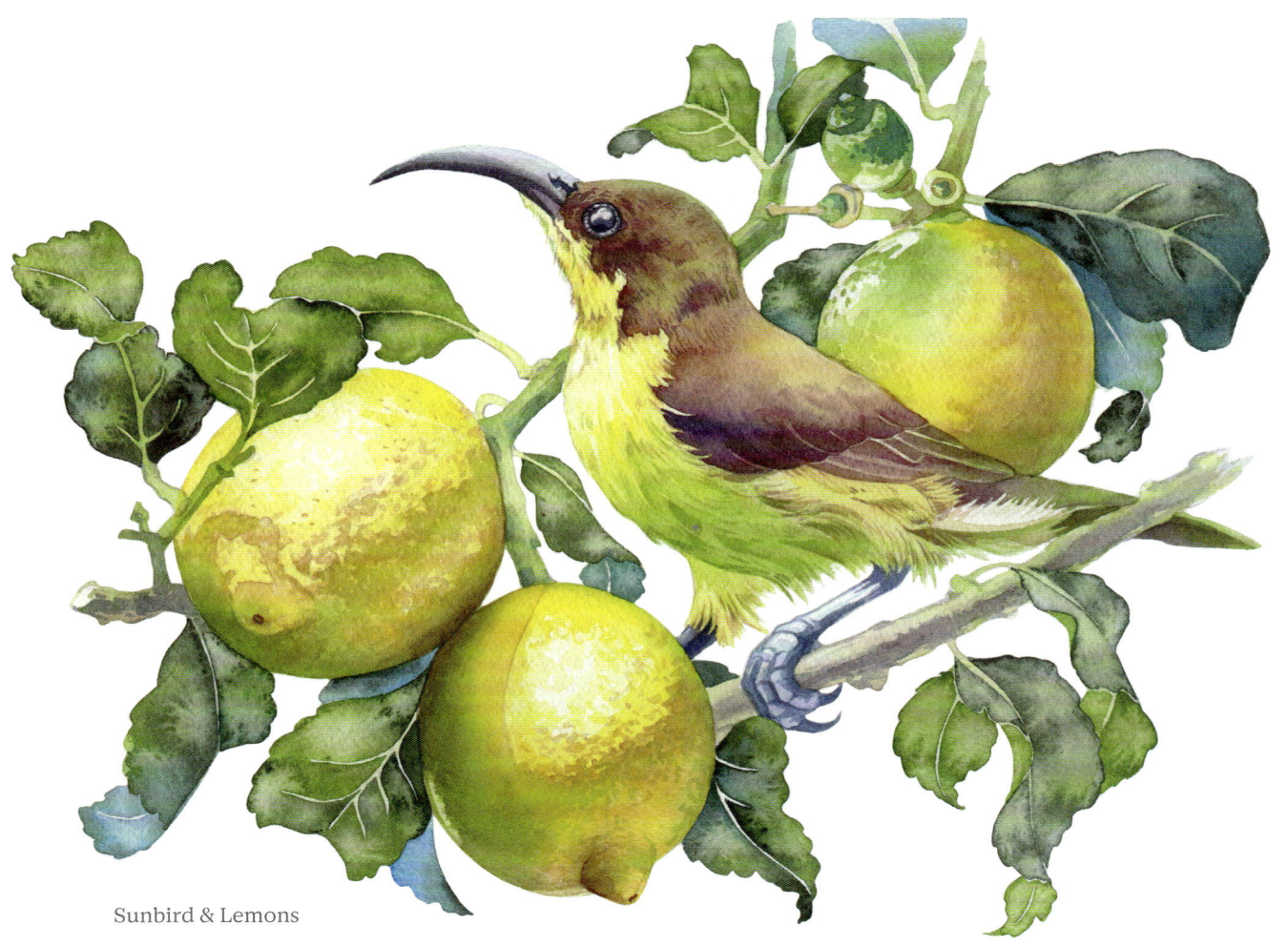

Sunbird & Lemons

Case Study: Sunbird & Lemons

In this composition, I applied Green Apatite Genuine in combination with Perylene Green and Aqua Green all over the lemon leaves. Heavier particles settled into the valleys of my paper, leaving behind wonderful granulation and texture that complements the smooth washes on the bird and the fruits. The interplay between granulating and non-granulating areas adds a dynamic quality to the artwork, drawing the viewer's eye and inviting closer inspection.

Video Available ▶ rockynook.com/watercolor-secrets

3.11 Burnt Sienna: Earthy Elegance

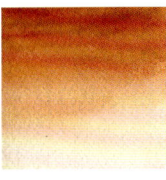

Burnt Sienna

Pigment: PR101
Lightfastness: I – Excellent
Transparency: Transparent
Staining: 1 – Nonstaining
Granulation: Non-granulating
Brand: Although typical Burnt Sienna watercolors are made with granulating PBr7, some brands use synthetic iron oxides to enhance vibrancy and transparency. I use the Winsor & Newton version of Burnt Sienna made with transparent red iron oxide (PR101). It offers a warm, rich brown hue with reddish undertones that doesn't granulate.

Origins and Characteristics

- The name of the pigment comes from "terra di Siena" or "Siena earth," referring to the city of Siena in Tuscany where it was originally extracted during the Renaissance. Sourcing and producing Earth pigments was a thriving industry at that time, and the range of colors was expanded to produce Burnt Sienna through the roasting of Raw Sienna. This heating process results in a transformation that deepens the color of Raw Sienna and enhances its warmth.
- **Lightfastness:** Burnt Sienna is generally lightfast, ensuring that artworks retain their vibrancy and integrity over time.
- **Layering and Mixing Potential:** It has excellent layering capabilities, allowing artists to build up depth and texture by applying thin glazes of diluted color. As a nonstaining color, it can be easily lifted off to reveal the white paper even after the wash is dry. Burnt Sienna mixes well with a variety of other pigments, yielding a range of nuanced tones. One of the most popular watercolor mixes includes combining Burnt Sienna and Ultramarine Blue to produce lively neutral grays.

Applications in Watercolor

- **Animal Studies**: Burnt Sienna proves invaluable for capturing the rich, varied textures of animal fur, and it's been a staple in my palette when painting pet portraits. For example, you can use it to paint tiger fur, adding stripes with saturated Indigo. It even works for light/almost-white animal fur. Try mixing very diluted Burnt Sienna with touches of Indigo to achieve the desired depth and shading on the sleek fur of a Siamese cat.
- **Landscapes:** In landscapes, Burnt Sienna lends itself beautifully to creating earthy textures and sandy terrain that evoke a sense of natural beauty and tranquility. Whether you're painting rocky cliffs or sun-drenched deserts, Burnt Sienna adds warmth and depth to the landscape, imbuing it with a timeless elegance that captivates the viewer's imagination.

HELPFUL TIP

Balance Burnt Sienna with vibrant accents. While I naturally gravitate toward vibrant and bold colors, I recognize the important role that Burnt Sienna plays in my palette. I find it particularly useful for rendering the diverse array of animals that inhabit my compositions. My favorite way of introducing this neutral color into my expressive style is to juxtapose it with vibrant greenery, bold red, cr dark blues for extra contrast.

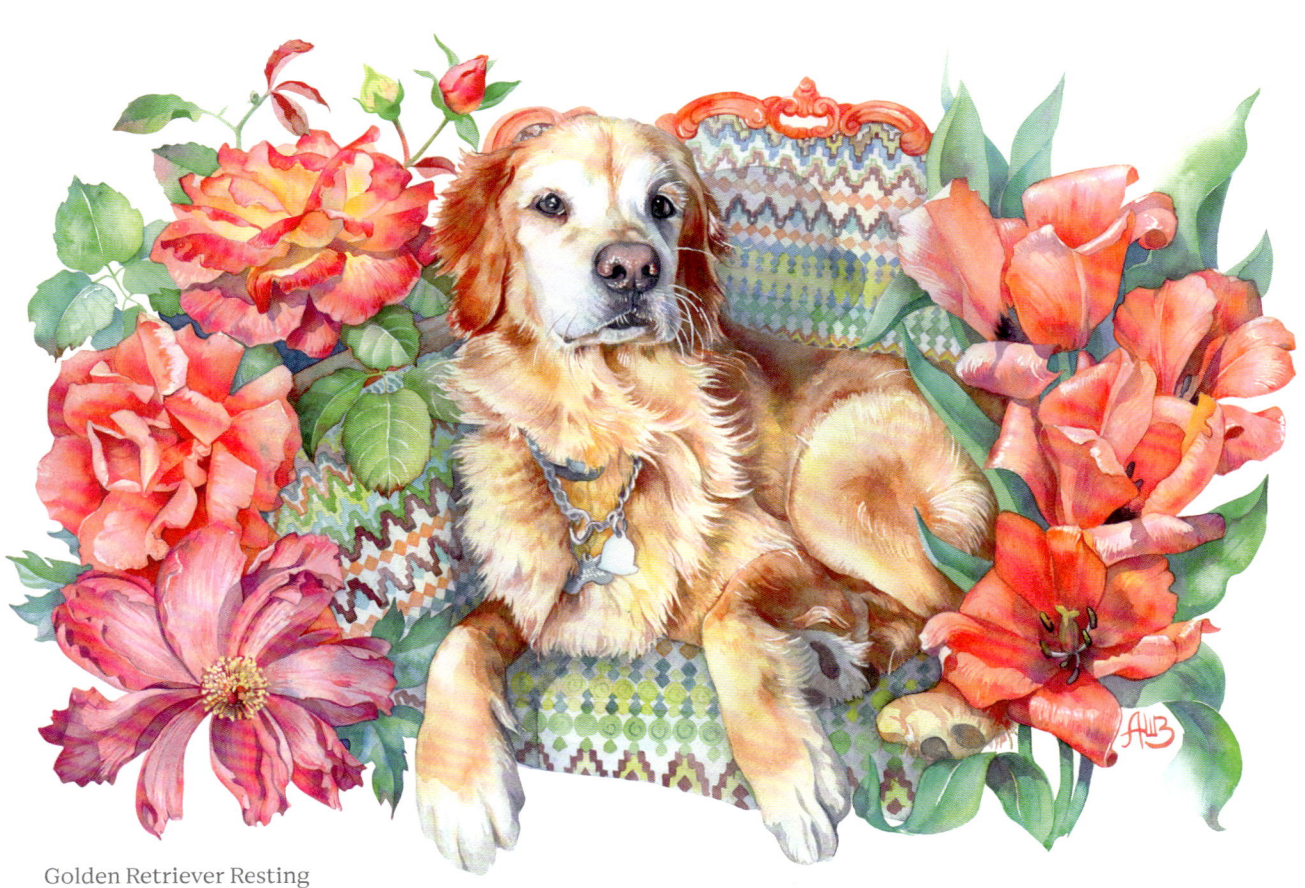

Golden Retriever Resting

Case Study: Golden Retriever Resting

In this pet portrait, I used Burnt Sienna as the primary pigment for the dog, layering it with subtle hints of yellow and ochre to capture the sunlight catching on the fur. I also glazed layers of Phthalo Blue and Indigo for the dark shadows.

3.12 Quinacridone Coral: Luminous Warmth

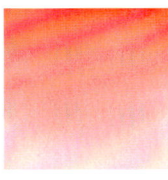

Quinacridone Coral

Pigment: PR209
Lightfastness: I – Excellent
Transparency: Transparent
Staining: 2 – Low Staining
Granulation: Non-granulating
Brand: My favorite version of this warm Quinacridone is from Daniel Smith. Note that PR209 is sometimes referred to as red, including Quinacridone Red in the Winsor & Newton range, and Quinacridone Red Light in the Schmincke range.

Origins and Characteristics

- Along with other synthetic pigments in the Quinacridones family, Coral was developed in the mid-twentieth century.
- **Excellent Lightfastness:** Exhibiting excellent lightfastness, Quinacridone Coral ensures that artworks retain their brilliance and vibrancy over time, making it suitable for archival purposes.
- **Layering and Mixing Potential:** With its transparent and versatile nature, Quinacridone Coral lends itself well to layering, allowing you to build up depth and complexity in your paintings. It also mixes harmoniously with other colors, yielding a range of nuanced hues and tones. Try mixing it with Quinacridone Gold to produce warm, sun-kissed hues ideal for capturing fruits or tropical flowers. Alternatively, you can add Phthalo Blue to create soft purples and mauves, perfect for depicting twilight skies or the shadows of dusk.

Applications in Watercolor

- **Botanical Art:** Quinacridone Coral adds a touch of luminosity to floral subjects, infusing them with a radiant warmth. For example, I love painting delicate blossoms of peach and apple trees with Quinacridone Coral, layering them with hints of magenta and orange to create a soft, ethereal effect that evokes the fleeting beauty of spring.
- **Sunrise or Sunset Skies:** In landscapes, Quinacridone Coral transforms skies into breathtaking tapestries of color, capturing the fleeting beauty of sunrise or sunset in all its radiant splendor.
- **Mixing Skin Tones:** In portraits, Quinacridone Coral will help you achieve natural and lifelike skin tones with a warm, glowing undertone.

HELPFUL TIP

Try Quinacridone Coral with a yellow underpainting. In my botanical studies, I often use yellow as an underpainting color for coral flowers. This creates a subtle glow that adds warmth and radiance to the petals, enhancing their natural beauty and allure.

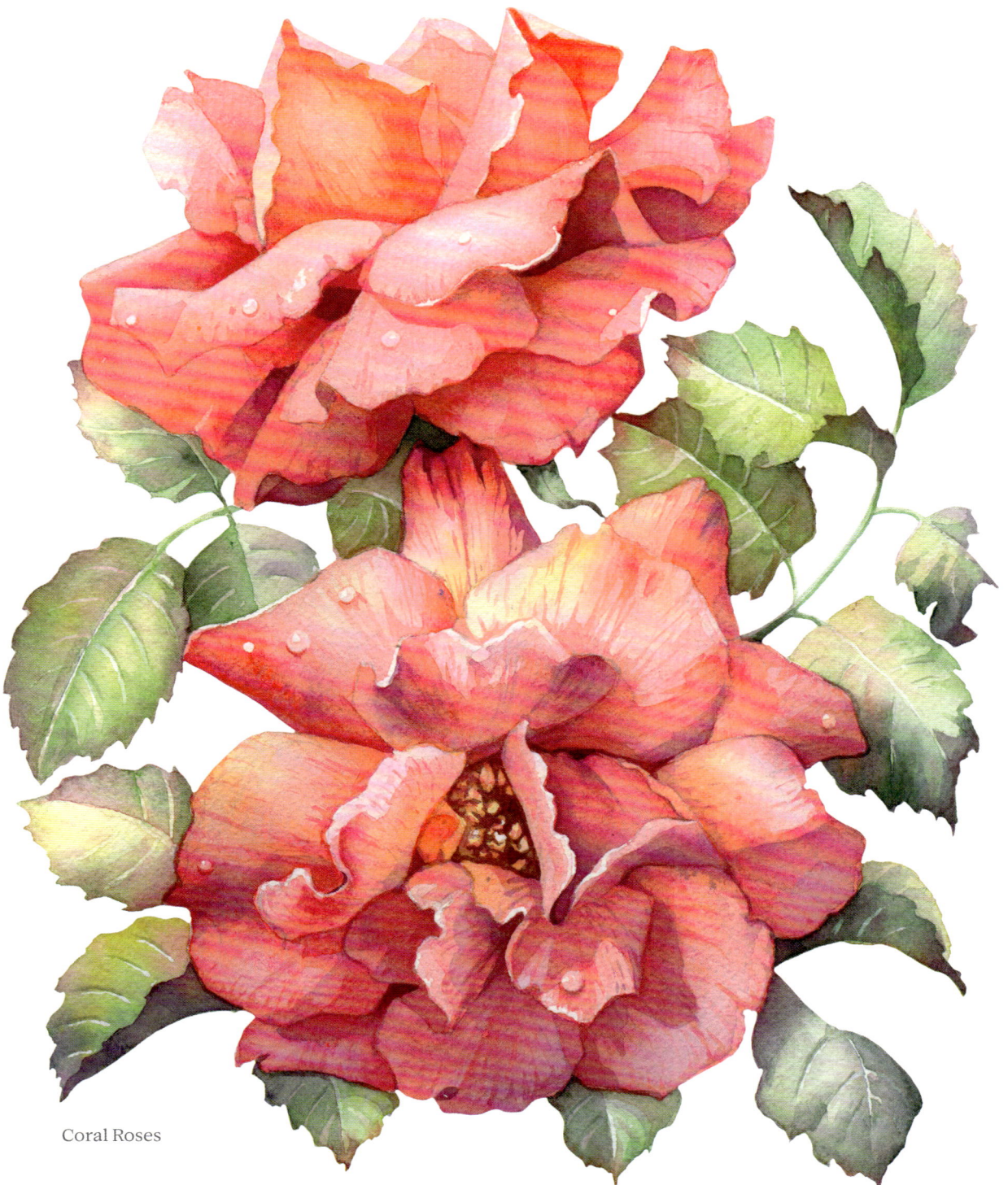

Coral Roses

Case Study: Coral Roses

In this rose study, I applied a thin wash of Hansa Yellow to the areas where the sunlight hits the rose petals directly, and then followed with a wash of Quinacridone Coral to establish the base color. Once the initial wash has dried, I built up additional layers using varying concentrations of Quinacridone Coral mixed with touches of other reds to create depth and texture.

3.13 Aqua Green: Serene Waters

Aqua Green

Pigment: Phthalo
Lightfastness: I – Excellent
Transparency: Transparent
Staining: Staining (W&N does not provide exact staining information)
Granulation: Minor
Brand: This Phthalo pigment is currently only offered by Winsor & Newton. You can try a similar, albeit more intense and blue-leaning alternative called Phthalo Turquoise from Winsor & Newton or other manufacturers.

Origins and Characteristics

- Aqua Green, sometimes referred to as Palomar Turquoise, was first crafted by Windsor & Newton around 2015. Although the Color Index hasn't been assigned yet, we know that it emerges from a Phthalo family (as of 2024 it is known as Palomar Turquoise). Therefore, it possesses all of the distinct characteristics of Phthalocyanine pigments, including excellent lightfastness and transparency.
- **Endless Range:** Its soft, blue-leaning hue evokes a sense of serenity and depth, reminiscent of misty forests and cool waters. Aqua Green has a very dark masstone when fully concentrated. However, it can be easily diluted, providing endless possibilities for creating nuanced shades and tones.
- **Layering and Mixing Potential:** In my experience, it lends itself well to glazing and wet-on-wet applications, allowing you to build up depth and complexity in your layers. It also mixes harmoniously with other colors, particularly other Phthalos.

Applications in Watercolor

- **Seascapes:** The most obvious application of Aqua Green is in capturing the subtle, greenish hues of tranquil waters. You can easily blend it with other blues, including Indigo and Phthalo Blue Green Shade, to create depth and movement in your seascapes.
- **Landscapes:** Aqua Green also lends itself beautifully to painting serene forests and mountain landscapes. Try mixing it with touches of warmer green to create spring foliage bathed in sunlight.
- **Portraits:** Interestingly, Aqua Green works really well as a shadow color when painting portraits. I often add translucent glazes of this Phthalo around the darkest areas of the face, particularly for skin tones with a green undertone.

HELPFUL TIP

While Aqua Green is typically favored in seascapes, don't hesitate to incorporate it into your botanical studies as well. I find that its blue-leaning hue always adds a touch of tranquility to green leaves, softening the contrast between the petals and the background foliage. Its transparent nature ensures smooth and even application, allowing for seamless blending of colors, while its high tinting strength enables you to achieve deep washes with minimal pigment. In fact, Aqua Green has become one of my go-to choices for botanical backgrounds.

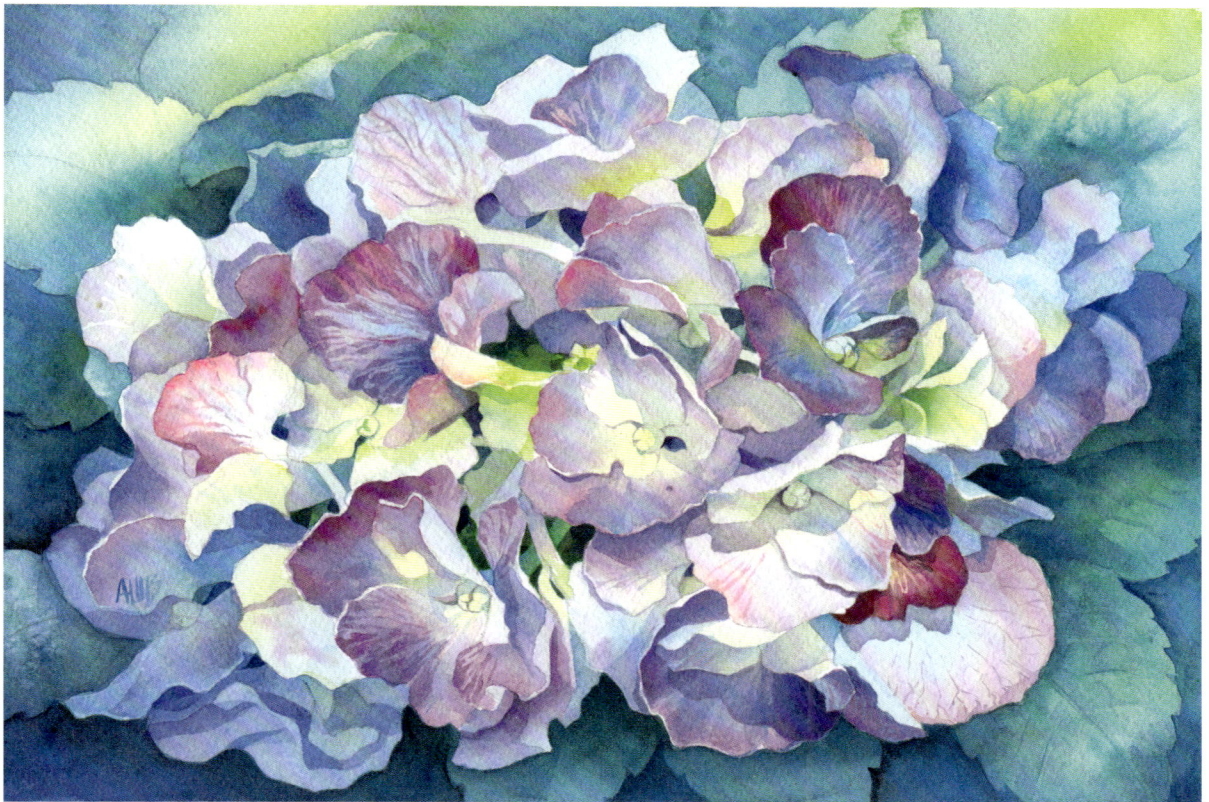

Hydrangea Flower

Case Study: Hydrangea Flower

This hydrangea flower, with its intricate clusters of petals and vibrant hues, presented a delightful challenge and became my first opportunity to test Aqua Green. I applied several washes of Aqua Green around the flower to establish the background, using varying concentrations to create depth and dimension. The pigment's high tinting strength allowed for subtle gradations of color, enabling me to capture the intricate interplay of light and shadow. I seamlessly mixed in Indanthrone Blue and added splashes of warm Green Gold throughout. Additionally, I applied Aqua Green to some of the petal shadows. Its transparent nature allowed for smooth and even application, creating soft, luminous accents that complemented the vibrant hues of the flower.

3.14 Why I Never Gave Up on Fluorescent Pink

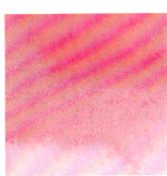

Opera Pink

Pigment: PR122
Lightfastness: Fugitive
Transparency: Transparent
Staining: 1 – Nonstaining
Granulation: Granulating
Brand: I use PR122 from Daniel Smith (called Opera Pink) and Winsor & Newton (called Opera Rose).

This version of PR122 combines the base Magenta pigment with a touch of fluorescent dye called Rhodamine B. The resulting combination exhibits an unparalleled vibrancy, making it ideal for creating eye-catching "glowing" pink accents in your paintings. While the exact origins of the name may be uncertain, the association with the colorful world of opera adds an extra layer of intrigue to this captivating hue. In addition to unparalleled vibrancy, fluorescent PR122 has many desirable characteristics, including transparency and subtle granulation. Yet beneath its alluring facade lies a contentious debate surrounding its use—a debate that sheds light on the complexities of artistic practice and the delicate balance between aesthetic allure and practical considerations.

- **The Fugitive Nature:** It's widely acknowledged that using fugitive pigments, such as Opera Pink, comes with inherent risks. These pigments are prone to fading over time, especially when exposed to direct light without adequate protection. Testimonials and experiments affirm the unfortunate truth: The luminous charm of Opera Pink may diminish with prolonged exposure, leaving behind a mere echo of its former brilliance.
- **Practical Considerations:** For artists who want to sell their work, the use of fugitive pigments poses a dilemma. You never know where your painting will end up—maybe in a sunny room or a dimly lit hallway. I don't recommend selling watercolor artwork that features fugitive pigments, since you cannot guarantee the conditions under which the piece will be displayed.
- **Why Keep Using It?** Despite the inherent risks, manufacturers continue to offer fluorescent PR122 in their palettes, driven by a myriad of factors. Pure aesthetics play a significant role—the sheer beauty of this pigment is undeniable, tempting artists with its allure and potential for creative expression. Moreover, in commercial illustrations where artwork is digitized, concerns about fading become less pressing. Once a painting is scanned or printed, it stays bright and vibrant forever.

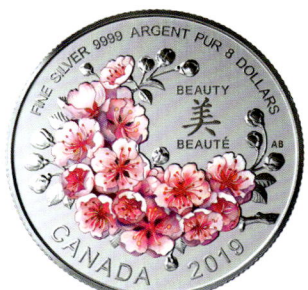

2019 "Brilliant Cherry Blossom" $8 Canadian Silver Coin
Coin image and concept/final drawing © 2024 Royal
Canadian Mint. All rights reserved / Image de la pièce et
dessins préliminaires et définitifs © 2024 Monnaie royale
canadienne. Tous droits réservés

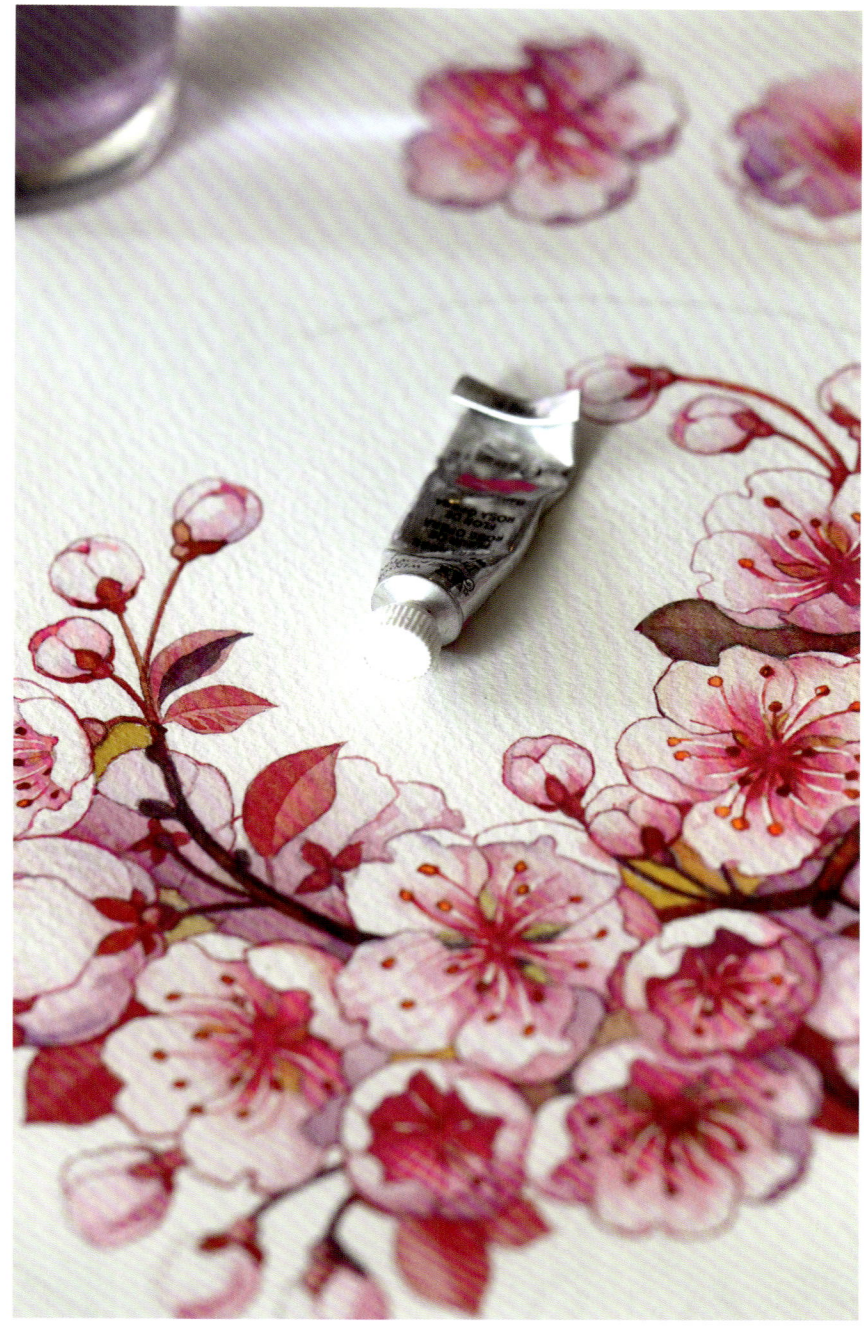

Brilliant Cherry Blossom Watercolor Illustration in Progress

Case Study: Using Opera Pink in Commercial Illustration

I've embraced fluorescent PR122 both in my personal work, as a joyful pursuit, and in the creation of commercial art. One notable project involved painting the iconic Cherry Blossom for the Royal Canadian Mint. This illustration was featured on $8 silver coins using selective color and engraving techniques. While the original watercolor may fade over time, the coin will remain as vibrant as ever, preserving the beauty of Opera Pink for generations to come.

4

Tools That Matter

4.1 Introduction

Welcome to my studio! Although it can be quite messy at times, it's my favorite spot in the house. This is where I store all my painting supplies, along with inspirational books, Canadian coins I designed, microphones and cameras I use to film art classes, and, of course, the beautiful Lego flowers my children crafted to help me decorate the room.

In this chapter, I will share my favorite watercolor materials—the ones I find indispensable or particularly suitable for my watercolor style. We will discuss various types of paper, paint brushes, watercolor mediums, mixing surfaces, and often-overlooked cleaning agents. I will explain why I prefer particular products, what makes them special, and how they help me bring my artistic visions to life. Some of them will open up possibilities for new watercolor techniques, like painting particularly tricky white details; others will make it easier to overcome common challenges like drying time and smudges. I will also mention the product that I use daily, although it was never meant for watercolor in the first place. I discovered it accidentally and it's been a game-changer in my work!

While I'll certainly provide insights into how my preferred supplies can be used to achieve specific effects and techniques, it's important to note that every watercolor journey is unique. What works wonders for me may not necessarily align with your individual style, budget, or artistic needs. Ultimately, the joy of art lies in the exploration and discovery of what resonates most profoundly with your creative spirit. When in doubt, I encourage you to visit your local art store and talk to staff—this is how I discovered most of my favorite watercolor brands. Remember, experimentation is key and there are always innovative products to test and enjoy.

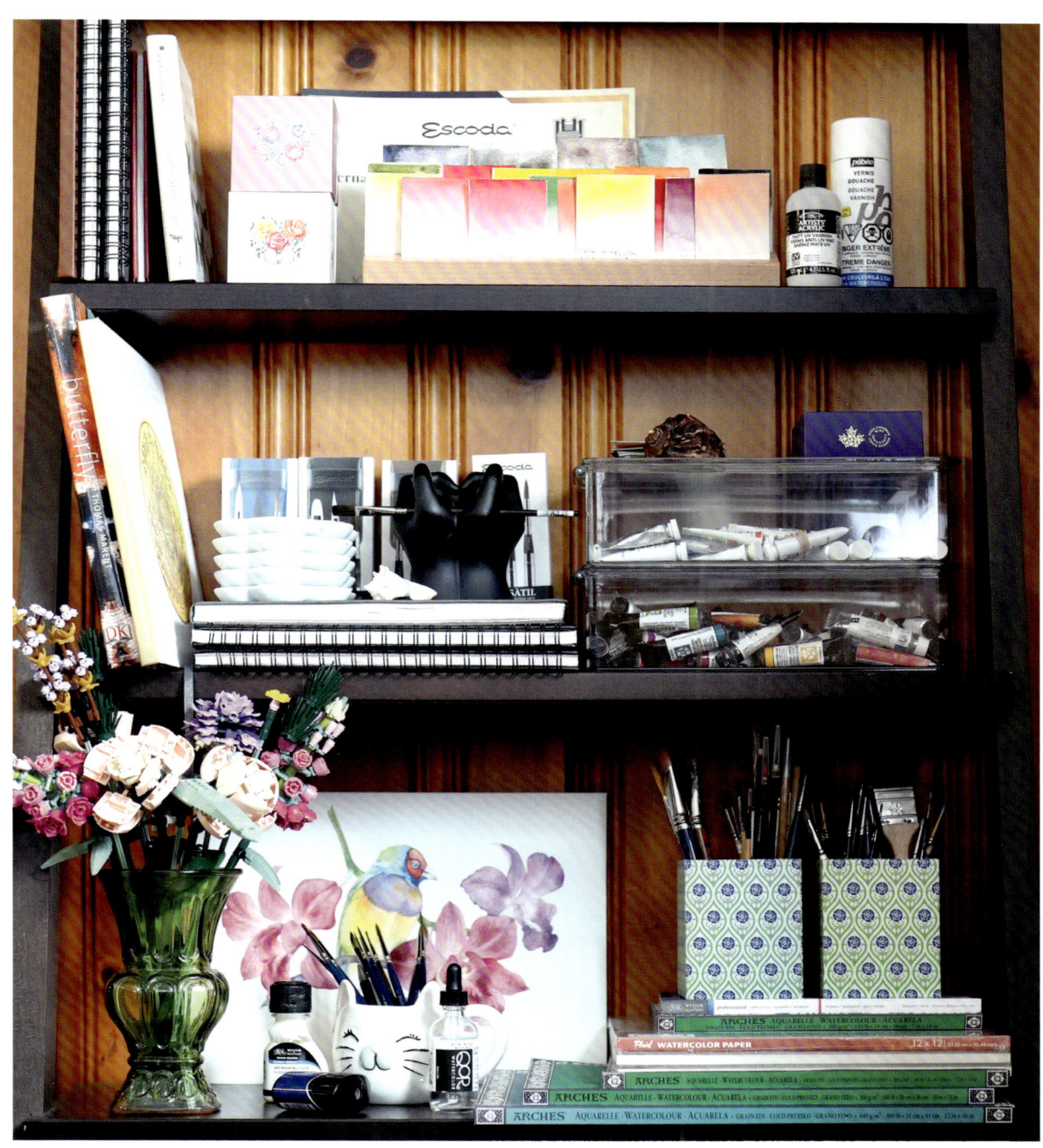

4.2 It's All About the Paper!

If there is one watercolor supply that matters above all else, it's your paper. The choice of your working surface is a crucial decision that influences both the experience and the final outcome of your painting. While there's no one-size-fits-all answer, I can provide insights into the advantages of using cotton versus wood pulp, explain why I prefer using paper blocks versus loose paper sheets, and recommend common cost-saving strategies for getting the best paper surface within your budget. In the next section, we will explore the unique traits of cold, hot, and rough watercolor paper.

Is Cotton Essential?

Painting on the wrong surface—whether its mixed media or student-grade paper—will tend to produce suboptimal results. Even the most expensive professional pigments will look rather dull on a wood-pulp surface, while even light layering will likely result in muddy colors due to lifting. Cotton papers are acid-free and archival, ensuring that your paintings withstand the test of time without yellowing or deteriorating. Most importantly, wet-on-wet watercolor techniques don't work on a wood-pulp surface because it's not treated to absorb excessive moisture. Instead of producing beautiful color transitions, your heavy washes might damage the paper surface. Therefore, I recommend always using 100% cotton paper to achieve the best results, while reserving 50% cotton sheets for swatching, color tests, and technique practice.

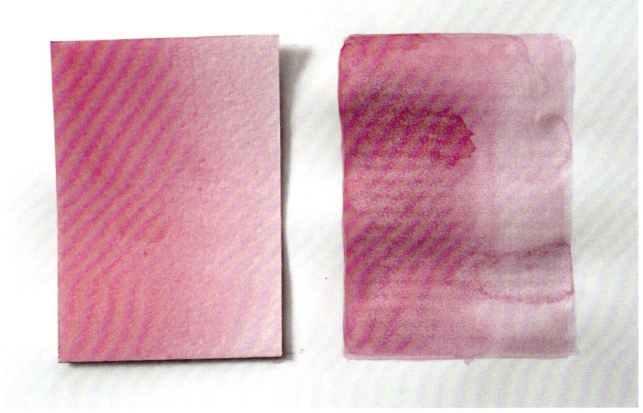

Watercolor Wash on 100% Cotton Paper versus the Same Wash on Cellulose Paper

Paper Weight

The weight of the paper (measured in pounds or grams per square meter) also plays a role in your painting process. Heavier papers (300lbs or 600gsm) are more resilient and can handle multiple washes. Thinner papers (100lbs or less) tend to warp with multiple color applications. I found a happy medium around 140lbs (300gsm), as this weight provides sufficient durability to absorb up to three washes without excessive warping, while also being more reasonably priced compared to the 300lb alternatives.

Manufacturing Process and Price Considerations

Watercolor cotton paper is crafted through a meticulous, multistage process to ensure durability, absorbency, and general suitability for watercolor painting. This includes pulp preparation to break down raw cotton, beating to refine the fibers, and sizing to control the paper's absorbency and improve its ability to hold watercolor pigments. Throughout the process, attention to detail, the quality of raw materials, and adherence to specific manufacturing standards contribute to the production of a high-quality surface uniquely suitable for watercolor painting. Admittedly, this complicated production process also makes cotton paper rather expensive. There are several ways to save, from buying larger sheets in bulk to be cut down into smaller size pieces, to choosing 140lbs weight instead of ultra-expensive 300lbs sheets.

Paper Format

- **Loose Sheets:** Watercolor paper is typically sold in sheets, allowing you to choose different sizes and quantities tailored to your artistic preferences. Loose sheets are commonly used by artists who prefer to work on larger surfaces and are willing to invest the time in pre-stretching their paper. Note that when not properly stretched beforehand, loose sheets, especially 300lbs in weight and lower, are prone to warping when wet. Stretching involves wetting the paper and then taping it down onto a flat surface until it dries, which can be time-consuming and cumbersome.
- **Paper Blocks (My Choice!):** Watercolor blocks are pads of watercolor paper that are bound together with a strong adhesive. The paper is attached along the edges, preventing it from warping excessively when it comes into contact with water. I find this feature to be particularly advantageous because it eliminates the need for stretching the paper before painting. While blocks are slightly more expensive than loose sheets, their convenience and time-saving benefits make them my preferred choice for watercolor work.
- **Sketchbooks:** While not specifically designed for watercolor painting, some sketchbooks do contain paper suitable for watercolor techniques. Note that sketchbook paper is typically thin and may warp or buckle when exposed to significant amounts of water. Still, sketchbooks can be a convenient option when I need a portable format to work outdoors or feel like experimenting with watercolor alongside other mediums.

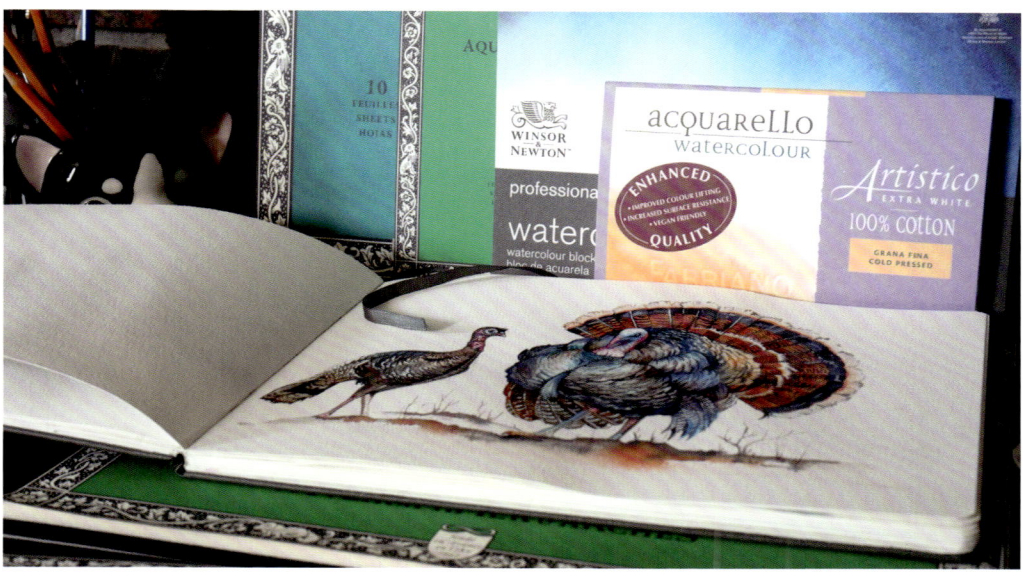

My Favorites

- For pigment testing, experimentation, and explorations: Artistico Cold Pressed blocks from Fabriano (140 lbs).
- For personal work: White Cold Pressed blocks from Arches (140 lbs).
- For commercial work that requires a smooth surface for scanning: Bright White Hot Pressed blocks from Winsor & Newton (140 lbs).
- For traveling and plein-air sketching: The Perfect Sketchbook from Etchr (140 lbs).

4.3 Paper Personalities: Hot vs. Cold vs. Rough

Understanding the unique characteristics of hot-pressed, cold-pressed, and rough finish will allow you to tailor your selection to your unique style and specific requirements of your project. Let's explore their impact on strokes, drying time, and specific applications in botanical, landscape, and other types of art.

Hot-Pressed Watercolor Paper

- **Texture:** Hot-pressed paper undergoes a high-temperature pressing during production, resulting in a very smooth surface.
- **Strokes:** The fine grain of hot-pressed paper allows for the most precise and detailed brushstrokes.
- **Drying Time:** Hot-pressed paper tends to dry very quickly compared to other types, making it suitable for artists who prefer a faster pace in their work.
- **Wet-on-Wet Washes:** The fast-drying quality of the hot-pressed paper makes it rather difficult to execute complex wet-on-wet washes and color-blending effects directly on paper.
- **Scanning:** Due to its smooth surface, the hot-pressed paper offers the best option for scanning your work without transferring the texture to the digital file.

Cold-Pressed Watercolor Paper (My Favorite)

- **Texture:** Cold-pressed paper strikes a balance between a smooth and textured surface.
- **Strokes:** The slightly textured surface allows for more expressive strokes; however, you may experience some difficulty with particularly intricate lines.
- **Drying Time and Wet-on-Wet:** Cold-pressed paper has a moderate drying time, providing you with solid foundation for wet-on-wet techniques.
- **Scanning:** A slightly textured surface makes it somewhat difficult to digitize watercolor artwork because the scanner's sensor captures not only the pigment on the paper surface, but also the depth of the texture. The effects are particularly pronounced if you leave a lot of white space or soft background color transitions.

Rough Watercolor Paper

- **Texture:** Rough paper offers a coarse and irregular surface. The texture is achieved by minimal pressing during production.
- **Strokes:** The pronounced texture allows for the most expressive and bold brushstrokes.
- **Drying Time and Wet-on-Wet:** Due to its textured surface, rough paper offers the longest drying time, ideal for the most complex wet-on-wet effects.
- **Scanning:** Rough paper is virtually impossible to scan without capturing the irregular surface with highly pronounced peaks and valleys. While capturing the texture of rough watercolor paper can provide a faithful representation of the original artwork, it may not always be desirable, especially in commercial art contexts.

Which Paper Finish Is Best for You?

Your choice of watercolor paper is not merely a matter of practicality—it's a reflection of your artistic style and preferences. Whether you prefer the subtle tooth of cold press, the smoothness of hot press, or the pronounced texture of rough paper, your selection will shape the look, feel, and overall aesthetic of your watercolor paintings.

Three Paper Swatches: Hot vs. Cold vs. Rough

Hot-pressed paper is excellent for illustrations where precise lines and quick drying time are crucial. For example, the smooth surface is great for capturing intricate details in botanical work. Quick drying is an important feature for plein-air painting and would be suitable for landscape and urban artists who enjoy working outdoors. The smooth surface is essential for commercial applications where scanning and further digital manipulations are required. I recommend hot-pressed paper for commercial artists and those who enjoy working on highly detailed pieces without extensive drying time.

Cold-pressed paper is the most versatile option and is my #1 choice for all types of work except commercial art. Its moderate texture strikes a delicate balance between smoothness and roughness, offering just enough tooth to capture pigment and create captivating brushwork, while still allowing for precise detailing when desired. Its forgiving surface absorbs water and pigment gracefully, allowing for controlled washes, vibrant color blending, and effortless lifting of paint for corrections or highlights. This versatility makes cold-pressed paper suitable for a wide range of artistic styles and techniques, from portraits to landscapes, and even botanical art. I recommend cold-pressed paper as the most balanced choice in general, and especially for beginner artists.

Rough watercolor paper is well-suited for styles and applications that embrace texture and spontaneity, such as impressionistic landscapes and loose abstracts. Its coarse texture lends itself well to large, expressive paintings, particularly landscapes and seascapes that convey the roughness of natural elements. If you are drawn to experimentation, you will find rough paper to be a perfect match for your creative vision, enabling you to push the boundaries of traditional watercolor painting and forge your own path of creativity.

4.4 Choosing the Right Pencil for Watercolor Paper

Sketching is often the first step in the painting process, laying the foundation for the artwork to come to life. Choosing the right pencil is essential to ensure your lines are visible yet easily adjustable or erasable. The key consideration when selecting a pencil for sketching on watercolor paper is graphite strength. The right grade of graphite will ensure that your sketch lines are present but subtle, without leaving heavy graphite residue that can muddy up watercolor washes.

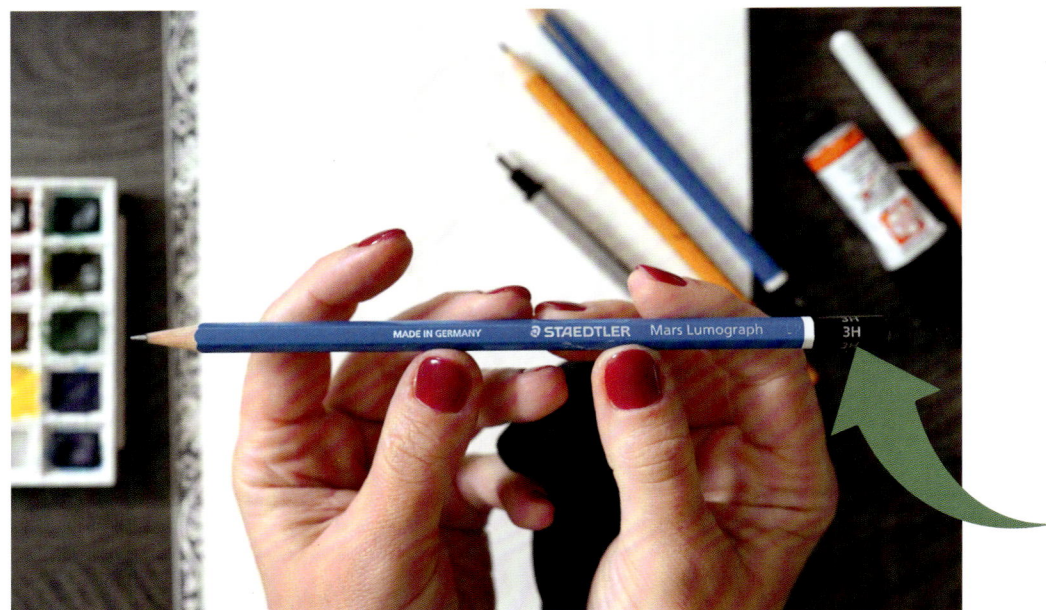

Pencil with 3H Mark

Understanding Graphite Grading Scale

Graphite pencils are graded based on their hardness or softness, which determines the darkness or lightness of the marks they make on paper. You'll often see a combination of letters and numbers printed on a pencil to indicate its graphite strength.

- **H Series:** Graphite pencils in the H series are harder and produce lighter marks. The higher the number (e.g., 2H, 3H, 4H), the harder the pencil and the lighter the mark it makes. These pencils are easy to erase, giving you flexibility to adjust your sketch as needed before applying watercolor paint.
- **B Series:** Graphite pencils in the B series are softer and produce darker marks. The higher the number (e.g., 2B, 3B, 4B), the softer the pencil and the darker the mark it makes. While these pencils are excellent for expressive drawing techniques, I don't recommend them for watercolor sketching. They tend to leave more pronounced marks that are difficult to erase without damaging the paper. They also produce heavy residue that can easily taint your watercolor wash.

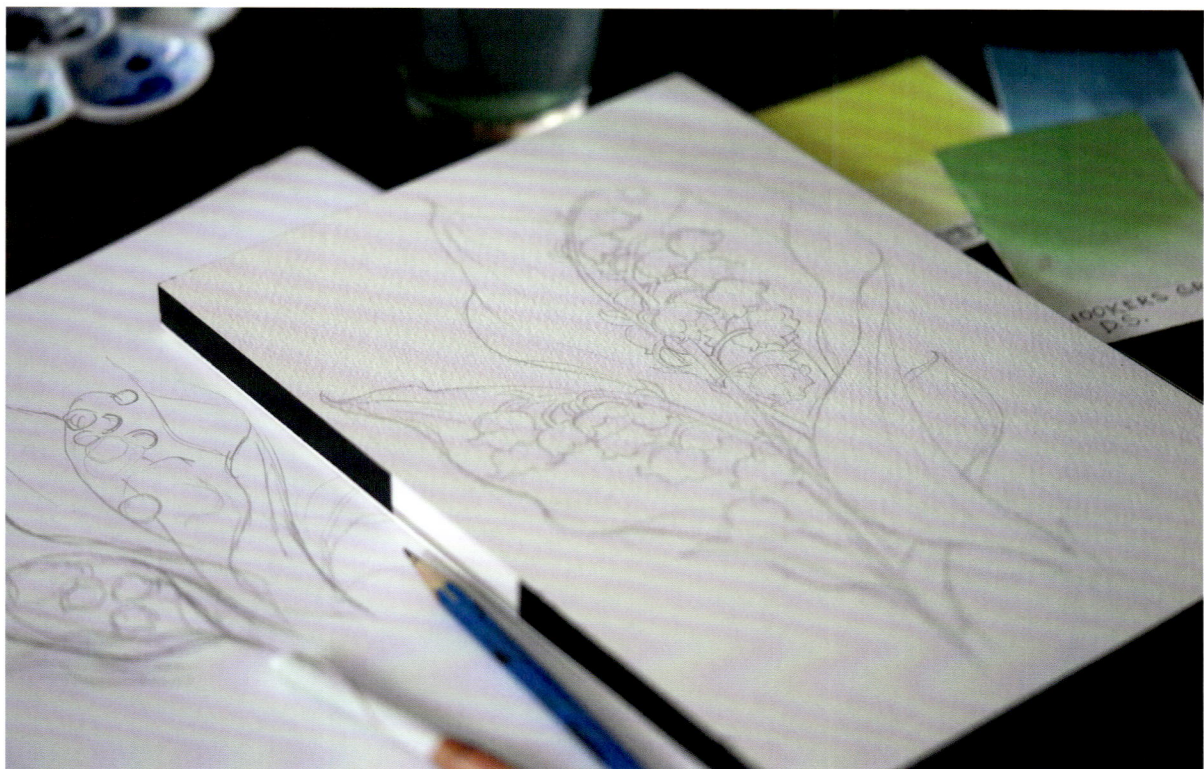

My Favorites: 3H and 4H wooden graphite pencils from Staedtler and Koh-I-Noor.

HELPFUL TIPS

- Take into account the texture of the watercolor paper you're using. Rough or cold-pressed papers may require softer 2H pencils to ensure adequate line coverage, while smoother hot-pressed papers may work well even with harder 4H or 6H pencils.
- Don't sharpen your pencils too much. If the tip is too precise, it can leave scratches on your watercolor paper, interfering with subsequent paint washes.
- Don't press the pencil too hard while drawing or transferring the lines. The excessive pressure can result in grooves, damaging the soft cotton surface of your paper.
- Instead of traditional graphite, consider using watercolor pencils for making your sketches. These pencils are specifically designed to interact with water and can be partially dissolved during the painting process, seamlessly integrating the sketch lines into the final painting.

4.5 Remove Pencil Marks without Ruining Your Paper

Watercolor paper is designed to absorb and hold water, allowing the paint to blend beautifully across its surface. However, excessive use of erasers can damage the paper fibers and compromise its ability to absorb water evenly. This can lead to inconsistent washes, impacting the overall quality of your artwork. Moreover, over-erasing can weaken the paper, rendering it susceptible to tearing or pilling when wet. When making alterations to your sketch, exercise gentle pressure to mitigate potential damage.

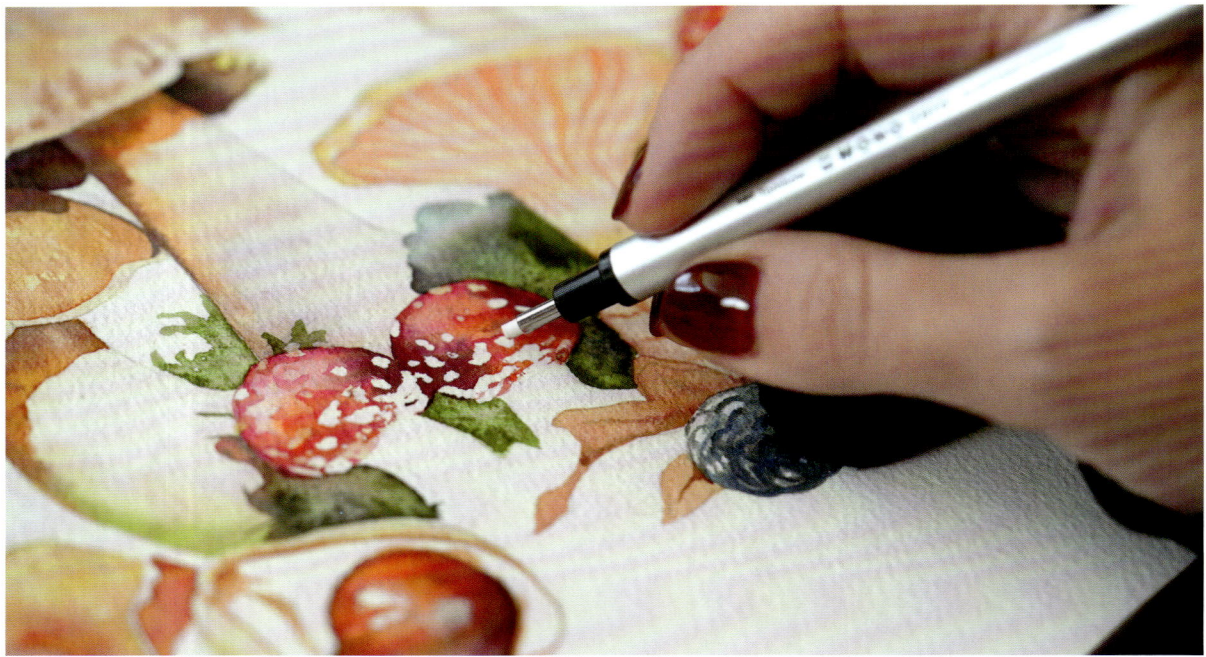

Tombow MONO Zero Retractable Eraser

In my view, the most effective erasers are those capable of precise removal of pencil lines while preserving surrounding areas. I recommend retractable erasers in a penlike design for their ability to target small areas without affecting adjacent portions of the paper. Alternatively, if you prefer larger erasers, opt for kneaded or soft vinyl types, which are less abrasive compared to standard erasers.

My Favorites: The Tombow MONO Zero retractable eraser (2.3mm) is my favorite eraser for precision touch-ups. I also use soft kneaded erasers from my local art store, DeSerres.

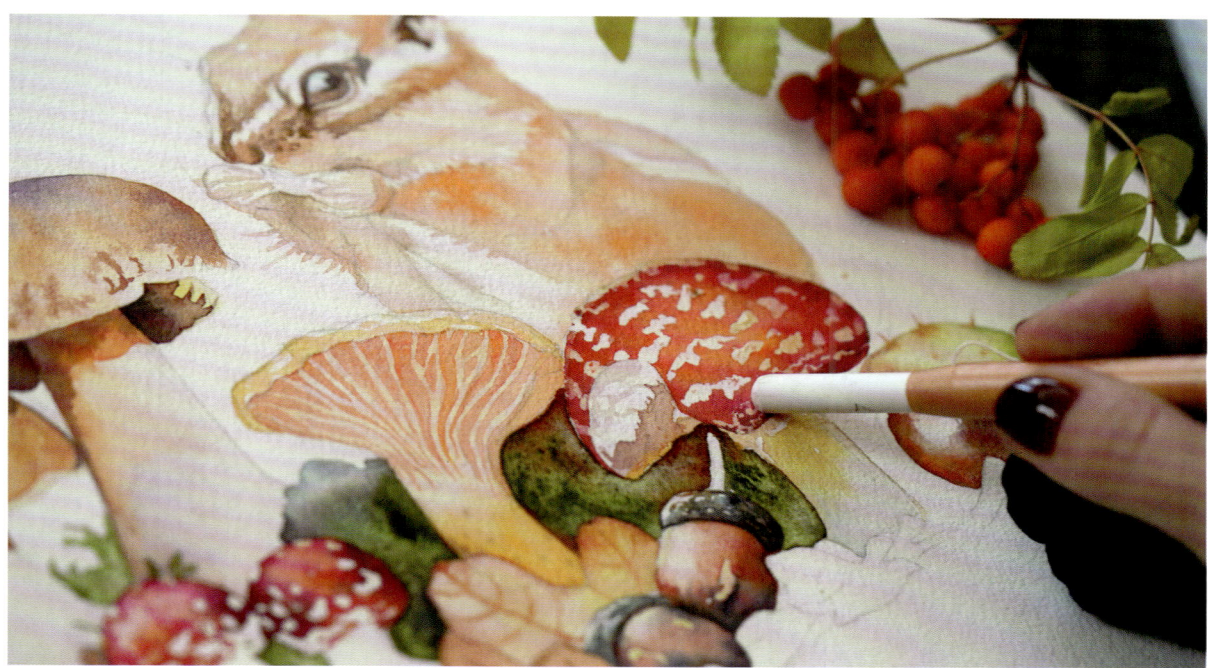

HELPFUL TIPS

- Rather than erasing excessively, I recommend waiting until your painting nears completion before addressing unnecessary lines. This approach will allow you to assess the painting holistically and determine which lines are truly unnecessary and detract from the composition.
- Avoid using your fingers to remove eraser residue, as the heat and oils from your hands can smudge the paint and harm the paper's surface, leading to uneven washes later on. Instead, employ a large, flat brush or a soft, clean dishcloth to gently brush away the residue.
- Over-erasing on watercolor paper can roughen the surface, creating areas with reduced paint absorption capabilities. Refrain from applying excessive color washes over these segments to maintain consistency across the paper.

4.6 Brush Shapes and Strokes

Watercolor brushes come in various shapes and sizes, each designed for specific purposes, allowing you to create a wide range of effects. Although some of these are really fun to experiment with, the reality is you only need a couple of classic shapes to create the most complex paintings with watercolor. Nevertheless, I will briefly mention some of the most common brush shapes and the types of strokes they can create before showing you my favorites.

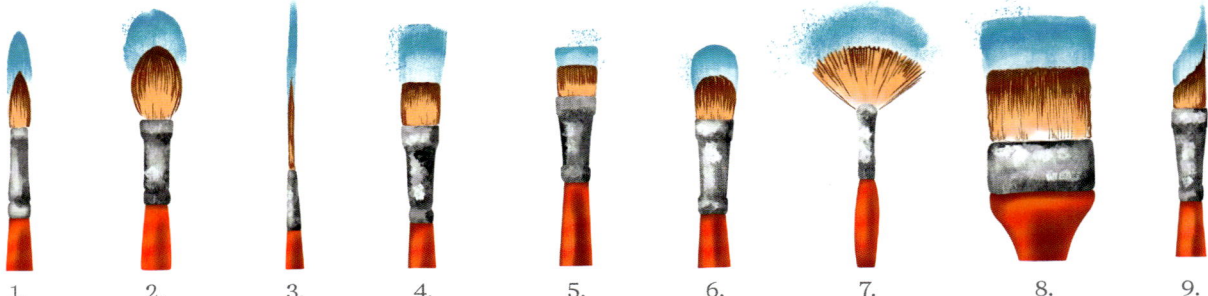

1.   2.   3.   4.   5.   6.   7.   8.   9.

Brushes and Strokes

- **Round Brush (1):** The most versatile of all brushes, it has a pointed tip and a full belly. The tip allows for precise, fine lines, while the belly can hold more water, enabling broader strokes.
- **Mop Brush (2):** This particularly large variation of a round brush holds a significant amount of water and pigment, making it most suitable for loose applications.
- **Rigger (Liner) Brush (3):** The thinnest round brush will allow you to paint extra-long strokes—perfect for fine details, precise outlines, and even lettering.
- **Flat Brush (4):** This brush has a squared-off tip with straight edges. This shape works best for covering large areas with quick and even washes of color. The straight edge is useful for creating sharp edges, making it an indispensable tool for painting geometric shapes and urban landscapes.
- **Bright Brush (5):** Similar to a flat brush, but with shorter bristles. This brush is suitable for controlled strokes with less flexibility, as well as lifting technique.
- **Filbert Brush (6):** Another variation on a flat brush, but with an oval tip. This shape is ideal for soft blending and transitions, and it can also be used for painting lovely petals with one stroke.
- **Fan Brush (7):** The bristles of this brush are spread out like a fan in a semicircle shape. It works great for experimenting with wet-on-dry textures and various abstract effects. Although this brush can be used for soft blending in watercolor, I find that it works best with thicker mediums, such as oil and acrylics.
- **Wash/Hake Brush (8):** These extra-wide flat brushes allow you to wet large segments of paper evenly, maintain a damp surface for wet-on-wet techniques, or lift excess moisture from the paper as needed.
- **Dagger (Sword) Brush (9):** Long, flat, and pointed, this brush resembles a dagger with angled edges. This irregular shape can be useful for capturing organic lines and shapes with varied width—for example, leaves and branches. The tip can also be used for detailed work and fine lines.

My Favorites

My go-to brush shapes include variations of round and flat brushes in smaller sizes that best fit my precise style and relatively small paper size. I find that traditional rounds—the ones with pointed tip and a full "belly"—can take care of the majority of my painting needs. If I could only have five brushes, I would choose the following:

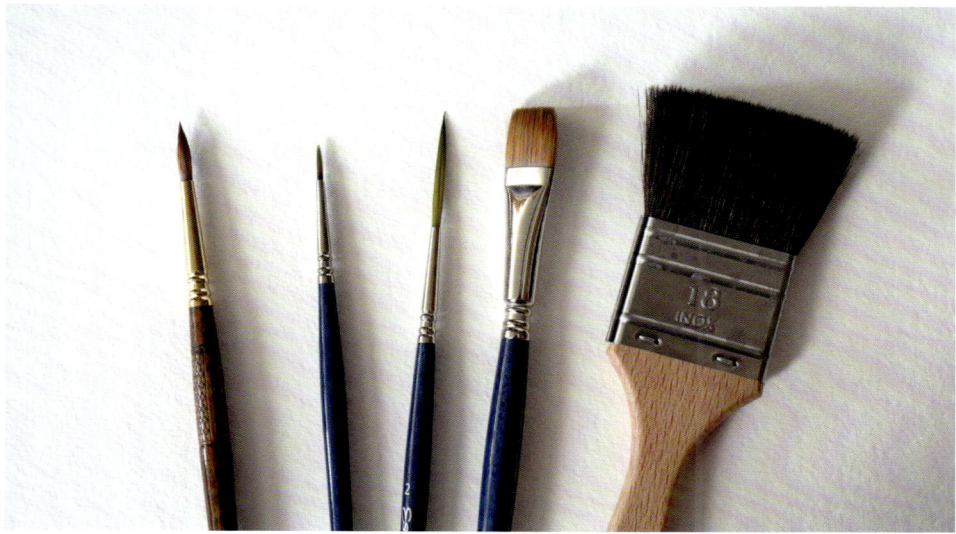

My Favorite Brushes

Classic Round: A classic round brush in size #4 is the one that does the most heavy lifting in my work. I prefer natural or partially natural bristles in this size, as they provide the most precision while holding just enough water for larger washes.
My Choice: Escoda Reserva Sable Round in size #4.

Precision Round: A round brush in size double-zero is always handy for creating fine outlines in the final layer. I find that synthetic bristles work best for detailed work, especially for bird feathers and leaf outlines.
My Choice: Escoda Chronos 90% Synthetic Round in size #1.

Rigger: Rigger brushes allow me to paint continuous sweeping strokes while reducing any potential wobbliness due to my hands shaking. These brushes are particularly useful when I paint human hair, animal fur, or flowers with intricate petal veins.
My Choice: Escoda Chronos Synthetic Rigger in size #2.

Flat: Occasionally, I introduce a flat brush into my process, mostly for lifting techniques.
My Choice: Escoda Chronos Flat in size #1/2.

Flat (Large): An extra-large flat brush is a recent addition to my collection. It's ideal for covering large areas of paper quickly and efficiently, making my background washes more even.
My Choice: Escoda Ultimo Synthetic Flat in size #18.

4.7 Natural versus Synthetic Bristles: What Makes a Real Difference

When it comes to choosing paintbrushes, one of the fundamental decisions you'll face is whether to opt for natural or synthetic bristles. Both types offer unique characteristics and advantages, but understanding the differences between them can help you make an informed choice that suits your specific needs and preferences. In this section, I will outline the key distinctions between natural and synthetic bristles to uncover what makes each type stand out.

Natural Brushes

ADVANTAGES

- **Overall Quality:** Natural brushes, particularly those made from Kolinsky sable hair, are renowned for their exceptional quality.
- **Precision:** They hold a fine point, allowing for more precise details compared to their synthetic counterparts. Note that sable tends to be more precise, while squirrel is less suitable for fine details due to inherent softness.
- **Water Retention:** Natural bristles tend to offer superior water retention. Squirrel brushes, in particular, have excellent water-absorbing properties, allowing for large washes and broad continuous strokes without the need for constant reloading.
- **Water Release:** The release of water is generally smooth and controlled, contributing to precise edges, smooth washes, and highly detailed work.
- **Softness and Flexibility:** Squirrel is known for its exceptional softness, making it suitable for extremely delicate glazes. Sable hair is quite flexible, albeit stiffer compared to squirrel.

DISADVANTAGES

- **Cost:** Natural bristles can be expensive and are often hard to find, depending on where you live.
- **Ethical Concerns:** Many artists avoid sable brushes due to ethical concerns related to the harvesting of animal hair.
- **Durability:** Sable brushes are moderately durable and can withstand the rigors of repeated use if cared for properly. Squirrel brushes may not be as durable, especially if subjected to heavy use.

Synthetic Brushes

ADVANTAGES

- **Cost:** Synthetic brushes are typically more budget-friendly than natural brushes.
- **Ethical Considerations:** They are cruelty-free—a preferred option for those who want to avoid animal-derived materials.
- **Durability:** Synthetic bristles are often more resilient, especially when it comes to maintaining their shape and performance over time.

DISADVANTAGES

- **Overall Quality:** Unfortunately, there is a high degree of variation in quality among synthetic brushes currently available on the market.
- **Water Retention:** Even the most expensive synthetic brushes may not hold water as well as natural brushes, impacting their performance with certain techniques.
- **Water Release:** Synthetic brushes are less predictable, providing less control over the water release. In my experience, this can lead to unexpected results, including water "puddles" or even unwanted drops of pigment.
- **Limited Softness:** While advancements have been made, synthetic brushes may still lack the softness and natural feel of high-quality natural brushes.

Case Study: Two Bullfinch Birds Painted with Synthetic & Natural Brushes

Ultimately, the choice between natural and synthetic brushes often comes down to personal preference, artistic style, and individual priorities. In my experience, the advantages of natural brushes, particularly water release and absorption issues, tend to get diminished as you get more experienced with watercolor. Without a doubt, you can achieve good results regardless of the bristles you choose, as illustrated in the example at right: the bullfinch on the left was painted with a Kolinsky sable Escoda Reserve brush, while the one on the right was painted with a synthetic Escoda Versatil in the same size. While the natural sable provided me with a more smooth and consistent flow of paint during the painting process, the overall effect is comparable.

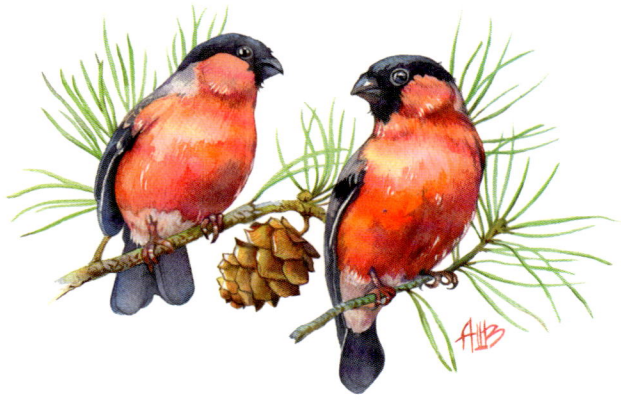

Two Bullfinches Painted with Different Bristles

HELPFUL TIPS

- When choosing the right brush, consider the type of work you primarily engage in. Synthetics generally work best for wet-on-dry technique and finer details, while natural bristles shine in loose wet-on-wet applications and large washes.
- Evaluate your budget and how frequently you plan to use the brushes. Synthetic brushes are generally more affordable, easier to find, and fun to experiment with.
- When opting for synthetic bristles, always look for well-established brands with good quality control. Companies like Winsor & Newton and Escoda have invested heavily in the development of synthetic bristles that are best at mimicking the natural properties of animal fur.
- Finally, don't forget to factor in personal preferences regarding ethical considerations.
- If you are not sure about the type of bristle to choose, you can try a "blend." For example, Escoda Chronos offers a combination of sable (10%) and synthetic (90%) bristles—the best of both world at a relatively affordable price.

4.8 Travel Brushes: Your Plein Air Companion

Did you know that some brushes can be folded to protect the soft bristles? With a travel brush set in hand, you can indulge in your passion for painting wherever your travels take you, whether it's capturing a stunning landscape or sketching the charming details of a new city. These so-called travel brushes are usually compact and lightweight, making them easy to carry, store, and transport. Whether you prefer the collapsible or retractable design, travel brushes provide convenience and versatility, allowing you to create beautiful artworks wherever inspiration strikes.

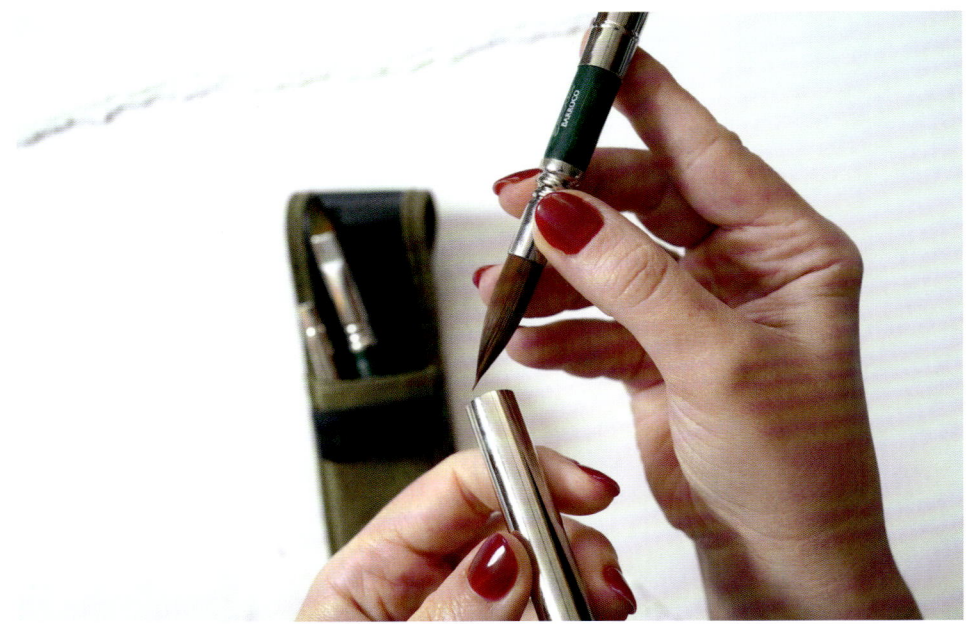

Collapsible Escoda Travel Brush

Two Common Types of Travel Brushes

- **Collapsible Brushes** are designed with two components: one part containing the bristles on one end and another part that can be disassembled to either cover the bristles or extend the handle. This collapsible design makes these brushes compact and portable, ideal for artists who want to paint outdoors or while traveling. With the ability to protect the bristles during transport and extend the handle for comfortable use, collapsible brushes offer convenience and versatility in a single tool.
- **Retractable Brushes** feature a different mechanism where the end pulls back inside the handle rather than moving the cover to become the handle. This design allows for quick and effortless deployment of the bristles, making it easy to switch between painting and storing the brush. Retractable brushes offer the same portability and convenience as collapsible brushes, with the added benefit of a streamlined design that eliminates the need for separate components.

Use Cases for Travel Brushes

- **Traveling on Vacation:** Imagine you're going on vacation or visiting family in a different town, and you want to bring your watercolor supplies along to capture the beauty of your surroundings. In this scenario, a travel brush set would be incredibly convenient. The compact size and portable nature of travel brushes make them easy to pack in your luggage or carry-on bag without taking up too much space. Additionally, the protective case or retractable mechanism of travel brushes ensures that the bristles remain undamaged during transit.
- **Plein Air Painting:** Traditional brushes may be cumbersome to transport and difficult to lay out neatly, especially in outdoor settings where wind and uneven terrain can pose challenges. However, with retractable or collapsible brushes, you can easily tuck them into your pocket or art bag, minimizing clutter and maximizing efficiency. This allows you to focus on your artwork without worrying about the condition of your tools, making plein air painting a more enjoyable and stress-free experience.
- **Urban Sketching:** When sketching on the streets or in crowded urban environments, space may be limited, and traditional brushes can be cumbersome to carry. Travel brushes offer a compact and portable solution, allowing urban sketchers to capture fleeting moments and architectural details with ease.

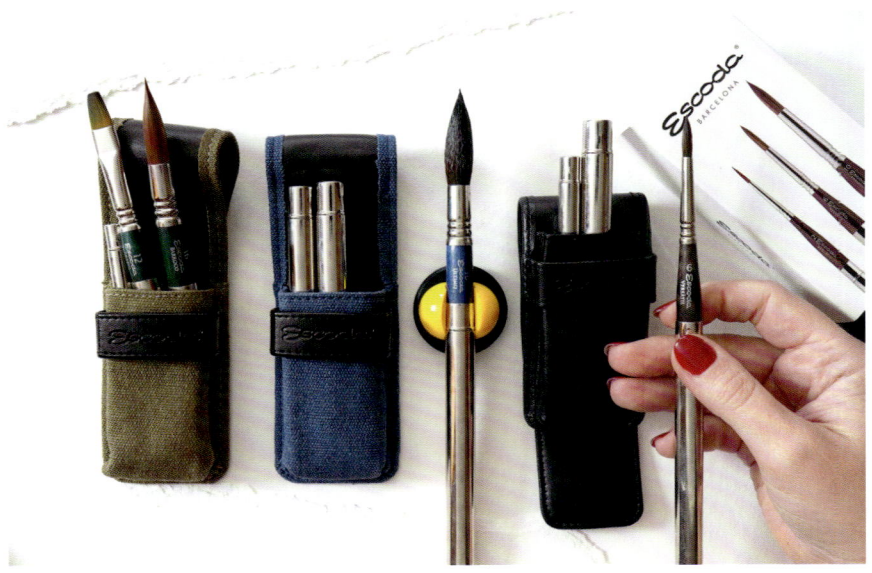

Escoda Travel Brush Sets

My Favorite Travel Brushes

One of my favorite travel brush sets comes from Escoda, a renowned manufacturer known for their high-quality brushes. These sets typically feature a variety of shapes and sizes, allowing you to choose the perfect combination for your watercolor style. The compact size of these durable pouches makes them well-suited for plein air painting or outdoor sketching, where space and portability are essential.

Video Available 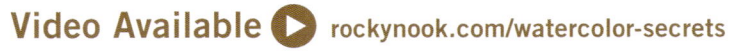 rockynook.com/watercolor-secrets

4.9 Extend the Life of Your Brushes and Avoid Muddy Colors

You might have noticed that, with time and use, your brushes gradually lose their precision and shape. To make matters worse, pigments from various colors tend to accumulate at the base of the brush, causing interference with fresh color mixing and resulting in dull, muddy watercolor washes. Even thorough rinsing with clear water doesn't completely remove these stubborn pigments from the brush's base. The good news is that there's a solution that can significantly extend the lifespan of both natural and synthetic brushes. Follow these steps every couple of weeks, using a mild hand soap or, even better, a specialized paintbrush soap:

Prepare: Begin by rinsing the brush under lukewarm running water to remove excess paint. Gently massage the bristles with your fingers to dislodge any lingering paint particles.

Rub and Swirl: Use your fingers to delicately lather up the soap, working it into the bristles. Alternatively, you can gently rub the brush against the soap bar in the direction of the bristles. Be cautious not to scrub too vigorously, as this can harm the bristles.

Rinse and Repeat: Rinse the brush under running water once more, using your fingers to eliminate any remaining soap. You can tap the brush on tissue paper to check for any lingering paint residue. Continue this process until the water runs clear or you no longer detect traces of paint on the tissue paper.

Reshape and Dry: Ensure there are no traces of soap left in the brush and tap it on tissue paper to eliminate excess water. After cleaning, reshape the brush using your fingertips and allow it to dry.

This routine is effective for most art mediums, particularly watercolor, acrylics, and gouache. By following these steps every couple of weeks, your brushes will enjoy a longer lifespan, while your colors will maintain their cleanliness and vibrancy.

HELPFUL TIP

Some brush soaps can act as conditioning agents that allow you to better shape and hydrate the bristles after cleaning. For example, the 2-in-1 cream soap and conditioner from Escoda uses extra virgin olive oil to help you put the hairs in the original position to ensure longevity of the brush shape. Having a pointy brush tip will add more precision in your work!

My Favorite Soap: My go-to soap bar is made by Escoda.

Video Available 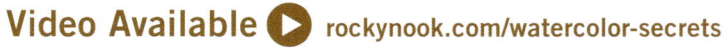 rockynook.com/watercolor-secrets

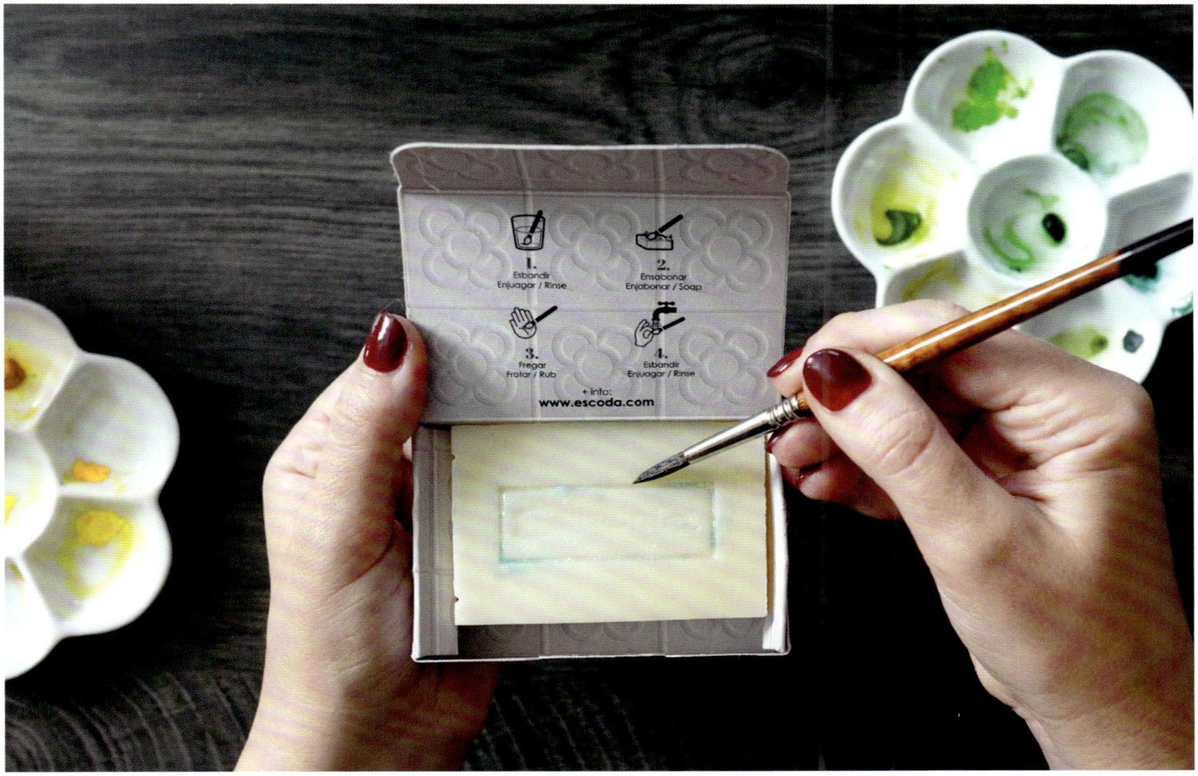

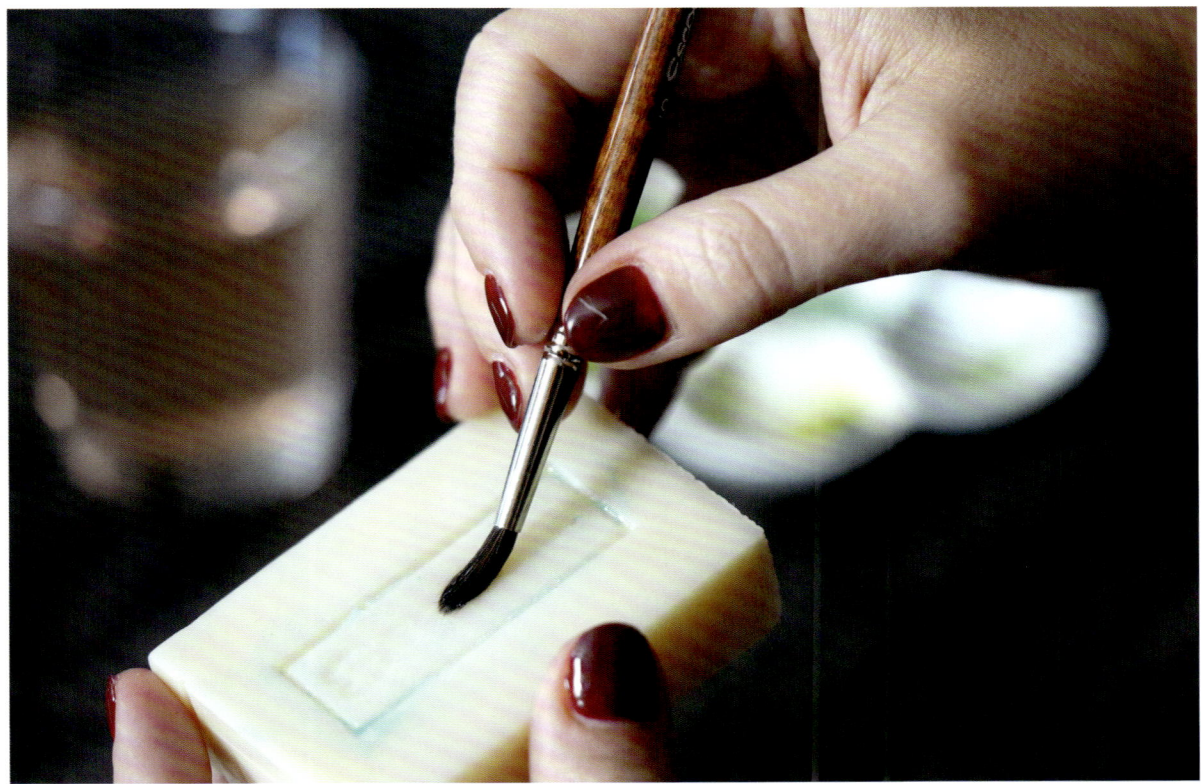

4.10 Synthetic Ox Gall: My Secret Weapon

We've all encountered the frustration of our paper drying too quickly, hindering our ability to achieve seamless and smooth wet-on-wet color transitions. Additionally, covering large background areas becomes a struggle as the paper dries before we can complete the segment, leading to disjointed and patchy results.

I have a secret weapon in my arsenal that I'm excited to share with you: Synthetic Ox Gall. It's a special watercolor medium that extends the drying time of your washes and even improves the paint flow. I recommend incorporating Synthetic Ox Gall into your watercolor practice, especially if you reside in extra-dry climates or struggle with wet-on-wet techniques. It's been a game-changer for me, particularly during dry summer months in Toronto. Here are five compelling reasons why Synthetic Ox Gall is my go-to solution for combating the drying paper dilemma:

- **Better Wet-on-Wet Experience:** With Synthetic Ox Gall, you can plan and execute complex color transitions using the wet-on-wet technique with ease. The extended drying time allows you to blend multiple colors over several minutes without rushing.
- **Seamless Background Coverage:** Say goodbye to patchy backgrounds! With Synthetic Ox Gall, you can cover large background areas seamlessly, ensuring that your entire segment stays wet until you finish. This enables you to make adjustments and enhancements as necessary, without worrying about dried patches.
- **More Complex Techniques:** You can expand your repertoire with more advanced techniques like wet-on-damp, which require prolonged drying time. Synthetic Ox Gall ensures that your paper remains wet enough to accommodate tricky time delays, empowering you to experiment with hard and soft blends.
- **Consistency in Dry Climate:** Even in the hottest and driest months, Synthetic Ox Gall keeps your paper wet and workable. As someone who regularly experiences dry climate, I can attest to its reliability in maintaining optimal painting conditions regardless of external factors.
- **Enhanced Pigment Flow:** One of the most remarkable qualities of Synthetic Ox Gall is its ability to improve pigment flow, resulting in stunning wet-on-wet blends. The paint glides effortlessly across the paper, creating mesmerizing textures and gradients that elevate your artwork to new heights.

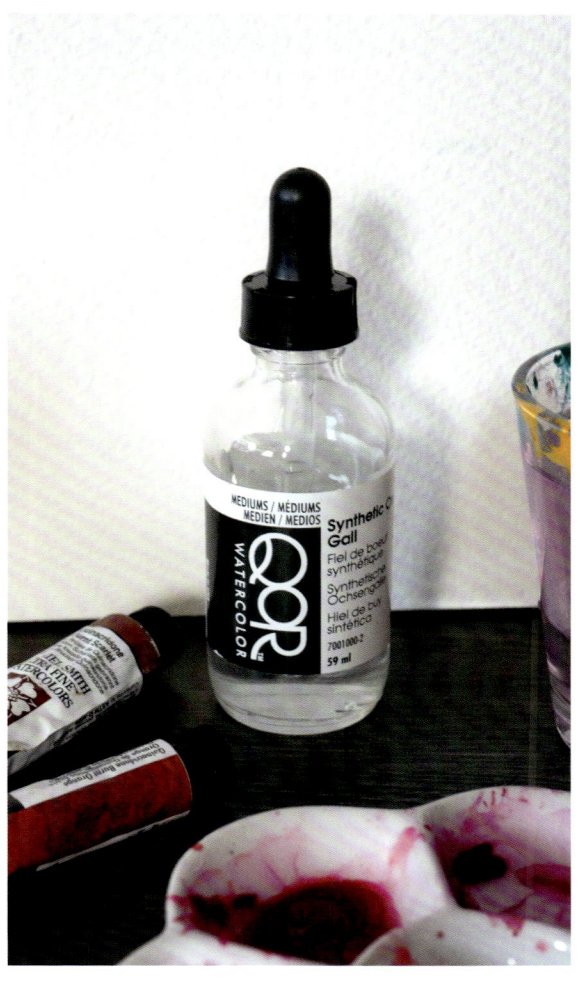

HELPFUL TIPS

- **Less is more!** Don't overuse the medium—just 2–3 drops in a 250ml jar of water will do the trick. It can actually damage your paper if you use too much.
- **Use Occasionally.** You don't need to use Ox Gall in every painting, as it can actually keep your paper damp for too long when you don't need it. I bring the medium out in the summer, usually for wet-on-damp work or for particularly large paintings where smooth background coverage is required.

My Favorite: Synthetic Ox Gall from QoR Watercolors.

4.11 Masking Fluid: When and How to Use It

The transparent beauty of watercolor lies in its luminosity, and preserving unpainted areas is crucial to achieve this effect. Watercolor masking fluid—a colorless rubbery medium typically made with latex—acts as a guardian, temporarily shielding specific sections of paper from absorbing paint. Whether it's preserving highlights in a portrait, maintaining the sparkle in water reflections, or creating intricate veins on a flower petal, masking fluid is a wonderful and useful addition to your watercolor toolkit. In this section, I will share the application techniques, various use-case scenarios, and my favorite tips for using masking fluid in my work.

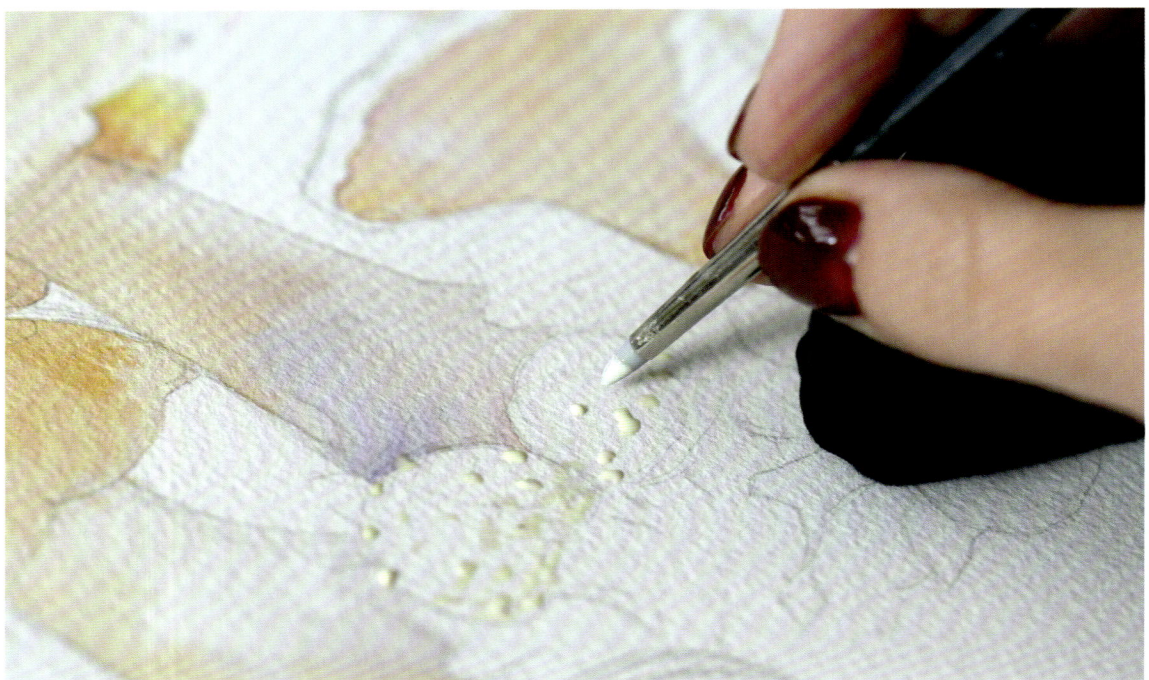

Masking Fluid Applied to Preserve the White Spots on Redcap Mushrooms

Step-by-Step

1. **Preparation:** Ensure your paper is completely dry before applying masking fluid. Shake the masking fluid bottle gently to achieve a smooth consistency. Avoid shaking it too much as it can create tiny air bubbles that take a long time to settle.
2. **Application:** Use a thin wooden stick or a specific masking fluid applicator to apply the fluid precisely to the areas you wish to preserve. You will need to work quickly, as masking fluid dries fast. In the above example, I am applying small dots of fluid to preserve the white spots on redcap mushrooms, before painting a wash of red color.
3. **Drying:** Allow the masking fluid to dry completely before applying watercolor. Once it dries, it forms a barrier that repels watercolor paint.
4. **Painting:** Apply watercolor washes as usual, knowing the masked areas will remain untouched.
5. **Removal:** Once the painting is dry, gently peel off the masking fluid with an eraser.

My Favorites: My favorite masking fluid is Art Masking Fluid from Winsor & Newton. My applicator of choice is a so-called rubber color shaper from Royal Sovereign (in size #0 for extra precision).

Use Cases for Masking Fluid

- **Fine Details:** The most common scenario for using masking fluid is to create intricate details that would be otherwise difficult to paint around. For example, when painting exotic flowers, I often mask the light petal veins before applying vibrant washes of color.
- **Preserving Highlights:** You can use the fluid to capture the brilliance of light by masking areas where highlights will appear. For example, I sometimes preserve the white highlights on the eyes before applying full color to the iris.
- **Creating Texture:** Experiment with texture by applying masking fluid in patterns or shapes before painting. This can add a lot of detail and visual interest when painting still lifes with fabric details. You can also experiment with layering masking fluid to create complex patterns in abstract compositions.

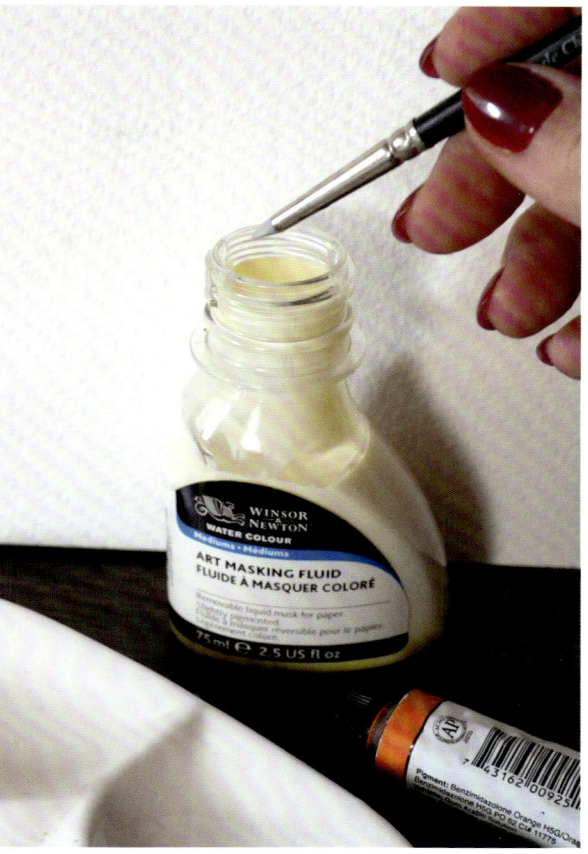

Winsor & Newton Art Masking Fluid Bottle and Royal Sovereign Applicator

- **Complex Reflections:** You can achieve realistic water reflections by masking off portions of the water's surface with fluid, and then painting them separately using a distinct color scheme that doesn't blend with the blues of the water.

HELPFUL TIPS

- **Test Before Application:** Always test the masking fluid on scrap paper before using it on your artwork to ensure it won't damage the paper. Less expensive papers, especially cotton and woodpile mixes, tend to rip when the fluid is removed.
- **Protect Your Brushes:** Avoid using your good paint brushes to apply masking fluid. The rubbery substance is difficult to remove and can easily ruin the bristles. Instead, invest in a soft, fine-tipped rubber applicator that can be cleaned with ease. As I mentioned above, my favorite applicator is a rubber color shaper from Royal Sovereign in size #0 for extra precision.
- **Add Color:** For those seeking an extra layer of guidance, colored masking fluids are a game-changer. These versions dry with a tint, allowing you to see exactly where you applied the fluid, providing visual cues and making it easier to plan intricate designs or layered compositions.

4.12 Glove: Your Anti-Smudge Guard

Picture this: You're working on a delicate watercolor wash and suddenly your hand accidentally grazes the wet paint. Although rare, these incidents can be incredibly frustrating, particularly when vibrant paints are smudged and the whole painting is ruined. What happens more often, however, is a gradual transfer of heat, dirt, and residual oils from the painting hand onto the surface of your painting, resulting in a slow deterioration of the paint washes that you don't notice until it's too late.

To prevent this, many artists opt to place tissue paper under their active painting hand, providing a buffer between the hand and the paper. Others rest their hand on a wooden plank or specially designed hand rest to avoid direct contact with the paper surface. A few years ago, I discovered a new way of dealing with the issue: an anti-smudge glove. Whether you're a beginner or a seasoned artist, I highly recommend incorporating anti-smudge guards into your painting toolkit. In my experience, they can make a world of difference in maintaining the integrity of your watercolor paintings.

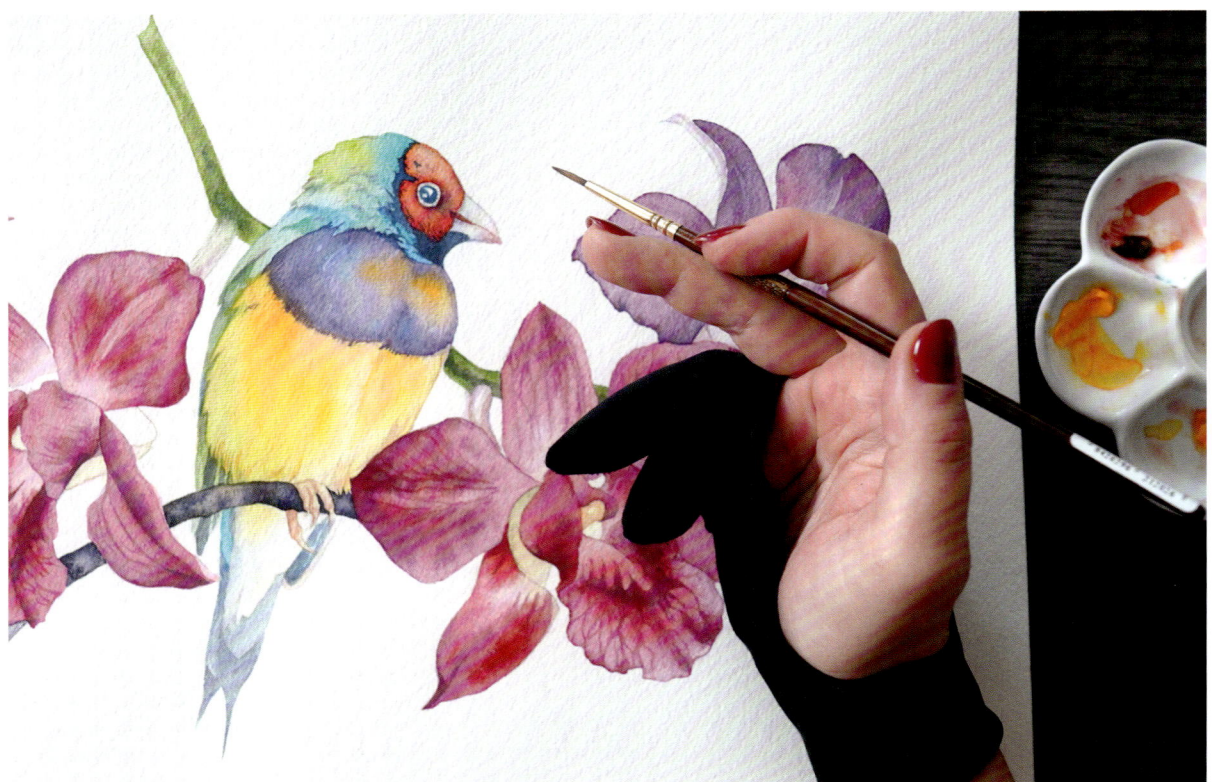

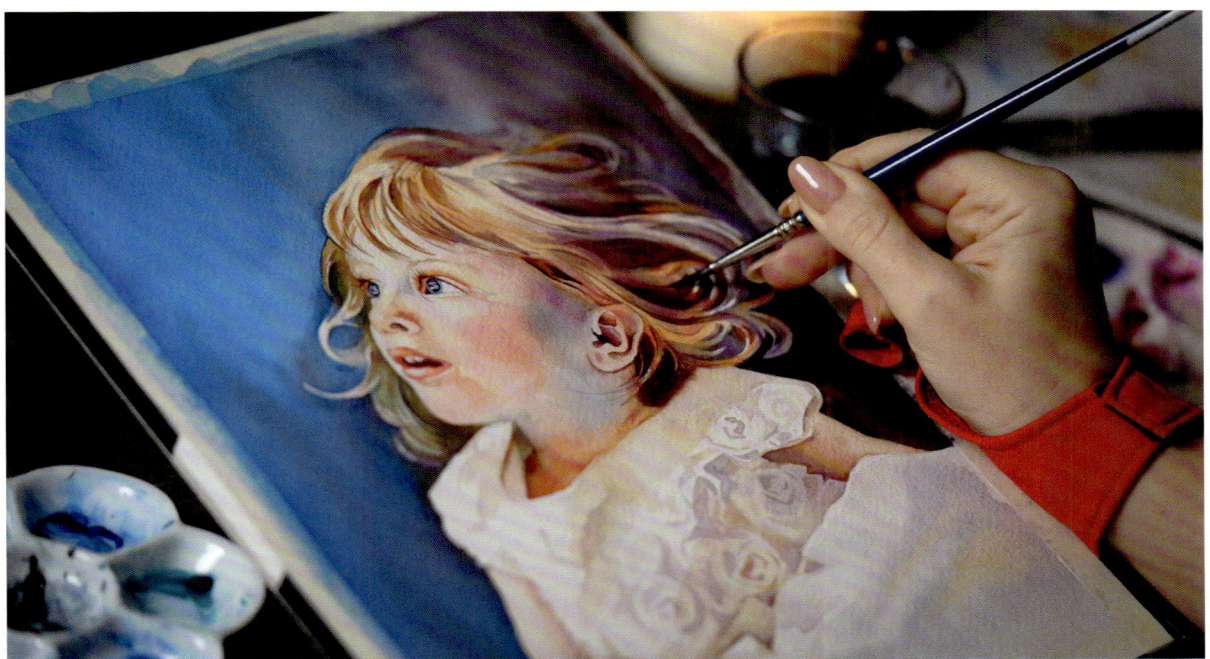

Unexpected Origin

Originally designed for graphic artists working on iPads and drawing tablets, these gloves have found an unexpected but highly beneficial application in my painting practice. I stumbled upon anti-smudge gloves by accident while working on a commercial project that involved digital drawing. Frustrated by smudges on my tablet screen, I decided to give these gloves a try. To my surprise, they worked like a charm! Intrigued, I decided to incorporate them into my watercolor practice, and the results were fantastic—not only did the gloves prevent smudges, but they also provided a smooth surface for my hand to glide over the paper, enhancing my painting experience.

How They Work

Anti-smudge gloves are typically made from a smooth, stretchy fabric that reduces friction between the hand and the paper surface. This minimizes the transfer of heat from your hand to paper and reduces the risk of accidental smudges, while allowing for precise brushwork and control. The gloves come in different sizes to fit comfortably on any hand, and there are even versions designed specifically for left-handed artists.

4.13 Palettes: Your Mixing Surface Matters

When you first start using watercolors, you will most likely encounter metal and plastic palettes, whether in a standalone format or on the reverse side of your paint set. Although cheap, durable, and easy to find, these palettes, especially the plastic variety, will stain over time. White porcelain palettes offer several unique advantages over other materials trays, making them my preferred choice for watercolor work.

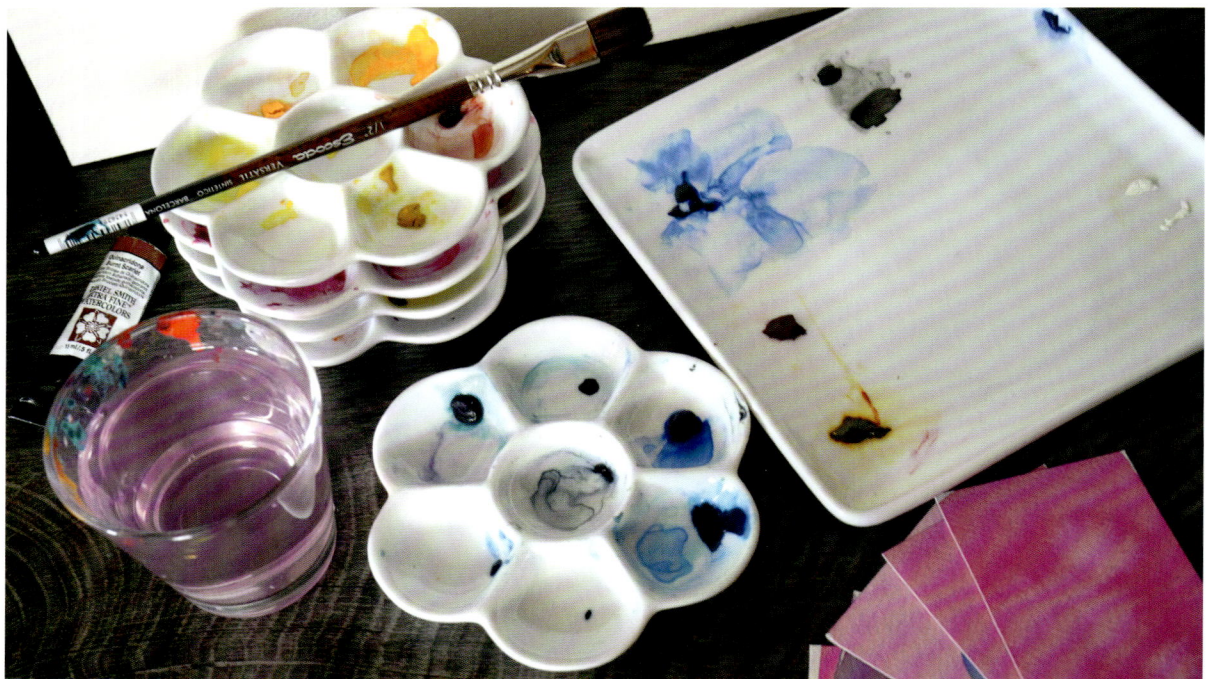

My Porcelain Palettes

Advantages of Porcelain

- **Stain-Resistance:** Porcelain's smooth and non-porous surface makes it resistant to absorbing pigments. This property prevents colors from deeply staining the palette and allows for effortless cleaning. Paint can be easily wiped off with a damp cloth, leaving the palette clean and ready for the next use.
- **Water Consistency:** Porcelain surfaces don't absorb moisture from the paint, keeping the water and pigments in your palette from evaporating too quickly. This feature helps to maintain the paint's consistency over extended painting sessions.
- **Color Clarity:** The nonreactive nature of porcelain ensures that the colors retain their true intensity and purity. This feature will allow you to mix and assess colors accurately against the pure-white surface, even in low-light scenarios.

Disadvantages of Porcelain

- **Weight:** Porcelain palettes tend to be quite heavy, making them difficult to travel with.
- **Durability:** Porcelain can also break or chip when dropped, so plastic palettes are still my preferred surface for plein air work.

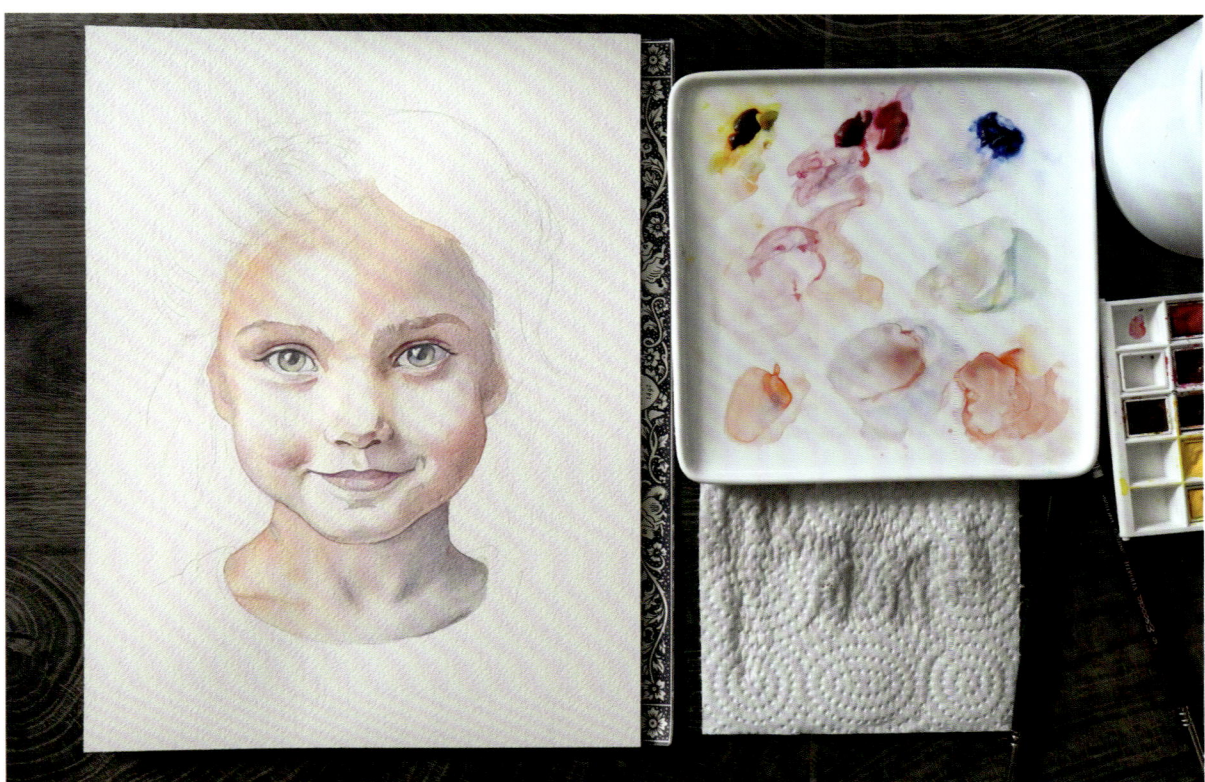

My Approach to Palettes

I rarely work with primary colors or premix my pigments ahead of time. Therefore, I rarely need large and open mixing surfaces. Instead, I rely on a variety of convenience pigments and use the charging technique to mix colors directly on paper when necessary. With this in mind, I prefer to organize my pigments into smaller porcelain palettes with separate wells for each pigment. This approach allows me to control the water-to-pigment ratio more precisely and achieve the desired consistency for each individual color.

HELPFUL TIPS

- **Format:** When choosing a palette, consider the size and layout. Many palettes come with multiple wells and a variety of large and small mixing areas, catering to different painting preferences.
- **Customization:** Look for palettes with removable or interchangeable mixing surfaces. Some palettes allow you to customize the mixing areas or replace wells if needed.
- **Regular Cleaning:** Whether you are using plastic, metal, or porcelain, it's essential to clean your palette regularly to prevent pigments from building up on the surface.

5

Essential Techniques

5.1 Introduction

Within the realm of watercolor, the interplay of pigment and water gives life to endless artistic possibilities. At the heart of every technique we explore lie two fundamental approaches:

- The **wet-on-wet** technique embodies fluidity and spontaneity by uniting a wet surface with wet paint to create an organic blend of colors.
- The **wet-on-dry** method uses wet paint on a dry surface, introducing a level of precision and detail that complements the inherent fluid nature of wet-on-wet.

As you progress in your artistic journey, you'll discover that every advanced technique is a nuanced variation of these two foundational approaches. I encourage you to embrace wet-on-wet and wet-on-dry as the pillars of your watercolor journey. These techniques lay the groundwork for your artistic expression, providing the flexibility to capture the delicate interplay of pigments or the precision required for intricate details.

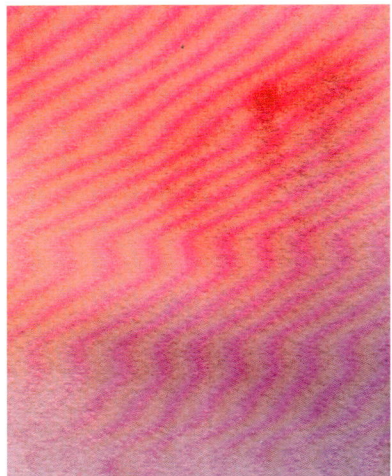 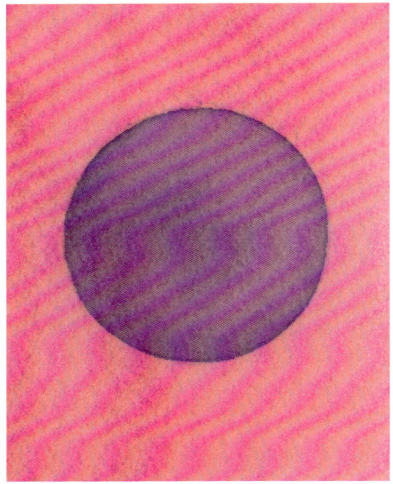 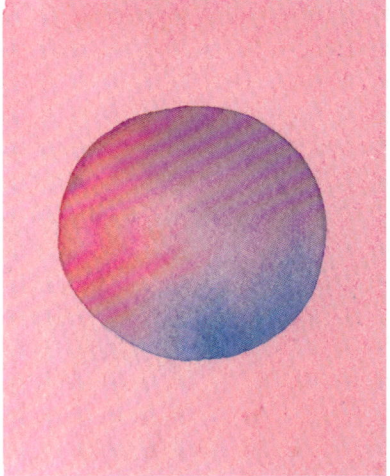

Wet-on-Wet   Wet-on-Dry   Combination of Wet-on-Wet and Wet-on-Dry

In this chapter, we delve into a vast array of watercolor effects, each presenting a unique variation born from the foundational strokes of wet-on-wet and wet-on-dry. Mastery of timing and pigment saturation will help you achieve a spectrum of effects, from gradients to textures, blooms, and controlled washes. The type of brushstrokes you use and even gravity will also affect the results you achieve. Techniques such as charging, the delicate art of mixing multiple pigments on paper, or glazing, where transparent layers grace dry foundations, all build upon the core principles of wet-on-wet and wet-on-dry. By combining both techniques, you will harness the strengths of each approach, resulting in dynamic and versatile watercolor artworks.

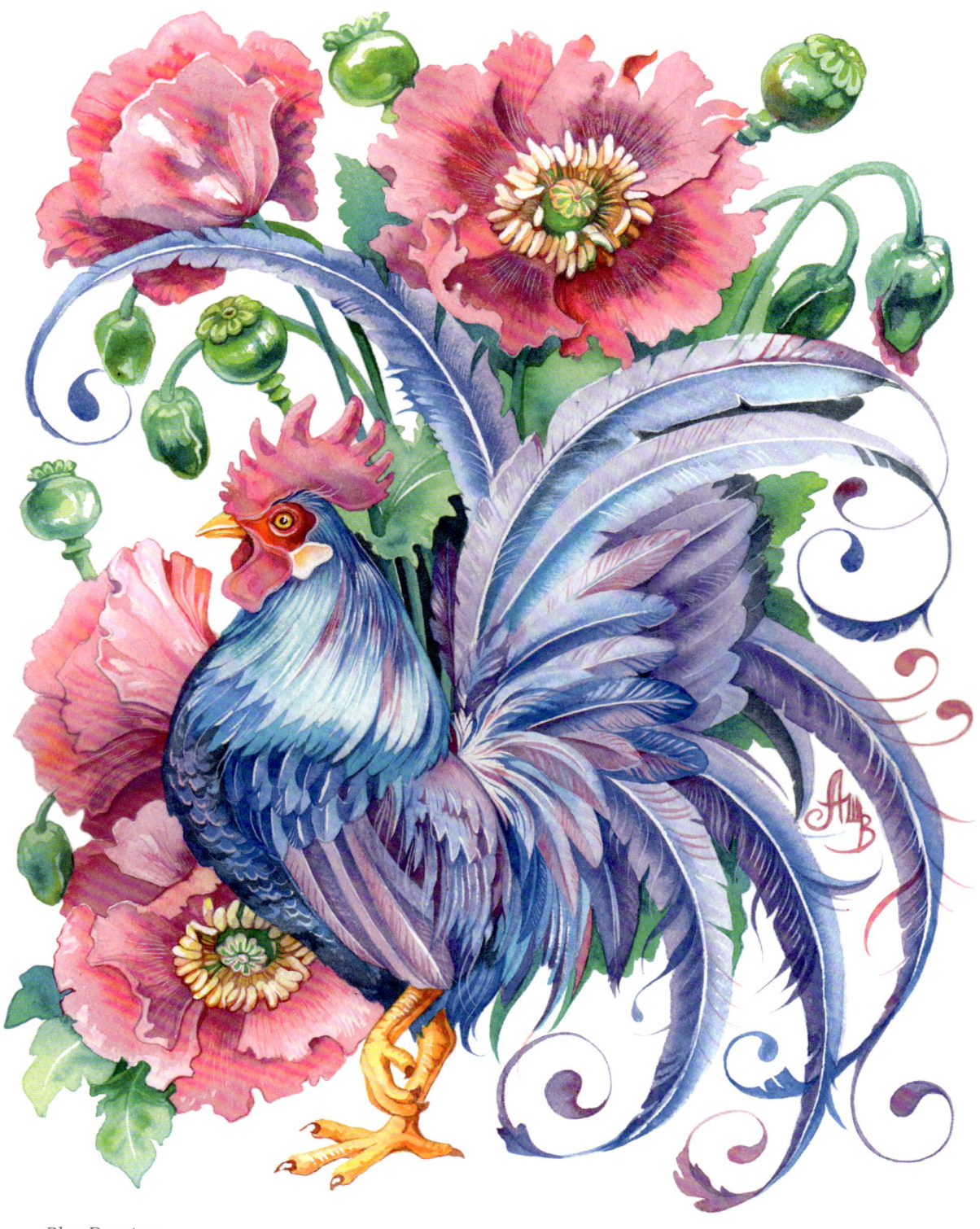

Blue Rooster

5.2 Wet-on-Wet Technique Fundamentals

Wet-on-wet is a fundamental watercolor technique that involves applying wet paint onto a wet surface, allowing colors to blend and create soft, diffused effects. It is known for its spontaneity and often unpredictable results. As a cornerstone of watercolor painting, wet-on-wet exists in a variety of forms, often serving as the base layer for subsequent washes executed through the wet-on-dry technique.

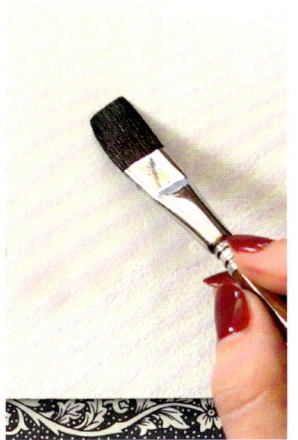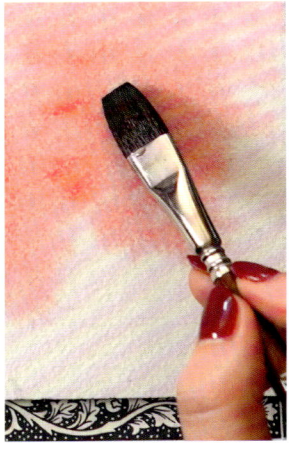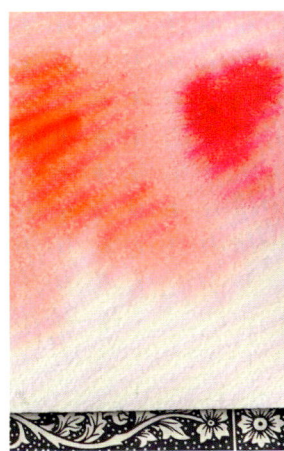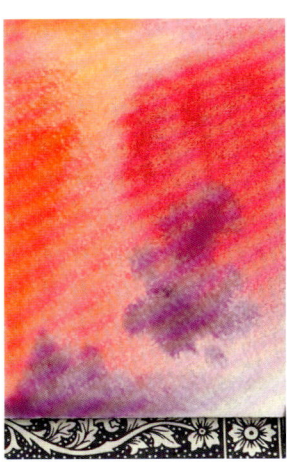

Wet-on-Wet Blend, Step-by-Step

Step-by-Step

1. **Wet the Paper:** Start with a piece of watercolor paper. Use a clean brush to evenly wet the entire surface of the paper with water. The paper should be damp but not excessively wet.
2. **Apply Wet Paint:** While the paper is still wet, apply watercolor paint using a brush loaded with diluted pigments. The wet surface allows the colors to spread and blend, creating soft edges and seamless transitions.
3. **Experiment:** Explore different color combinations and pigment concentrations. Watch as the colors mingle and flow, creating beautiful gradients and unpredictable patterns.

HELPFUL TIPS

You can use gravity to create new and exciting effects with wet-on-wet technique. For example:

- **Apply Gravity:** Tilt or rotate the paper to guide the direction of paint flow while your paper is wet. This adds an element of control over the blending process, allowing you to create more dynamic color transitions. This is particularly effective for the pouring and charging variations of the wet-on-wet technique. (See pages 103 and 96 for more on these techniques.)
- **Dry Standing:** Leave your paper standing upright or on a slight angle (~45 degrees) to create a really smooth gradient. The particles of paint will flow down gradually, leaving a beautiful dark-to-light transition. This is useful for variegated washes where a slight tilt in your paper surface will ensure a better flow and blending of colors.

- **Explore Granulation:** Depending on the type of paint you use, the effects of gravity may be more pronounced. Super-granulating pigments respond particularly well to tilting and drying upright because of their tendency to "separate" into distinct color areas during the drying process.

Video Available ▶ rockynook.com/watercolor-secrets

My Favorite Wet-on-Wet Variations

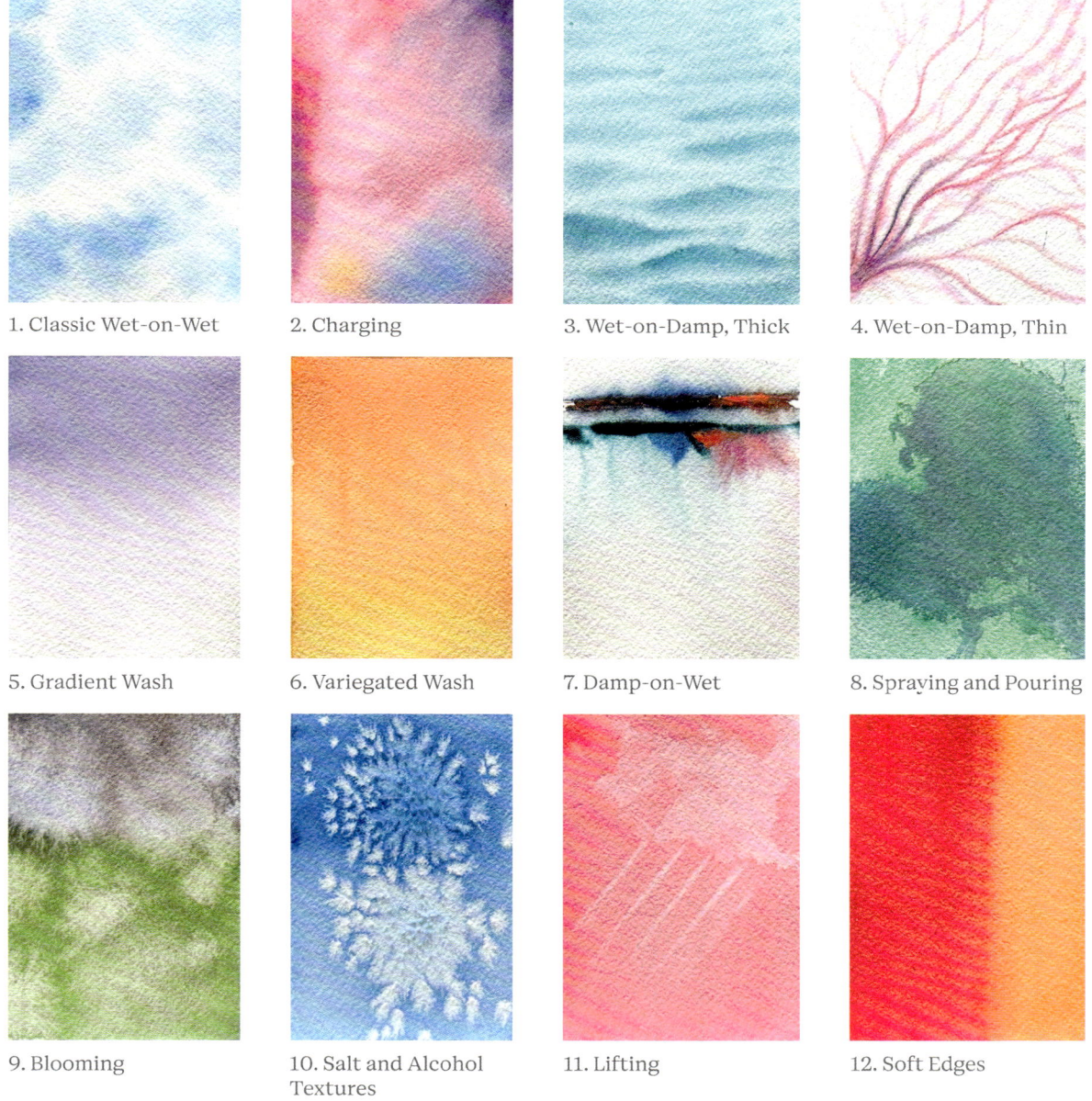

1. Classic Wet-on-Wet	2. Charging	3. Wet-on-Damp, Thick	4. Wet-on-Damp, Thin
5. Gradient Wash	6. Variegated Wash	7. Damp-on-Wet	8. Spraying and Pouring
9. Blooming	10. Salt and Alcohol Textures	11. Lifting	12. Soft Edges

Twelve Wet-on-Wet Variations

5.2 Wet-on-Wet Technique Fundamentals *(continued)*

- **Classic Wet-on-Wet (1):** The simplest version of wet-on-wet technique involves wetting the entire paper surface with clear water, and then applying diluted paint. This is great for creating dreamy backgrounds, soft skies, or loose abstract washes.
- **Charging (2):** In this variation of traditional wet-on-wet, several colors are applied consecutively onto the wet surface, with varying degrees of saturation. This approach allows for more controlled color placement while still achieving blended effects.
- **Wet-on-Damp, Thick (3):** Use a large round brush to apply more saturated paint on a slightly damp surface. This approach is useful for creating soft hair texture and realistic waves.
- **Wet-on-Damp, Thin (4):** Load your thinnest brush (e.g., rigger brush) with a thicker, drier pigment and apply it to the damp surface. This technique will create sharper details while maintaining a sense of realism with a soft, "barely there" blending. This approach works well in botanical art for capturing petal details and leaf veins.
- **Gradient Wash (5):** Create a gradient wash by applying a light color at one end of the paper and a darker color at the other. Tilt the paper to encourage the colors to blend gradually, resulting in a smooth transition.
- **Variegated Wash (6):** You can blend several colors within a single wash, creating a dynamic and visually engaging effect. This technique adds depth to your composition and provides an interesting foundation for the main elements of your artwork.
- **Damp-on-Wet (7):** Place an undiluted (straight from the tube) blob of paint on your paper, then blend it up or down with clear water using a large flat brush. The resulting gradient will be more expressive compared to a traditional wet-on-wet wash.
- **Spraying and Pouring (8):** Try spraying your paper with a diluted color mixture to create unpredictable wet shapes that can absorb additional color. You can add several pigments into the wet area using a syringe, and rotate the paper to guide the flow of the paint. This allows you to control the direction of the color blending, emphasizing certain areas or creating specific patterns.
- **Blooming (9):** Encourage "blooming" effects by dropping additional water onto the wet paint. This will produce soft, irregular edges, perfect for adding texture and abstract background washes.
- **Salt and Alcohol Textures (10):** While the paint is still wet, sprinkle salt onto the surface. The salt absorbs moisture, creating unique textures and patterns as it interacts with the paint. Alternatively, you can drop alcohol to disrupt the flow of pigments, leading to unique and visually appealing effects.
- **Lifting (11):** While your paint is still wet, use tissue paper or the edge of a damp brush to reveal the underlying white of the paper. This is useful for creating highlights and correcting mistakes.
- **Soft Edges (12):** Create soft edges between contrasting blocks of color by painting them close together. Timing is key with this approach: your first pigment should be slightly damp before you place the second one next to it.

5.3 Wet-on-Dry Technique Fundamentals

The wet-on-dry technique involves applying wet paint onto a dry surface. This way of painting offers precision and control that perfectly complements the wet-on-wet method discussed in the previous section. By exploring its variations and applications, we can unlock a world of possibilities, from intricate details to atmospheric depth and perspective.

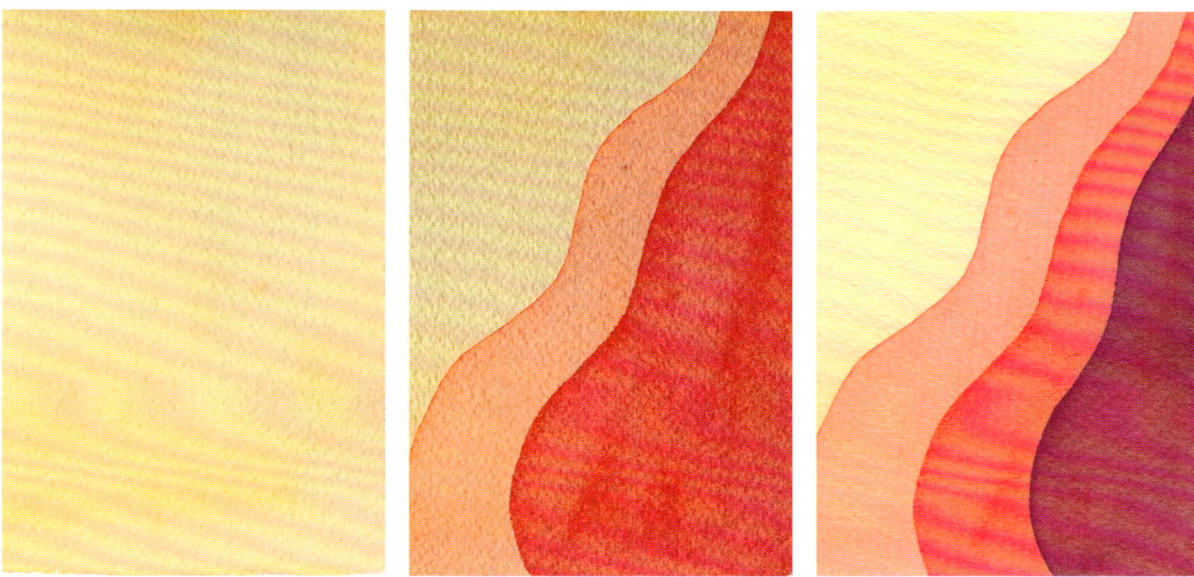

Wet-on-Dry Process

Step-by-Step

1. **Prepare Your Materials:** You can begin with dry watercolor paper, or paint on a previously painted layer (typically made with wet-on-wet technique) that is now dry. Pre-mix the colors you intend to use or simply activate your pigments with clear water.
2. **Apply Paint to Dry Paper:** Using a brush, apply wet paint directly onto the dry paper or previously painted surfaced. The paint will stay where you place it, allowing for sharp edges and fine details.
3. **Experiment:** Add more layers to build up color, texture, and detail with precision. Vary your brushstrokes to create different textures and effects. Explore both broad strokes using a flat brush and fine lines using your fine round brush to maximize the technique's versatility.

HELPFUL TIPS

- **Water Control:** Be mindful of the water-to-pigment ratio in your brush to maintain control over the paint's behavior on dry paper. Use less water and smaller brushes when aiming for fine lines. Add more water and opt for a flat brush when glazing larger sections of color.

- **Patience is Key:** Allow layers to dry completely before adding more paint! This ensures that colors remain distinct and don't bleed into each other unintentionally.
- **Combo Techniques:** You can introduce elements of wet-on-wet into your wet-on-dry applications. For example, when glazing shadows using wet-on-dry application, you can charge multiple pigments into your "active" wet layer to create intricate color transitions and add visual interest.

My Favorite Wet-on-Dry Variations

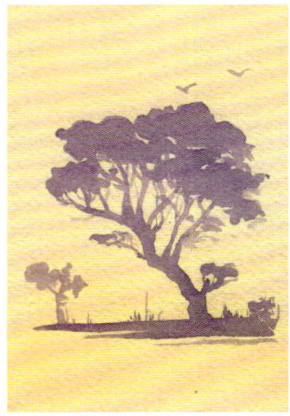 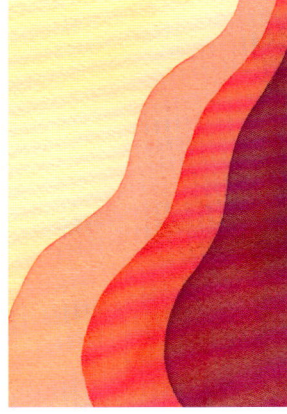 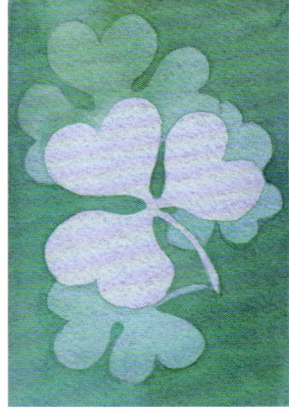 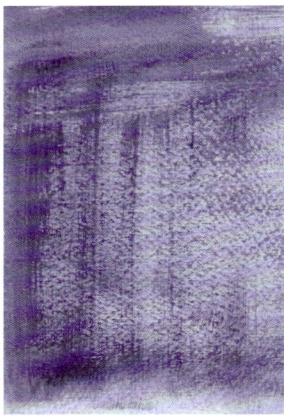

Fine Details   Glazing / Layering   Negative Painting   Textured Effects

- **Fine Details:** When aiming for realistic depictions or intricate details, wet-on-dry excels. It is particularly useful in botanical illustrations, architectural renderings, and portraiture where fine details, textures, and sharp lines are essential to capture the subject realistically.
- **Glazing / Layering Transparent Colors:** With wet-on-dry, you can apply colors to dry paper several times, allowing each layer to dry before adding the next. This technique, called glazing, is crucial for building depth and richness in watercolor paintings. It enables us to gradually intensify colors, create depth, and add complexity to compositions while maintaining full control over the process. For more information on glazing techniques, including the X-Ray method, see pages 112–115.
- **Negative Painting:** Wet-on-dry is ideal for negative painting, a technique where you paint around the subject to define its shape. This method is valuable for creating highlights, defining forms, and adding clarity and depth to the composition. For more information on negative painting, see page 116.
- **Textured Effects:** The dry-brush technique, another variation of wet-on-dry, creates textured effects by using a brush with minimal water. This technique is excellent for suggesting rough surfaces, adding texture to objects, or conveying the tactile feel of certain elements within the artwork.

5.4 Wet-on-Damp: The Most Underrated Watercolor Technique

The wet-on-damp technique in watercolor involves applying paint onto a surface that is moist but not overly wet. Unlike wet-on-wet, where the paper is thoroughly wet, with wet-on-damp, the surface has a slight dampness. This approach allows for a degree of control over the diffusion of pigments, offering a balance between the blending characteristics of wet-on-wet and the precision of wet-on-dry.

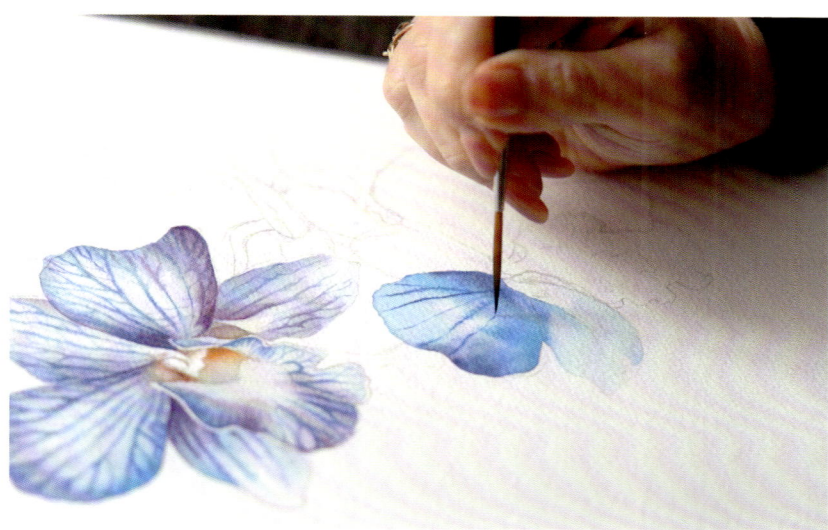

Wet-on-Damp Process

Step-by-Step

1. **Prepare Your Paper:** Although wet-on-damp technique can work on any paper surface, in my experience, the cold-pressed finish produces the best results.
2. **Wet the Paper:** Use a clean brush to evenly wet the entire surface with water. You can also use a very light mix of your favorite non-granulating color to create a light background tint.
3. **Experiment with Drying Time:** Wait a few seconds for the water to sink into the surface of your paper. For cold-pressed paper, I recommend between 30 and 45 seconds of drying time before applying the paint. You may need to adjust the timing depending on your paper brand and local climate.
4. **Apply Wet Paint to Damp Paper:** While the paper is still wet, apply watercolor paint using the tip of your favorite round brush. The colors you use for wet-on-damp technique should be more concentrated compared to classic wet-on-wet applications. If you used a background tint, apply more saturated pigment and less water for your wet-on-damp strokes. The paint will stay where you place it, but the edges of your stroke should blend slightly with the damp surface.

HELPFUL TIPS

All round brushes with fine tips generally work well for wet-on-damp technique. However, certain brush shapes add more flexibility and create more interesting effects.

For instance, you might discover that rigger brushes are most effective for creating elongated organic lines, such as petal veins or grass stems. The distinctive shape of the rigger brush will help you achieve more stable and smooth strokes, compensating for any potential unsteadiness that may arise while applying the paint in wet-on-damp conditions.

On the other hand, you might discover that short round brushes, particularly in sizes #0 or even #00, provide increased stability and precision for finer wet-on-damp strokes. Smaller brushes don't absorb as much pigment and water, minimizing the risk of accidents and preventing pigment from spreading too far. The drawback of this method is the need to reload your brush more frequently.

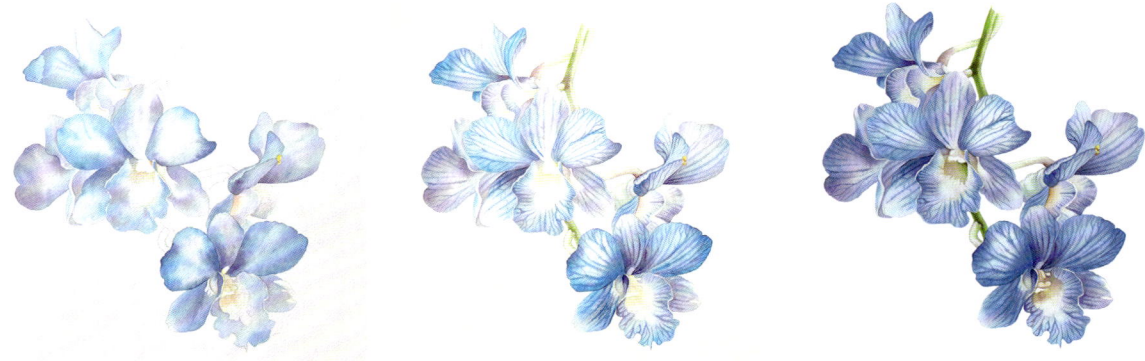

Blue Orchids

How I Use Wet-on-Damp

I painted this blue orchid branch using a variety of staining pigments on cold-pressed paper. The wet-on-damp technique helped me create the faded petal veins on the second layer.

In the first layer, I painted every petal with clear water, adding saturated blues and purples around the edges using the charging variation of the wet-on-wet technique. The pigments I used included my favorite non-granulating Phthalo Blue Green Shade (PB15:3), Phthalo Blue Red Shade (PB15), and Quinacridone Violet (PV55). You could experiment with using Ultramarine in this case, but note that granulation properties of typical Ultramarines may interfere with your wet-on-damp strokes and even obscure some of the lines due to extra texture. In the center of each flower I added a subtle hint of Yellow Ochre (PY43) and Scarlet Lake (PR188) using wet-on-wet technique.

For the second layer, I wet the surface of each petal and then waited about 45 seconds for the clear water to sink in. Note that this process of rewetting the paper did not disturb the underlying paint because I used highly staining pigments in the first layer. I added the blue veins using the same Phthalo Blue, but this time I loaded the brush with fully saturated pigments. Note that my lines became sharper and more defined as the water kept evaporating from the surface. This process took several minutes for each petal until my cold-pressed paper was dry and I could no longer observe the subtle blending effects. While the petals were drying, I painted the stems using Sap Green and Perylene Violet.

For the third and final layer, I added a soft glaze of blue and purple wet-on-dry, to add definition and shadows on each petal. I also painted additional shadows on the flower stems.

Video Available 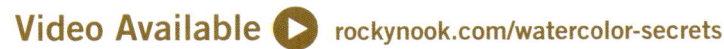 rockynook.com/watercolor-secrets

5.5 Charging Technique: A Splash of Magic

Charging involves introducing different saturated pigments onto a partially dried color wash to create vivid color transitions, adjust the hues, harmonize the palette, or simply add extra visual interest in your work. This technique is very useful for botanical subjects, abstract art, and anything that requires intense color play.

Wet-on-Wet vs. Charging vs. Wet-on-Damp

The key difference between wet-on-wet, charging, and wet-on-damp, is timing and your desired effects. All three methods involve working with wet paint on a wet surface, but the results are a slightly different. Wet-on-wet technique is typically used with one or two pigments and clear water, and it creates smooth and thorough blends. Charging technique, on the other hand, involves working with several pigments and slightly less water on the surface. The charging technique allows you to place contrasting colors next to each other rather than blending them fully. Lastly, wet-on-damp requires a significant delay in timing, so the pigments don't spread much and the strokes are more visible.

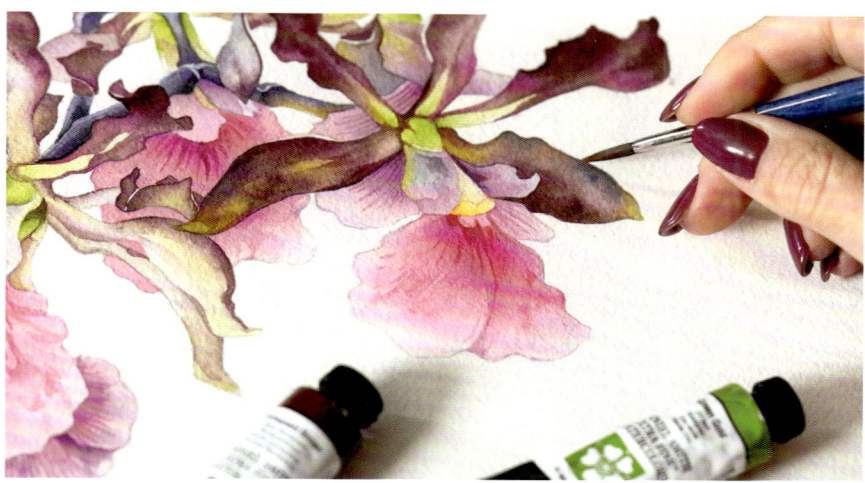

Charging Process

Step-by-Step

1. **Wet the Paper:** Use a clean brush to evenly wet the entire surface with either clear water or a well-diluted pigment of your choice.
2. **Apply Wet Paint:** Apply a splash of saturated paint and watch it spread.
3. **"Charge" Additional Pigments:** Apply another wet pigment on top of the initial wet paint. Experiment with dilution—a softer touch of new color will create a more subtle blend, while a bolder application will result in better contrast and visual separation between the colors you are working with.

Applications in Watercolor

- **To Adjust Hues & Create Visual Interest:** The first and most common scenario in which you might use the charging technique is to slightly adjust the hue of an existing color wash, adding extra vibrancy to specific areas of your painting. You can charge analogous colors like green and yellow, or stick to a more unified palette by charging various shades of red.

- **To Add Subtle Shadows:** Cool pigments, especially blues, always come in handy when you want to create shadows or help make objects look like they are receding into the background. Instead of glazing your shadows separately, you can charge these darker colors into a segment of an object while your paper is still wet. This will help you create more subtle shadow effects with a softer transition between light and dark.
- **To Harmonize the Palette:** You can use the charging technique to make the palette of your painting more cohesive. For example, if you have a strong splash of color in one area of the painting, you can charge the same color into other areas to create a subtle visual echo. This can help you harmonize the overall palette and add color continuity throughout your composition.

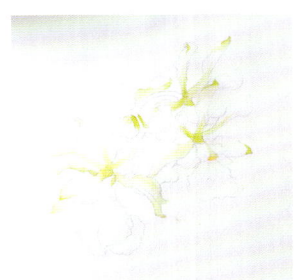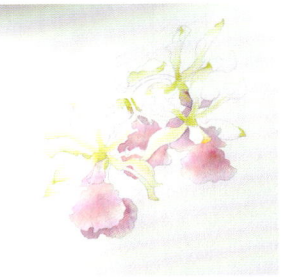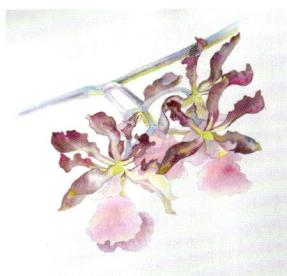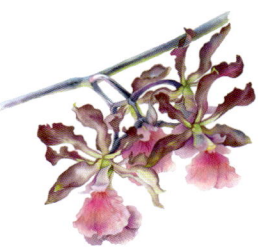

Chocolate Orchids

How I Use Charging Technique

In this painting of the chocolate orchid, I used the charging technique in a variety of ways throughout each segment of the flower.

On the pink petals (orchid "lips"), I first covered each segment with a light wash of Opera Rose (PR122). Using a gentle touch and a damp brush, I charged a slightly darker and more intense pink—Quinacridone Magenta (PR122)—into the center of the drying wash. Notice that my Magenta doesn't reach the edges of the petal, creating a very soft, natural blend. I repeated this process one more time in the final step, adding more texture and definition to the pink petals. I also charged some Quinacridone Violet (PV55) on the background pink "lips" to create a subtle shadow effect using a cooler hue.

On the dark violet petals, I used the charging technique in a different way to accentuate the color temperature variations and add visual interest to the main petals. First, I covered each petal with a slightly diluted Perylene Violet (PV29). This time I waited a bit longer for the water to sink in, until my paper was more damp than wet. I then "charged" the petals with fully concentrated Perylene Violet around the edges, followed by splashes of very saturated Quinacridone Magenta and Indanthrone Blue (PB60).

To harmonize the overall palette, I continued charging similar colors throughout, adding splashes of Blue and Magenta even on the branches. Notice that in some areas I even charged Green Gold (PY150, PY3, PG36) into my Violet. This pigment was used in the first underpainting layer, in the center of each flower.

Video Available 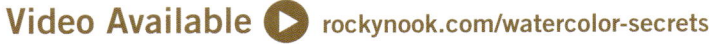 **rockynook.com/watercolor-secrets**

5.6 Salt Technique for Extraordinary Textures

Incorporating salt into your watercolor paintings allows for a playful exploration of texture, producing unique and visually captivating effects. The salt absorbs moisture from the paint, creating patterns and granulation effects. Whether you're creating realistic landscapes or abstract masterpieces, salt textures will elevate your watercolor game, adding an element of surprise and creativity to your artworks.

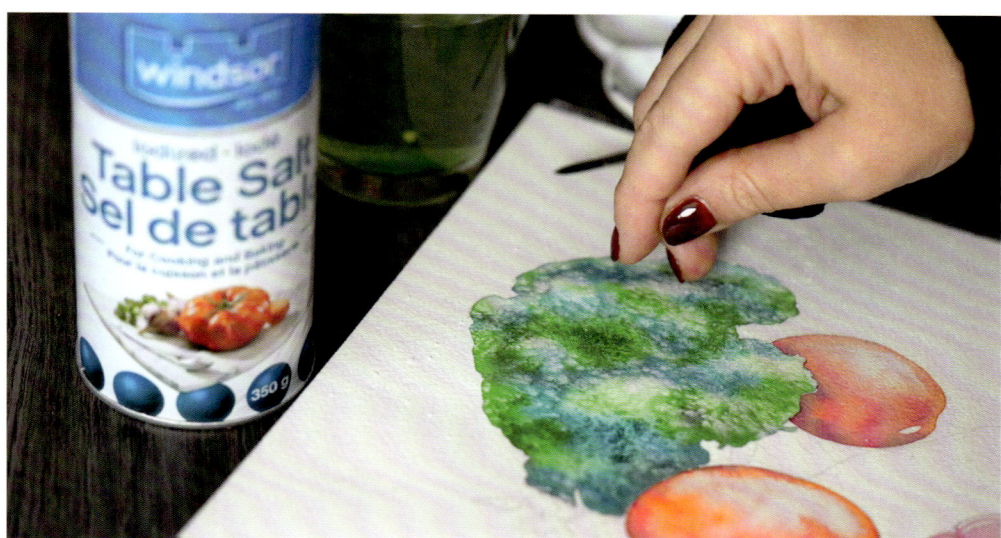

Using Salt to Create Broccoli Texture

Step-by-Step

1. **Prepare Your Paper:** Wet the area of your watercolor paper where you want to apply the salt. You can use a clean brush to evenly moisten the paper.
2. **Add Color:** Apply watercolor paint onto the wet surface using traditional wet-on-wet method. Use various colors and experiment with different concentrations for a rich and dyramic result.
3. **Sprinkle Salt:** While the paint is still wet, sprinkle salt evenly over the painted area. Be playful with the amount of salt you use; more salt typically results in more pronounced textures. Experiment with different stages of wetness to achieve various textures.
4. **Observe and Adjust:** Allow the salt to sit on the paper and interact with the wet paint. You will observe the salt absorbing moisture, creating fascinating patterns and textures as it moves the pigment. At this stage you can carefully add additional colors while your paper is still wet.
5. **Let It Dry:** Allow the artwork to dry completely. As it dries, the salt will leave behind unique textures and granulation effects in the painted area.
6. **Remove Salt:** Once the paint is dry (~2-plus hours), you can remove the salt crystals using a soft cloth or tissue paper. Be gentle, as the particles of salt can scratch the paper surface if you apply too much pressure.
7. **Add Details:** You can now add additional colors using wet-on-dry method, adjusting tonal values and introducing new shadow layers to further define the form.

Applications in Watercolor

- **Dynamic Seascapes:** You can apply salt to wet areas depicting ocean waves to simulate the foamy, textured look of crashing waves.
- **Winter Scenes:** Use salt in areas representing snow or frost in winter landscapes, creating a crystalline texture.
- **Backgrounds and Abstract Art:** Experiment with salt in abstract compositions to introduce unpredictable and intriguing textures. My favorite use of salt is to add visual interest to watercolor backgrounds, adding a soft texture to abstract washes and framing more realistic and detailed objects in the foreground.

HELPFUL TIPS

Different types of salt, such as fine table salt or coarse sea salt, can yield distinct textures. Explore the effects each type creates:

- **Sea Salt:** Coarse sea salt creates larger, more pronounced textures. It's perfect for simulating the rugged texture of rocks and ocean waves, or for adding bold, expressive details to your artwork.
- **Table Salt:** Fine table salt, on the other hand, produces finer textures. It's ideal for creating subtle, delicate patterns, making it a fantastic choice for portraying soft backgrounds or gentle atmospheric effects.
- **Epsom Salt:** Epsom salt, with its unique crystal structure, introduces a different dimension. Experimenting with Epsom salt can result in intricate, star-like patterns, making it perfect for creating cosmic or celestial scenes.

How I Use Salt

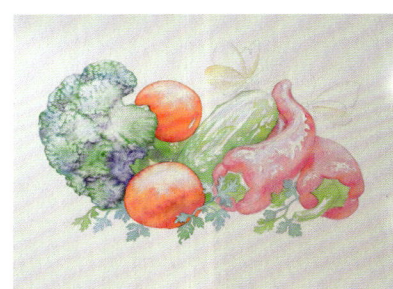 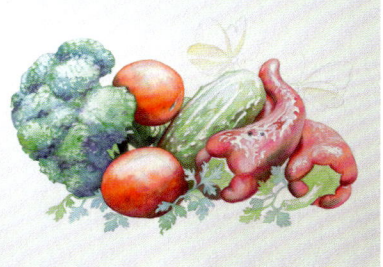 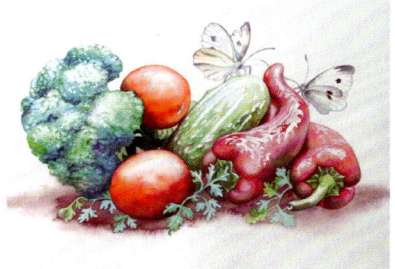

In this broccoli painting, I experimented with table salt and two shades of green: a cooler, blue-leaning Aqua Green from Winsor & Newton (Phthalo), and a warmer, yellow-leaning Hooker's Green from Daniel Smith (PG36, PY3, PY150, PO48). I applied the salt only on the highlights (the protruding broccoli clusters). While my paper was still wet, I added a splash of Dioxazine Purple from QoR Watercolors (PV23) in the shadow areas.

Video Available ▶ rockynook.com/watercolor-secrets

5.7 Gravity to the Rescue

Leveraging gravity in watercolor painting can lead to intriguing and organic effects, creating dynamic textures and gradients. There are several ways to incorporate gravity into your wet-on-wet washes, from tilting the paper to encourage subtle paint movement, to using syringes and spray bottles for more expressive flow of pigments and very dynamic effects.

Step-by-Step

- **Prepare Your Paper:** Choose quality watercolor paper, as it absorbs and reacts to water more effectively. If you plan on applying several washes, make sure your paper is stretched to avoid warping. You can also use a watercolor block where each sheet of paper is glued on the side to prevent the buckling effect.

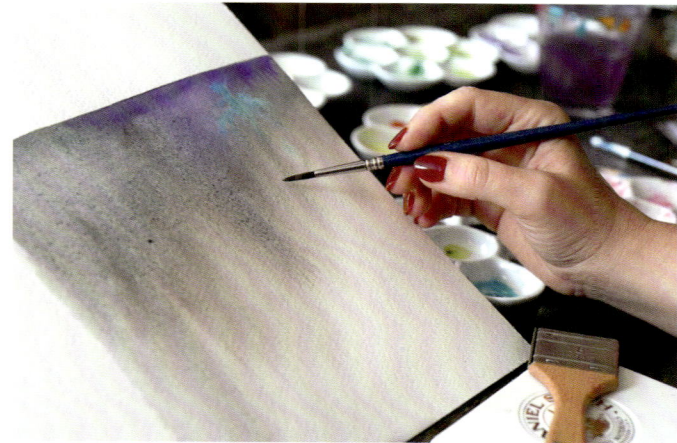
Tilted Paper Allows Gravity to Move the Paint

- **Prepare Your Paints:** Use a variety of colors, ensuring they are watered down to different consistencies for diverse effects. You may want to prepare your mixes in a separate container to last through particularly large washes.

- **Prepare Your Materials:** Have at least two clean water containers to control the amount of clear water and paint. A selection of brushes, including a larger mop and/or flat brush, is useful for applying broad strokes influenced by gravity. For additional effects, you may want to use a syringe to apply larger amounts of water and paint. Spray bottles are useful, too, if you want to introduce extra bursts of clear water into your mix. Lastly, you will need a fair amount of clean tissue paper to remove excess water from the bottom of your working area.

- **Wet the Paper:** Wet your paper thoroughly with clear water or diluted color using a large flat brush.

- **Paint a Tilted Wash:** Introduce concentrated watercolor onto the upper edge of your paper, letting it drip downward. Tilt the paper to guide the drips, creating expressive lines and textures.

- **Dry in a Tilted Position:** Leave your artwork to dry tilted to encourage further flow of paint. Try leaving it on an easel at various angles to experiment with how gravity affects the drying paint.

HELPFUL TIPS

- **Drop Extra Color (Brush Method):** Load your brush with concentrated paint and gently tap it above the paper. Allow droplets to fall onto the wet surface, creating interesting patterns as the paint disperses.

- **Drop Extra Color (Syringe Method):** Placing a new pigment mix with the tip of your syringe, instead of your brush, will create a more dynamic burst of color.

- **Drop Extra Color (Pouring Method):** You can pour new colors mixed with a generous amount of water into your wash while your paper is still wet. Note that this approach brings extra moisture to your working surface, extending the drying time significantly.
- **Spray Water:** Use a spray bottle to moisten your drying paper. As the water droplets land, they interact with the damp paint, creating textural effects. Tilt the paper to influence the direction of the water.
- **Clean Your Surface:** As your colors move down with gravity, excess water might collect at the bottom, producing undesirable results; it might even drip down on your desk or seep into the underlying pages of your sketchpad. Use tissue paper to absorb the excess moisture at the bottom of your paper.

How I Use Gravity with Watercolor

I love using gravity to create dynamic, textured backgrounds in my landscape work. In this painting, I poured wet paint on wet paper using a syringe instead of a brush to achieve a sense of movement and intricate reflections on the water.

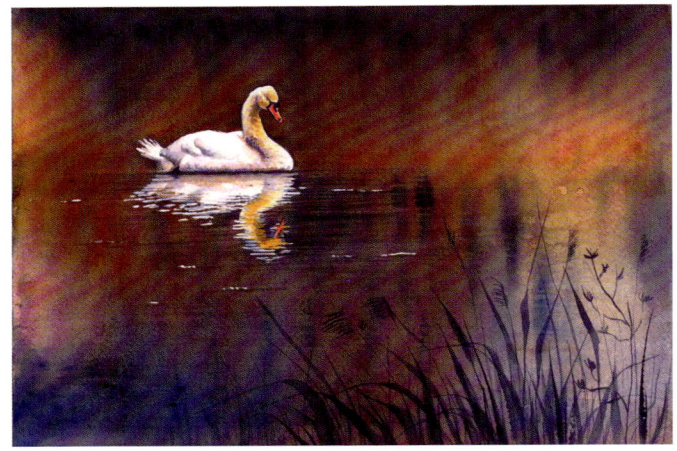

White Swan

Before applying my background gradients, I masked the silhouette of the swan using the Art Masking Fluid from Winsor & Newton. I also preserved the small reflections on the water around the swan using a few strokes of the same fluid.

I prepared the background using very diluted oranges: Quinacridone Burnt Orange (PR206) and Quinacridone Gold (PO48, PY150). I then added complimentary blues—Indanthrone Blue (PB60) and Indigo (PB60, PBk6)—to mark up the grasses and water reflections. My paper was tilted to encourage the flow of pigment from top to bottom, creating the first set of subtle gradients.

Next, I dropped more saturated colors onto the wet surface to simulate moving reflections in the water. In some areas, I poured my diluted blues directly from my palette, creating larger, more static gradients. Using a syringe allowed for smaller, more controlled gradients immediately under the trees in the background. I kept my paper tilted and rotated it throughout the process to accentuate the extra-long reflections on the water's surface.

I left the painting in a tilted position to dry, allowing the paint to flow naturally and creating realistic and soft transitions.

After the background was done, I erased the masking fluid, added small feather accents and shadows on the swan, and painted the grass using wet-on-dry method.

Video Available 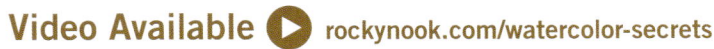 rockynook.com/watercolor-secrets

5.8 Lifting Technique: Corrections & Soft Highlights

The lifting technique in watercolor art involves the lightening or removal of paint from the paper surface to create highlights, correct mistakes, or enhance specific details. This versatile method relies on the unique quality of some watercolor pigments to be reactivated with water even after drying.

Step-by-Step

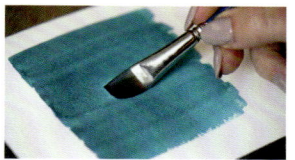 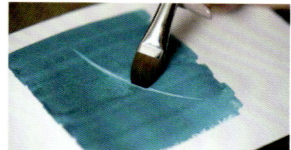 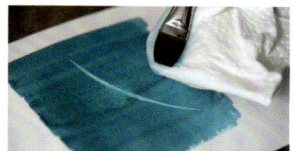 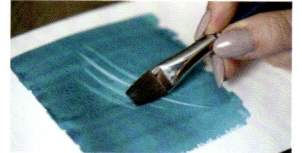

1. **Prepare Your Surface and Materials:** Select the surface you want to work with—this can be a freshly painted wash, or a dry segment of your painting. Prepare a stiff, preferably synthetic, flat brush and a jar of fresh water.
2. **Lift the Paint:** Use the brush to gently lift the desired amount of paint off the surface. Your brush should be damp, but not dripping with water. To get rid of extra moisture, I recommend tapping it on tissue paper before applying the lifting technique.
3. **Repeat the process:** If the first stroke didn't produce the desired effect, clean your brush again to remove paint residue, and apply the lifting technique again.

Applications in Watercolor

- **Small Details:** Lifting technique works particularly well for creating intricate light details on dark surfaces. For example, I often use it to add elongated veins on green leaves and red flower petals.
- **Soft Highlights:** This technique works well for creating large highlights. You can achieve realistic water reflections by painting the watercolor scene as usual, and then lifting off a portion of the blue color where the wave reflection should occur.
- **Correcting Mistakes:** If a color is too intense or an area needs correction, the lifting technique provides a solution. Dampen the area with a clean, wet brush and lift off excess pigment gently. This method allows for subtle adjustments without damaging the paper.

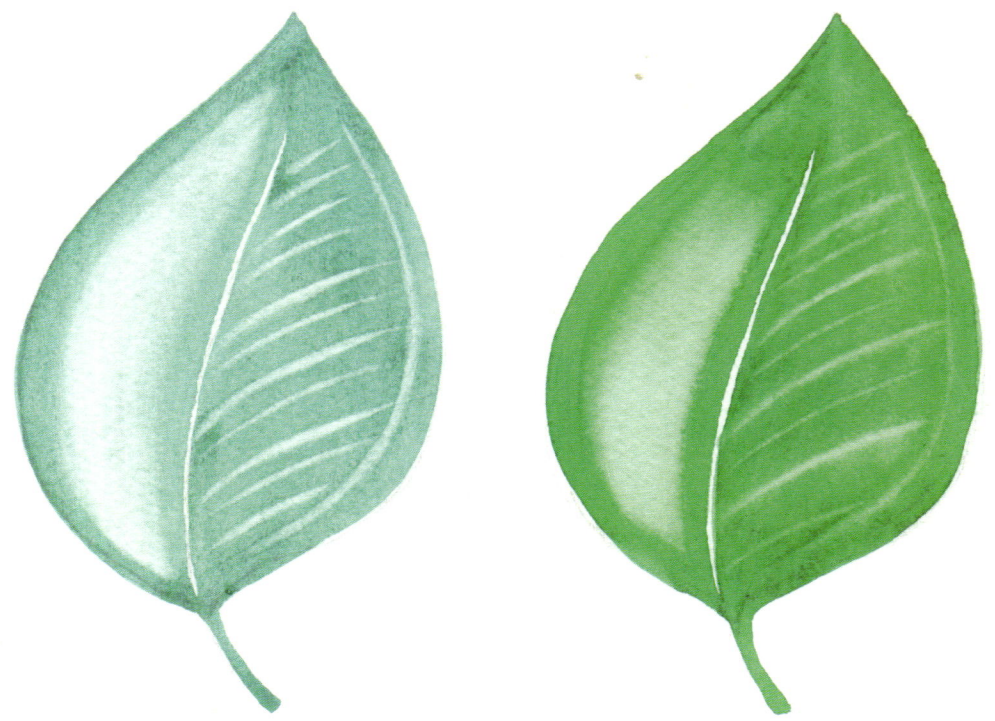

Veridian Green Leaf vs. Phthalo Green Leaf,
Painted with Lifting Technique

HELPFUL TIPS

- **Paint Considerations:** Low-staining watercolors respond well to lifting, while high-staining watercolors are much harder to lift, especially after the paint is dry. In the example above, I painted the leaf with a base green color, and while it was still wet, used a fine wet brush to gently lift off paint along the areas where veins would be. I also lifted a large segment on the other side after the paint was dry. Note that low-staining Veridian Green on the left lifted easily, while high-staining Phthalo Green gave a more muted effect by adhering to the surface of my paper more effectively, making it harder to move.
- **Brush Considerations:** Depending on your goal, some brushes work better for lifting purposes than others. Hard-bristle brushes, such as sable and synthetic, tend to work better for lifting small lines and highlights. Softer brushes, like squirrel, are better for lifting larger surfaces because they absorb and release water effectively without damaging the paper fibers. You might find that brush shapes matter too. For example, I find that applying a sharp edge of my flat brush works better for elongated highlights, compared to dragging a round brush back and forth. For larger areas, you may forgo brushes altogether and rely on tissue paper. This method works particularly well for creating soft cloud effects.
- **Paper Considerations:** High-quality watercolor paper is crucial for successful lifting. Papers that are 100% cotton with good sizing allow for more controlled lifting without excessive damage to the surface.

How I Use Lifting Technique

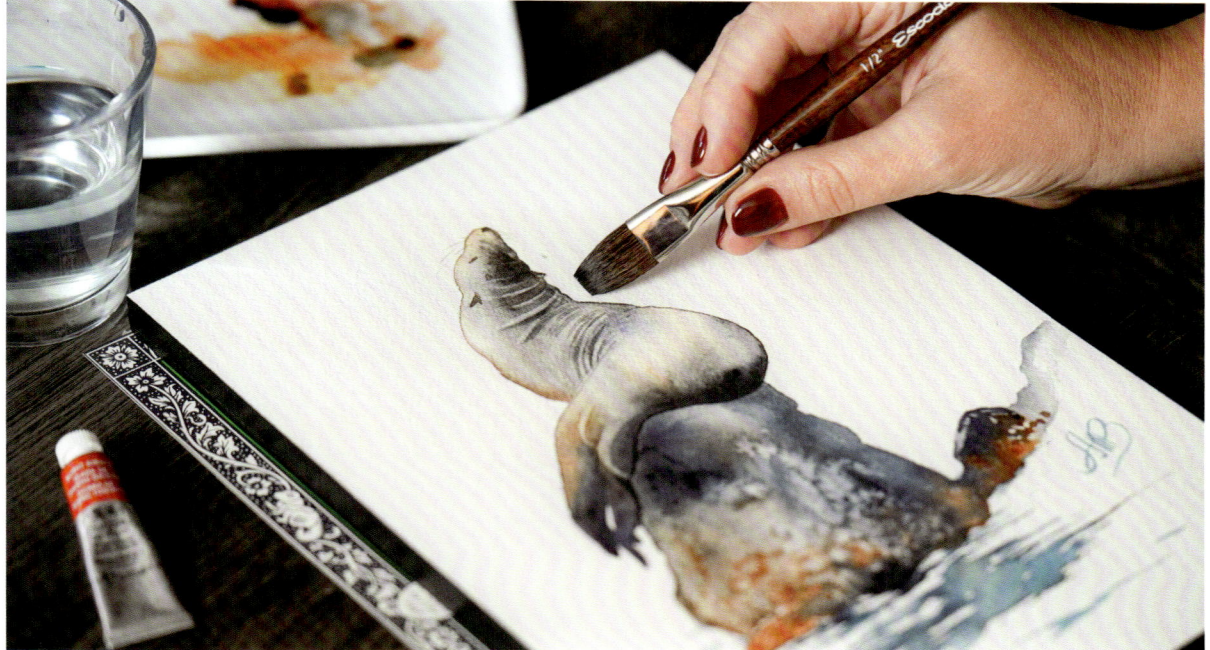

Sea Lion on the Rock

In the Sea Lion painting above, I used my flat synthetic Escoda brush in size #1/2 to lift several highlights on the wet animal. I was able to curve the edge of the brush slightly to follow the direction of the skin folds with precision. The original layer was painted with a beautiful Tundra Violet (PB29, PBr6) from Schmincke. This pigment is highly granulating and lifts easily, allowing a lot of flexibility for painting wet and reflective surfaces, while maintaining fantastic texture and visual interest with just one wash.

Video Available ▶ rockynook.com/watercolor-secrets

5.9 Layer by Layer: The Art of Watercolor Glazing

Glazing technique involves applying successive layers of watercolor to modify values (lights and darks) and color appearance in the final painting. Each new glaze creates deeper tones, often changing the colors and value balance completely. Glazing is one of the best ways to create realism and depth with watercolor, whether you are painting a small flower or a large, intricate composition with lots of objects.

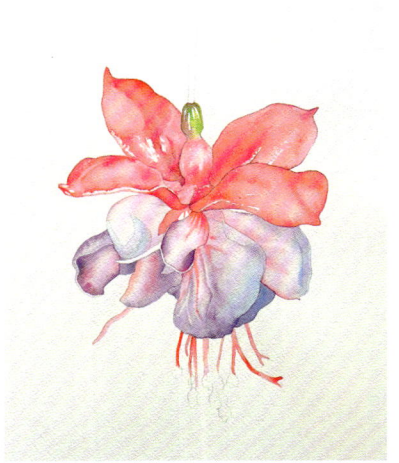 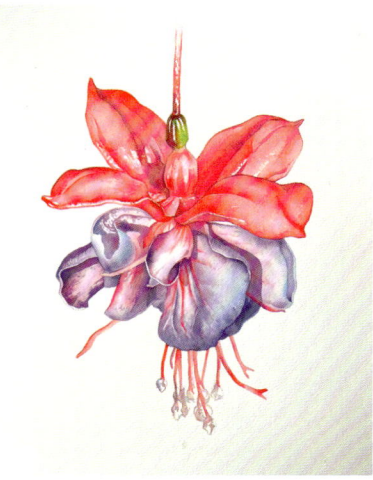 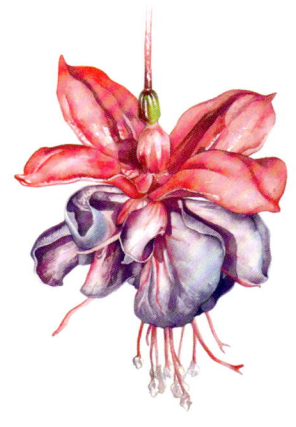

Fuchsia Flower

Video Available ▶ **rockynook.com/watercolor-secrets**

Step-by-Step

1. **Paint the Background:** Using wet-on-wet technique, paint the background layer. Here, you can blend multiple colors, but make sure to keep them very diluted to leave yourself enough room to add more layers.
2. **Add Darker Details:** For the darker details, use wet-on-dry method. Focus on the larger shadows and most vibrant parts of your subject. Amplifying darker tones will add a sense of three-dimensional form. You can continue introducing additional colors into the active wash using wet-on-wet method, but this is less desired.
3. **Finish With Accents:** Here, you can bring your pigments to full saturation, using less water and focusing on the darkest shadows and finest details.

HELPFUL TIPS

- **Drying Time is Essential!** Let each layer of color dry FULLY before applying the next! If you start glazing on top of a wet layer, you risk lifting the background pigments. You can use a hairdryer to speed up the drying time, or work on another painting while you wait.
- **Paper Quality:** If you plan to paint more than two layers of color, make sure your watercolor paper is thick enough to absorb water several times without buckling. You want to use 100% cotton paper, 140lbs (300gsm) or heaver.

- **Light Brushwork:** Glazing technique requires a light touch because you don't want to disturb the underlying layers of paint. Try not to scrub the paper with your brush, and avoid repeatedly brushing over the previous layers. This is particularly important if your underlying layers were created with low-staining pigments that don't adhere to the surface as well as their high-staining counterparts.
- **Pigment Properties:** Consider the following pigment properties when planning your glazes:
  - » *Transparency:* Avoid semiopaque and opaque pigments on layer two and above because they may block or distort the underlying color washes. Stick to transparent pigments, like Quinacridones and Phthalos, as you progress through your layer sequence.
  - » *Staining:* Less-staining pigments can be disturbed and even lifted off if you glaze on top of them, so try to avoid them for background layers.
  - » *Granulation:* Granulating pigments tend to obscure the underlying colors by introducing heavy texture. You may use them successfully on the background layer if you are adding transparent colors above.

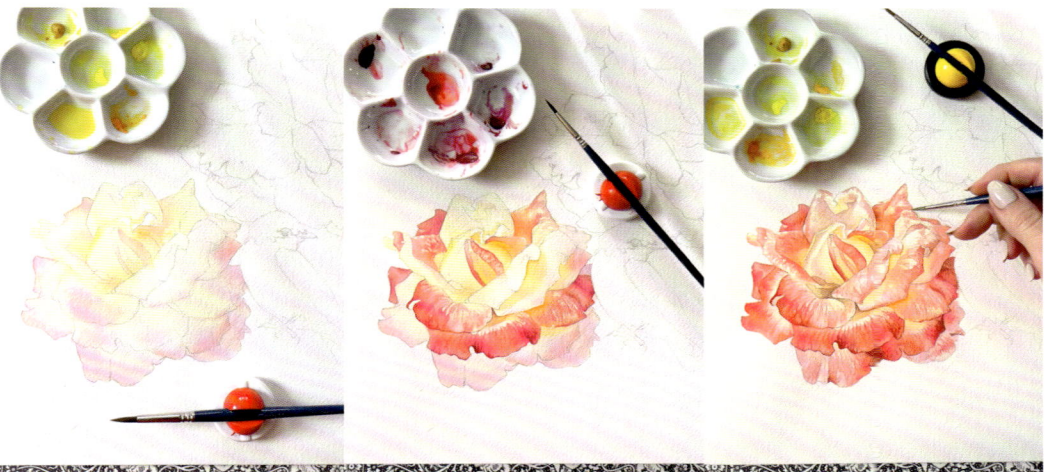

Summer Rose

How I Use Glazing Technique

In this rose painting, I used wet-on-dry technique to build intricate color blends and texture on the rose petals.

First, I prepared the background by applying a light wash of Cadmium Yellow Medium Hue (PY53, PY151, PY83) and Quinacridone Red (PV19) using a traditional wet-on-wet method.

After this first layer was completely dry, I used various shades of red to add vibrant coloring to each petal using wet-on-dry method. My strokes follow the natural shape of the petal: from the edges toward the center of the flower. This controlled application was perfect for capturing unique color transitions that I observed in the reference photo.

Finally, I glazed additional details using wet-on-dry technique, adding more nuanced color variations with controlled blending of transparent colors in the third wash. Notice that I was able to gradually achieve full color saturation while maintaining full control over my color placement.

Video Available ▶ rockynook.com/watercolor-secrets

5.10 X-Ray Technique: Translucent Delights

X-Ray technique is a fun, beginner-friendly way of depicting natural subjects by applying thin, watered-down layers of color to show overlapping objects (e.g., flower petals, insect wings, translucent feathers, etc.). You can think of it as a unique variation on the classic glazing process that takes full advantage of the translucent nature of the watercolor medium.

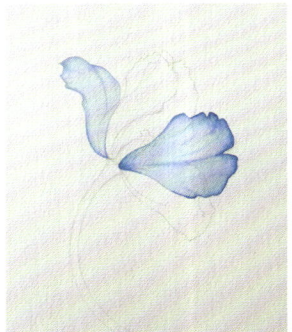 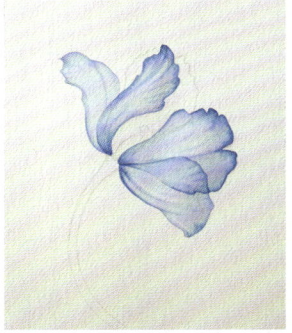 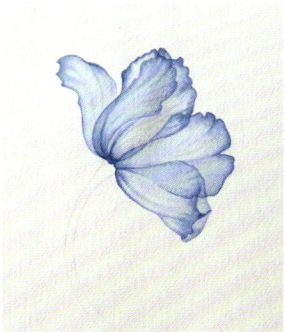 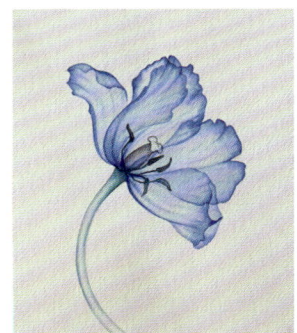

Video Available ▶ **rockynook.com/watercolor-secrets**

Step-by-Step

Here is how you can create an X-ray flower just like this using only a few watercolor pigments:

1. **Draw an Outline:** Include the "invisible" elements that you want to show. For example, when painting a flower, draw some of the background petals, making sure the outlines reach the base of the flower stamen.

2. **Prepare Your Paints:** Mix a light petal color by combining water (~95%) and your favorite non-granulating blue pigment (~5%). Make sure to have enough paint to last you through the entire first layer. In addition to your light color mixture, prepare more saturated petal color by squeezing a small amount of paint on your palette and activating it with a small amount of water.

3. **Paint Non-adjacent Petals:** Paint your first petal with the light mixture using a bigger round brush. Wait a few seconds to let the water sink in—the surface of the petal should be damp, but not dripping with water, before you proceed. Before the petal is dry, take more saturated paint with the tip of your brush and trace the edge around the wet petal. The color should be spreading very slowly toward the center. If it spreads too fast or too far, wait about 15 seconds and try again. Repeat this process, but only for the petals that are not adjacent (not touching one another). Let everything dry completely.

4. **Add Overlapping Petals:** After the first set of petals is completely dry, repeat the process on the next layer of petals. Once again, you have to make sure the petals you are working on in this session are not overlapping.

5. **Accentuate the Details:** After the petals are fully dry, you can add beautiful accents like petal veins and stamens by gently glazing diluted paint over the dry petals. Don't overdo it! Adding too many details will overpower the transparent effect.

HELPFUL TIP

The X-Ray technique works best with non-granulating and fully transparent pigments. Granulating pigments create visible texture even when diluted, and this can affect the transparent nature of your overlapping layers. Opaque and semiopaque pigments tend to block the background layers, once again interfering with the overall effect. They are more appropriate for the small accents and finishing touches that are not meant to be see-through. You can find out about the transparency and granulating properties of your colors by checking the pigment information on the tube or the manufacturer's website. For more information on pigment transparency and granulating properties, see pages 10 and 8.

How I Use X-Ray Technique

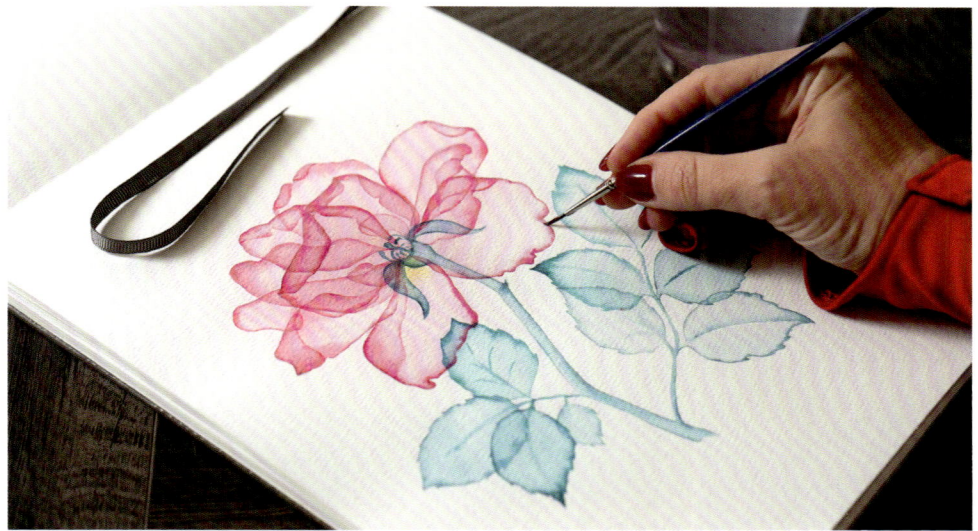

Pink Rose

In this example, I used the X-Ray technique to paint a translucent rose in my cold-pressed watercolor sketchbook from Etchr.

I used a larger round brush to wet the background on the first set of petals. To better show the boundaries of each petal, I added a small amount of Quinacridone Red (PV19) into my water.

Using fully saturated red, I then added a vibrant border around the silhouette of each petal. Note that I switched to a smaller round brush to get more precision in my outline.

After the first set of petals was fully dry, I painted additional overlapping petals. As an extra detail, I decided to add some folds using the same technique.

I painted the stem and leaves using the same X-Ray technique, this time switching to a new set of pigments: Aqua Green from Winsor & Newton (Phthalo) and Phthalo Turquoise (PB15:3/PG7) from QoR Watercolors.

In the final step, I created a few soft shadows and accentuated some of the overlapping areas between the petals by making them slightly darker. I also added a glaze of warm Cadmium Yellow Medium Hue (PY53, PY151, PY83) from Daniel Smith to create glow inside the flower.

Video Available ▶ rockynook.com/watercolor-secrets

5.11 Negative Painting: A New Way of Seeing

Negative Painting is a method of painting an object without filling it in with color. Instead, you are surrounding an object (or a segment of an object) by applying your pigment around it, revealing a lighter silhouette on paper. This technique requires a radically different way of seeing because you are working only with negative space, never touching the primary shape with your brush.

Applications in Watercolor

Although negative painting is used across all visual mediums, there are three scenarios where this approach is absolutely indispensable for watercolor artists.

Scenario #1: Revealing Light Details

The most popular use of negative painting technique arises from a particular limitation of watercolor medium—namely, the fact that we can't add lighter details on top of dark color blocks due to the transparent nature of our paint. Instead of introducing white pigment, which would ruin the overall luminosity of your work, the best option is to paint around the lighter segment with darker color wash. In the example at right, I created several intricate lines and sections on a sphere by using the tip of my brush to sculpt the negative space around them. This technique is particularly useful for painting intricate subjects, such as leaf veins, bird feathers, and various architectural details that contain thin, light blocks of color on top of darker segments. For more information on the use of negative painting on bird feathers, see page 141.

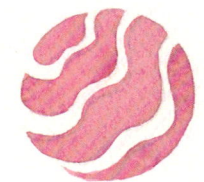

Scenario #1

Scenario #2: Reserving White Highlights

As a variation of the first case study, negative painting can be used to reserve the white space of your paper to create realistic highlights. In this example, I painted a sphere with solid color, but left a small white spot completely dry, painting around it with the tip of my brush. Reserving this small highlight instantly adds a sense of volume to the shape, making it look more three-dimensional. This application of negative painting is great for adding extra shine and dimension to any glossy object without using white paint. It works particularly well for human and animal eyes because including small reflections makes them look more realistic. You can soften the edges around the highlight by running a clean damp brush along the border between light and dark. For more information about why it is not ideal to use white in watercolor art, see page 234.

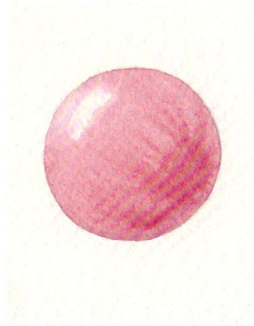

Scenario #2

Scenario #3: Framing Backgrounds

Revealing background objects by painting around them is my favorite way of using negative technique. It works by outlining the silhouette with a darker color, creating a background layer that frames the foreground objects without applying any strokes on those objects. In this example, I covered the entire surface, including the sphere, with a lighter color. After this layer was dry, I

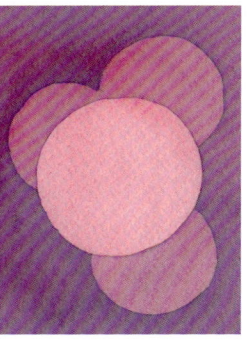

Scenario #3

applied another wash of color, only this time, I avoided touching the sphere with my brush. The result is a lighter shape emerging from a darker foreground. You can repeat this process several times by painting smaller background segments and revealing additional shapes in the background. This technique is my absolute favorite for creating rich atmospheric backgrounds with a variety of organic shapes behind the main character (e.g., a bird or a flower branch). For more examples of this application, see page 217.

How I Use Negative Painting

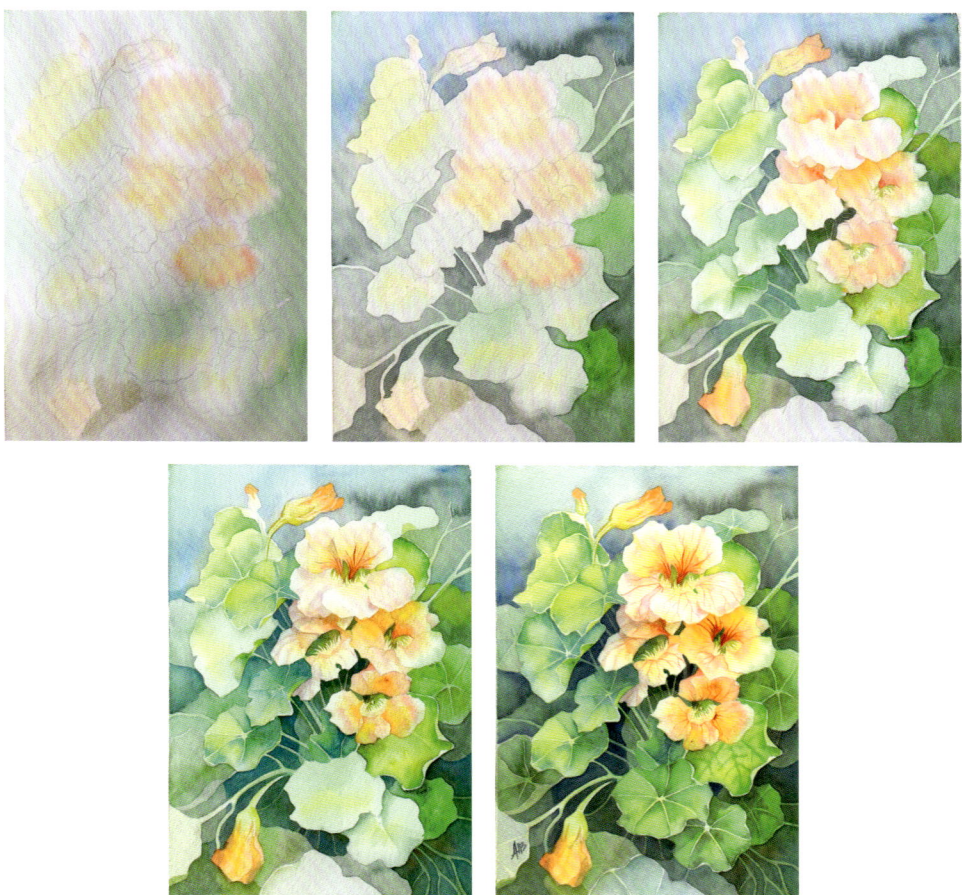

Nasturtium Flowers

In this nasturtium composition, I used negative painting in three ways:

- I applied darker greens around the leaf veins to reveal lighter green lines in the center.
- I painted sections of dark green inside each flower to frame the thin yellow stamens.
- Finally, I used blues, greens, and even browns to paint around the entire plant, focusing on capturing the thin stems with precision. In some cases, I applied several washes, partially covering the leaf shapes in the distance, creating a better sense of depth.

Video Available 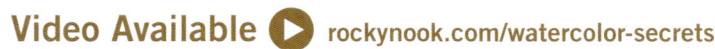 rockynook.com/watercolor-secrets

5.12 Underpainting Technique

The underpainting technique involves creating an initial layer of color on paper before adding the main layers. This preliminary layer serves multiple purposes across different artistic mediums, influencing the overall tone, mood, and texture of the final artwork. For watercolor artists working with transparent layers, the underpainting provides a base that interacts with subsequent glazes, adding luminosity and depth to colors. I often use this technique to influence an underlying color temperature of my main subject and to enhance various lighting scenarios.

Step-By-Step

1. Apply a light underpainting layer on the areas you want to accentuate. Avoid fully saturated colors—you want to leave enough room to build values (lights and darks) on top. Let the underpainting layer dry completely before painting on top of it.
2. Follow with your transparent or semitransparent pigment, glazing them on top of the underpainting to reveal the colors underneath. Note that warm, especially yellow, pigments will add a warm glow, while blue and purple pigments will create a shadow effect.

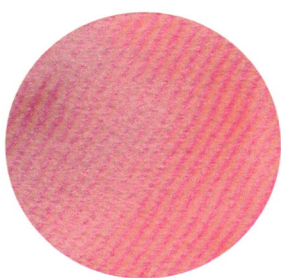

1. Without Underpainting

Applications in Watercolor

- **Add Glow:** Using warm colors like yellows and oranges in the underpainting stage can infuse the entire artwork with a radiant effect. This is particularly effective for highlighting objects that receive direct sunlight. For example, when painting cityscapes during the night, a yellow underpainting can capture the reflective quality of artificial lights, giving the scene a dreamy atmosphere. In nocturnal scenes, a warm underpainting adds a touch of mystery, creating a compelling representation of moonlight casting its glow on a landscape.

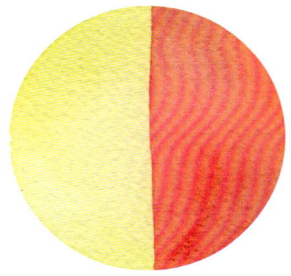

2. With Yellow Underpainting

- **Convey Coolness and Shade:** Using blue in the underpainting can simulate cool shadows and shaded areas. This technique is ideal for capturing the serene, tranquil ambiance of scenes in the shade or during overcast weather. In watercolor paintings of snowy forests, a cool blue underpainting can emphasize the shadows among the green trees, capturing the serene quietude of a winter woodland.
- **Build Depth:** Underpainting aids in establishing the spatial relationships between objects, enhancing the sense of depth in the painting. For example, a blue underpainting is particularly effective in creating the illusion of distant elements, such as mountains or bodies of water receding into the background.

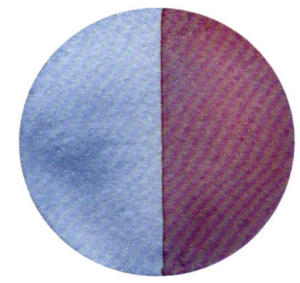

3. With Blue Underpainting

- **Unify the Palette:** Some artists use a colored underpainting throughout the entire surface of the painting to harmonize the intended color scheme. Although this method is more common in oil and acrylics, it can be used in watercolor to influence the overall atmosphere of the piece. For example, toning your paper with a light wash of Golden Ochre can help you establish a warm base for a vibrant autumnal landscape or a sun-kissed portrait.

- **Add Contrast and Visual Interest:** Pairing warm underpainting with cool shadows can create a dynamic contrast, making the shadows appear cooler in comparison. Conversely, complementing warm highlights with a cool blue underpainting makes the warm tones pop and brings interest to specific areas of the composition. This striking contrast can be used effectively to add visual interest and depth in your compositions.

HELPFUL TIPS

Consider relative color temperature when planning your underpainting. Warm orangey-yellows look great under medium and warm reds. For example, Hansa Yellow Medium or Hansa Yellow Deep can be used under Quinacridone Coral to add a very natural glow on rose petals. However, these warm yellows don't mix as well with cooler pinks, and might appear almost muddy brown. Consider switching to cooler yellows if you plan on painting a cool pink flower. For example, if the petals on your orchid are painted using Quinacridone Magenta (PR122), you can use a cool Lemon Yellow (PY175) from Daniel Smith or Cadmium Yellow Primrose (PY35) from QoR Watercolors for your underpainting layer.

My Favorite Underpainting Colors: For cooler-toned underpaintings, these colors provide a subdued foundation, enhancing the vibrancy of subsequent warm hues: Phthalo Blue Green Shade (PB15:3) or Dioxazine Purple (PV23) from QoR Watercolors.

The following pigments work well as a warm base layer: Hansa Yellow Medium (PY97) and Lemon Yellow (PY175) from Daniel Smith for cooler sunlit effects, or Yellow Ochre Light (PY43) and Golden Ochre (PY42) from Winsor & Newton for a more subtle natural glow.

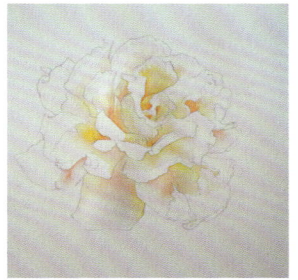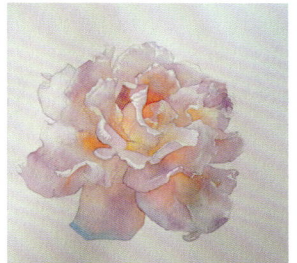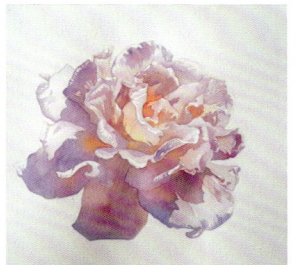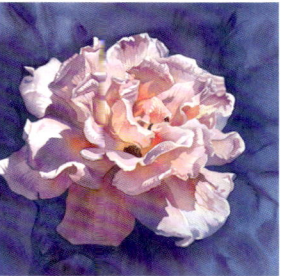

Glowing Rose in Four Steps

How I Use Underpainting Technique

In floral compositions, a yellow underpainting can simulate the natural translucency of petals, contributing to the impression of a sunlit garden. My favorite technique involves applying various shades of yellow, and sometimes orange, before painting the flowers with various red variations of Quinacridone.

In this painting, I used range of warm hues to create a sense of warmth and luminosity in the center of the rose. My underpainting colors included Hansa Yellow Deep (PY65) from Daniel Smith and Scarlett Lake (PR188) from Winsor & Newton.

I then used cooler shades of violet and purple for the shadows to accentuate the warm light inside the rose.

The final step included several washes of Indanthrone Blue (PB60) for the background to further heighten the contrast and add depth to the painting.

6
Favorite Subjects

6.1 Introduction

As an artist deeply enamored with the natural world, I find endless inspiration in the intricate patterns of flowers, the graceful curves of leaves, and the majestic presence of animals and birds. In this chapter, I will demonstrate some of my favorite subjects and explain the related palettes and techniques I use.

Flowers, Stems, and Leaves

Colorful organic shapes hold a special allure for me for several reasons. First, they offer a sense of spontaneity and freedom, allowing me to express myself intuitively without constraints. Second, they reflect the intricate beauty of nature, reminding me of the harmony and balance that exists within the natural world. Lastly, they provide endless opportunities for watercolor experimentation and discovery, pushing me to explore new pigments and test complex techniques.

Fruits and Vegetables

Fruits and vegetables, with their vibrant colors and varied textures, make for a delightful subject to practice on. In addition, they possess inherently appealing shapes and forms, making them an excellent accessory in many compositions.

Birds and Animals

Birds, with their grace and vitality, add a touch of whimsy and vitality to my artwork, inviting viewers to connect with the natural world on a deeper level. In this chapter, I will share my favorite tips on feather anatomy that will help you pick the best techniques for capturing your favorite birds. I will also provide a few insights to help you capture the endearing personalities of dogs and cats on paper.

Faces: A Fascination Beyond Expertise

While I may not consider myself an expert in portraiture, I am endlessly fascinated by the human face. Human faces, with their myriad expressions and emotions, offer a unique challenge and opportunity for artistic exploration. In this chapter, I will demonstrate how to apply layering technique to paint realistic faces and share my favorite skin-tone combinations.

Let It Snow

I find immense joy in translating atmospheric effects onto paper, particularly the hushed serenity of a snowy landscapes. Join me as I uncover the secrets to creating compelling snow textures. In addition, I will share some folk-inspired techniques for creating charming holiday ornaments that will delight both beginner and seasoned artists alike.

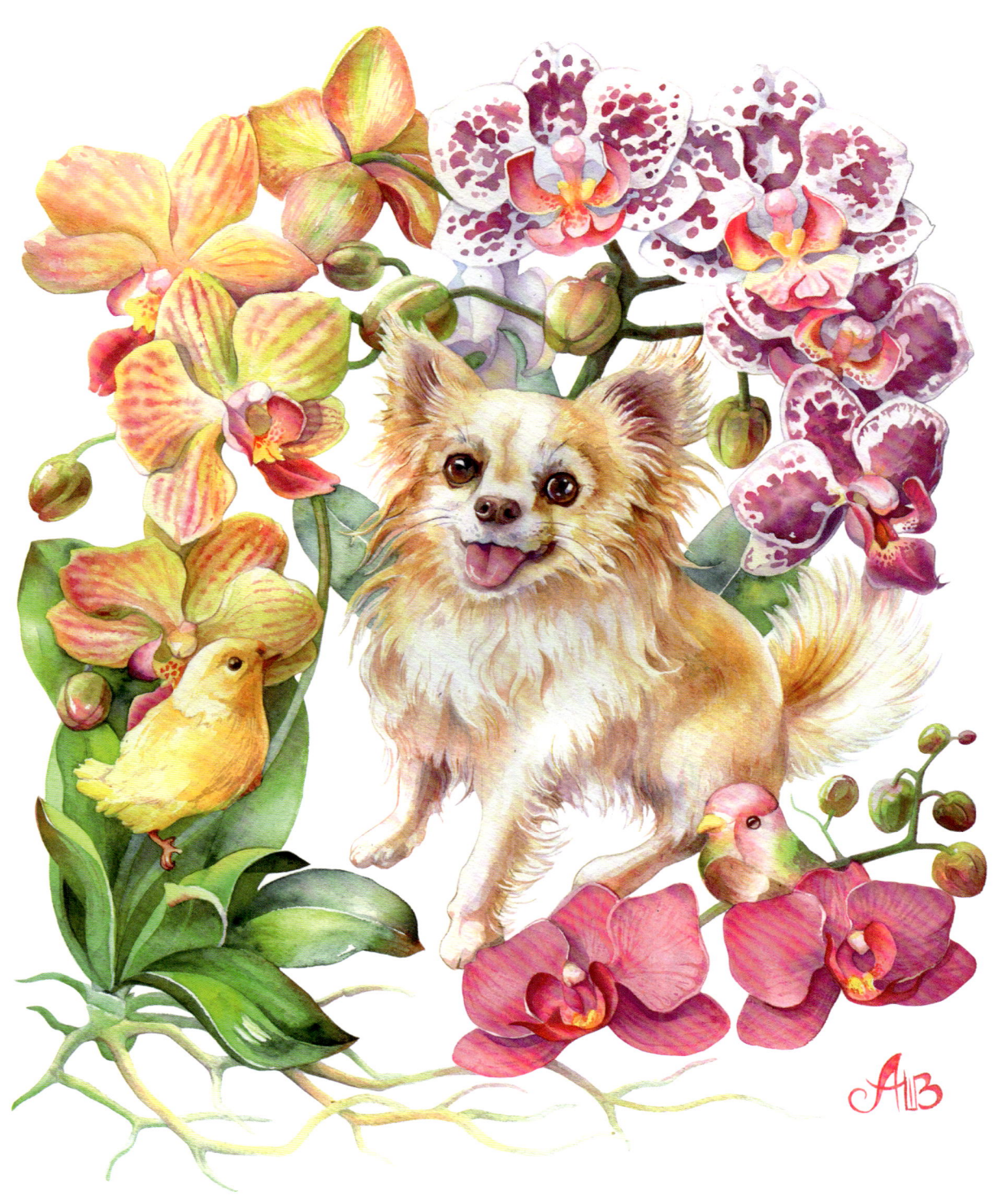

Chihuahua Portrait with Orchids

6.2 Flower Petals

Botanical watercolor art has been a source of fascination for me for many years. The delicate balance between precision and creativity, the intricate details of petals, and the challenge of capturing the essence of each bloom have kept me captivated throughout my watercolor journey. In the next three sections, we'll explore different types of flower petals, leaves, and stems, as well as various watercolor techniques that can help you capture the beautiful variations of flower species we find in nature. I hope that my passion for botanical watercolor art inspires you to embark on your own artistic exploration and find joy in the mesmerizing world of plants.

Single-Stroke Petals

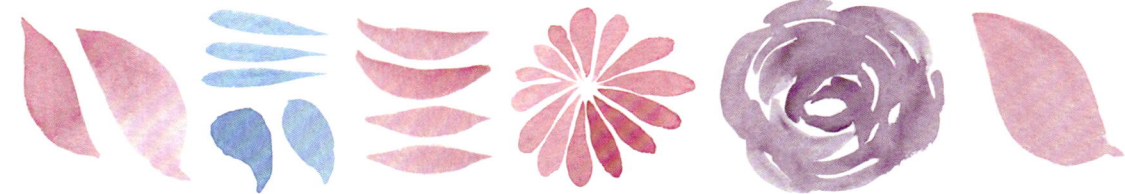

This beginner-friendly method relies on the shape of your brush to capture the essence of the flower petal. Thick round brushes create elongated oval shapes with pointed tips, suitable for daisies and chrysanthemums. I captured the distinct shapes by using precise brushstrokes, focusing on tapering the strokes toward the tips of the petals. Flat brushes are more suitable for wider round petals, including roses and camellia flowers. Here, I applied gentle, circular brushstrokes that reflect the softness and roundness of these petals.

Wet-on-Wet Single-Layer Technique

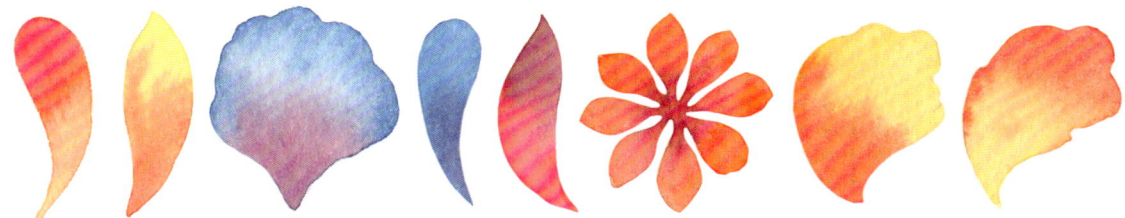

You can enhance the color transitions by adding wet-on-wet technique to the single-layer application. In this example, I applied a warm orange color all over the petal shape using a larger round brush in size #4. While my paper was still wet, I added more concentrated reds directly into the base wash using the tip of the same brush. Wet-on-wet application of multiple pigments will give you enough flexibility to capture the most complex petal shapes without having to apply several washes of color.

Wet-on-Damp Petal Veins

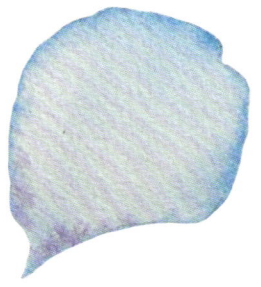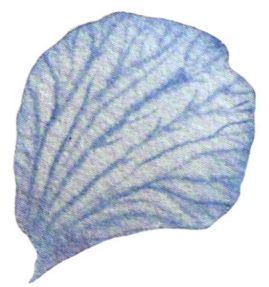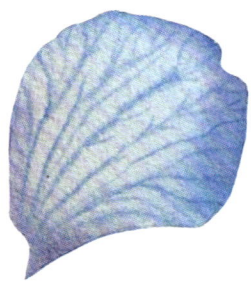

Capturing petal veins requires a degree of water control and careful timing. In this example, I applied a wash of light Phthalo Blue Green Shade all over the petal using a larger round brush in size #4. After about a minute and a half (while my paper was slightly damp), I followed with more saturated pigment using the tip of my smaller round brush in size #00. Once the first layer is dry, you can add shadows by applying more saturated colors using wet-on-dry method. This approach works well for Stargazer lilies, orchids, and other intricate flowers that display well-defined veins and narrow segments of vibrant color. See page 101 for more information on the wet-on-damp technique.

Combination Approach for Complex Petals

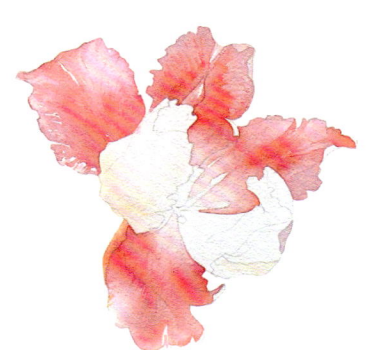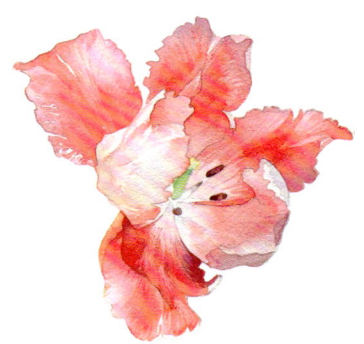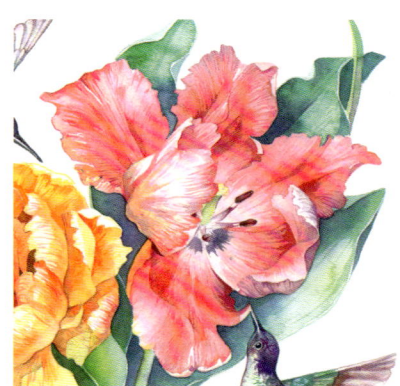

The most intricate flowers require a combination of different techniques, including variations of wet-on-wet and wet-on dry, applied in successive layers. Start with your lightest colors, applying a single wash all over the petals. You can cover the entire flower this way, or work on one petal at a time. If you want to create highlights, leave those segments dry by painting around them. Add more saturated pigments using wet-on-wet technique to add subtle color variations. After the first layer is dry, introduce darker colors using a smaller brush to ensure precision. In this example, I applied a thin wash of pinks and reds, then followed with more saturated reds using negative painting to capture the shadows and borders between the petals. In the third layer, I applied even more saturated colors wet-on-dry to enhance the shadows, create folds around the edges, and emphasize thin veins on some of the petals.

6.3 Flower Stems

Mastering the art of watercolor flowers extends beyond capturing petal shapes; it involves a comprehensive grasp of painting stems to bring your botanical compositions to life. Stems provide the necessary structure and grounding for your colorful petals, allowing them to bloom organically on the paper. In this section, I will share my favorite techniques for painting stems, from beginner one-stroke applications to more advanced multilayer techniques for complex stems. Remember, the interplay between delicate petals and sturdy stems is what breathes life into your botanical watercolor creations.

Single Strokes for Simple Stems

Thin, elongated stems, often found in smaller field flowers, can be easily captured with a single-layer application. Experiment with varying sizes, amounts of pressure, and angles to discover the versatility of your brushes, ensuring your stems vary in thickness from the tip down to the base. In this example, stems 1 and 2 were painted using a round brush in size #2. Stems 3 through 5 were painted using an elongated rigger brush in size #2. Note that the length of rigger brushes allows for more fluid and continuous strokes, making them ideal for rendering the extended and elegant lines. Stem 6 was painted using a thicker round brush in size #4.

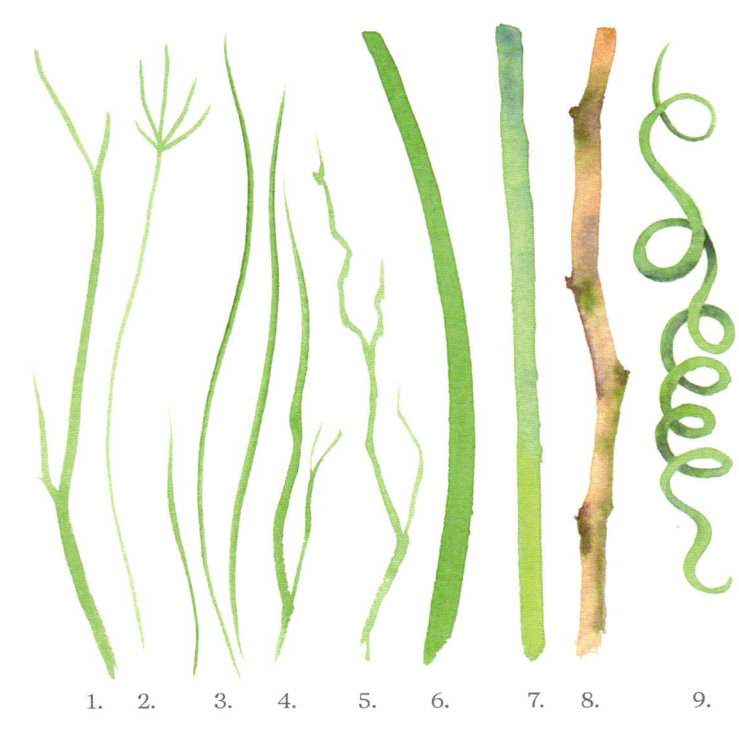

1.   2.   3.   4.   5.   6.   7.   8.   9.

Basic Stems

Wet-on-Wet for Thick Stems

For thicker stems, including tulips and peonies, I utilize the wet-on-wet technique that allows the paint to bleed and blend naturally. Note that darker hues will likely be concentrated on top of the stem, immediately under the flower petals that cast large shadows. In example 7, I applied a thin layer of Hooker's Green (PG36, PY3, PY150, PO48) from Daniel Smith, adding drops of Aqua Green (Phthalo) from Winsor & Newton on top to create shadows and dimension. I painted stem 8 with Burnt Sienna (PR101) from Winsor & Newton, and added drops of Perylene Violet (PV29) and Hooker's Green using wet-on-wet technique.

Two-Layer Approach for Curvy Stems

Shorter round brushes are your best companion for painting the twisting curves of the vines. I paint them in stages, connecting each part of the curve with the tip of my brush. I then follow up with darker colors to add shadows for the background segments using wet-on-dry method. For stem 9, I used Hooker's Green in the first layer, and then followed with Indanthrone Blue (PB60) to add shadows on the background segments.

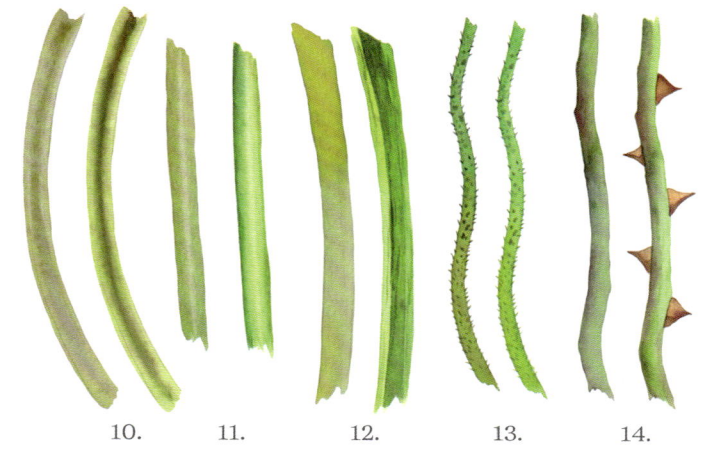

10.   11.   12.   13.   14.

Advanced Stems

Lifting for Extra Dimension

Lifting technique will help you create subtle highlights on thicker stems. For stem 10, I applied a diluted layer of Hooker's Green all over the shape, adding Perylene Violet as a subtle shadow in the center. I then used my flat brush to gently remove the color along the edges. For stem 11, I used the same method, but in reverse: I added darker colors along the edges, and lifted the colors along the central part to create the backlit effect. In both examples, I performed the steps twice to boost the colors and reinforce the contrast.

Wet-on-Dry for Complex Texture

Layering can be very useful when painting thicker stems, allowing you to build depth, shadows, and texture. For example, I used layers of Perylene Green (PBk31) on top of lighter Hooker's Green to define darker segments of the peony stem (12). The poppy stem (13) called for short precise strokes to capture the hairs on the stem. I added the reddish thorns along the rose stem (14) after the green layer was completely dry to prevent a bleeding effect.

Negative Painting for Background Stems

Negative painting is my favorite technique for capturing flower stems on a colored background. In this example, I applied a light wash of Green Gold (PY150, PY3, PG36) from Daniel Smith all over the background, including the stems. After this layer was dry, I followed by applying a glaze of Hooker's Green, this time painting around each stem to reveal its shape. I then applied another layer, this time adding blue to enhance depth. The third layer helped me reveal additional stems in the background.

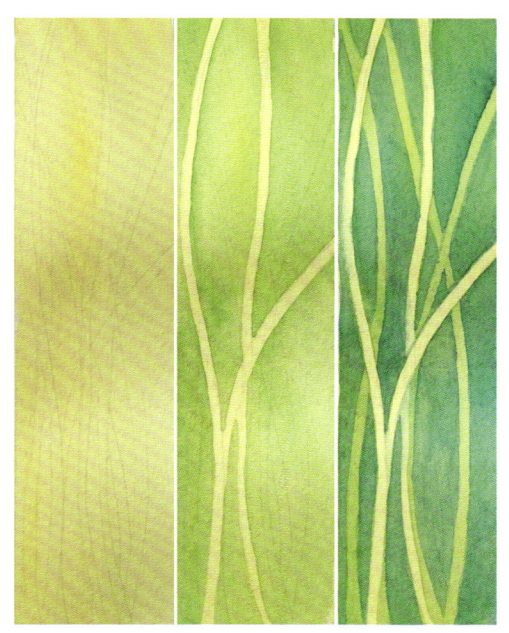

Negative Painting Stems

6.4 Macro Flowers

Painting extreme flower close-ups is one of my favorite ways to practice watercolor. Macro references offer a unique perspective on traditional botanical watercolor. Sometimes, getting really close to your favorite subject can completely change the experience, allowing you to test new techniques and see colors from a different angle. I highly recommend this approach because it can be very forgiving and, in many respects, even easier to paint. This perspective allows you to practice light and shadow transitions without worrying about the overall form. In this section, I will share two case studies, explain my color choices, and describe the specific techniques I use.

Case Study: Gladiolus Close-Up

In this painting, I focused on a single funnel-shaped bloom of the flowering gladiolus spike. Concentrating on the intricate shadows was instrumental in helping me achieve a heightened sense of realism and a convincing three-dimensional shape.

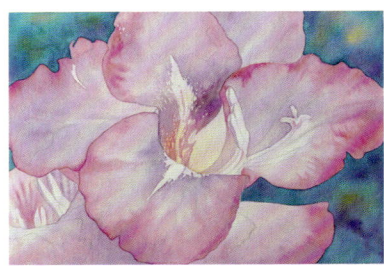

Step 1: In the first layer, I created a very light map of color on the petals using a delicate combination of diluted Quinacridone Magenta (PR122), Quinacridone Violet (PV55), and Dioxazine Purple (PV23). In the center of the flower, I applied muted Ochre to impart a warm glow and to balance the vibrant pinks. For the background, I used a blue-leaning Aqua Green—a transparent Phthalo pigment that allows for easy layering to achieve a sense of depth. To enhance depth and maintain palette continuity in the background, I introduced splashes of Dioxazine Purple, which I had already used on the petals.

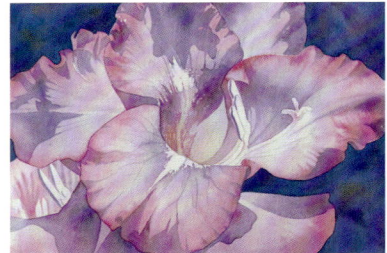

Step 2: The second step involved carefully painting the largest petal shadows and applying another glaze of purple on the background. Note that glazing several layers on the background allowed me to build even coverage and achieve a very dark, almost opaque look.

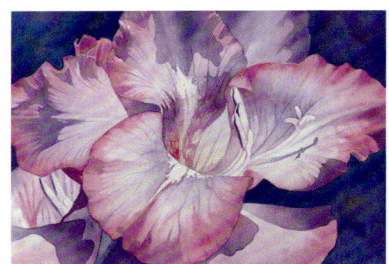

Step 3: In the third layer, I accentuated the darkest areas of the petal shadows and meticulously painted thin veins using my smallest brush. I also applied the final glaze of Dioxazine Purple to bring the background color to full saturation, ensuring it complemented the foreground.

Step 4: In the final—optional—step, I applied a thin glaze of Quinacridone Magenta mixed with fluorescent variation of PR122 called Opera Pink to intensify the vivid pink on the petal edges. This final touch boosted the overall vibrancy and added a striking finish to the painting.

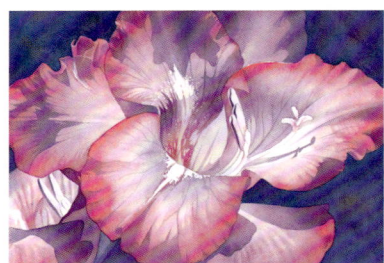

Gladiolus Close-Up

Case Study: Tulip Close-Up

In this tulip study, I used several transparent reds to capture a variation of color temperature on the petals. The most vibrant red you see is Carmine (PR176) from Daniel Smith, while there is warmer Quinacridone Coral (PR209) in the center, and cooler Quinacridone Magenta (PR122) on the distant petals in the background. The darkest petal shadows were painted with Perylene Violet (PV29).

Step 1: In the first layer (images 1 and 2, at right), I applied clear water to each petal and then dropped in saturated reds closer to the base using the wet-on-wet method. My colors could flow freely toward the edge, leaving the tip of each petal almost white. I also introduced a soft wash of Yellow Ochre (PY43) in the center of the flower before painting the dark stamens.

Step 2: In the second layer (image 3), I applied more saturated Carmine using the wet-on-damp technique to accentuate the petal texture. I introduced rich Perylene Violet to define some of the darkest shadows between the petals, and used a combination of Perylene Violet and Hansa Yellow Deep (PY65) for the stamens in the center.

Step 3: In the final layer (image 4), I added Dioxazine Purple (PV23) to my palette to further accentuate the shadows and the darkest details in the center, including small speckles of pollen. I also painted thin strips of concentrated reds to add texture to the petals using the wet-on-dry method.

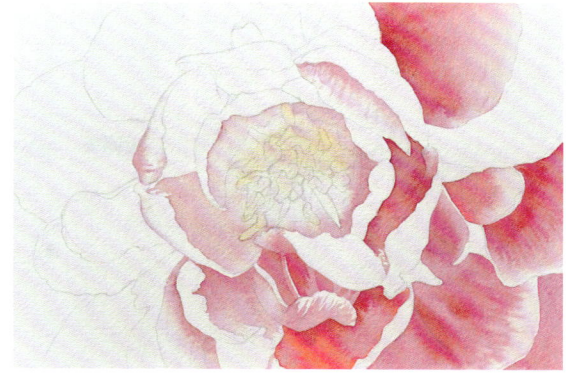

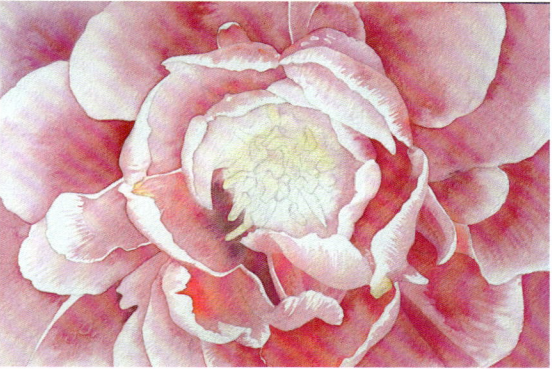

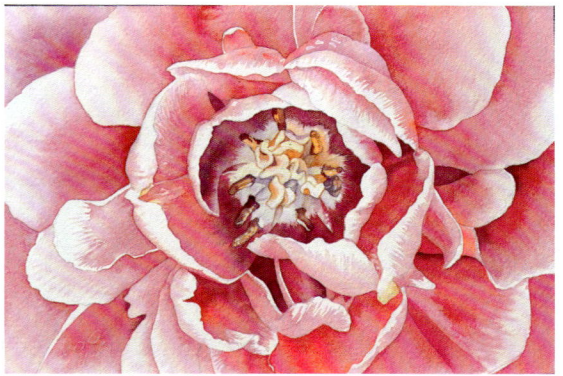

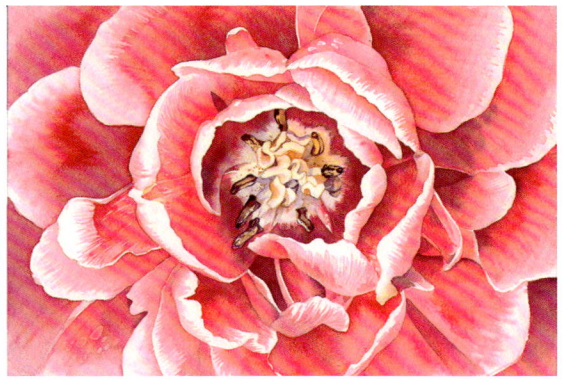

Tulip Close-Up

6.5 Foliage: Convenience vs. Mixed Greens

I must confess, I used to avoid painting leaves at the start of my watercolor journey, focusing on the colorful flowers instead. The truth is, creating natural-looking greenery can be quite tricky, especially when there are many intricate and overlapping details involved. In addition, human eyes tend to perceive more shades of green than any other color, making it hard to choose the right pigments. Over time, I learned to apply color theory to master the right balance of hues and values in my green mixes. Moreover, negative painting became my best friend when tackling tricky organic details. In this section, I will explain my favorite techniques for painting greenery, from beginner-friendly, one-step applications to more advanced layering techniques.

Mixing vs. Convenience Greens

Before we start, let's review the basic principles of color theory in the context of greenery. There are two basic ways to achieve natural-looking green hues: by mixing primary yellows and blues, or by using convenience greens straight from the tube. Either method is valid, depending on your style and artistic preferences. I use both methods in my work, often relying on granulating greens as a shortcut for creating complex textures with ease.

My Favorite Green Mixes

My favorite primary mix is Cadmium Yellow Primrose (PY35) (sometimes referred to as Lemon Yellow) mixed with Phthalo Blue Green Shade (PB15:3) from QoR Watercolors. For a warmer and more granulating look, I prefer Cadmium Yellow Medium Hue (PY53, PY151, PY83) mixed with Ultramarine (PB29) from Daniel Smith.

Lemon Yellow + Phthalo Blue Green Blue Shade

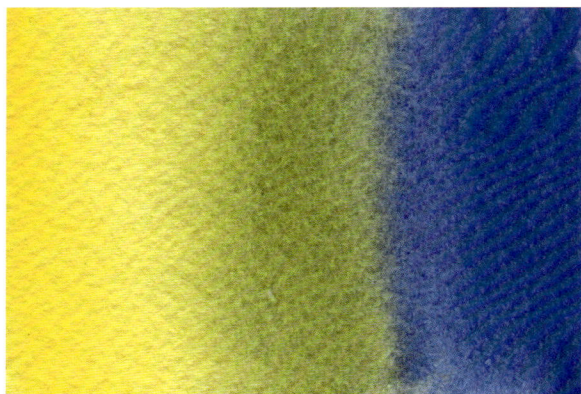

Cadmium Yellow Medium Hue + Ultramarine

My Favorite Convenience and Single-Pigment Greens

My favorite single-pigment greens include granulating Green Apatite Genuine (mineral) from Daniel Smith, the dark and moody Perylene Green (PBk31) from Daniel Smith, and a more muted blue-leaning Aqua Green (Phthalo) from Winsor & Newton. My go-to convenience mixes include granulating Cascade Green (PBr7, PB15), the most versatile Hooker's Green (PG36, PY3, PY150, PO48), and the warm Green Gold (PY150, PY3, PG36) from Daniel Smith.

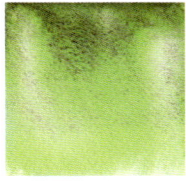 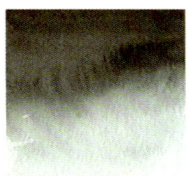  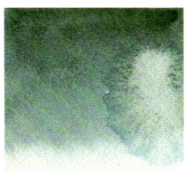  

Green Apatite Genuine from Daniel Smith (Mineral)

Perylene Green from Daniel Smith (PBk31)

Aqua Green from Winsor & Newton (Phthalo)

Cascade Green from Daniel Smith (PBr7, PB15)

Hooker's Green from Daniel Smith (PG36, PY3, PY150, PO48)

Green Gold from Daniel Smith (PY150, PY3, PG36)

HELPFUL TIPS

- Avoid using vibrant greens straight from the tube. Pigments like Phthalo Green Yellow Shade (PG36) or Viridian Green (PG18) provide an excellent base for mixing with primaries, but tend to look harsh and unnatural when applied in their pure form.
- Do mix reds and violets into your greens to create a range of warm brownish hues. My favorite "dry leaf" mixtures include Quinacridone Burnt Orange (PO48) and Perylene Violet (PV29).
- Try granulating greens to create easy organic textures with just one wash. Explore super-granulating varieties like PrimaTek™ from Daniel Smith to find your new favorite granulating green.
- Extend your palette to include different hues within the same color family for a more visually interesting effect. Notice and capture the variations in color temperature even on the simplest green leaves: segments that directly face the source of light will appear more yellow, while bluish greens will be concentrated in the shadow areas.

6.6 Leaf Techniques: From Beginner to Advanced

Single-Stroke Leaves

You can use a variety of round and slanted flat brushes to create easy single-color leaf shapes. In this example, I used Hooker's Green (PG36, PY3, PY150, PO48) from Daniel Smith—one of my favorite convenience greens—to paint a simple organic shape, leaving a thin border in the middle to indicate the leaf stem.

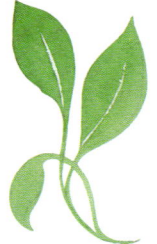

Granulating Wash

Here, I used a variety of granulating pigments to create rich texture with a single layer of color. The pigments I used are Green Apatite Genuine (mineral) from Daniel Smith, Cascade Green (PBr7, PB15) from Daniel Smith, and Desert Green (PR108, PG26) from Schmincke. Adding drops of clear water into the drying wash helped me enhance the granulating effect.

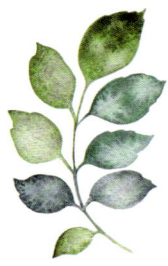

Wet-on-Wet Charging

In order to create striking color transitions, I introduced several colors into a freshly painted wash of Hooker's Green: Green Gold (PY150, PY3, PG36) for highlights and Indanthrone Blue (PB60) for shadows. I also charged Perylene Violet (PV29) and Burnt Sienna (PR101) to create dry patches.

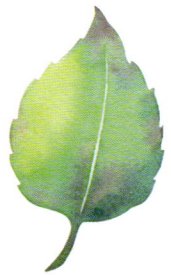

Wet-on-Damp

Wet-on-damp technique is my favorite way to create leaf veins. Here, I painted a light wash of color using mainly Yellow Ochre (PY43) and Burnt Sienna (PR101). Before this first layer was dry, I added very saturated strips of Permanent Brown (PBr25) with a very thin round brush.

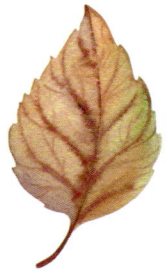

Lifting Technique

In this example, I covered the leaf outline with some vibrant Phthalo Green Yellow Shade (PG36), adding Perylene Violet (PV29) with the charging technique. With the edge of my flat brush, I then lifted strips of paint from a fresh wash to create thin strips of lighter color that mimic leaf texture.

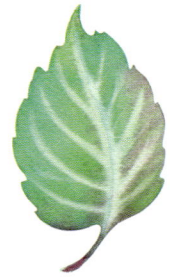

Wet-on-Dry

On these ginkgo leaves, I started by applying a light wash of ochres and greens. After this layer was dry, I followed up with very saturated colors to add thin veins using traditional wet-on-dry method. Elongated round brushes in size #0 work best for adding these types of organic details. In the third layer, I added subtle shadows around the edges, using ochres and oranges to boost the vibrancy.

Negative Painting

Using negative painting technique is the easiest way to create light veins on larger and more complex leaves. Start by applying a light wash of your base color all over the leaf shape, and let it dry thoroughly. Follow up with darker pigment around the outlines, leaving the vein areas dry. In this example, I used a combination of Hooker's Green (PG36, PY3, PY150, PO48) from Daniel Smith and Aqua Green (Phthalo) from Winsor & Newton to create a subtle nuance in green hues.

Masking Fluid

In this example, I applied a light wash of various reds to create the base tone. I then applied masking fluid to conceal the leaf veins using a thin rubber applicator. Next, I painted a solid wash of red all over the entire leaf, waited for it to dry, and then erased the mask to reveal the light details. For the third, layer I added subtle details using my darkest colors.

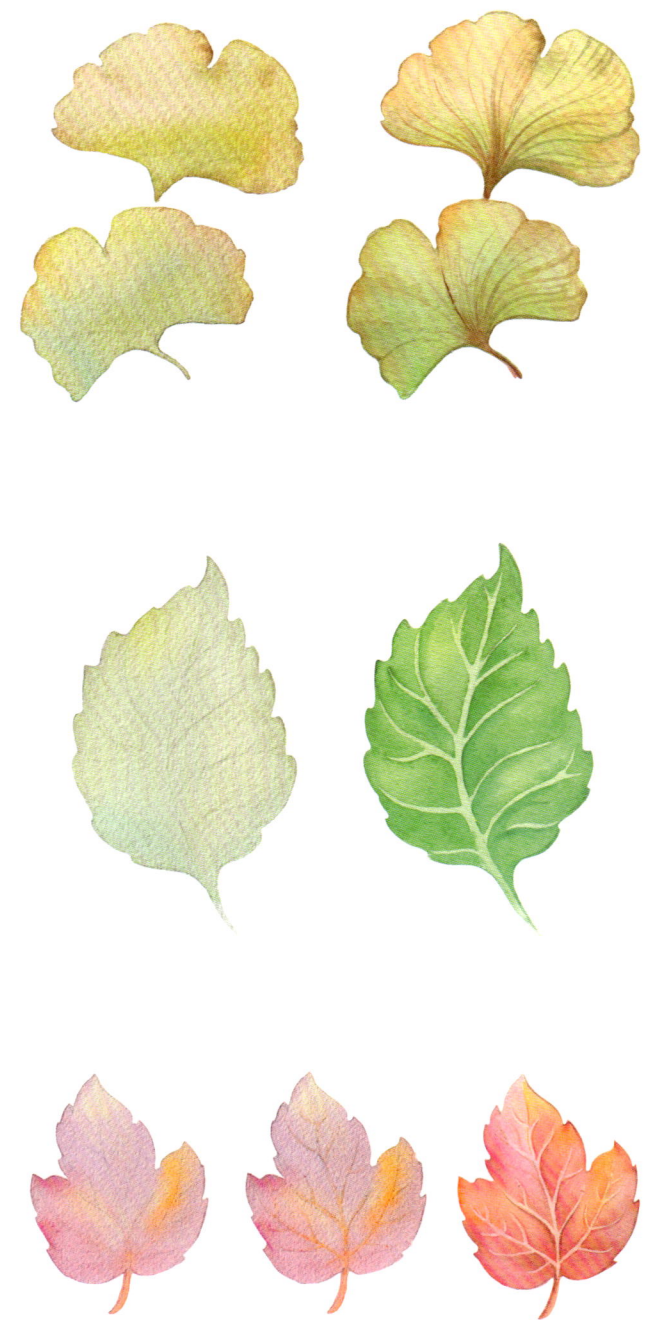

Video Available 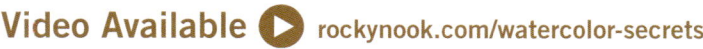 rockynook.com/watercolor-secrets

6.7 Complex Leaves

No matter what your current skill level is, you can paint even the most complex greenery by applying watercolor techniques you are most familiar with. In this comparative study, I painted the same peony leaf twice to demonstrate both beginner and more advanced approaches to the same subject. Remember, you can always modify your approach to fit your style, available time, and even palette constrains.

Case Study #1: Depth and Definition in Three Layers

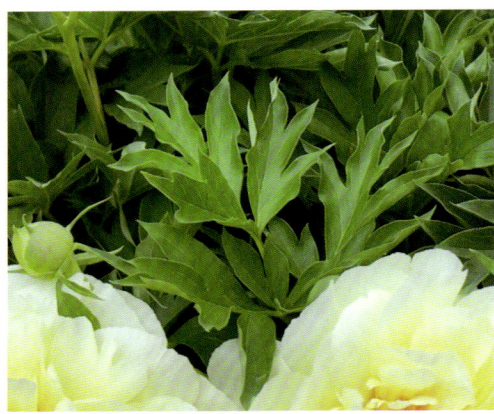

Peony Leaf Reference Photo

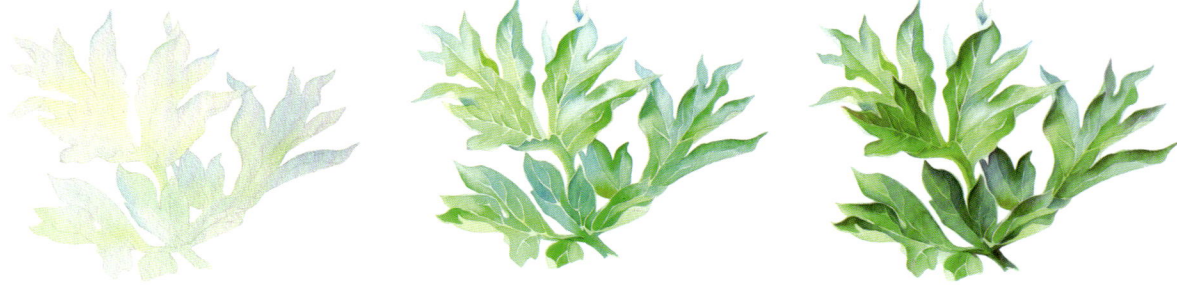

Peony Leaf in Three Steps

In this example, I painted a green peony leaf using three layers of color, a variety of pigments, and a combination of wet-on-wet and wet-on-dry techniques, including negative painting.

STEP 1: Start with an underpainting, using the lightest green you see in your reference image (e.g., the color of leaf veins and leaf highlights). You can vary your green color temperature by adding different amounts of yellow and blue into your base green using wet-on-wet method. In this version, I used Hooker's Green (PG36, PY3, PY150, PO48) as my base color, Green Gold (PY150, PY3, PG36) for highlights and areas most illuminated by the sun, and Aqua Green (Phthalo) for darker shadow areas as well as blue-leaning leaf tips.

STEP 2: Once the first layer is dry, paint the mid-tones using wet-on-dry technique. Focus on adding definition in the darkest areas by applying a slightly more saturated version of your base green color. Avoid the lightest areas and blend your darker strokes with a clean damp brush to create a seamless transition from light to dark. Vary green values (lights and darks) by noticing the direction of light and the relative positioning of each leaf "section" between the veins. In this step, you can also use negative painting technique to apply darker colors around the leaf veins.

STEP 3: For the final layer, you can enhance the contrast by adding more saturated color in the darkest areas of the leaf. I added Perylene Green (PBk31) and Prussian Blue (PB27) to capture some of the lower segments that are facing away from the light. You can also make subtle adjustments in color temperature by glazing transparent layers of yellow and red to add natural warmth. In this version, I glazed Quinacridone Coral (PR209) to create brownish shadows and Bordeaux (PV32) to enhance moody, dark areas on the stem and bottom leaf segments.

Case Study #2: Blooming, Charging, and Granulation with One Layer

In this example, I painted the same peony leaf using a single layer, a variety of pigments, and a combination of my favorite wet-on-wet techniques.

Base Color: For each segment of the leaf, I started by applying diluted Hooker's Green (PG36, PY3, PY150, PO48), and then switched to a cooler Aqua Green (Phthalo) at the bottom where shadows looked more prominent overall.

Charging: Before the base color was fully dry, I dropped more saturated colors wet-on-wet, introducing Green Gold (PY150, PY3, PG36) and Aqua Green, and even splashes of darker Indanthrone Blue (PB60). This approach allowed my pigments to blend directly on paper, adding variations in value and color temperature.

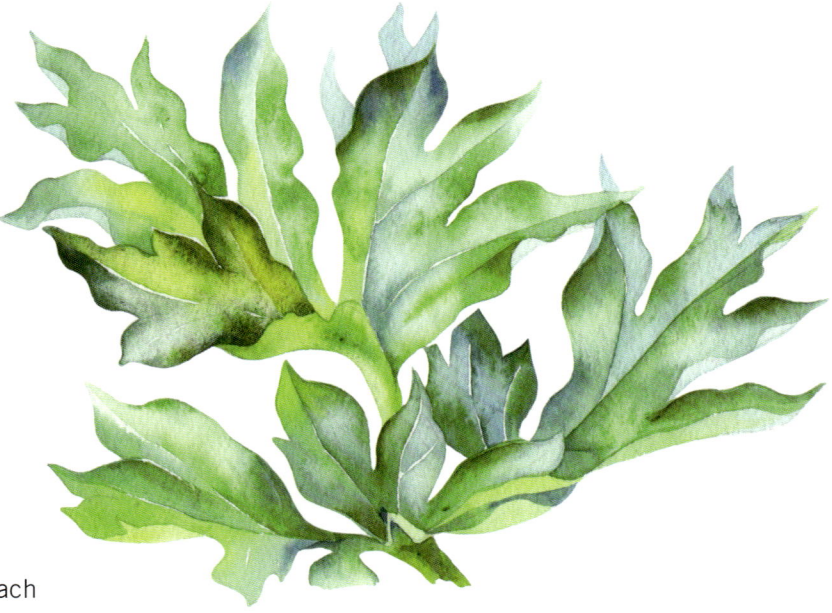

Peony Leaf in One Step

Blooming: In order to achieve lighter tones, I used blooming technique by dropping clear water into the areas that are facing toward the light. This was done while my background paint was still wet so the water could push the green particles out, creating a highlight.

Granulation: Note that in one segment I applied granulating greens—Green Apatite Genuine and Cascade Green—to add extra texture and visual interest. This approach is particularly useful for beginner artists who want to create rich textures without getting lost in several layers of color.

Video Available ▶ rockynook.com/watercolor-secrets

6.8 Tropical Greenery

Lush tropical foliage often looks different from the typical leaves we find in cooler climates. Painting exotic plants like Monstera and Philodendron requires a nuanced approach, and often a unique selection of pigments. In this section, I will help you see and notice these special aspects of tropical plants so you can paint them with confidence.

Lean Into the Tropical Palette

The first thing you may notice about tropical leaves is their distinct coloring. More vibrant compared to typical greenery, tropical plants boast an entire range of colors, from dark turquoise to lemon yellow, and even splashes of vivid red. My favorite tropical greens include Green Gold, Phthalo Green, and Phthalo Turquoise. Additional colors I often introduce into tropical greenery include Quinacridone Magenta and Coral.

   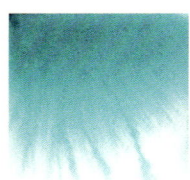 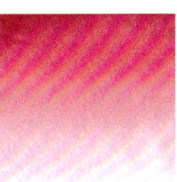 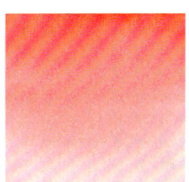

Green Gold from Daniel Smith (PY150, PY3, PG36)

Winsor Green Blue Shade from Winsor & Newton (PG7)

Winsor Green Yellow Shade from Winsor & Newton (PG36)

Phthalo Turquoise from QoR Watercolors (PB15:3/PG7)

Quinacridone Magenta from QoR Watercolor (PR122)

Quinacridone Coral from Daniel Smith (PR209)

Capture Glossy Highlights

Exotic leaves often have a very smooth and glossy surface, which tends to reflect sunlight. Make sure to capture these spots by preserving the white of your paper. You can soften the edges around the highlights with a damp brush or keep them sharp and defined.

Accentuate the Veins

Tropical plants tend to hold large amounts of water, making the leaves much thicker compared to the ones we see in cooler climates. The best way to capture leaf edges and veins is to use the negative painting technique. If you don't enjoy working around the thin strips of color with your brush, you can use masking fluid to preserve light veins, and erase the fluid after the work is complete.

Layer Reds (Instead of Mixing)

Some of the more complex tropical greenery includes the color red and it requires a special approach to layering. To maintain pure and intense reds right next to vibrant greens, apply them in separate washes, allowing plenty of drying time in between.

Focus on the Silhouette

My final tip is to notice the intricate shapes of the tropical leaves and highlight them by using deeper saturated colors around the edges. I often glaze darker shades of blue in my final layers to bring more attention to the leaf silhouettes.

Case Study: Scarlet Ibis and Tropical Leaves

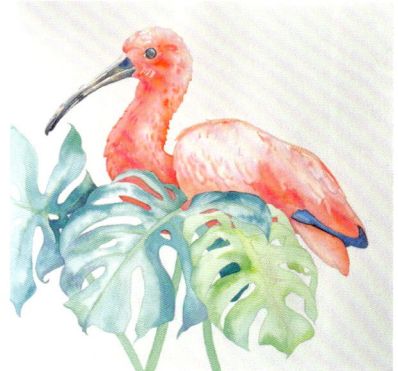 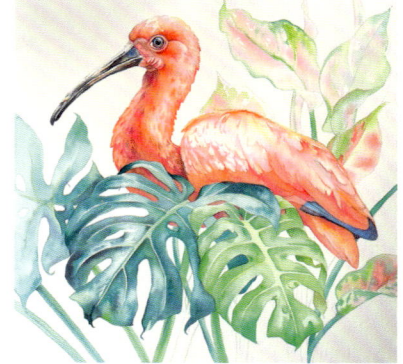 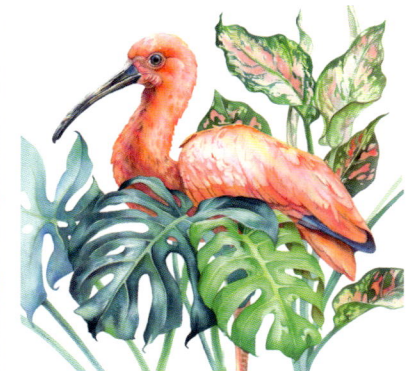

Scarlet Ibis and Tropical Leaves in Three Steps

In the example above, I included two types of tropical leaves to complement the scarlet ibis:

- I covered the entire Monstera plant with a light wash of color first: Phthalo Turquoise (PB15:3/PG7) from QoR Watercolors on the left and Phthalo Yellow Green (PG36, PY3) from Daniel Smith on the right. After the leaves were dry, I continued building darker green washes, leaving elongated yellowish veins dry by painting around them. For the Monstera plant on the left, I also included splashes of Indigo to create deeply intense blue shadows in the final layer.
- I used Quinacridone Coral (PR209) for the vivid red details on the Aglaonema leaves. Quinacridones are highly staining, so my Coral stayed firmly in place without getting diluted as I continued to apply green details on top using wet-on-dry method.

Video Available ▶ rockynook.com/watercolor-secrets

6.9 Birds and Feather Varieties

Birds, with their vibrant feathers and graceful movements, have long been my watercolor muse. I love to combine them with various flowers and fruits, often adding intricate greenery to create complex compositions that can occupy me for days at a time. In this section, we will delve into the intricate world of painting bird feathers, so you can explore various techniques that bring these delicate creatures to life. Each technique offers a unique way to represent bird feathers, so don't hesitate to combine them or adapt them to suit your artistic vision.

Understanding Feather Anatomy

First, let's take a moment to appreciate and understand the variety of bird feathers. Note that feathers are not just colorful adornments—they are complex structures that serve distinct functions on the body of the bird. For example, down feathers provide warmth and protection, while colorful contour feathers provide camouflage against predators. As artists, what we see on the surface, and therefore what we paint, are primarily the first two feather varieties that cover the exterior of the bird:

- **Contour Feathers:** These short feathers are distributed evenly over the body of the bird, making up the overall shape. The part we see is colored, while the base is colorless. The overall effect is usually soft and delicate color transitions, requiring a lot of blending and wet-on-damp brushstrokes. The texture can be enhanced using wet-on-dry technique.
- **Flight Feathers:** Elongated wing and tail feathers contribute to the silhouette, often displaying intricate color patterns. Note that one side of the wing feathers is usually wider to provide better mobility in flight. Wet-on-dry technique variations work best here to capture sharp color transitions and to define individual feather details.

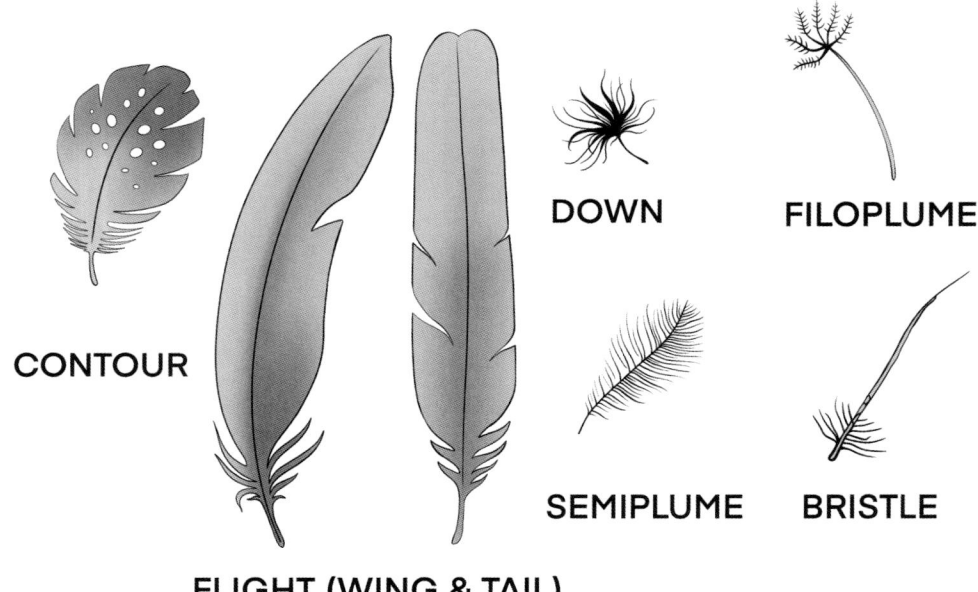

Types of Bird Feathers

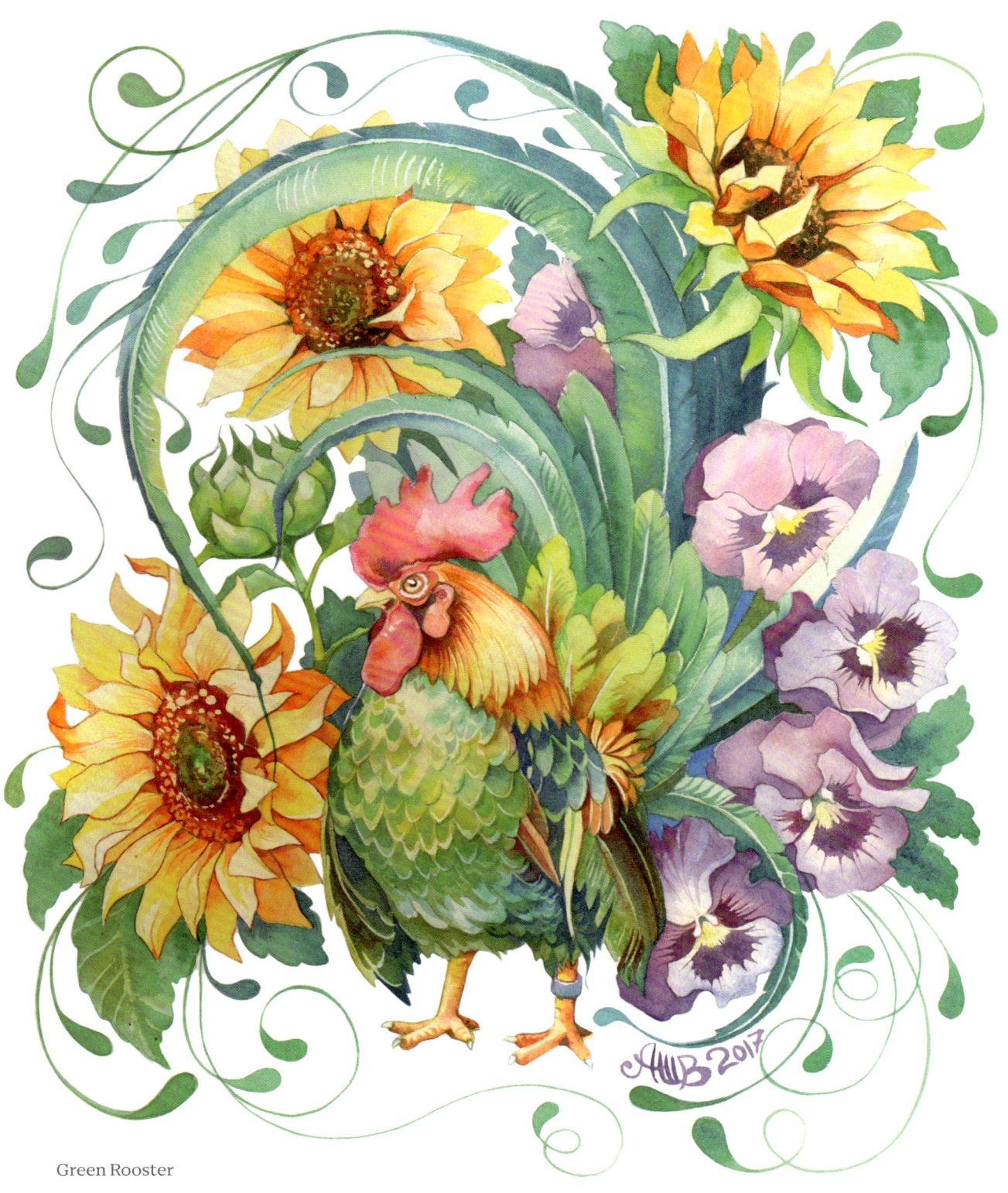

Green Rooster

Wet-on-Damp Wash for Soft Contour Feathers

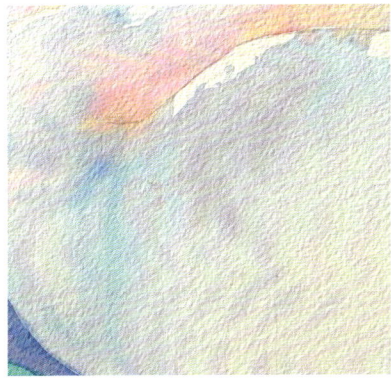  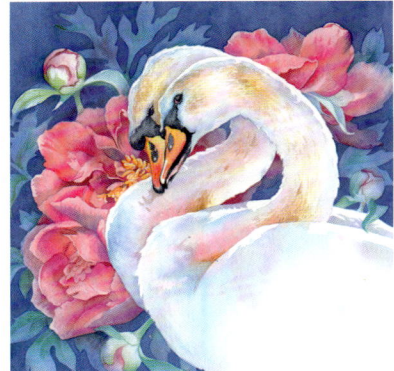

Swans

Soft contour feathers, particularly the ones found on a bird's chest and belly, are best captured by using wet-on-damp technique:

- Wet the entire feather area with clean water or a very diluted pigment.
- Drop in your chosen feather colors while the paper is still wet. Allow the colors to blend and bleed into each other, creating a soft and natural feather texture.
- As your paper is slowly drying, use a finer brush to add details like shadows or subtle variations in color using more saturated pigments.

Wet-on-Dry Strokes for Extra Texture and Definition

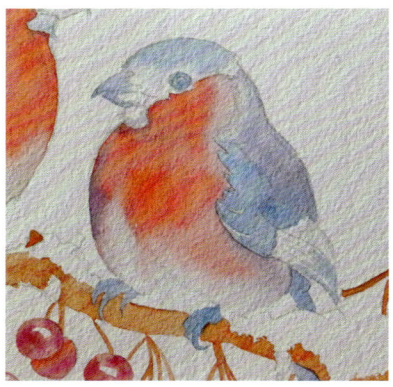 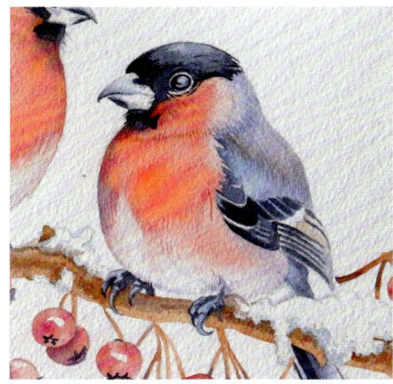 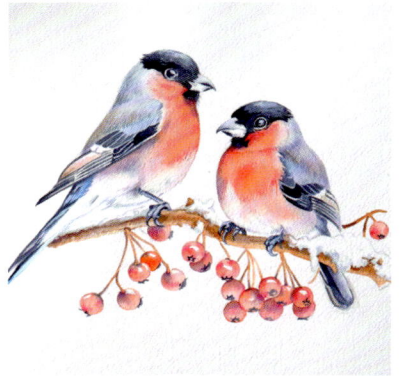

Bullfinches

Wet-on-dry technique works well for creating texture on the contour features and adding depth:

- Paint the base layer of color using wet-on-damp technique as described above.
- Follow with the second layer of color, using more saturated pigments. Use quick, short, and controlled strokes to build up darker areas. Extra-thin brushes in size #0 or #00 work best for this technique. Vary the pressure to mimic the texture of the plumage, always positioning your brush in the direction of the feathers.
- Follow the process one more time to add extra depth using darker colors.

Wet-on-Dry Layers for Multi-Colored Feathers

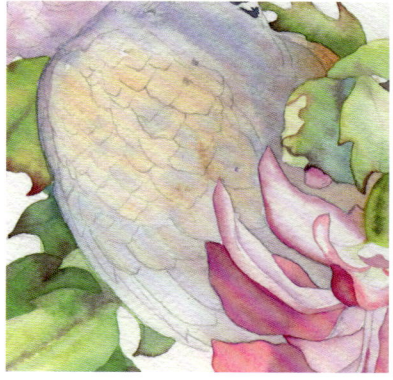 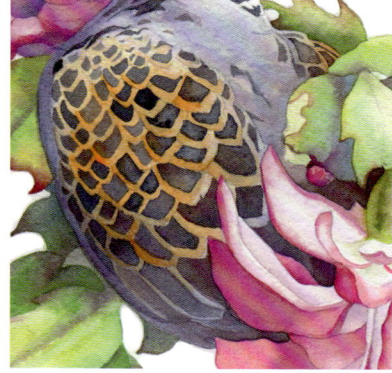 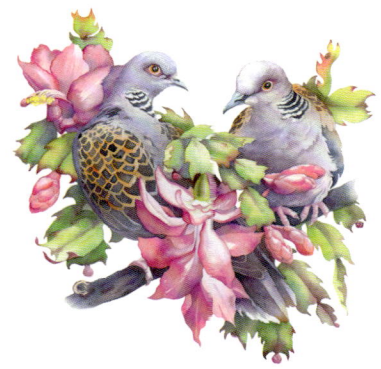

Turtle Doves

Wet-on-dry technique is the best method for adding intricate patterns on both the contour and the flight feathers:

- Paint the lightest colors of the feather first. Your pigments should be relatively diluted, to allow you to build extra colors in the next layer.
- Once the first layer is dry, load a small round brush with more concentrated pigment and paint additional color patterns using wet-on-dry method.

Negative Painting for Monochromatic Flight Feathers

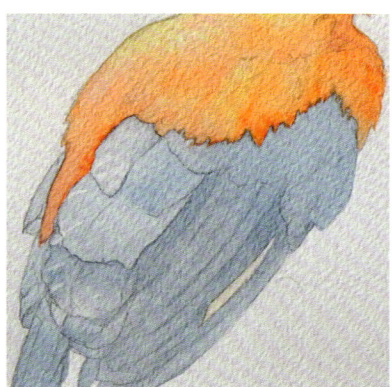 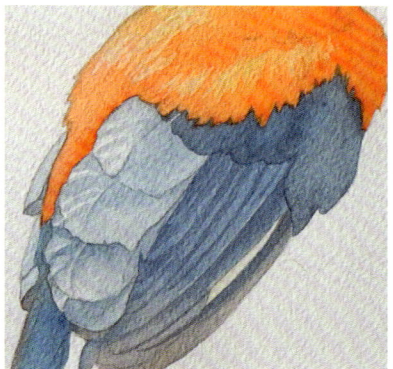 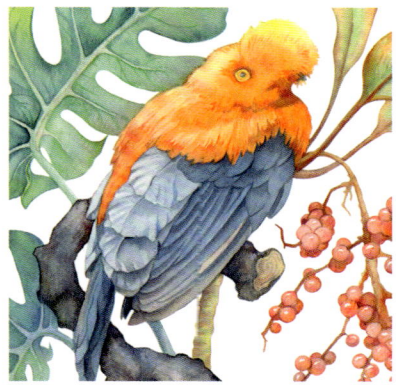

Cock-of-the-Rock

You can use negative painting to define individual feathers. This technique works particularly well for capturing larger flight feathers that display monochromatic coloring:

- Start by applying your base color all over the segment of feathers. For example, you can cover the entire wing with a light wash of Indigo, like I did in this example.
- Paint around the feather shapes using more saturated pigment, allowing the negative space to reveal the intricate details.
- You can repeat this process several times, gradually building deeper shadows and reinforcing the feather silhouettes.

6.10 Painting Complex Birds

Painting complex birds requires careful glazing and a combination of wet-on-dry and wet-on-wet techniques. In this section, I will share my favorite tips and guide you through a step-by-step case study of a particularly intricate bird I painted recently. You will learn how to achieve realistic textures, vibrant colors, and lifelike details by layering your watercolors effectively.

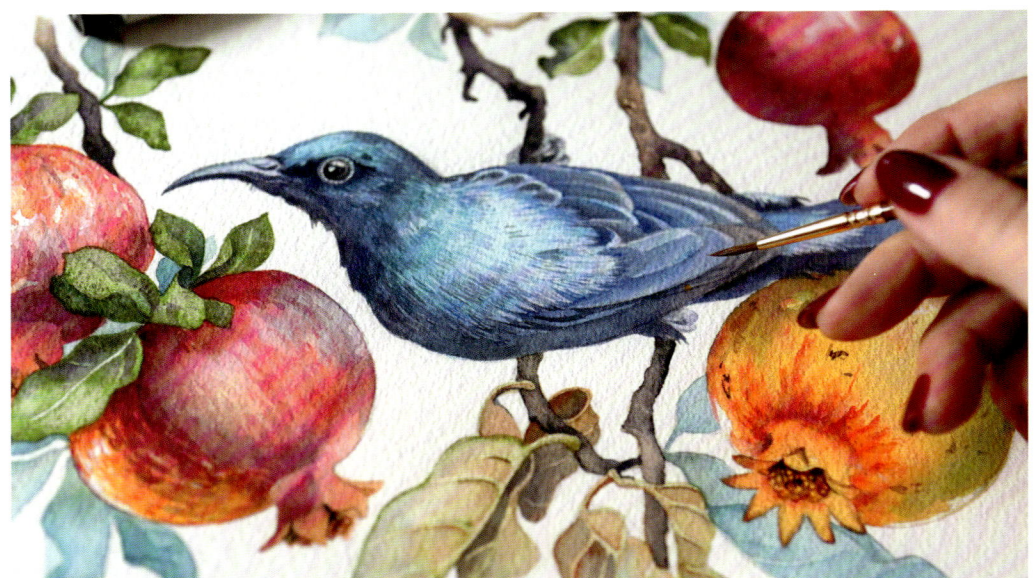

Blue Sunbird in Progress

Study References

Look at reference images of the specific bird you are painting to understand the pattern and coloration of its feathers. Pay attention to how light interacts with the feathers. Paint around the highlights using negative painting technique, and glaze shadows using wet-on-dry to create a three-dimensional effect.

Embrace a Variety of Pigments

Select a palette that encompasses a wide range of hues, allowing you to capture the diverse colors found in bird plumage. Muted earthy tones will help you capture the subtle color nuances on birds found in temperate climates. For example, you may want to explore Ochres and Umbers to capture the subtle nuances of eagle or sparrow feathers. On the other hand, birds that inhabit lush, warm habitats require a more vibrant palette. You will need a variety of Phthalos and Quinacridones to capture the full color spectrum of tropical birds.

Invest in Thinner Brushes

A combination of flat brushes for background washes and small round brushes for details will provide versatility in rendering feather textures. You will likely need to invest in extra-thin brushes in sizes #1 or even #0 for detailed work. I often use Escoda Chronos round brushes in size #00, as they offer both precision and flexibility for painting particularly fine feather textures.

Case Study: Blue Bird

In this composition, I painted four layers of color to build intricate texture on the sunbird. Throughout the process, I gradually increased pigment saturation and switched from larger to smaller round brushes.

- **Layer 1:** In the first layer of color, I applied a diluted wash of Phthalo Blue Green Shade (PB15:3) all over the bird's body. I then dropped in Phthalo Turquoise (PB15:3/PG7) and Dioxazine Purple (PV23) to capture the soft color transitions using wet-on-damp method.

- **Layer 2:** After the base layer was completely dry, I applied successive glazes of transparent colors to enhance subtle gradients I observed in the contour feathers and to build extra depth. In the second layer, I introduced Quinacridone Burnt Scarlet (PR206) to add warmer brown spots on the wings. Note the use of negative painting, particularly on the tail feathers.

- **Layer 3:** For the third layer, I continued building texture using more concentrated versions of my base pigments. I also started introducing Indigo for the darkest shadows on the feathers, as well as the details on the eyes and the beak. I applied translucent layers of Phthalo Turquoise (PB15:3/PG7) and Phthalo Blue Green Shade (PB15:3) over some of the lighter segments to achieve richer tones.

- **Layer 4:** I waited until the rest of the composition was done to reassess the overall color balance and make final adjustments on the bird. I added extra saturated Indigo to reinforce the silhouette of the bird and some of the darker shadows between the feathers.

Video Available 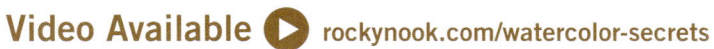 rockynook.com/watercolor-secrets

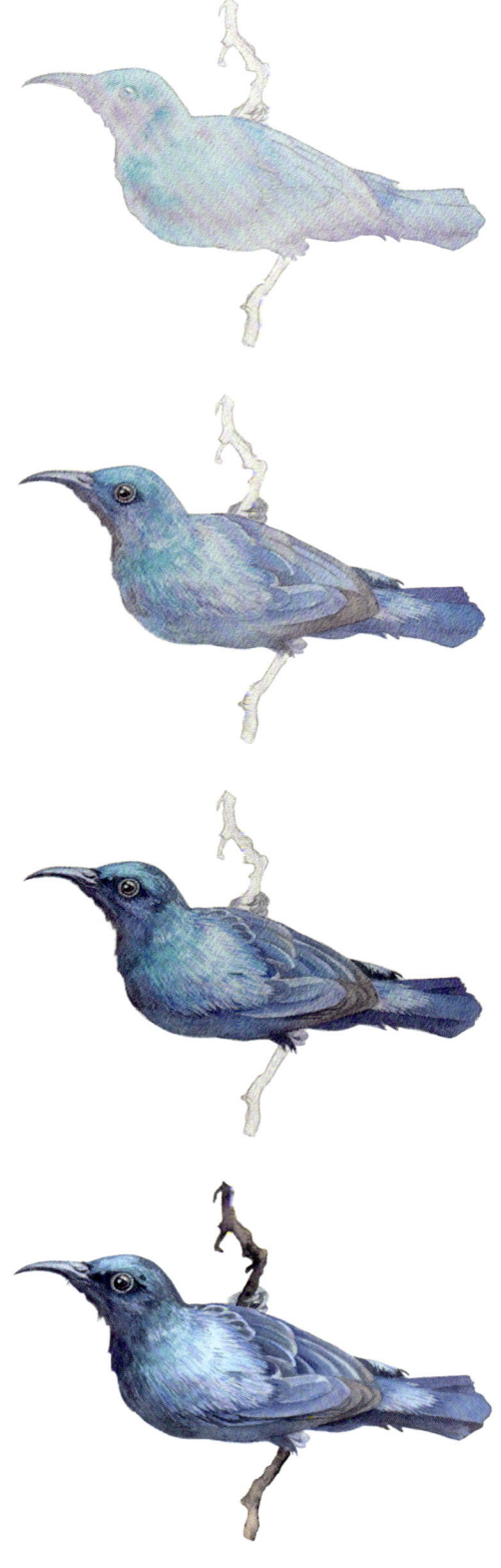

Blue Sunbird in Four Steps

6.11 Tips for Painting Fruits and Berries

Few subjects bring me as much joy as capturing the vibrant colors and luscious textures of nature's bounty. From the smooth curves of apples to the intricate patterns of citrus peels, each fruit offers a unique artistic challenge and opportunity for creative expression. By embracing vibrant colors, layering techniques, and attention to detail, you can create stunning fruit-themed compositions that are as tantalizing to the eyes as they are to the taste buds.

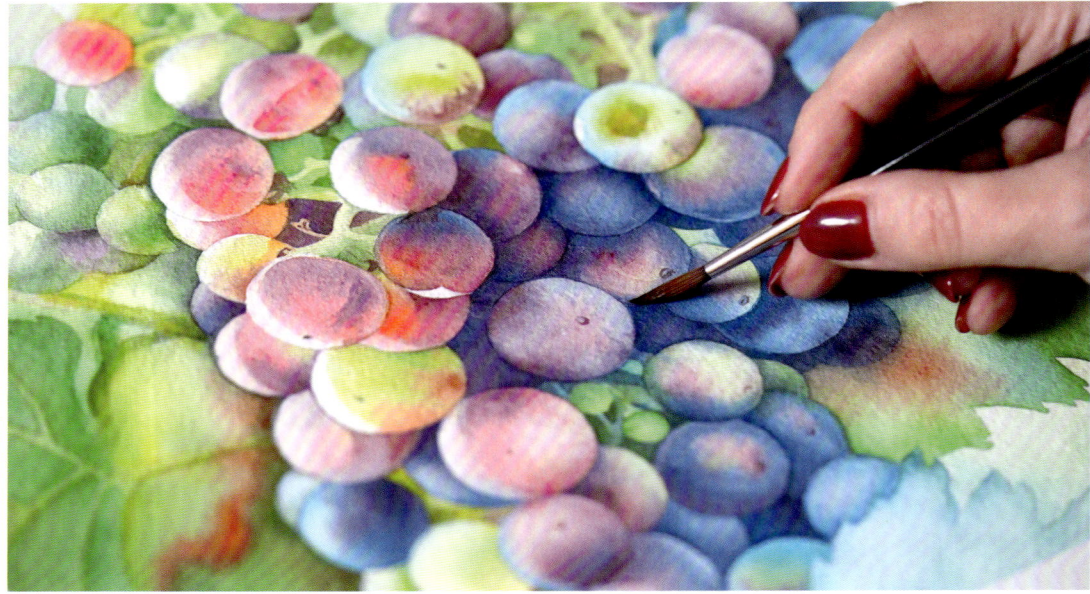

Grapes in Progress

Observation is Key

Before picking up your brush, take the time to closely observe the fruit you intend to paint. Instead of relying on photo references, I often take a trip to the local farm or purchase some fruit at the market. This gives me the best opportunity to notice the subtle gradations of color, the play of light and shadow, and the texture of the peel or flesh. Paying attention to these details will enrich your painting with realism and depth.

Choose Vibrant Colors

Watercolor's inherent transparency and luminosity make it an ideal medium for capturing the vivid hues of ripe fruits. Experiment with a diverse palette of colors, leaning on Quinacridones and Hansas to achieve the most vibrant shades.

Embrace Layering

Even the simplest one-color fruits, like yellow bananas, can be used to practice the layering technique. Begin with light washes to establish the base colors of your fruit, then layer progressively darker tones to enhance shadows and highlights. This approach lends a luminous quality to your paintings and captures the translucent quality of fruit flesh.

Focus on Texture

Pay close attention to the texture of the fruit's surface, whether it's the smooth skin of a peach or the rough rind of a pineapple. Use a variety of brushstrokes and techniques to convey texture, from soft washes for smooth surfaces to dry brushstrokes for rougher textures.

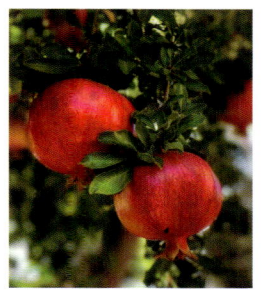

Case Study: Pomegranates

In this case study, I will show you my typical process for painting fruits, from creating a pencil outline to adding step-by-step watercolor washes to slowly build form and texture.

Create an Outline: Observe your reference photo, noting the overall shape, the direction of light, and the small details you want to capture. If the fruit is particularly large, you may want to include even the smallest scratches and imperfections in your outline. In my outline, I often simplify the surrounding details—in this example, I decided to reduce the number of leaves so I could focus on rendering the pomegranate fruit in detail.

Step 1: Start with a light wash of color, painting around the highlights. The white of your paper should serve as your brightest white, particularly for shiny fruits with many reflections. In this example, the top pomegranate had several visible highlights, so I painted around them using a negative painting technique. The bottom one did not have any obvious areas of pure white, so I covered the entire surface with my underpainting layer. You can use a single pigment or experiment with additional pigments to map out the main areas of light and dark. I used Quinacridone Red (PV19) as my base color, adding splashes of Hansa Yellow Deep (PY65) around the highlights. For the shadow areas, I used Burnt Sienna (PR101) and Phthalo Blue Green Shade (PB15:3).

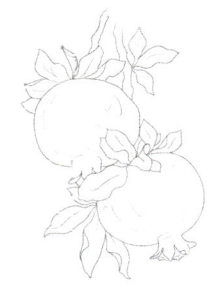

Step 2: For the second layer, I usually add another wash of color, this time focusing on the darkest areas of the fruit. In this example, I applied additional layers of Quinacridone Red and Hansa Yellow Deep, avoiding the lighter segments, and blending my saturated pigments toward the highlights using a clean, damp brush. Note that the shadow pigments applied in the first layer still show through this fresh glaze. I used granulating Green Apatite Genuine (mineral) to create simple but textured leaves with one layer.

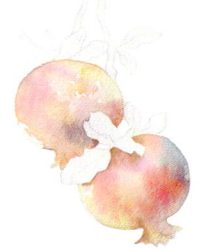

Step 3: I finished the pomegranates by building additional glazes of Permanent Alizarin Crimson (PR177) on the darkest segments of each fruit. This semiopaque pigment helped me block some of the underlying layers and create matte segments where I needed them. I then switched to a smaller round brush to build extra texture by applying short strokes of Perylene Violet (PV29) over the shadows and the dry stamens. To unify the palette, I also applied the same violet to the leaf shadows and added background leaves using Aqua Green (Phthalo).

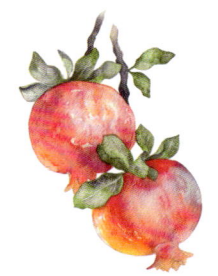

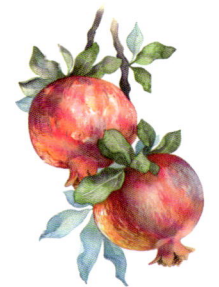

Pomegranates: Reference Photo, Outline, and Three-Step Painting

6.12 Tips for Painting Watercolor Pets

There's something truly special about immortalizing our beloved pets in works of art. Whether it's the playful antics of a bounding pup or the serene gaze of a contented cat, pets have a unique ability to touch our hearts and inspire our creativity. In the early days of my watercolor journey, pet commissions became my artistic playground. They allowed me to explore and practice a wide range of techniques while teaching me the importance of patience, attention to detail, and the power of observation.

Experiment with Composition

Beyond the reference photo of your pet, the canvas becomes your realm of artistic expression. Embrace the freedom to incorporate additional elements into the composition, enriching it with depth and visual intrigue. As a devotee of botanical beauty, I often intertwine flowers and foliage that harmonize with the hues of the fur, lending a decorative flourish to the scene. Consider exploring more realistic backgrounds or employing abstract splashes of pigments to artfully frame your subject.

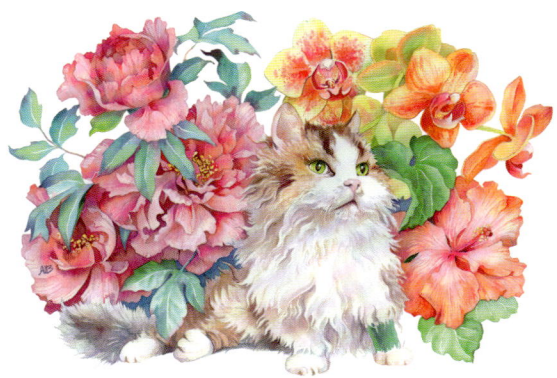

Gus: Cat Portrait Commission

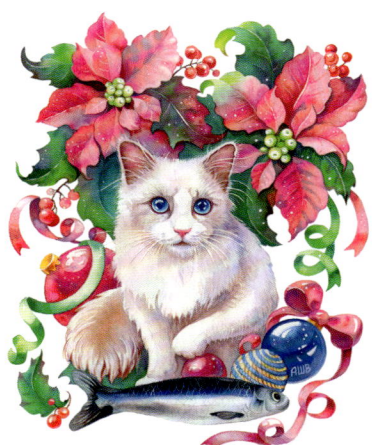

Iris: Cat Portrait Commission

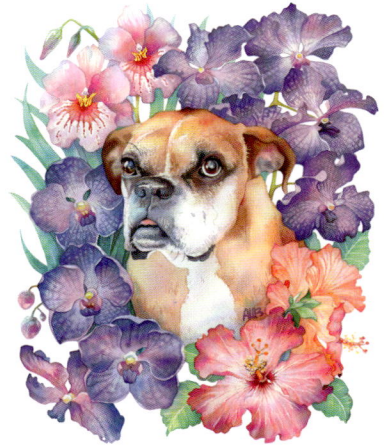

Dog Portrait Commission

Include Personal Objects

I often include favorite toys and articles of clothing in my pet portraits. Whether it's a colorful ball or a monogrammed chain, these elements help me capture not just the physical likeness, but also the unique spirit and personality of each pet.

Bring Extra Focus to the Eyes

It's essential to capture the expressiveness and depth of the animal's gaze to truly convey their character. Take your time to observe the nuances of their eyes—the shape, color, and subtle reflections. Use a fine-tipped brush and layers of translucent color to build up the intricate details, paying close attention to highlights and shadows to bring the eyes to life.

Negative Painting for Fur

One of the most effective techniques for painting fur in watercolors is negative painting. Instead of painting the individual strands of fur, focus on painting the spaces around them, gradually building up layers to create the illusion of depth and texture. Start with light washes for the base fur color, then gradually darken the surrounding areas to define the fur's contours. Negative painting allows you to capture the softness and volume of fur with subtlety and finesse.

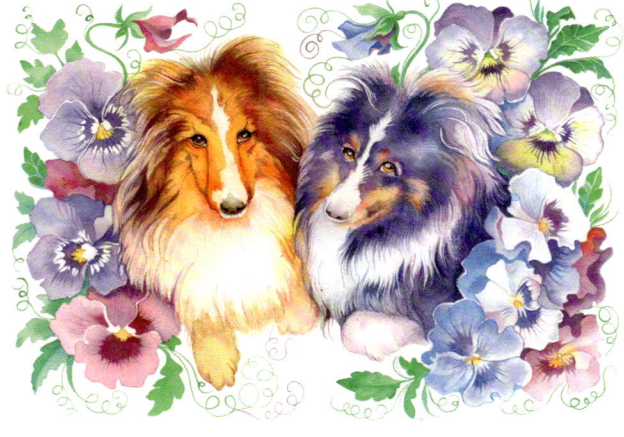

Shelties Portrait Commission

Masking Fluid for Extra Detail

For adding intricate textures to pet portraits, consider employing masking fluid. This versatile tool can accentuate highlights in the nose or delineate lighter strands of fur. Apply it meticulously with a fine brush or rubber applicator to create patterns or highlights where fur texture is pronounced. Once dry, overlay the masked areas with washes of color, then delicately remove the masking fluid to unveil the textured fur beneath. This method imbues your pet portraits with dimension and realism, amplifying their visual impact with every stroke.

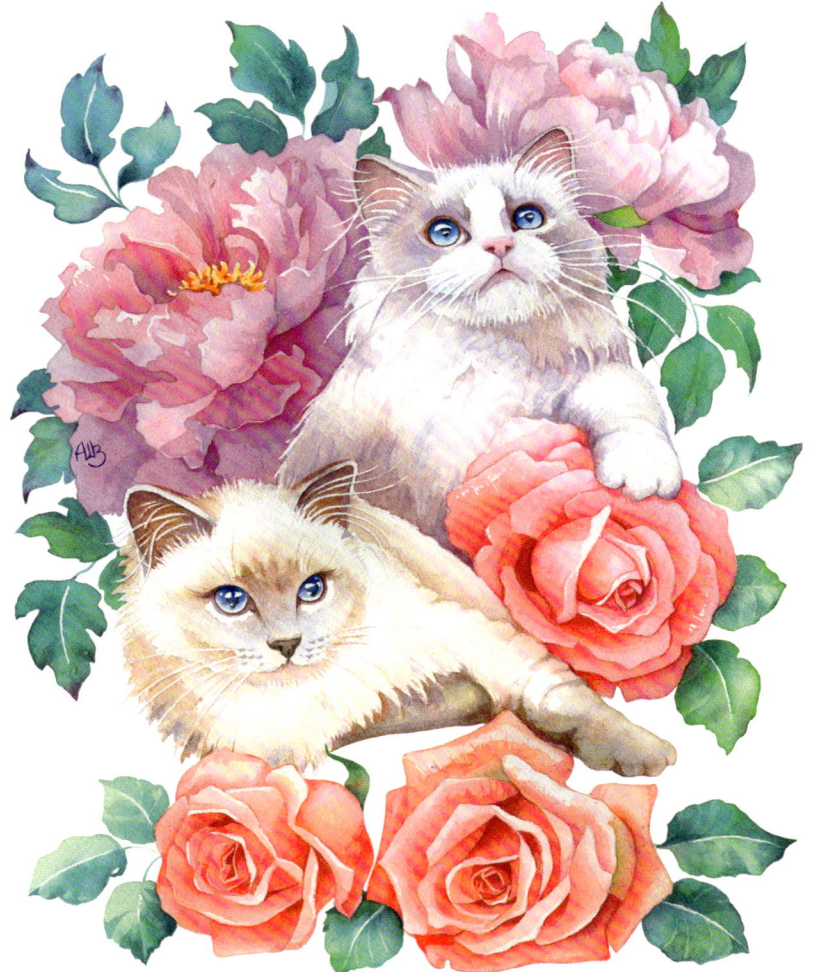

Two Ragdolls: Cat Portrait Commission

6.13 Tips for Painting Portraits

I have a passion for painting faces, though I'll readily admit that I'm far from being an expert. What draws me in isn't the pursuit of mastery, but rather the journey itself. With each new portrait I create, I find myself encountering something fresh—a revelation of the unseen, whether it's a new technique discovered or a unique blend of skin tones. What's truly special about painting faces with watercolor is the intimate connection it fosters. Each portrait becomes not just a representation of the subject, but a reflection of my own interpretation of human character and emotion. Watercolor, with its unpredictable nature, always injects a delightful element of surprise into the process. Despite not claiming mastery, my fascination with painting faces with watercolor endures.

Accurate Outlines

Organic shapes are very forgiving, but our brains are wired to notice even the smallest imperfections in human faces. A minor error in anatomy might affect your results no matter how skillfully you apply the paint. This is why I recommend getting an accurate pencil outline before applying the paint. You may want to trace your subject, focusing on the overall proportions of the face and the details of the eyes. As long as your image is copyright free, tracing will provide a better foundation for your watercolor learning, allowing you to focus on mastering the skin tones.

Skin Before Hair

I like to start my portraits by applying a soft wash of color on the skin, before painting the hair. The trick is to get just under the hairline with your lightest tone, and follow with the hair strands after the skin layers are dry. This way, you can ensure the transition from skin to hair is seamless and doesn't create any awkward borders.

Getting through the "Awkward" Stage

Before we apply the darkest values, the face often doesn't look "right," and that can be unsettling for the eyes. This awkward stage—right before we apply the darkest details—is inevitable, but it might challenge your confidence. This is where I often start questioning my progress and have to remind myself to trust the layering process. Allow your initial layers to dry out completely before adding the smaller details like the nose shadows and the lash line.

Slow Layering

The common temptation is to paint the entire face in one sitting. However, patient layering pays off, especially when it comes to portraits. Start by applying your lightest skin tones first, and gradually add shadows so you can avoid going too dark too soon. Leave small details—like the eyebrow hairs and wrinkles—until the end.

Background Color Tricks

Introducing a splash of color into the background of your portrait can work wonders in adding depth and accentuating the highlights on the subject's face. Among the plethora of colors available, blue stands out as a reliable choice due to its ability to evoke a sense of distance. One of my favorite tactics involves strategically applying a touch of Phthalo Blue Green Shade (PB15:3) somewhere along the eye line. This particular pigment boasts remarkable vibrancy, effortlessly drawing attention to the eyes.

Another technique I frequently employ is the juxtaposition of sharp and soft edges. By maintaining a crisp edge on the side of the face illuminated by the strongest light, and gently softening the opposite side, as demonstrated in this portrait of Sophie, a sense of dimensionality and depth is achieved.

Blues and Greens in Skin Tones

It's essential to recognize that skin tones often encompass subtle blue and green undertones. Light doesn't merely skim the skin's surface; it penetrates and scatters within its layers, reflecting back out in nuanced hues. This sub-surface scattering is particularly noticeable in shadowed areas, accentuating cooler tones. Additionally, regions of the skin with lower concentrations of melanin—the pigment responsible for skin color—such as around the eyes or cheeks, may exhibit lighter tones with hints of blue or green. Environmental factors further influence the perception of skin tones—natural daylight, for instance, tends to amplify these cooler hues, whereas artificial lighting may emphasize warmer, orange tones. Understanding these complexities is crucial for artists striving to capture the intricate subtleties of human skin in their artwork.

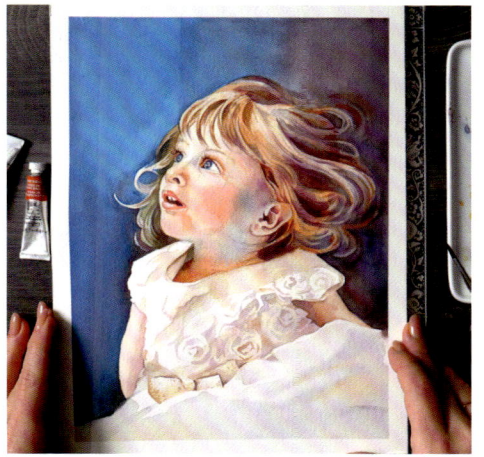

Sophie

Case Study: Child Portrait

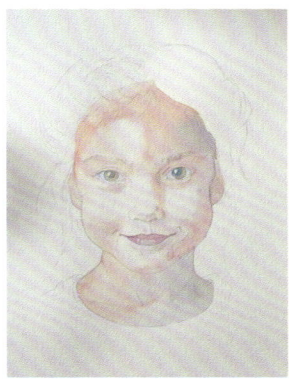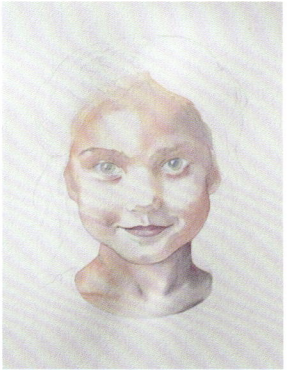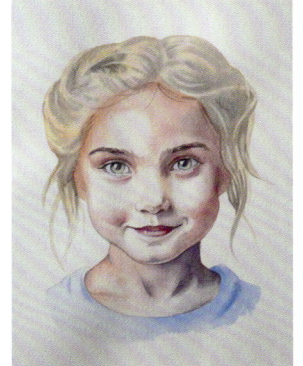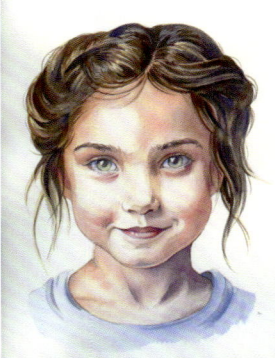

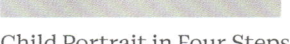
Child Portrait in Four Steps

In the study shown here, I painted a young girl using four layers of color on the skin. For the first layer, I used the primary triad of Quinacridone Gold (PO48, PY150) from QoR Watercolors, Permanent Alizarin Crimson (PR177) from QoR Watercolors, and non-granulating Ultramarine Finest (PB29) from Schmincke. In the second and third layers, I introduced Brown Madder (PR179) from Winsor & Newton as a shortcut for my light skin tone, and I continued using the primary triad to render the shadows, as well as other details like lips and eyes. In the final layer, I also added Perylene Violet (PV29) from Daniel Smith for the darkest shadows, and a combination of Yellow Ochre (PY43) from Winsor & Newton and Raw Umber (PBr7) from QoR Watercolors for the hair strands.

6.14 Mixing Skin Tones

The question of mixing skin tones is perhaps the most common inquiry when it comes to watercolor portraits. Can just three pigments truly provide the expansive range of colors necessary to authentically capture the nuances of a human face? The short answer is yes. Primary yellow and primary red serve as the foundation for blending a plethora of oranges and pinks, establishing a solid basis for medium to light skin tones. Secondary greens and purples prove invaluable for crafting shadows and achieving olive skin tones. Depending on the dilution, these tones can be adjusted to match the specific nuances of your subject, ranging from lighter to darker shades. By blending all three primaries, a spectrum of browns and neutrals is obtained, essential for rendering darker skin tones.

Primary Triads

Nonetheless, as I've discovered through experience, there exist subtleties and constraints when adhering to the primary triad method. First, the selection of pigments within your triad influences the resulting blends, dictating a distinct "mood" in the final hues. For instance, one combination may yield warm and understated tones, while another may produce vibrant and dynamic shades, suiting different artistic styles accordingly.

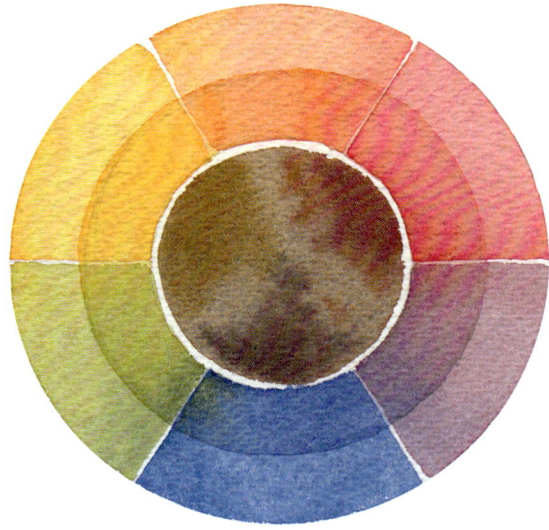

Three Primaries Case Study #1

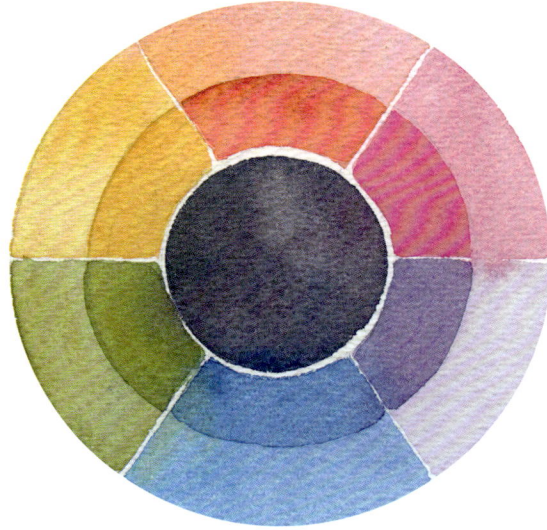

Three Primaries Case Study #2

Primary Yellow: Quinacridone Gold from QoR Watercolors (PO48, PY150)

Primary Red: Permanent Alizarin Crimson from QoR Watercolors (PR177)

Primary Blue: Ultramarine Finest from Schmincke (PB29)

Primary Yellow: Yellow Ochre from Winsor & Newton (PY43)

Primary Red: Quinacridone Magenta from QoR Watercolors (PR122)

Primary Blue: Phthalo Blue Red Shade from QoR Watercolors (PB15:6)

Convenience Mixes

Another constraint of the primary triad method lies in the requirement for meticulous and frequently time-consuming mixing to maintain uniformity of hues throughout layers. While certain artists may not find this process burdensome, others may seek shortcuts, opting to incorporate additional pigments. This preference, alongside personal stylistic inclinations, explains why the palettes of your favorite portrait

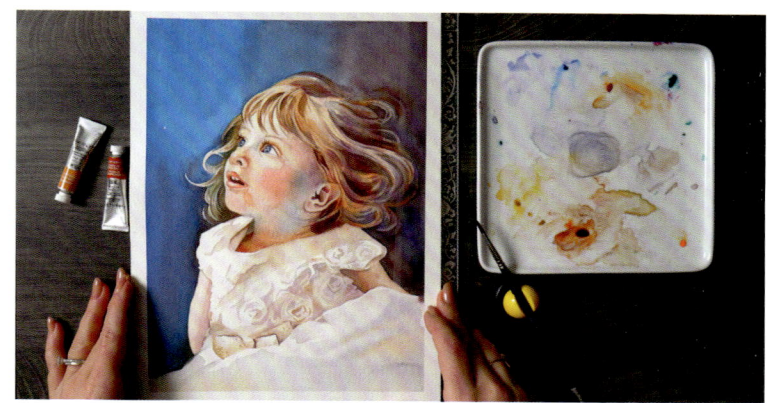

Portrait of Sophie

artists may feature an array of colors beyond the primaries. These supplementary hues allow for greater flexibility and efficiency in achieving desired tones, accommodating varying artistic approaches and preferences. My personal favorites when it comes to skin tone convenience pigments include: Brown Madder for all base skin tones, Perylene Violet for darker skin tones, and Aqua Green and Phthalo Blue Red Shade for green and blue color accents within the shadows.

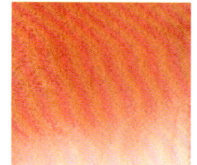 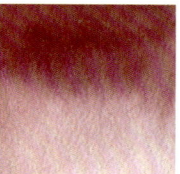  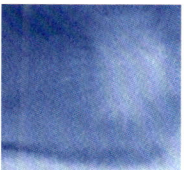

Perylene Maroon, a.k.a. Brown Madder from Winsor & Newton (PR179)

Perylene Violet from Daniel Smith (PV29)

Aqua Green from Winsor & Newton (Phthalo)

Phthalo Blue Red Shade from Daniel Smith (PB15:6)

Remember, there is no right or wrong approach to painting portraits with watercolor! In fact, you can paint an entire portrait using only one color—think about black-and-white photography and how effective it is at capturing the essence of the human face by relying on the contrast between lights and darks. However, for those keen on exploring the full spectrum of colors, learning and practicing human face anatomy can greatly enhance your portrayal's realism. Understanding how light interacts with the face, illuminating certain features while casting shadows on others, is equally crucial. By embracing these fundamentals and experimenting with different techniques, you will embark on a journey of discovery, infusing your portraiture with depth, emotion, and authenticity. So, use what you have on your palette today, and explore the art of portraiture with joy and curiosity.

6.15 Tips for Painting Animal, Bird, and Human Eyes

Our brains are naturally wired to focus on the eyes due to their crucial role in social interaction and emotional communication. From an artistic perspective, the significance of the eyes cannot be overstated—they are often the first thing people notice even in the most complex compositions. Whether you are painting a wild animal, a beloved pet, or a human subject, the eyes serve as focal points that draw viewers into a piece, capturing attention and evoking a sense of connection. Therefore, mastering the art of painting eyes is essential for artists seeking to create engaging and emotionally resonant artwork.

Plan Your Layers

Regardless of your watercolor style or level of experience, you will likely need at least two washes of color to capture the intricacies of eye shape. Start with a very light wash to cover the whites of the eyes, while avoiding highlights and reflections. My favorite pigment for this initial wash is Phthalo Blue Green Shade (PB15:3). Subsequent washes can be darker, allowing you to gradually build up values and capture the subtle variations of color within the iris.

Capture the Highlights

Incorporating a bright highlight is a simple yet effective technique for accurately depicting the spherical shape of the eye. You can achieve this either by painting around the bright spot with the tip of your brush using the negative painting technique, or by using masking fluid to conceal the highlights. Alternatively, you can apply white gouache after the main layers of color have dried. I prefer to position the highlight slightly off-center and closer to the upper lid, as light typically originates from above.

Don't Neglect the Shadows

Don't overlook the importance of shadows when painting eyes. It's not just about capturing their color and basic appearance; you need to understand and capture the full effect of light on the eye area. Take a close look at your refer-

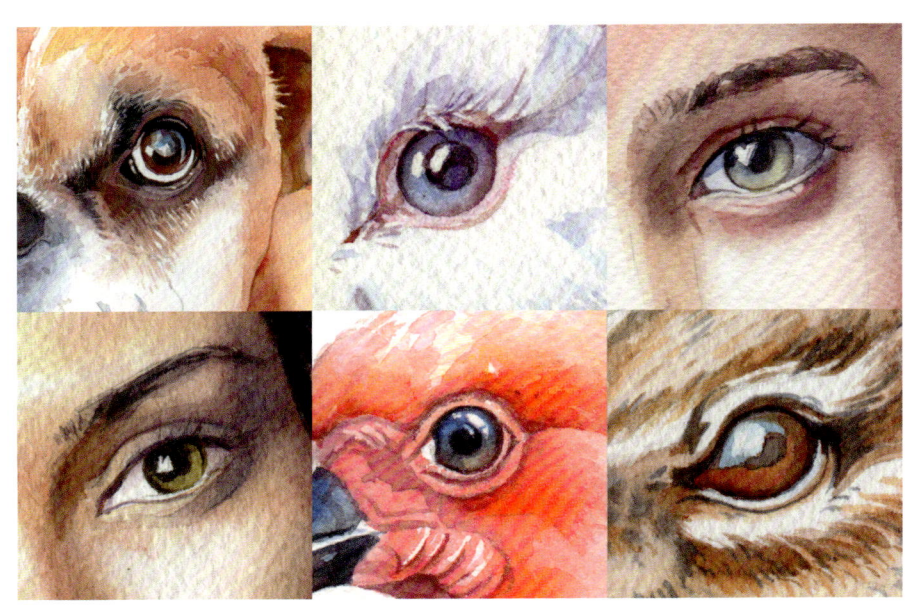

ence—whether you're painting a bird or an animal, there are usually shadows and even wrinkles around the eye and eyebrow area. Try to recreate these by gently applying darker glazes of color to create a more realistic setting. If space allows, consider adding a subtle shadow under the top lid within the whites of the eyes.

Accentuate with Visual Tricks

Sometimes the eyes can appear small and indistinct, blending into the overall composition. However, there are tricks to bring them to life. For instance, when painting a brown bird, adding vibrant orange strokes around the eyelids can prevent them from getting lost amid a sea of feathers. Similarly, when painting a white rabbit, defining fur details around the eyelids can draw attention to the eyes.

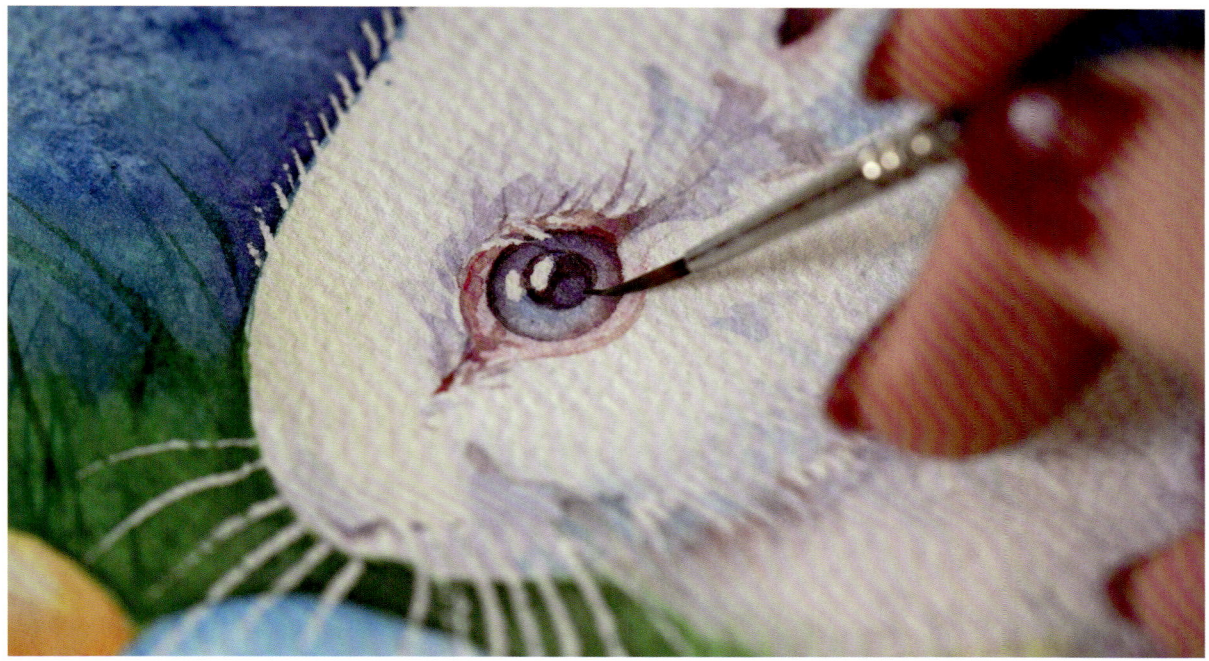

Avoid Pure Black

My go-to pigment for the darkest parts of the eye is usually Indigo. It blends well with the blue under-painting on the iris and the dark shadows on the eyeball. Additionally, it contains black, allowing for a full range of values needed for eyelashes and the darkest details. I recommend avoiding pure black pigments straight from the tube, as they can look harsh and unnatural.

Slow Down

Mastering the art of painting eyes is all about patience and precision. Whenever I approach the eye area, whether in quick watercolor studies or more detailed pieces, I always slow down. Why? Because getting this small part of the painting right is absolutely key for everything else to fall into place seamlessly. Even though the eyes may seem like just a tiny part of the face, they hold incredible importance. They can truly make or break a painting. That's why I recommend reaching for your finest, most precise brushes and taking your time to layer your paint carefully. By focusing on perfecting this small but crucial detail, you'll set the stage for the success of your entire composition.

6.16 How to Paint Realistic Snow

Painting snowy scenes can be both challenging and rewarding—capturing its unique luminosity and texture requires a thoughtful approach. In this section, I will describe my favorite tips and techniques, including a more realistic approach to help you create stunning snowscapes full of depth and atmosphere, and a variety of decorative techniques suitable for holiday cards and surface design projects.

Observe Color Reflections

When we observe snow in real life, we rarely see it as pure white. Most frequently, it reflects the color of the sky, giving it a light gray or light blue appearance. In addition, the ambient light of sunrise and sunset can cast orange and pink tones. This warm light interacts with the cool hues of the snow, giving it a slightly warm purple tint. Furthermore, snow often reflects the colors of nearby objects. If there are trees, buildings, or colorful objects nearby, their hues will also be reflected in the snow. For example, pine trees will tend to add green to the blue snow shadows below.

Prepare the Snow Palette

Avoid using stark white straight from the tube. Instead, mix your blues, greens, and purples with lots of water to achieve luminosity. My favorite pigments for capturing snow include: Cobalt Blue (PB28) and Phthalo Blue Red Shade (PB15:6) for traditional snow scenes, Cobalt Teal (PG50) for vivid icy patches, Dioxazine Purple (PV23) for warm shadows, Indigo (PB60, PBk6) for cool shadows, and Perylene Green (PBk31) for pine-tree shadows on the snow.

 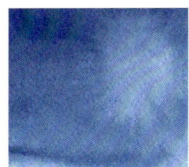   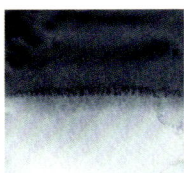 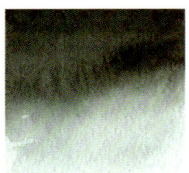

Cobalt Blue from Winsor & Newton (PB28)

Phthalo Blue Red Shade from Daniel Smith (PB15:6)

Cobalt Teal from QoR Watercolors (PG50)

Dioxazine Purple from QoR Watercolors (PV23)

Indigo from Daniel Smith (PB60, PBk6)

Perylene Green from Daniel Smith (PBk31)

Sketch to Set the Scene

Outline the composition lightly, using a very hard pencil (3H or 4H). Avoid applying too much pressure, as your pencil lines will be particularly visible under light watery layers. Focus on the major shapes and forms, considering the interplay of light and shadow in the snow-covered scene. Do include outlines of major shadows, as they will help you define large masses of white snow.

Skip the Highlights and Paint the Shadows

Painting snow is an exercise in understanding and rendering intricate shadow patterns, which are essential for conveying the texture, form, and mood of the snowy landscape. Use negative painting technique to paint around the white areas of untouched snow and bright highlights, and use very diluted pigments for the darkest areas, always considering the direction of light to render the shadows accurately. If needed, use masking fluid to preserve the white on the most intricate highlights.

Enhance Details

Review the overall painting and add details selectively. Adjust contrast, refine edges, and balance tones to ensure the snow feels realistic and integrated into the scene. You can introduce white gouache to add tiny snowflakes or individual snow particles, or use a dry brush technique to add granular details in shaded areas.

Case Study: Polar Bear Resting

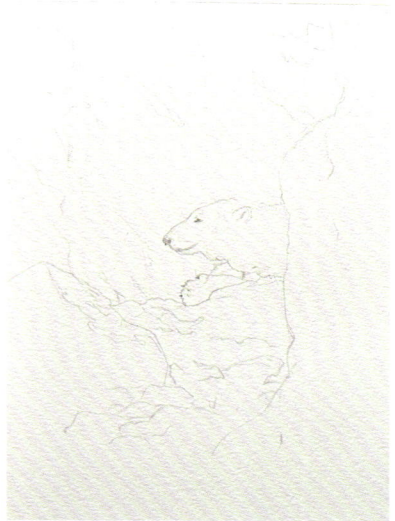 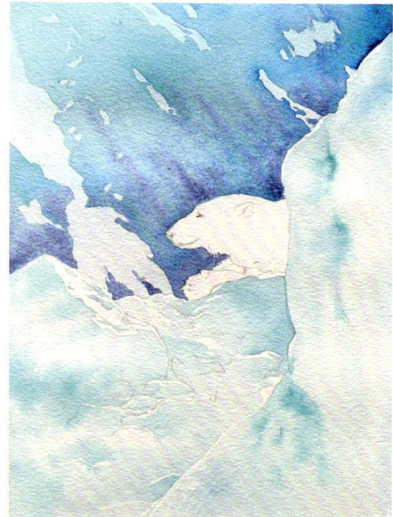 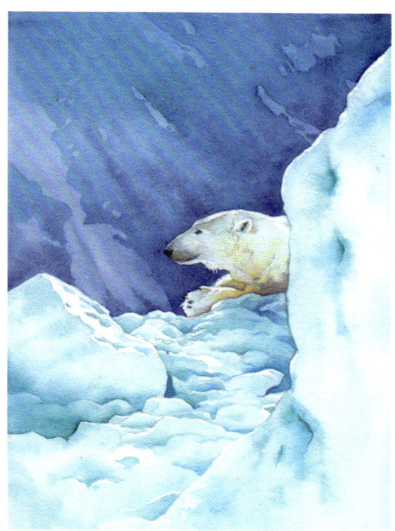

Polar Bear Resting in Three Steps

In this study, I used a variety of pigments, textures, and techniques to differentiate between foreground and background snow. On the foreground snowbanks, I applied Cobalt Teal (PG50) using wet-on-wet technique, only capturing the darker shadow areas. I opted for warmer tones or more defined brushwork to create a sense of closeness. There were multiple spots I left completely dry, painting around them to preserve the brightest highlights. Then I used larger strokes of granulating Cobalt Blue (PB28) to recreate snow hills in the distance. Note that I had to work quickly to add colors while the surface was still wet, letting the colors blend softly for a serene backdrop. I followed with several washes of transparent Phthalo Blue Green Shade (PB15:3) and Phthalo Turquoise (PB15:3/PG7) to suggest the layers of snow and accentuate the shadows between snow-covered elements.

6.17 Stylized Snow for Holiday Projects

In addition to painting realistic snowscapes, I enjoy painting stylized winter compositions using a more decorative approach to watercolor. In this section, I will share my favorite specialized techniques, including salt and white gouache, with some elements of Eastern European folk art. These are incredibly fun to experiment with, especially around the holiday season.

Folk Art Strokes

One of my favorite methods for painting snow is based on my training in Ukrainian folk art. It involves overlaying white pigment over traditional watercolor washes to create abstract shapes that resemble snow. White gouache works best here, as it is more opaque compared to traditional watercolors.

Speckle Dab

Another method frequently used by folk artists involves placing white dots of various sizes to mimic falling snowflakes. Use the back of your brush or an old pencil to pick a small amount of wet paint, and then dab it lightly onto paper to create small, speckled textures. For a more realistic effect, consider layering the dots. Start with smaller dots in the background and gradually build up density in the foreground. This will give your artwork a sense of depth, mimicking the way snowfall appears in nature. Note that white watercolor dots will tend to fade slightly, creating a more muted result, while white gouache dots will create more defined and bright dots.

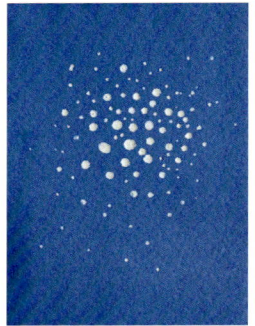

Splattering and Dripping

Instead of placing white dots onto dry surface, you can splatter paint into freshly painted washes for an illusion of falling snow. To do this, you will need an old toothbrush loaded with white pigment. Hold the toothbrush about 4–6 inches away from your paper and use your thumb to pull back and release the bristles, allowing the paint to splatter onto the surface. Experiment with different heights, angles, and distances to create variation in the size and density of the snowflakes. Alternatively, you can load a large painting brush and tap it gently on top of your paper so the white pigment can drip onto the wet surface.

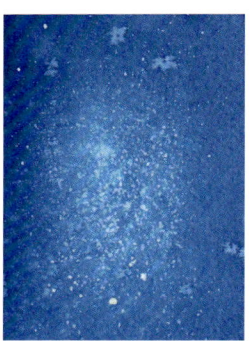

Salt

For a truly abstract and stylized approach, you can experiment with salt and wet-on-wet technique. Sprinkle fine-grain salt onto wet paint to create unpredictable textured effects resembling snow crystals sparkling in the sun.

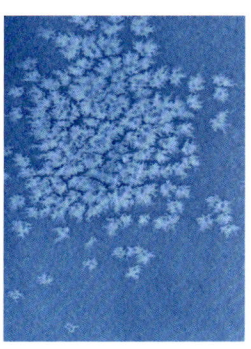

Case Study: Christmas Ornaments

In this illustration, I combined traditional watercolor layering technique with elements of Ukrainian folk art to create a cheerful a Christmas card. The bulbs were painted using a combination of primary colors—red, magenta, and blue. I applied several layers of diluted paint to build sufficient volume and define reflections on each sphere. After my watercolor layers were dry, I followed with white gouache to add decorative elements. On the red ornament, I painted stylized snowflakes by combining teardrop brushstrokes with small dots of paint using the back of my brush. The blue ornament features a more complex scene with a snowed-on village.

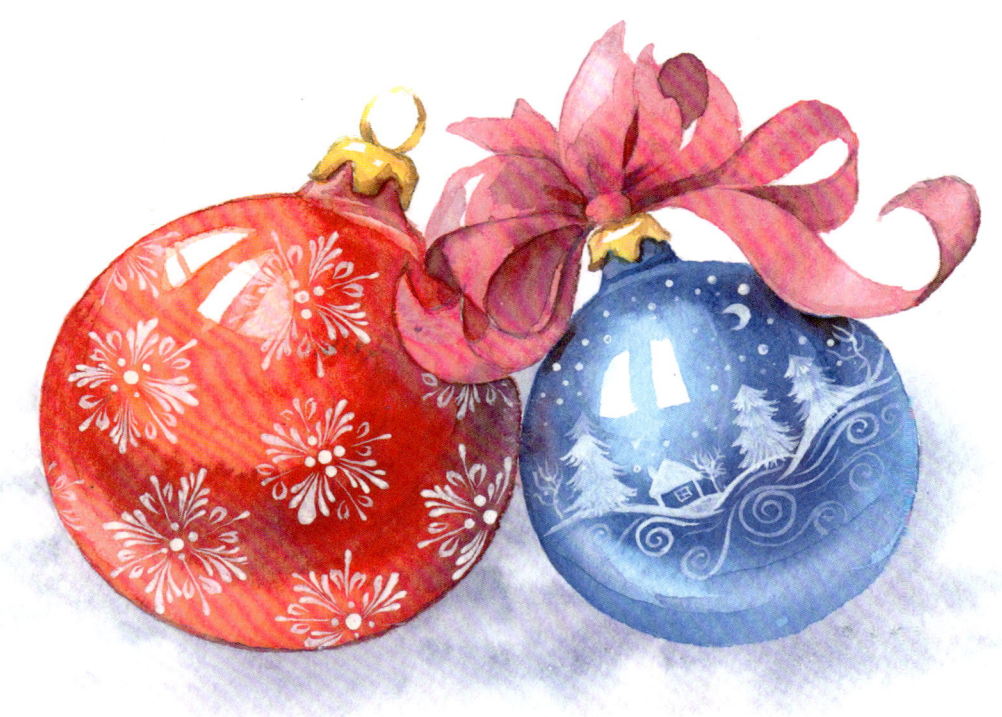

Christmas Ornaments

7

Dealing with Challenges and Common Frustrations

7.1 Introduction

Embarking on the watercolor journey is an adventure full of triumphs, but also some stumbling blocks. I assure you that even the most seasoned artists encounter frustrations along the way. In this chapter, I will share specific tips and techniques for addressing common challenges that all watercolor beginners face, including water control, crisp versus soft edges, and the very common tendency to "overpaint" or overwork your paper. Before we start, remember the following principles:

Embrace the Learning Curve

In the realm of watercolor, challenges can materialize in various forms. From managing washes and controlling pigment saturation to understanding the intricacies of paper absorbency and drying times, each aspect presents a learning opportunity. It's essential to recognize these moments as stepping stones toward your artistic growth. In the beginning of my watercolor journey, this realization was quite liberating. I keep reminding myself every day that all the watercolor masters I look up to once navigated the same waters. Every smudged stroke, every uneven wash, and every color that seems uncontrollable is a chapter in our watercolor story—a story of curiosity, creativity, and continuous improvement.

Practice and Celebrate

Practice remains the cornerstone of improvement. As brush meets paper, and colors blend and dance, each stroke contributes to honing techniques and resolving common issues. Remember that every artist's journey is unique. Patience and perseverance are invaluable companions, while repetition and dedication offer a gateway to overcoming most of your stumbling blocks. Don't forget to celebrate even the smallest victories along the way because every conquered challenge is a step toward mastery.

Look for Solutions

Understanding that most issues have solutions is very empowering. While practice is important, using tried and tested strategies tailored to address common issues will accelerate your progress. Don't be afraid to seek advice and guidance to help you overcome the hurdles more efficiently. Embrace all available resources, from online tutorials to local workshops with experienced artists.

Now let's delve into the common frustrations and issues that often greet beginners and occasionally pose a puzzle even to the more experienced hands.

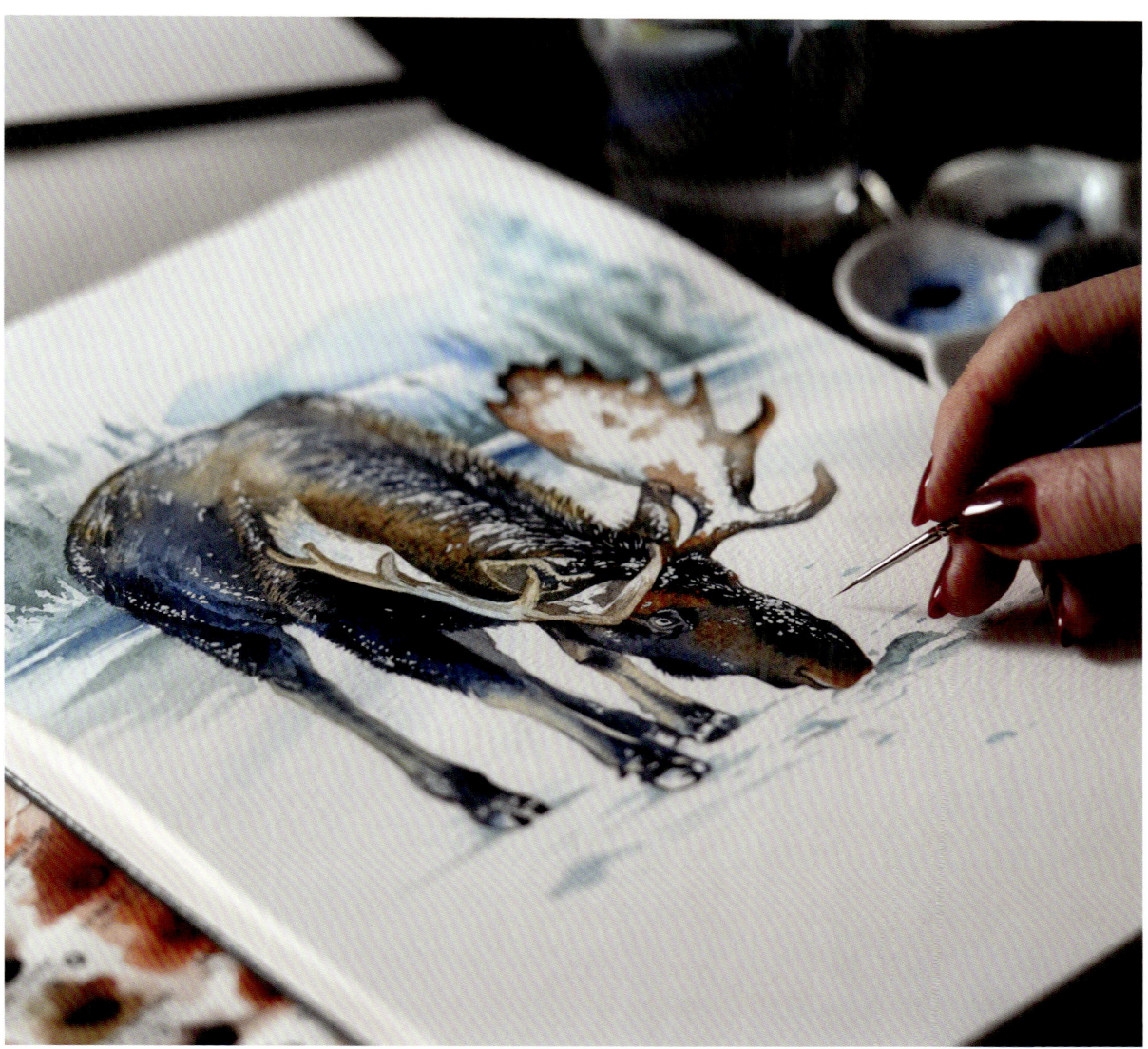

"Winter Moose" Watercolor Sketchbook Exploration

7.2 How to Avoid Overpainting

Overpainting is a common issue that can result in muddy colors, overworked areas, or even damaged paper. Here are some useful strategies that help me find a good balance between detail and restraint, allowing me to keep my watercolors light without compromising the vibrancy and details in the painting.

TIP #1: Avoid Erasing

This may seem counterintuitive at first, but excessive erasing often leads to overworking the paper later on. Watercolor paper is extremely delicate because it's made with cotton. Even a slight disturbance in the fibers caused by excessive erasing can interfere with color application. You may be tempted to paint over these patches, which only makes it worse by creating muddy and uneven blends. This is why it's important to minimize the use of erasers. You can do so in two ways: 1) use a hard graphite pencil (3H or stronger) to create very light and easily "liftable" lines; or 2) trace your outlines to avoid erasers altogether.

TIP #2: Layer from Light to Dark

Watercolors require a very delicate approach. Always start with light, watered-down washes to build the foundation of your artwork. Then gradually add more saturated paint, either on the same layer (using wet-on-wet technique) or as a separate layer (using wet-on-dry technique). This way you can better control the depth and details, reducing the tendency to overwork too early in the process.

TIP #3: Plan Appropriate Drying Time

Appropriate drying time between layers of paint is essential! Before I realized this simple rule, I used to compromise my work by rushing in with new colors before the first washes were dry. I recommend reserving at least one hour of drying time for smaller segments, and at least six hours for larger wet-on-wet blends. You can work on a different segment of the same composition or start a new one in the meantime. These days, I always have several paintings in process so I am never tempted to overwork too soon.

TIP #4: First Large, Then Small Brushes

Always start with larger brushes to block in shapes and areas of color, then switch to smaller brushes for more detailed work. Larger brushes encourage broader strokes and prevent getting lost in intricate details too soon. Smaller brushes hold less water, allowing you to render details without too much scrubbing.

TIP #5: Skip Single-Pigment Blacks

Avoid using black colors straight from the tube, as they tend to look harsh and unnatural. Moreover, pure blacks never blend harmoniously with other pigments, and that's one of the main things that leads to overworking and muddy washes on paper. Instead, experiment with alternatives or mix your own natural black (you can find several recipes on page 228).

TIP #6: Use Wet-on-Dry Technique to Make Things Darker

Building form and dimension requires additional layers of saturated paint. Artists often use wet-on-wet technique in this stage, rewetting entire areas of the painting and adding darker colors using broad wet-on-wet strokes. Unfortunately, this is one of those things that often leads to overworking by "exhausting" your paper and disturbing the underlying layers of paint. This is especially likely if you are painting on a

50% cotton surface, as opposed to a 100% cotton surface. I find it much easier to build tonal values using precise wet-on-dry strokes instead. I use a smaller brush and add smaller saturated strokes, applying wet paint to very limited areas that require more depth without using excessive amounts of water.

TIP #7: Limit Your Palette

Streamline your selection of colors to simplify the process, maintain clarity, and avoid overcomplicating your artwork. The definition of a limited palette varies among artists—while I perceive a palette of seven or eight pigments as restrained, some artists thrive with just the three primary colors (red, yellow, and blue). Nonetheless, trimming down your palette even slightly will prevent unnecessary complexities, minimizing the chances of overpainting and excessive manipulation of your paper surface.

TIP #8: Know When to Stop

Probably the most important tip for avoiding muddy colors and overpainting is to know when to stop. Recognize when the piece has reached a stage where additional work might not add significant value. Sometimes, leaving certain areas slightly unfinished or "suggested" can even add character.

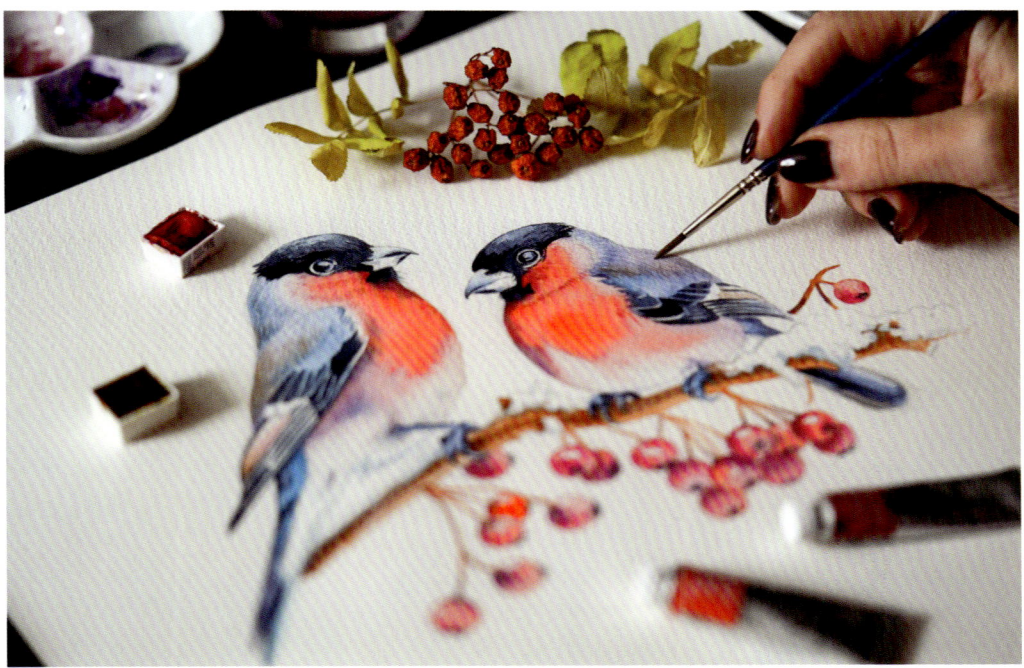

Two Winter Birds

Case Study: Winter Birds

In this painting, I used three layers of color on the birds (the focal point), but only two layers on the surrounding objects. The berries, in particular, were painted using one simple layer of red, complemented by a few darker-blue details. Although I am always tempted to add more details, the small white highlights were more than enough to indicate the surface is shiny and the shapes are round.

Video Available ▶ rockynook.com/watercolor-secrets

7.3 How to Create Crisp Edges and Fine Lines

Due to its fluid nature, watercolor can present challenges when you're aiming for crisp edges. However, with the right techniques and mindful practices, you can achieve sharp lines and clean borders even on textured paper.

TIP #1: Hot vs. Cold vs. Rough Paper: Choose Wisely

The texture of your watercolor paper influences color edge quality. Generally, lower-grade wood pulp and minimal cotton papers may result in messy edges no matter what you do. Some professional grade papers are easier to work with than others. When looking to create fine lines and crisp edges, consider the following:

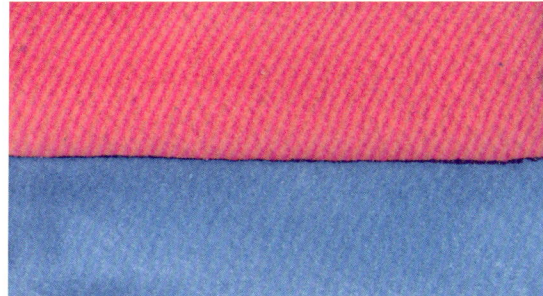

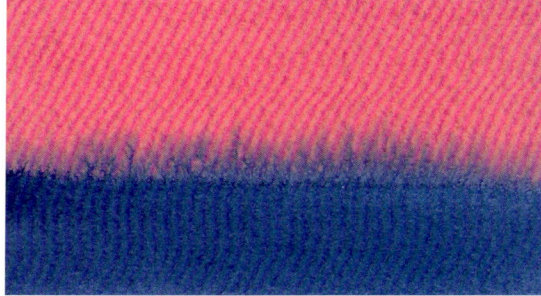

Crisp vs. "Bleeding" Edges

- **Rough paper**, with its pronounced texture, provides ample drying time for complex wet-on-wet washes. However, its coarse surface hinders precise lines, making it unsuitable for my detailed stroke and crisp edge-oriented style.
- **Hot-pressed paper** offers an ideal smooth surface for intricate details, particularly in botanical work. However, the downside of this paper is its quick drying time.
- **Cold-pressed paper**, my preferred choice, features a slightly grainy surface or "tooth." While it dries slowly, allowing beautiful wet-on-wet color transitions, the texture makes achieving smooth edges more challenging. I overcome this by using precise brushes and other strategies, described below.

TIP #2: Drying Time Is Essential

One of the most common mistakes beginners make is rushing to put new colors next to the freshly painted segments. This often results in particles of new pigment traveling from one block of color to another, creating a soft edge or washing away the boundary between two colors altogether. Remember that watercolor pigments tend to move with water. When looking for a crisp border between two adjacent colors, ensure the first color is completely dry before painting the next color.

TIP #3: Brush Shape Matters

Experiment with brush shapes and strokes to enhance the quality of your edges. Consider employing long, sweeping strokes utilizing the side of a flat brush when working on expansive color blocks that demand sharp, geometric lines with defined borders. For intricate details, opt for small round brushes, particularly when complemented by short, precise strokes, to achieve optimal results.

TIP #4: Use Overlapping Edges to Your Advantage

When planning your layers, incorporate a subtle overlap between adjoining color blocks. Starting with lighter hues and progressively introducing darker layers, wet-on-dry represents a natural and effective method for achieving seamless edges. This systematic approach serves to mask imperfections in your strokes and eliminate any discernible gaps between distinct color blocks.

TIP #5: Avoid Nonstaining Pigments

Using low-staining pigment can lead to "dissolved" edges, particularly in more advanced scenarios with multiple color layers. These pigments don't adhere to paper as well as their high-staining counterparts, becoming easily reactivated by subsequent glazes. This often results in unintended muddy areas within the artwork. This challenge can be addressed by deliberately avoiding low-staining pigments and opting for high-staining alternatives.

Case Study: Gouldian Finch and Orchids

This Gouldian Finch presented an interesting challenge of painting multiple overlapping blocks of colored feathers. I had to start with my lightest pigments first, and then I progressed to darker hues, ensuring ample drying time between each application.

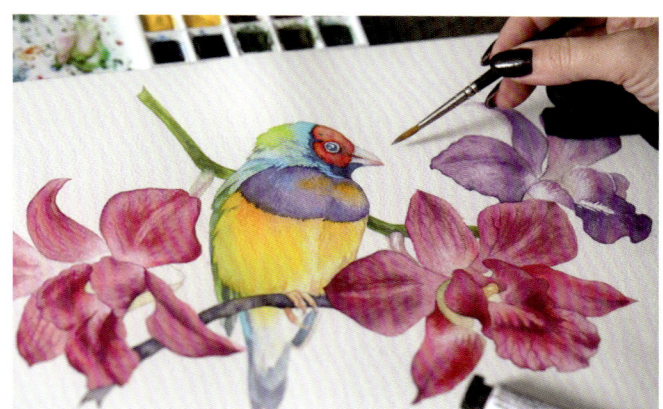

Gouldian Finch and Orchids

- **Step 1:** I started by painting a gentle wash of Cadmium Yellow Medium Hue (PY53, PY151, PY83), adding small green and orange accents using wet-on-wet method.
- **Step 2:** After this layer was dry, I followed with violet and green color blocks, extending these deeper pigments slightly over the yellow edge to eliminate any potential gaps.
- **Step 3:** To conclude, I introduced Indigo feathers and a brown branch at the center, purposefully overlapping the edges to eliminate any visible gaps between colors. The outcome is a series of sharp edges between adjacent blocks of vibrant feathers, devoid of any perceptible interruptions.

Note the error: I used Cobalt Blue Violet (PB28, PV19) to paint the segment of purple feathers on the bird's chest. Although quite beautiful, this low-staining pigment can be easily lifted. During the final layer, I applied a glaze of Quinacridone Gold (PO48, PY150) across the left side of the bird. In order to add shadow and enhance dimension, I had to cover some of the purple feathers along the way. The dry Cobalt became reactivated and lifted with my wet strokes, resulting in a slightly blurred edge and an unintended spot where the two pigments were meant to seamlessly overlap. A high-staining purple or violet alternative would have maintained its position undisturbed by additional washes. For example, Dioxazine Purple (PV23) would have allowed for the addition of the gold shadow across the bird's chest without compromising the intended boundary between purple and yellow.

Video Available 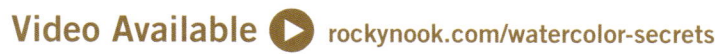 rockynook.com/watercolor-secrets

7.4 How to Avoid Dull and Muddy Colors

If you want to keep your watercolors fresh and vibrant, there are several things you can do to improve your results. In this section I will share my favorite methods for achieving vivid intense colors, including specific tools and techniques I use to avoid dull muddy colors, as well as the brands and pigments that provide the most vibrant look.

TIP #1: Use Two Water Containers

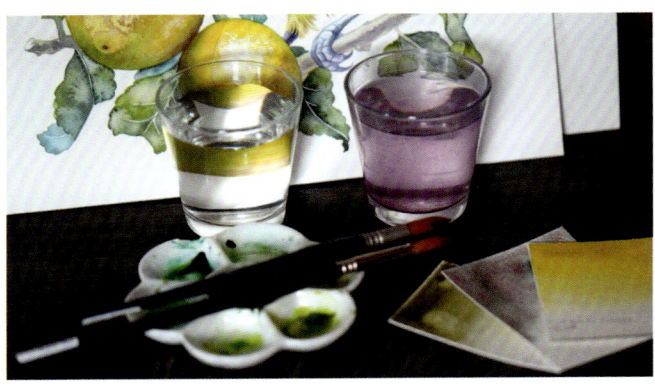

Watercolor pigments tend to get in and stay in the base of the brush, reducing the vibrancy and clarity of any subsequent pigments you may use. If you notice that your colors are getting muddy throughout the painting process, try using a dual container or simply opt for two jars of water instead of one. Use the first reservoir to clean your brush, and the second one to give an extra bath and make sure you get rid of all residual pigment before switching to the next layer.

TIP #2: Invest in Different Brushes for Warm and Cool Colors

You may not realize it, but pigments often stay in the brush hairs even after a thorough cleaning, causing muddy results especially when switching from one color family to another. If you've ever switched from intense Ultramarine to a warm Cadmium Yellow, you know the residual blue will instantly make your yellow more dull. To avoid this effect, I typically use two sets of brushes of the same size for different color families: one for cool washes (green, blue, and violet), and another for warm (yellow, orange, and red). Refer to page 82 to learn more about how to clean and condition your brushes more thoroughly so they stay clean and last longer.

TIP #3: Embrace the Glazing Technique

The glazing technique is the best way to avoid muddy colors because it involves slow and gradual building of transparent color layers. This wet-on-dry approach to painting reduces pigment cross-contamination across distinct color segments. It allows us to build color strength slowly and gradually, achieving deeper tones and saturated color segments in a controlled way. While you are doing it, the areas you cover might get progressively smaller, while your colors get more juicy and saturated. You can glaze pure green next to pure red without mixing the two, achieving areas of pure vibrant color throughout.

TIP #4: Mix on Paper versus Palette

Instead of mixing pigments on the palette, try mixing them on paper using the charging variation of the wet-on-wet technique. Start with a light layer of your main color, then slowly add other pigments with the tip of your brush while your paper is still wet. Your pigments will have less opportunity to overpower or mute one another. Instead, they will tend to stay relatively concentrated where you place them, and gently spread into other areas. You will end up with larger areas of concentrated pigment rather than a more muted mixture.

TIP #5: Use Complementary Colors

Complementary colors, situated on opposite sides of the spectrum, tend to enhance each other, intensifying their perceived brightness. For instance, by placing blues and oranges side by side, you can augment the vibrancy and intensity of each color. This phenomenon is not limited to blues and oranges; other examples of complementary pairs that enhance each other's intensity include red and green, and purple and yellow.

Case Study: Swallows and Roses

In this study, I introduced an underpainting of pure Phthalo Blue Green Shade (PB15:3) to boost the vibrancy of the blue feathers on the bird and counterbalance the muted umbers of the brown feathers. This choice of underpainting not only heightened the blue tones, but also provided a striking contrast against the more dull and subdued browns. Additionally, these splashes of vivid blue enhanced the perceived intensity of the warm reds on the

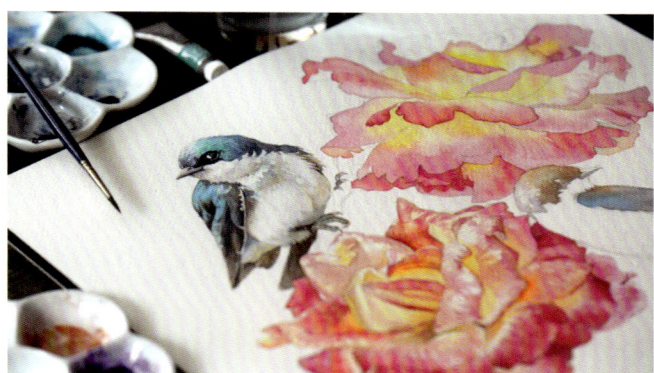

Swallows and Roses in Progress

rose petals, making the entire composition more visually engaging and harmonious.

TIP #6: Explore "High-Chroma" and High-Staining Pigments

To avoid dull and uninspired results, I recommend exploring high-chroma colors with a focus on high-staining varieties.

- **Chroma**, in the context of color theory, measures the purity or intensity of a color. Colors with high-chroma are often found in their purest form on the color wheel, away from neutral tones. For example, a pure pink like Quinacridone Magenta (PR122) would be considered high-chroma, while a dull, muted brown, like Perylene Maroon (PR79), would have lower chroma.
- **High-staining pigment** families, including Phthalos and Quinacridones, display more pigment strength compared to their low-staining counterparts. Their unique combination of vibrancy and transparency makes them perfect for building vivid layers of color while preserving the luminosity in your work.

Many manufacturers offer custom palettes uniquely curated to offer the most vibrant pigments that will help you create bold and energetic compositions. For example, the High-Chroma set from QoR Watercolors includes six exceptionally brilliant pigments, including three of my favorites: Transparent Pyrrol Orange (PO71), Quinacridone Magenta (PR122), and Dioxazine Purple (PV23).

Video Available 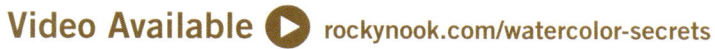 rockynook.com/watercolor-secrets

7.5 Improving Water Control

Water control is a crucial aspect of watercolor painting, influencing the outcome of washes, gradients, and overall painting techniques. Here are some strategies I use to enhance water control and my favorite tips for effective practice:

Overloading the Brush

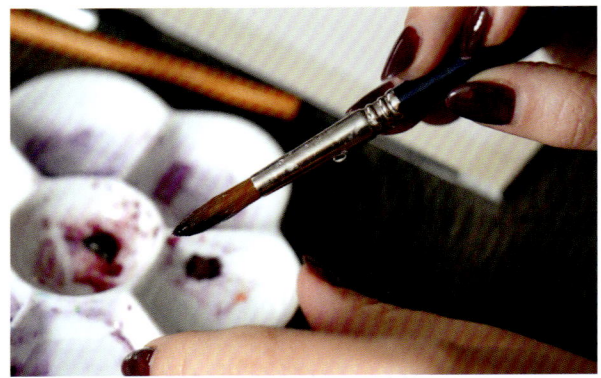

- **Challenge:** Using a brush saturated with too much water can lead to unpredictable washes, causing the paint to spread uncontrollably.
- **Tip:** Gradually load your brush with water and pigment so you are able to control the intensity and coverage of your strokes. The bristles should never feel "heavy" or dripping with pigment. If you continue to experience challenges, consider changing to a smaller brush size or even upgrading to a different bristle type. Remember that larger brushes hold more water, while smaller brushes provide greater control for detailed work. In addition, quality synthetics from reputable manufacturers tend to hold less water compared to natural brushes, while still providing excellent precision.

Uneven Washes

- **Challenge:** Achieving an even wash can be challenging, especially on larger areas when the paper dries unevenly or absorbs water inconsistently.
- **Tip:** Pre-wet the entire surface of the paper evenly, using a large flat brush to promote uniform coverage. Follow with smaller round brushes for more precise color placement. If needed, tilt the paper to control the flow of water and ensure more even pigment distribution.

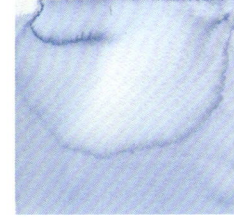

Uneven Wash

Unwanted Blends and "Backruns"

- **Challenge:** Blooms, backruns, and even muddy edges can occur when an area is too wet and a drier pigment is introduced, causing an unexpected diffusion of color.
- **Tip:** Remember that pigments move with water. Avoid placing saturated colors next to freshly painted washes to avoid undesirable blends. Remember, too, that fully saturated color mixtures tend to slow down and even prevent pigment flow in wet-on-wet applications. On the other hand, more watered-down mixes encourage fast and uncontrollable flow of pigments.

"Backrun"

Drying Too Quickly

- **Challenge:** In hot or dry conditions, watercolor can dry too rapidly, limiting your ability to blend or create smooth transitions.
- **Tip:** Work in smaller sections, keep your palette covered, and mist the paper lightly with a spray bottle throughout the painting process. In particularly dry conditions, consider using watercolor medium to extend the drying time. For more information on my favorite medium, see page 84.

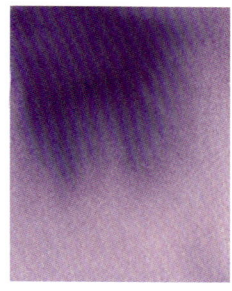

Uneven Drying

Wet-on-Wet Timing Exercise

One of my favorite watercolor exercises involves painting a series of controlled strokes on wet paper at different time intervals. It's a great way to master water control across different types of cotton, pigments, and brushes. This approach is also useful for learning the optimal timing of wet-on-wet techniques on your specific paper type. I use this as a test for every new paper brand that comes across my desk to fully understand the limitations and differences across individual manufacturers.

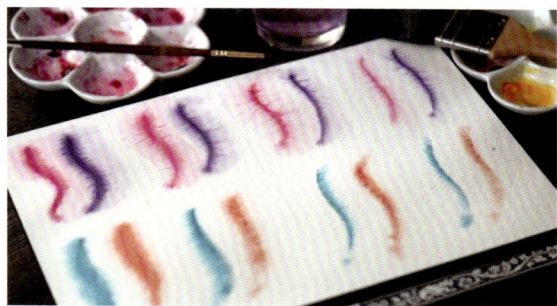

Controlled Brush Exercise with Timer

Step-by-Step

1. Divide your sheet of paper into four individual sections. Wet the surface with clear water, using a large flat brush to ensure even coverage. Start the clock!
2. Begin by adding thin strokes of color in the first section. Observe how far the paint spreads. If your brush didn't leave any defined marks, your paper may be too wet. In this case, wait another minute before moving on to the next section.
3. Repeat the process at the two-, three-, and four-minute marks. Note the differences in pigment dispersion for each time interval—from fully wet to slightly damp. This helps in developing control over water and pigment application, teaching you to manage timing, saturation, and water-to-pigment ratio effectively.
4. Note that you can test a range of colors in the same section. This exercise allows you to observe how different pigments react to water and practice achieving optimal timing for different brands, palettes, and color schemes. In addition, you can experiment with different brushes to better understand their loading capacity and identify any potential issues with pigment release.

Remember that mastering water control is an ongoing process. Regular practice and experimentation with different techniques will significantly enhance your ability to manipulate water and achieve the desired effects in your watercolor paintings.

Video Available 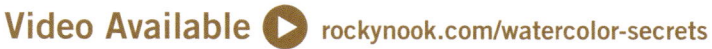 **rockynook.com/watercolor-secrets**

7.6 Mastering Tonal Values

Understanding Tonal Values

Tonal values refer to the range of lights and darks in your painting. Achieving a balance between these values is crucial for creating depth and capturing the essence of your subject. Whether you're painting a landscape, portrait, or still life, mastering tonal harmony is a skill that will significantly enhance your watercolor art.

Practice Value Scales

Before diving into a full-fledged painting, practice creating a value scale. This simple exercise involves painting a gradual transition from the lightest to the darkest tone. This visual guide will assist you in maintaining a consistent tonal range throughout and help you plan your layers of color accordingly.

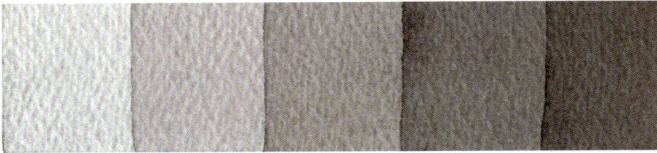

Tonal Values Scale – GRAY

Note that while some pigments appear vibrant and bright at first glance, their grayscale equivalents might reveal surprising characteristics. As you practice your value scales, I recommend focusing on the following two color families that present the most challenges in the context of tonal harmony:

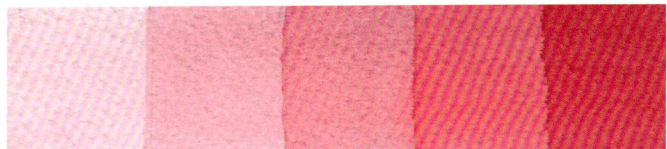

Tonal Values Scale – RED

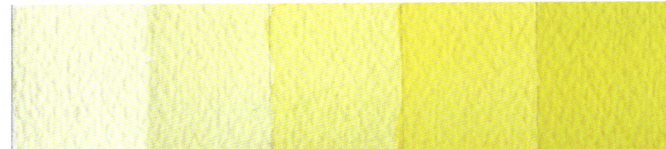

Tonal Values Scale – YELLOW

- **Red:** Red is often perceived as a lively and intense color, especially when fully saturated. However, as we will explore in lesson 9.7, "Working with Red Pigments," page 224, it appears close to 100% black when converted to grayscale. Be mindful of incorporating fully saturated red into your early washes, and practice value scales to understand its impact on the shadow areas.
- **Yellow:** Yellow poses a unique challenge in watercolor due to its inherent transparency and difficulty in building up dark values. No matter how many layers you apply, yellow may struggle to reach the depth seen in other colors. Explore value scales to observe the limitations of your yellow pigment when creating darker tones. Refer to lesson 9.8, "Working with Yellow Pigments," page 226, for more information on how to paint tricky yellow subjects.

Conduct a Grayscale Study

One of the most common pieces of advice in the context of tonal values is to conduct grayscale studies of your chosen subject. Using only one pigment will help you understand the true tonal values of each color on your palette. This will guide you in creating a more balanced composition when you use the full range of pigments available.

HELPFUL TIPS

While a full grayscale study is extremely beneficial, there are easier ways to apply the same principles when you are pressed for time or want to create quick value checks throughout the painting process. Prior to planning the layers, I often convert my reference photos to black and white using a free image-editing app on my phone. In addition, I recommend taking snapshots of your process work and using the same method to convert them to black and white. This will help you reassess the value balance at each stage and make adjustments as necessary.

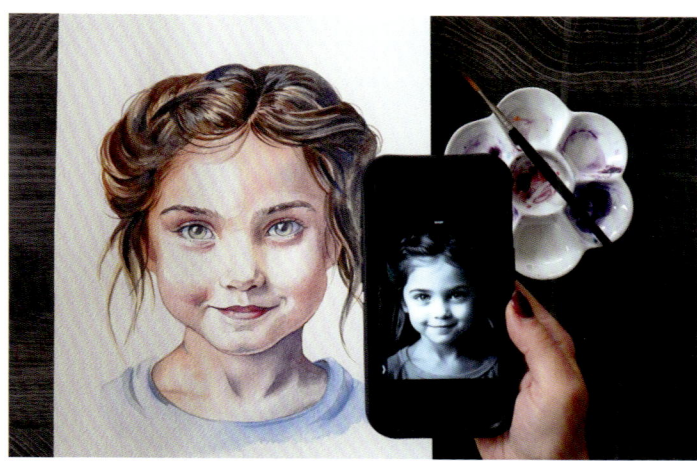

Avoid Low-Contrast and Overexposed References

As we will discuss in section 8.10, the lighting of your subject plays a pivotal role in shaping your painting experience. When considering tonal values, a photograph that is excessively dark or overly bright, lacking distinguishable shadows, can present difficulties in capturing a lifelike, three-dimensional form on paper. Select images and scenes characterized by distinct areas of light and shadow, providing a clear foundation for your value balance.

Experiment with Limited Palettes

Working with a limited color palette encourages focus on tonal values. By restricting your choices, you'll become more attuned to the varying degrees of light and shadow in your composition. This is especially beneficial for beginners honing their contrast skills.

Don't Judge Until Your Paint is Dry!

Don't forget that watercolor washes tend to settle into lighter tones as the water evaporates from the surface of your paper. This phenomenon is called a "drying shift," and some pigments are more prone to this than others. Therefore, it's best to assess your tonal values and the overall contrast after your painting is completely dry.

Build Layers Gradually

Finally, don't forget that the layering technique is a powerful tool for achieving the right tonal contrast. Start with lighter washes and gradually build up layers, allowing each one to dry before adding the next.

7.7 Are Blooms Really a Mistake?

Watercolor blooms, also known as "cauliflowers" or "blossoms," are unexpected and fascinating patterns that occur when wet pigment encounters another wet area on the paper. These beautiful "accidents" are created when excess water or pigment gathers on the paper, causing a unique dispersal of color. While beginners may see blooms as mistakes, experienced watercolor artists often embrace them as opportunities for unique and visually captivating effects. By understanding the science behind blooms and intentionally experimenting with their use, you can harness these beautiful imperfections to enrich and diversify your watercolor style.

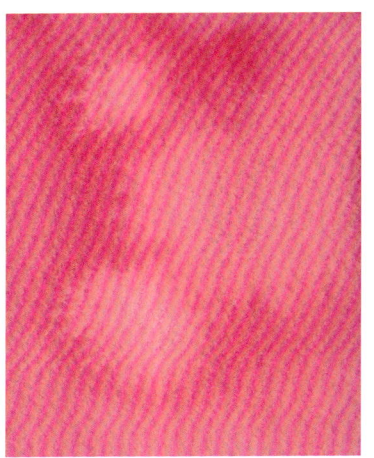 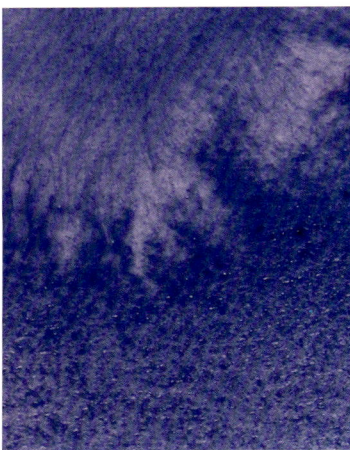 

Watercolor Blooms

How Blooms Happen

- **Water Drops:** Blooms commonly occur when drops of clear water land on a freshly painted wash. The water interacts with the drying pigment, pushing the paint particles outward to create irregular borders around the water drop.
- **Uneven Drying:** Blooms also emerge when a wet paint area meets a drier one, prompting the wet pigment to flow back into the drier region. This uneven drying process results in soft edges and intriguing textures.
- **Water Saturation:** Saturation of the paper with water or uneven paint application can contribute to blooms. When a highly saturated area encounters a less wet or drier section, pigments naturally diffuse, creating blossoms.

Turning Mistakes into Masterpieces

Instead of perceiving blooms as mistakes, consider them as serendipitous moments of beauty that add an organic and lively dimension to your painting. Embrace the unpredictable nature of watercolor by intentionally introducing blooms into your process, turning what might seem like an error into a unique feature. Here are some intentional uses of watercolor blooms:

- **Atmospheric Effects in Landscapes:** Introduce blooms in skies to create soft clouds and atmospheric effects. The irregular edges of blooms mimic the ethereal quality of natural clouds, adding depth to landscape paintings.

- **Abstract and Expressionistic Art:** Embrace the spontaneity of blooms in abstract or expressionistic paintings. Let the pigments flow freely, creating dynamic and visually interesting patterns that add energy and movement to the composition.
- **Textured Backgrounds:** Incorporate blooms into backgrounds to add texture and interest. The organic nature of the patterns can evoke a sense of depth and complexity, enhancing the overall aesthetic of your artwork.
- **Water Reflections:** Use blooms strategically to depict reflections on water surfaces. Allow the pigments to create natural variations that mimic the ripples and movement of water.

How I Use Watercolor Blooms

In my botanical work, I incorporate watercolor blooms to simulate the delicate texture of flower petals and leaves. Strategic placement of clear water drops on highly granulating washes, such as Cascade Green (PBr7, PB15), Ultramarine (PB29), or my favorite, Green Apatite Genuine (mineral), works exceptionally well for painting intricate flora with irregular surfaces.

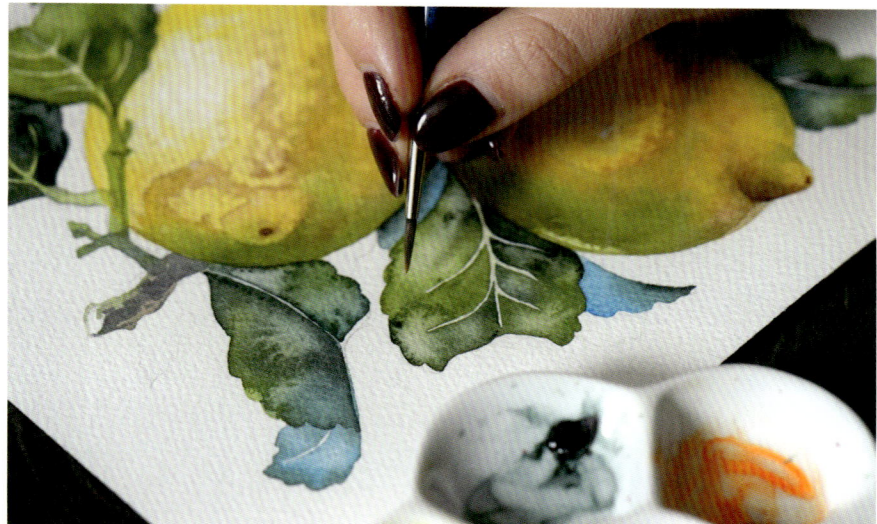

Close Up of Green Leaves with Intentional Watercolor Blooms

HELPFUL TIPS

- **Timing is Key:** Pay attention to the drying stages of your washes. Introduce wet washes at specific points in your painting process to encourage blooms where desired. If you drop your water right after applying the background color, the bloom will spread farther and the edges will be faint. If you wait a bit longer, the edges of your bloom will be more defined, but the bloom itself will be smaller.
- **Paper Considerations:** High-quality 100% cotton watercolor paper that can handle wet washes without excessive warping contributes to the effectiveness of blooms. Generally, blooming effects are more aesthetically pleasing on more-textured cold-pressed paper.
- **Pigment Considerations:** Granulating pigments tend to exhibit a more pronounced "cauliflower" effect.

7.8 How to Lift Smudges

While watercolor paint may not be erasable, correcting accidental brush marks and paint smudges is achievable through the lifting technique. Embrace mistakes as a natural part of the artistic process, and use this method to rectify errors without compromising the entire artwork. Here's a step-by-step guide, along with some helpful tips and preventive measures to improve your ability to maintain a clean painting surface.

Materials Needed

- **Clean Water:** Have at least one container of clean water on hand. Two containers work even better for lifting larger stains and highly saturated brush marks.
- **Brushes:** Use brushes to lift the paint.
- **Paper Towels or Tissues:** Use these to blot excess water.

Step-by-Step

1. **Wet the Area:** Use a clean brush to wet the area where the mistake occurred. Ensure the paper is damp but not excessively wet.
2. **Blot Excess Water:** Gently blot excess water with a paper towel or tissue. The surface should be damp but not saturated.
3. **Lift with Brush:** With a clean, damp brush, gently lift the unwanted paint by blotting and lifting it off the paper.
4. **Blot Again:** Blot the lifted paint with a paper towel to absorb the removed pigment.
5. **Repeat if Necessary:** If the mistake persists, repeat the process. Be patient and work gradually.
6. **Dry Completely:** Allow the area to dry completely before applying new layers of paint.

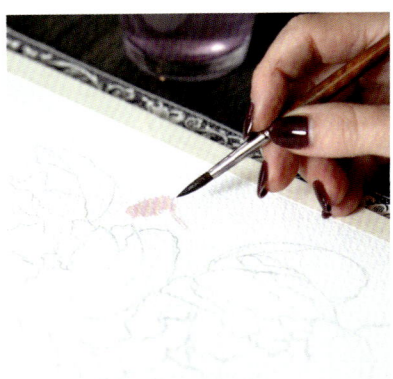 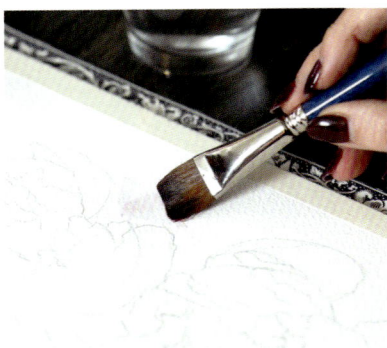 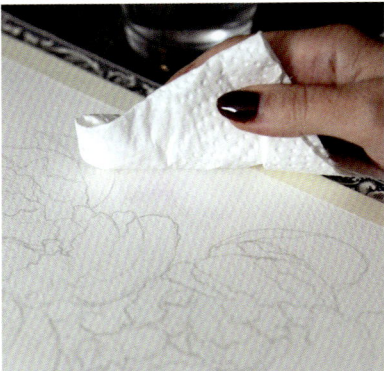

Lifting Smudges – Before, During, and After

HELPFUL TIPS

DOs

- **Act Quickly:** Address the mistake promptly, as wet paint is easier to lift than dry paint. This is crucial with vibrant, high-staining pigments like Phthalos and Quinacridones, as they adhere strongly to the paper surface and are challenging to lift after drying.
- **Get Creative:** Introduce a new detail instead of struggling with stubborn paint marks. Adding extra leaves or falling petals can cleverly mask accidental smudges without resorting to excessive scrubbing. This method allows you to correct errors seamlessly, turning mistakes into opportunities for artistic refinement.

DON'Ts

- **Don't Scrub:** Avoid scrubbing the paper vigorously to prevent damage to the cotton surface. Instead, rewet the paper and try lifting again a few minutes later.

Brush Considerations

- **Experiment with Different Shapes:** Test various brush shapes to find what works best for your specific lifting needs. Flat brushes excel at lifting larger areas and are suitable for correcting extensive sections, while round brushes in smaller sizes offer precision for targeting smaller marks.
- **Natural vs. Synthetic Bristles:** Natural bristles, like sable and squirrel, are softer and cause less damage to the paper, but may require multiple attempts for effective lifting. Harder synthetic brushes can be used cautiously for stubborn mistakes.
- **Eradicator Brush:** Consider the "eradicator brush," a specialized tool with stiffer synthetic bristles and a fine, pointed tip. Ideal for precise lifting, this brush allows selective removal or lightening of pigments in specific areas without disturbing adjacent paint. If control and precision are priorities, an eradicator brush is a valuable addition to your collection.
- **Brushes I Use:** When lifting smudges, I typically start by wetting the area with a large soft flat brush to activate the paint and the surface around the smudge. I then use a short synthetic flat brush to lift the paint slowly.

Preventive Measures

- **Anti-Smudge Guard:** Wear a glove on your working hand as an additional protective layer for the paper's surface.
- **Methodical Approach:** Adopt a left-to-right or right-to-left working method to avoid accidentally smudging fresh paint. If you are righthanded like me, start from the top-left corner and progress down to the bottom right. If you're lefthanded, reverse the process accordingly.
- **Scrap-Paper Testing:** Utilize a piece of scrap paper to test colors before applying them to the main painting. This practice minimizes unexpected results and allows you to refine your color choices.
- **Masking Fluid:** When working on detailed areas, consider using masking fluid to protect specific sections from accidental marks.

7.9 To Trace or Not to Trace?

Tracing outlines for watercolor painting is a topic that sparks ongoing debate within the art community. The controversy mainly revolves around the balance between the convenience of tracing and the artistic integrity that comes with independently honed drawing skills. In this section, I want to provide a balanced view on this topic and describe my own approach to tracing as it evolved through the years of practice.

Why It's Controversial

Artists often question whether tracing compromises the authenticity of their work or serves as a legitimate tool in the creative process. On one hand, tracing offers a convenient and time-saving method, allowing artists to prioritize the application of watercolor techniques. Conversely, some argue that mastering drawing skills independently is vital for artistic development, fostering a deeper understanding of form, proportion, and spatial relationships. Both perspectives are valid, and I encourage adopting a flexible approach to maximize your watercolor learning experience.

Copyright Considerations

Thoughtful and legal tracing for watercolor painting is a common, productive, and widely accepted practice. Many revered artists, including masters, used tracing or copying to refine their skills and study form and composition intricacies. Tracing acts as a bridge between technical proficiency and artistic expression, emphasizing watercolor's challenges. However, a crucial caveat is that source images ***must always be copyright-free or used with proper authorization***, ensuring ethical and legal practices.

Benefits of Tracing for Watercolor Artists

Note that tracing offers several important benefits compared to drawing outlines by hand.

- **Focused Learning:** Tracing allows artists, particularly beginners, to focus more on mastering watercolor techniques without the added challenge of intricate drawing skills. While both are essential skills, mastering them one at a time fosters a deeper understanding and proficiency in each discipline. This division of focus enables you to refine watercolor techniques, emphasizing the unique qualities of the medium without being encumbered by the complexities of drawing.
- **Accurate Foundation:** Tracing ensures accuracy in capturing the subject's proportions and details, providing a reliable foundation for watercolor application. This is particularly important in figurative art. For example, even subtle inconsistencies in facial proportions can be noticeable, making tracing an effective tool for ensuring accuracy in your portrait work.
- **Reduced Frustrations:** When the initial outline lacks proper proportion, you may encounter difficulties in establishing harmonious tonal values and layering watercolor effectively. This can often lead to frustration and a sense of discouragement, hindering progress in watercolor even if you possess strong technical skills.
- **Convenience:** Sometimes, we just want to paint! Tracing is an incredible tool that allows us to maximize painting time.

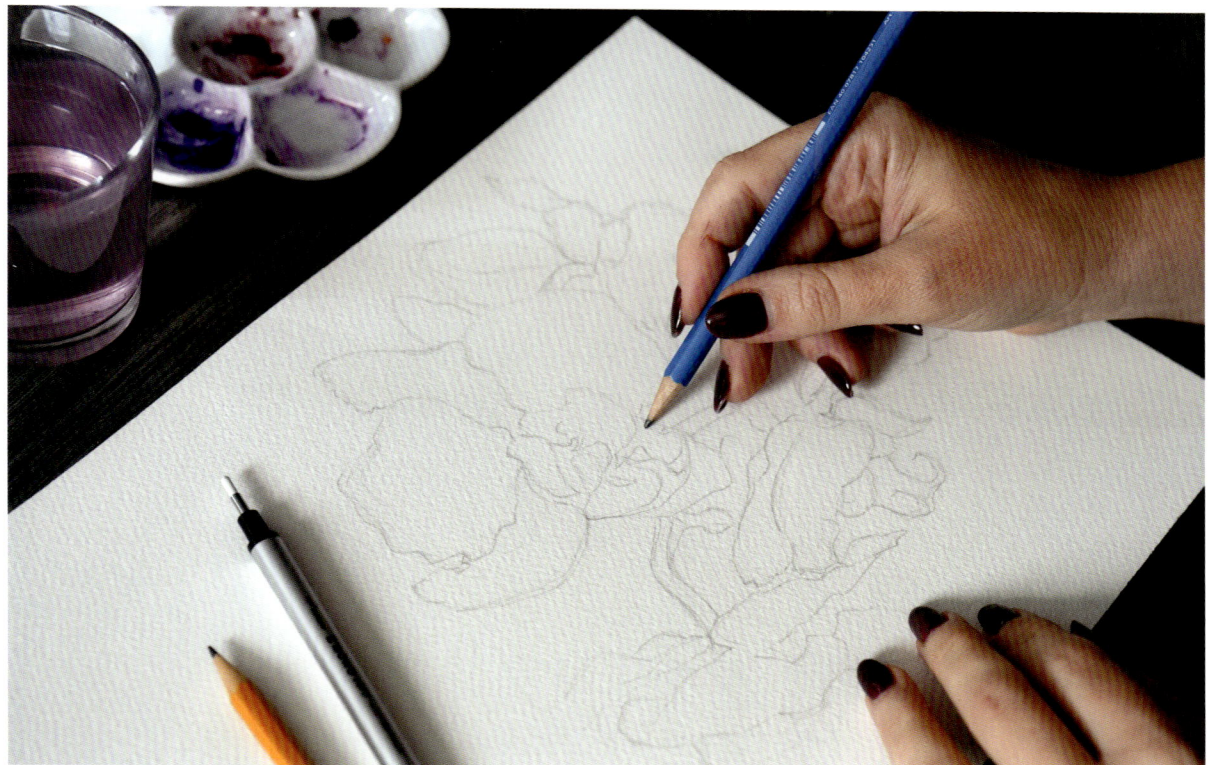

Drawing Orchid Outlines

Tracing in Watercolor: A Personal Journey

As I was embarking on my watercolor journey, I discovered the utility of tracing as a valuable tool, allowing me to focus on refining specific watercolor techniques. Concurrently, I dedicated time to honing my drawing skills independently, employing traditional tools such as pencils and ink pens.

Over time, my proficiency in drawing improved, leading me to adopt a more selective approach to tracing. While confident in my ability to hand-draw flowers and plants, I continued to use tracing for intricate subjects like animals and birds. One exception to my hand-drawn rule persisted—recognizing my technical limitations, I occasionally resorted to tracing faces, especially in portrait commissions where precision is paramount.

I can assure you that consistent practice will undoubtedly empower you to master the technical skills required for freehand outlines. However, patience is key, as certain subjects may pose more challenges than others. Organic shapes, for instance, tend to be forgiving, allowing for quicker improvement in proportion sketching. Separating the disciplines of drawing and watercolor allowed for a more effective learning experience, and the path you choose is entirely yours.

In conclusion, the choice to trace outlines in watercolor painting is deeply personal, with varied perspectives within the art community. While tracing offers convenience, it's juxtaposed against the value attributed to independently acquired drawing skills. As long as ethical considerations are observed and tracing is executed with skill and intention, it remains a valid method within your artistic toolkit.

7.10 Tracing Methods

Let's explore common approaches to tracing accurate outlines, including the use of a lightbox, tracing paper, and the grid. Each method provides unique benefits, catering to personal preferences, available tools, and drawing skill levels. I'll also share my preferred technique, applicable to any watercolor surface, including canvas. Remember, the key lies in consistent practice and experimentation to uncover the methods that align best with your artistic process.

Lightbox Method

A lightbox is a backlit device with a translucent surface that allows artists to trace images easily.

1. Place the image to be traced on the lightbox, securing it in place with masking tape.
2. Position a blank sheet of watercolor paper on top of the image.
3. Trace the lines, shapes, or details using a light graphite pencil.

Pros and Cons: The light shining through the box illuminates the image, allowing for an easy tracing experience. Although this method can be very effective for lighter paper weights (140lbs and under), it is not suitable for thicker textured paper (300lbs) or watercolor board.

Graphite Tracing Paper Method

1. Place a sheet of graphite tracing paper (coated side down) over the blank watercolor paper, pad, or canvas.
2. Place a printed image over the tracing paper facing up. Secure all three sheets with masking tape to prevent movement.
3. Using a pencil or stylus, carefully trace the lines of the image. As you do so, the graphite from the tracing paper will transfer onto your watercolor surface.

Pros and Cons: Graphite tracing paper proves to be a great option for canvas artworks, yet its application with delicate watercolor paper requires careful consideration. It's essential to exert sufficient pressure with your pencil to ensure successful graphite transfer onto the cotton surface. However, it's equally important to be cautious, as excessive pressure can unintentionally transfer surplus graphite onto the watercolor paper, causing undesired smudges or lines.

Grid Method

1. Divide both the original image and the blank watercolor paper into a grid of equal squares. For example, if the original image has a 4x4 grid, replicate the same grid on the blank paper.
2. Reproduce the image within each reference square onto the corresponding square on your watercolor paper. Focus on one square at a time to maintain proportions.

Pros and Cons: The grid method is effective for enlarging or reducing an image. However, it requires a significant amount of erasing due to extra pencil marks for the grid itself, which may damage your watercolor surface. To mitigate this, use a light touch while creating the outlines.

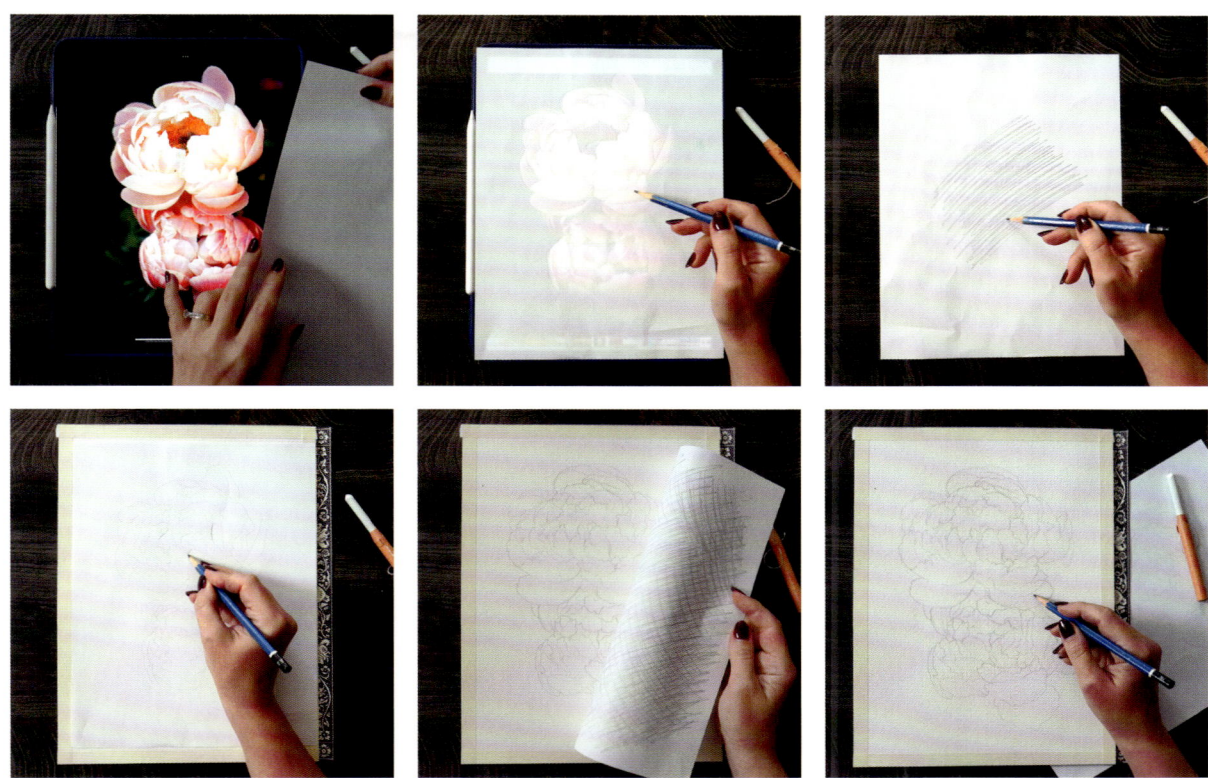

My Favorite Tracing Method Step-by-Step

My Favorite Method (Using a Printer)

Materials Needed: Printer (color or black and white), image to be traced, watercolor paper, masking tape, two graphite pencils (soft and hard), and a soft eraser.

Step-by-Step

1. Print an image you want to trace on regular white printer paper.
2. Flip the paper over so the printed side is facing down. Cover the entire area on the back of the paper with a pencil, ensuring even coverage. Use medium-staining graphite (2B–4B) to avoid leaving excessive smudges on watercolor paper.
3. Place your image on the watercolor paper with the printed side facing up. Secure it with tape or clips to prevent movement.
4. Using a sharp pencil or stylus, trace the outlines of the image on the front side of the paper. The applied graphite on the back will transfer the image onto the watercolor paper. Focus on capturing only the main outlines and basic proportions. The details can be added later!
5. Remove the printed image and clean up the lines using a soft eraser. You can add extra details and subtle shading at this stage, using a hard graphite pencil (2H or 4H).

My Favorite Method (Using an iPad)

Instead of a printed reference, you can use your iPad screen to trace any image (or part of the image) you want to paint.

Step-by-Step

1. Choose the image you want to trace on your iPad. Make sure the brightness is adjusted so you can clearly see the details. You may want to dim the lights in your room.
2. "Lock" the view using the "Guided Access" feature on your iPad to prevent accidental movement of the image on screen:
   a. *Turn on Guided Access:* Go to Settings > Accessibility > Guided Access.
   b. *Lock the Screen:* Open the image you want to trace. Triple-click the side (or Home) button to start a Guided Access session. Your iPad screen will now stay on the image you opened. It won't respond to touches or switch to another app until you end the session by triple-clicking the side (or Home) button again.

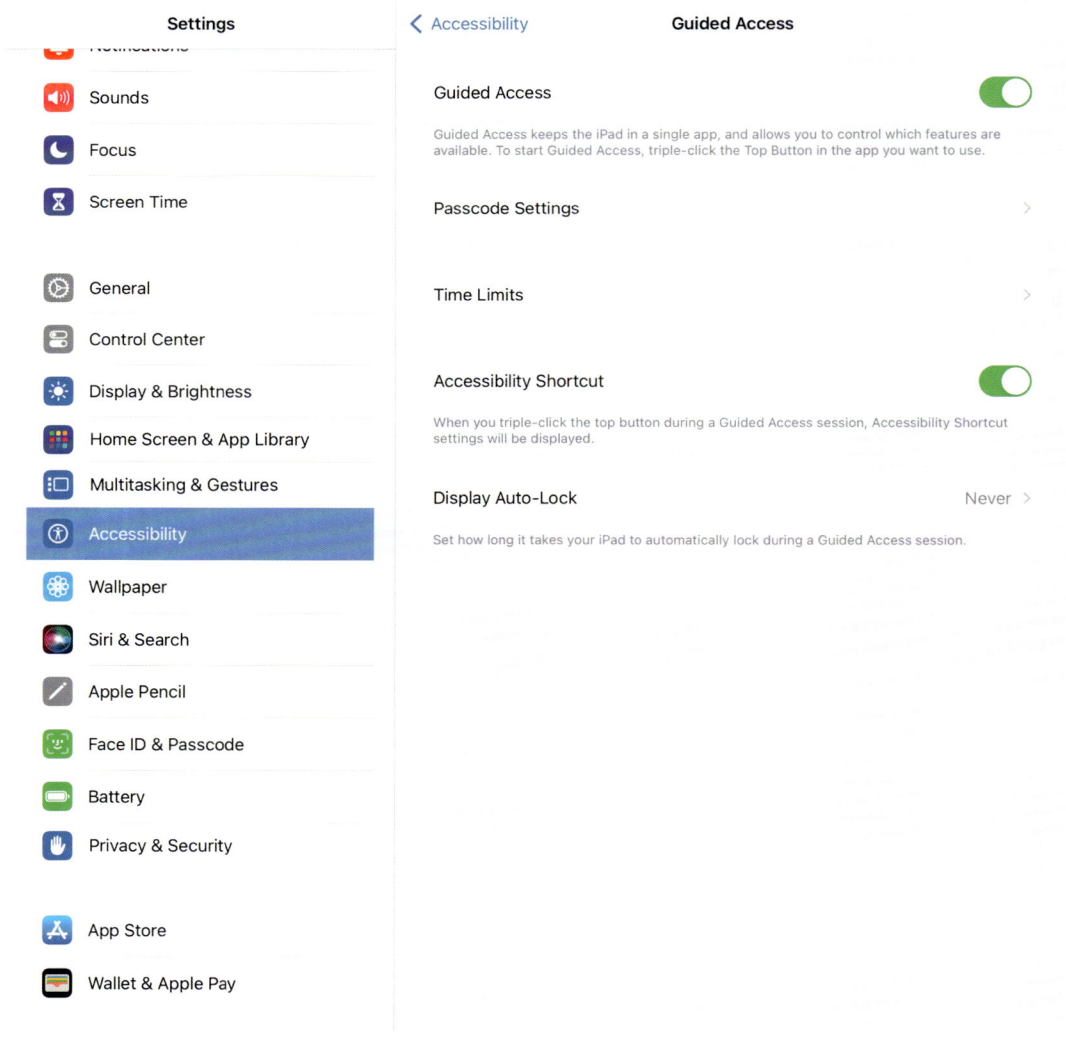

3. Place regular (not watercolor quality) white paper over the iPad screen. Printer stock works well for this method. Secure your paper with masking tape.

4. Carefully trace the outlines of the image onto the paper using any graphite pencil. Apply gentle pressure to avoid damaging the iPad screen.

5. Once you've completed tracing, lift one corner of the paper to ensure you've captured all necessary details. If not, carefully lift and reposition the paper to continue tracing.

6. Follow the rest of the steps as described in the Printer Method on page 179.

Video Available ▶ **rockynook.com/watercolor-secrets**

8

Composition Secrets

8.1 Introduction

As someone who loves creating intricate compositions, I spend my days thinking about how to blend colors and shapes in a way that's visually captivating. You might recognize my work for its detailed birds and flowers, often mixing references to create something unique. You might have even seen my designs on Canadian money or book covers at your local store.

In this chapter, I'll share some of my favorite tips for crafting these complex compositions. We'll dive into some basic theory, exploring concepts like rhythm, movement, and color harmony. I will also discuss the key influences that I rely on when looking for composition inspiration: Ukrainian folk art and the Gongbi style of Chinese watercolor. Plus, I'll give you a list of easy-to-access image sources that won't land you in copyright trouble.

You don't need to possess a mastery of watercolor to get started. In fact, it was through experimenting with arrangements of my beloved flowers that I first acquainted myself with the medium, long before my professional illustration career took flight. Due to their forgiving nature, organic forms always seem to look good together, no matter your skill level. From there, I gradually added birds, animals, and even people to my compositions. Wherever you begin, crafting compositions promises to be an immensely gratifying journey, complementing your learning adventure in any artistic medium.

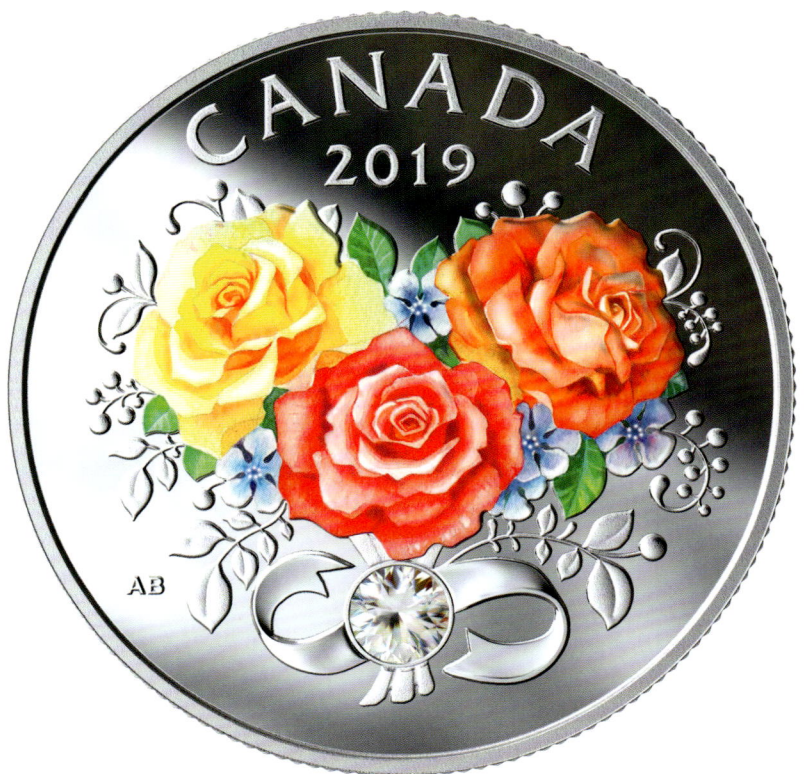

2019 "Celebration of Love" Canadian Silver Coin Design Featuring Watercolor Roses
Coin image and concept/final drawing © 2024 Royal Canadian Mint. All rights reserved / Image de la pièce et dessins préliminaires et définitifs © 2024 Monnaie royale canadienne. Tous droits réservés

8.2 Composition Structures (And How to Avoid Boring Ones)

Composition structure serves as the backbone of our artwork, dictating how elements are arranged within the frame. While traditional symmetrical and centered compositions have their place, they can often fall flat, lacking the energy and intrigue needed to captivate the viewer. To breathe life into your watercolor compositions, it's essential to explore alternative structures that embrace asymmetry, movement, and unexpected shapes. In this section, I will share my favorite arrangements that help me avoid the trap of boredom in my watercolor explorations.

Static Structures

In the beginning of my art journey, I preferred the safety of static shapes, always relying on the boundaries of my paper to dictate the arrangement of my reference images. As you can see in the image shown here, *The Year of the Horse*, placing my main subjects directly in the center of the frame resulted in rather predictable, albeit balanced, artwork. For the longest time, I favored these types of symmetrical structures for their sense of stability and order. Eventually I realized that while balance is essential, it doesn't necessarily equate to perfect symmetry. In fact, unbalanced compositions can often be more visually interesting, creating tension and dynamism that draw the viewer in. Over time, I learned to break free from the constraints of static structures and unlocked a world of creative possibilities that breathed new life into my compositions.

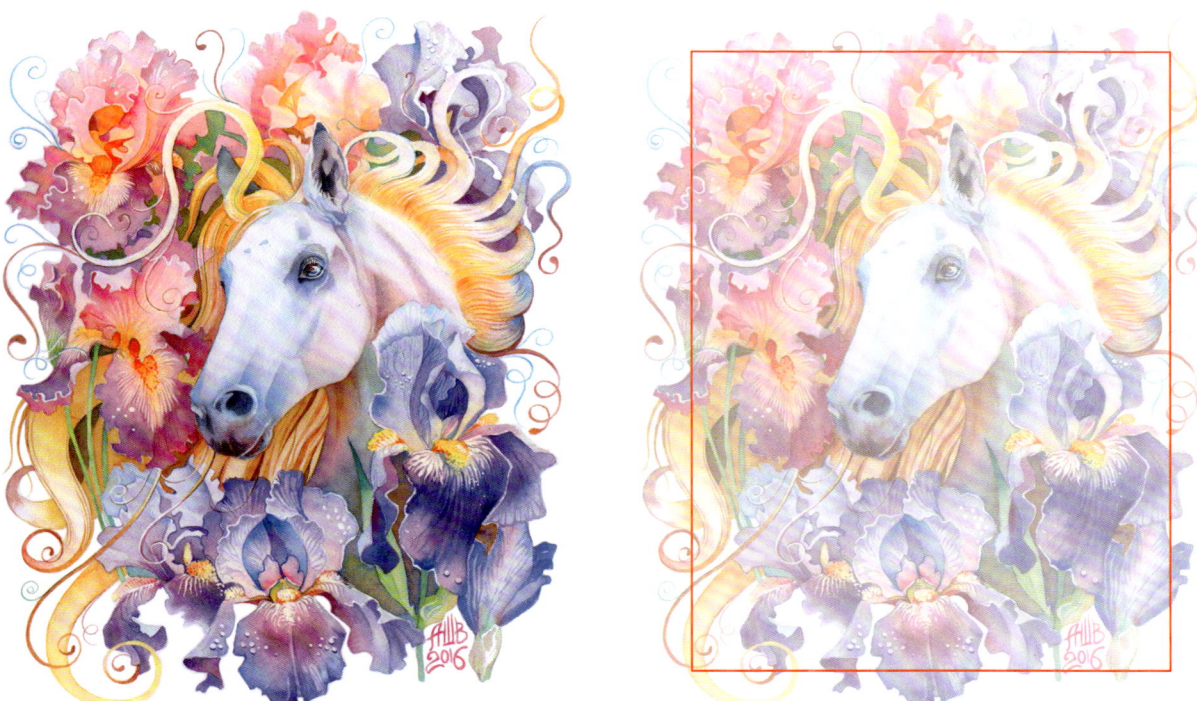

12 Zodiacs: Year of the Horse (rectangular-shaped composition structure)

Dynamic Structures

One effective way to break out of the boredom of traditional composition structures is to explore different shapes within the frame. Instead of confining your subjects to rectangular boundaries, consider incorporating circular, triangular, or irregular shapes that add visual interest and complexity to the composition. For example, arranging elements in a circular pattern can create a strong sense of movement and flow, while a triangular composition can convey stability and balance with a hint of tension.

Dynamic Structures: Heart

One of my favorite composition shapes is an upside-down triangle or a heart. It offers the familiar safety of a symmetrical arrangement on top, while creating a stronger sense of vertical movement toward the bottom than a traditional rectangular shape. You can recognize it in this painting of two doves.

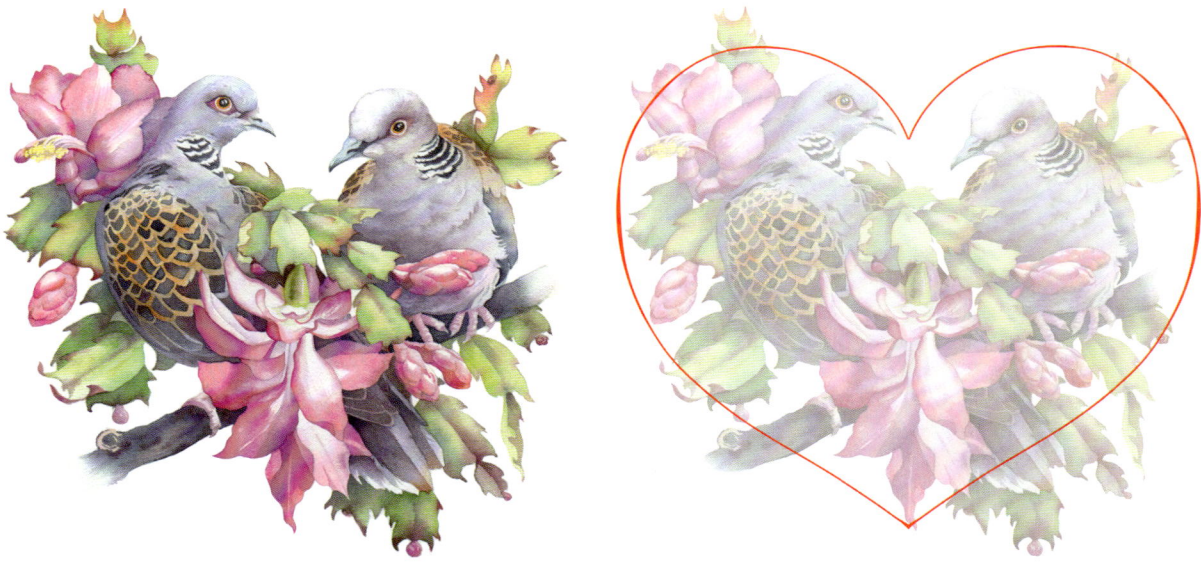

Two Turtle Doves (heart-shaped composition structure)

Dynamic Structures: Triangle

Instead of settling for traditional shapes, consider more asymmetrical structures. For example, triangular compositions offer a more dynamic alternative to rectangles, providing a sense of stability and balance with a hint of tension. I like to arrange elements in a triangular formation, enticing viewers to explore the interplay between the elements.

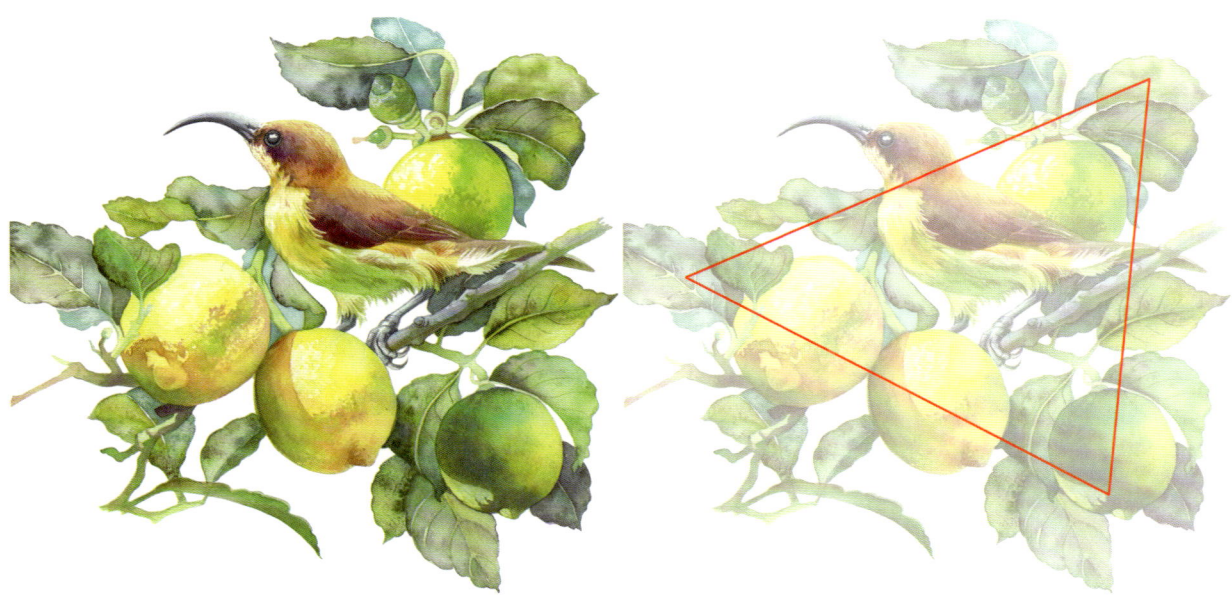

Sunbird and Lemons (triangular-shaped composition structure)

Dynamic Structures: X-Shape

I often introduce an X shape as an underlying structure for my rectangular canvases. By strategically positioning my elements on the opposing ends of the imaginary cross, I am able to inject a sense of tension and movement into my work, keeping viewers engaged and intrigued. Note that the objects are often paired in terms of their shapes and colors, creating visual pathways that lead the viewer on a journey of discovery across the two diagonal lines that meet in the middle.

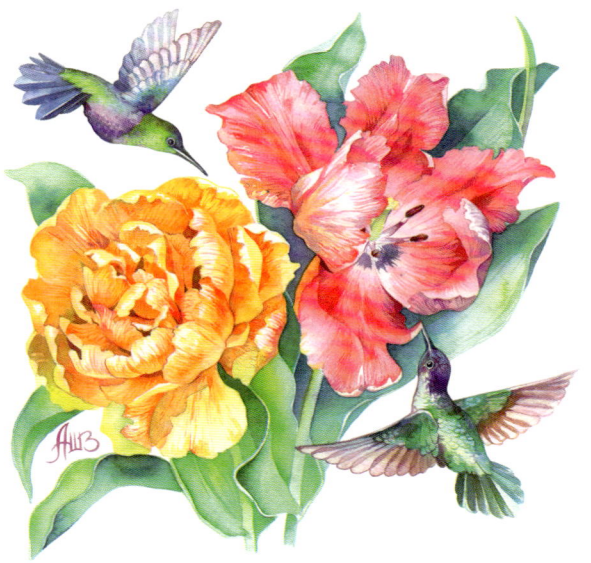
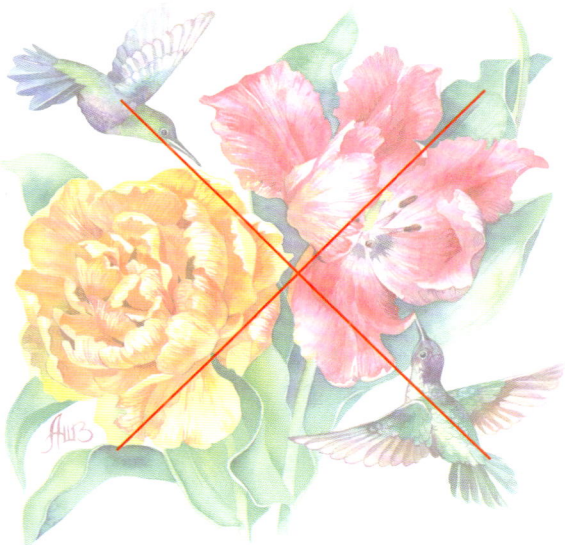

8.3 Movement in Composition

When designing my compositions, I often focus on the dominant sense of movement. Whether it's a gentle sway or a dynamic leap across the canvas, movement injects energy into my pieces, making them more compelling and memorable. Understanding how to harness movement can transform a static image into a dynamic experience, captivating the viewer and imbuing your artwork with life. Let's delve into why movement is crucial in composition and explore some examples using natural subjects.

Compelling Story

Finding a clear sense of movement helps me direct the viewer's gaze and control the visual narrative. It establishes a sense of progression, leading the eye from one element to another in a deliberate sequence, like a silent conductor. By strategically placing elements to create pathways or rhythms, you can orchestrate the viewer's journey through the artwork, ensuring they observe and interpret it as intended.

Visual Interest

Movement adds vitality and interest to a composition, preventing it from appearing stagnant or lifeless. It introduces a dynamic quality that engages the viewer's imagination, inviting them to explore the artwork actively.

Examples of Movement in Composition

- **Subtle Movement:** In a still-life composition, the arrangement of objects in a diagonal formation can lead the viewer's gaze from the foreground to the background, creating a sense of depth and movement within the frame.
- **Moderate Movement:** In a landscape painting, the gentle curve of a river winding through the scene will guide the viewer's eye toward the distant horizon, creating a sense of tranquility and continuity.
- **Bold Movement:** In an abstract painting, bold, sweeping brushstrokes in vibrant colors will help you add a sense of kinetic energy, transforming the canvas into a whirlwind of motion and emotion.

HELPFUL TIP

The boundary of your canvas may suggest the right direction for the structure of your scene and the movement within it. For example, a round canvas typically calls for a circular movement. Therefore, when painting within a circle, as I do for my coin designs, I often arrange individual elements in a spiral. On the other hand, when working within the boundaries of a rectangle, I often use the rule of thirds and position my shapes to reach for one of the tension points. When unsure about the right direction, I simply position my subjects to "reach for the sun," directing the gaze or an open flower crown toward the source of light.

In this example, the positioning of the bird reaching for pomegranates offers an excellent opportunity to utilize movement in composition to create a dynamic and engaging visual narrative.

- The elongated body of blue feathers creates a sense of stretching and reaching, suggesting dynamic motion within the stillness of the scene. The bird's extended neck conveys a sense of anticipation and action, as if it is in the midst of a graceful movement toward its desired destination.

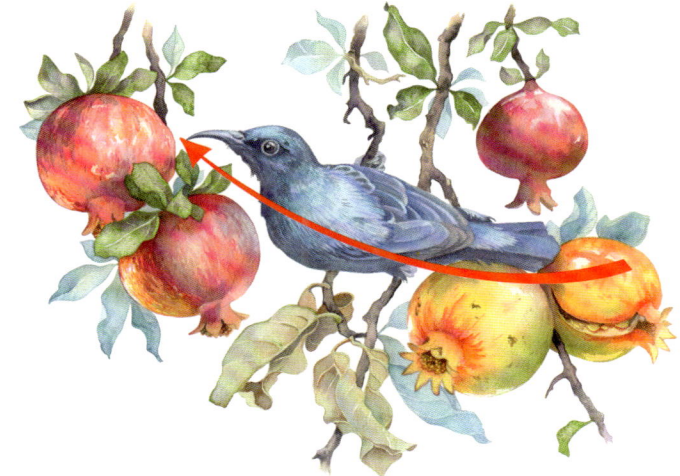

Blue Bird and Pomegranates

- The placement of shapes introduces a natural pathway for the viewer's eye to follow. The positioning of the fruit, combined with the bird's elongated form, guides the viewer's gaze from the center of the composition, where the bird is perched, to the top left, where the pomegranates hang tantalizingly out of reach. This visual journey mimics the bird's own movement as it navigates through the space, creating a seamless flow of energy from one point to another.
- The contrast between the vibrant blue plumage of the bird and the rich red hue of the pomegranates adds visual interest and emphasis to the focal point of the composition. The bright, saturated colors draw the viewer's attention toward the interaction between the bird and the fruit, highlighting the moment of connection between the natural elements.

In this scene, I added a sense of motion through the careful arrangement of elements and the strategic use of color that was not present in the original reference.

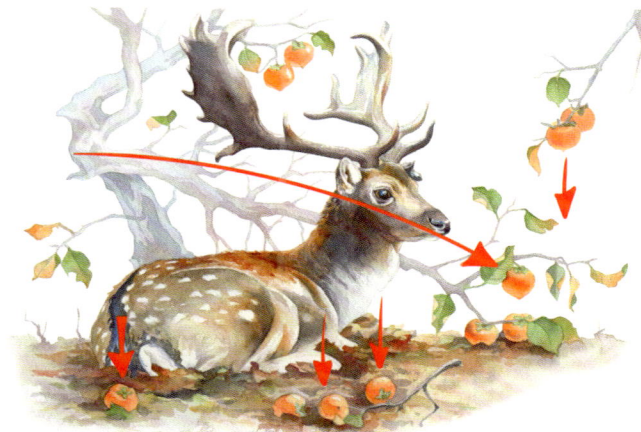

Deer and Persimmons

- To complement the deer resting in the foreground, I included a distant tree with ripe persimmons. This diagonal line created by the tree leads the viewer's gaze from one corner of the canvas to another, creating a sense of fluid motion from left to right.
- In addition, I placed several ripe persimmons on the ground, suggesting another type of motion— the fallen ripe fruit. These bright color accents echo the warm highlights on the animal and draw the viewer's eye toward them, encouraging further exploration.
- As a result of this subtle diagonal motion created by the branches, and the vibrant fruit shapes sprinkled strategically throughout, the artwork feels more alive, inviting the viewer to immerse themselves in the scene and experience the beauty of nature in motion.

8.4 Creating a Strong Focal Point

One of the most important aspects of composition is creating a strong focal point that draws the viewer's attention and anchors the entire artwork. By employing techniques such as color contrast, placement, size and scale, and leading lines, artists can effectively draw attention to the focal point and guide the viewer's gaze through the composition. In this section, I will demonstrate some of my favorite techniques for creating a powerful focal point that commands attention and captivates the viewer.

Positioning: Central

The most basic way to create a focal point is to position your main subject in the center of the composition. The downside of this approach is that it can feel quite static and even boring. For example, in this painting called *The Year of the Sheep*, from my *12 Zodiacs* series, I positioned the sheep exactly in the middle of the rectangular block of flowers.

12 Zodiacs: Year of the Sheep

Positioning: The Rule of Thirds

Instead of placing your focal point directly in the middle of the canvas, consider alternative approaches. For example, the rule of thirds is a useful guideline to follow, where you place the focal point at one of the intersections of the imaginary grid lines. This off-center placement adds visual interest and creates a more dynamic composition.

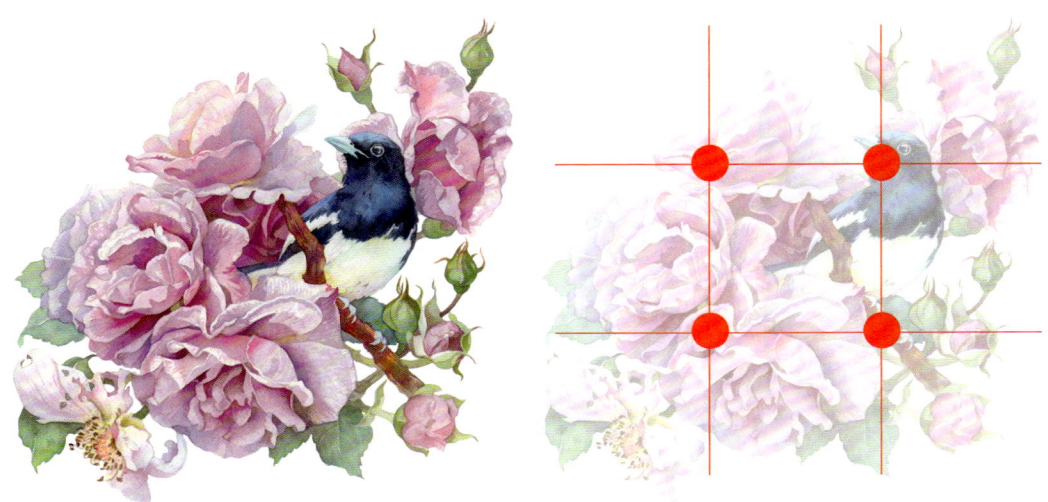

Magpie and Violet Roses

Contrast

You can amplify the contrast in value, color, or texture to make your focal point pop against the surrounding elements. My favorite way to create this effect is by placing a colorful element next to more muted objects. In this composition, I applied this principle in reverse, placing a dark blue butterfly amid a sea of vibrant red poppies.

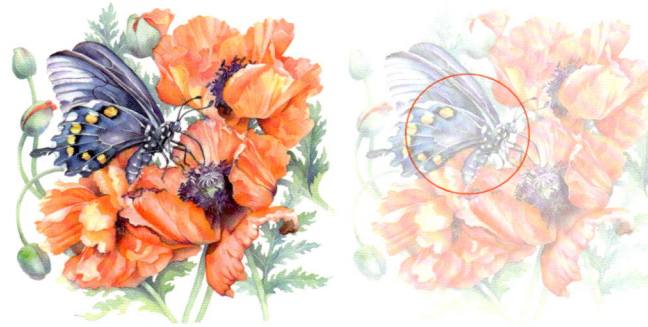

Butterfly and Red Poppies

Size and Scale

Make your focal point larger or more detailed than other elements in the composition to emphasize its importance. By increasing the size or scale of your focal point, you can ensure that it commands attention and dominates the composition. In this example, I made my dragonfly extra-large compared to the sweet pea flowers. By adding a generous amount of white space around the insect I was able to create additional contrast and emphasize the importance of this element in the composition.

Leading Lines

By incorporating leading lines, such as converging diagonal lines, you can create a visual pathway that guides the viewer's gaze directly to the focal point. In this illustration, the large pink flower in the center is my focal point, while the two doves are turning their heads in a way that

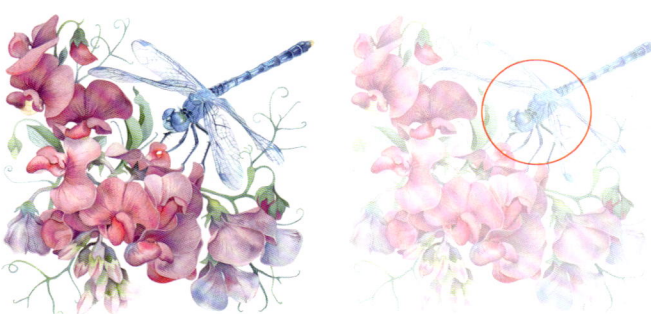

Dragonfly and Sweet Pea Flowers

reinforces the overall movement toward this point. The first dove is looking straight at the viewer with a sense of welcoming curiosity. This bird is inviting us to enter the world of the illustration and engage with the subject matter. Meanwhile, the second dove is focused intently on a vibrant pink flower nestled within the bush. By directing its gaze toward the petals, this bird draws the viewer's attention downward,

creating a natural sense of movement and progression. As the viewer's gaze follows the line of sight from the first bird toward the second, they are guided along a visual journey that culminates in the intricate details of the cactus flower. This progression from left to right, and then downward, creates a sense of narrative flow, leading the viewer through a logical sequence of exploration and discovery within the scene.

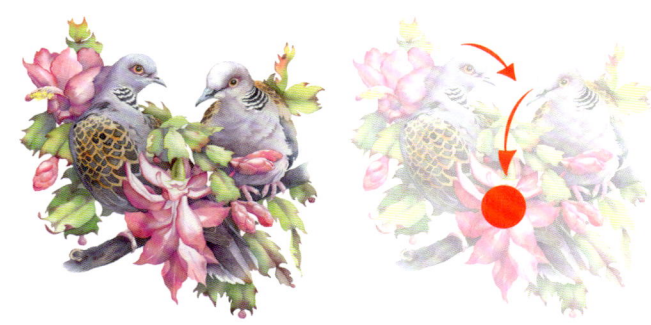

Two Turtle Doves

8.5 How to Use Gaze and Gestures in Composition

Movement in composition isn't limited to physical objects or shapes in motion; it can also be conveyed through gaze (if you are painting humans, animals, or birds), and even hand gestures (if you have a human subject). When painting living subjects, I always try incorporate the eyes and body movements into the composition to direct the viewer's attention toward specific focal points or areas of interest, and to create a better sense of narrative within my artwork. In this section, I will mention a few familiar examples of classic artists strategically orienting their subjects to guide the viewer through the visual story. I will also share several of my own studies featuring birds—my favorite subject.

Classic Examples of Gaze and Body Gestures in Composition

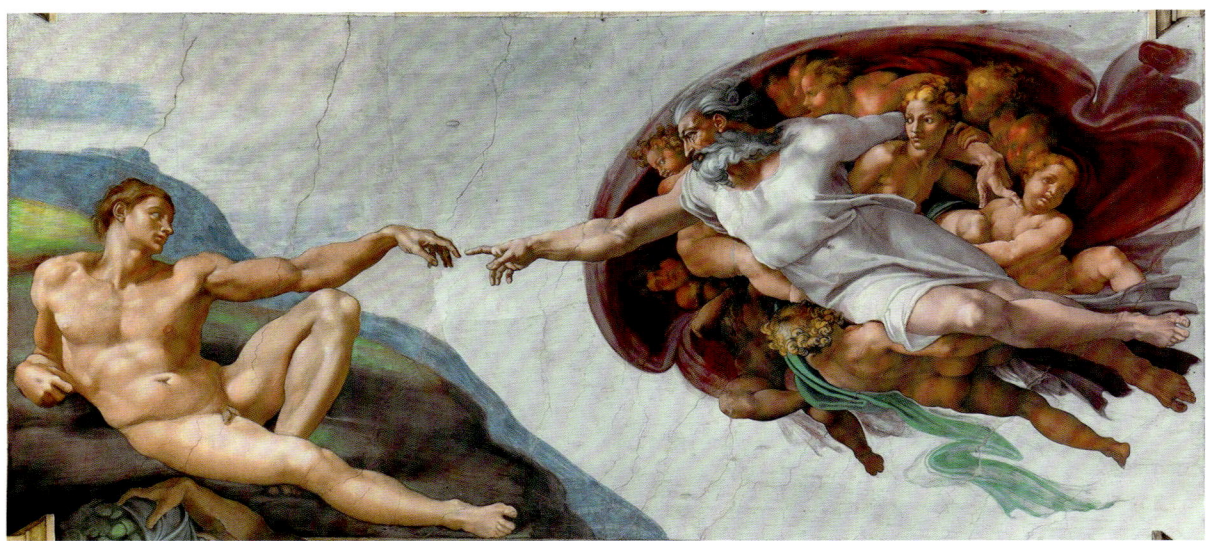

Michelangelo, *The Creation of Adam* (c. 1508–1512)

In Michelangelo's *The Creation of Adam* (c. 1508–1512) from the Sistine Chapel ceiling, the dynamic movement and hand gestures convey the biblical narrative with profound intensity. God's commanding gesture, depicted through an outstretched arm and open hand, imparts life to Adam, whose slightly bent arm and receptive hand mirror God's action with eager anticipation. The interplay between their gestures creates a sense of tension and drama, drawing viewers' gaze toward the focal point where the divine touch meets human receptivity, inviting contemplation on the mysteries of creation and the relationship between humanity and the divine.

In Johannes Vermeer's iconic painting *Girl with a Pearl Earring* (c. 1665), the young girl's gaze is directed toward the viewer with an intensity that is both captivating and intimate. The slight turn of her head and the tilt of

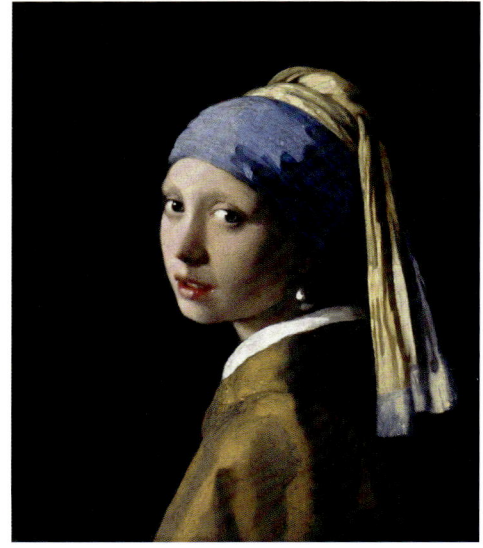

Johannes Vermeer, *Girl with a Pearl Earring* (c. 1665)

her body suggest a moment of pause, as if she has been caught in the midst of a private reverie. By positioning her gaze directly toward the viewer, the artist establishes a connection that transcends time and space, inviting us to share in the quiet contemplation of the moment.

HELPFUL TIPS

Have you ever noticed that you attention is always drawn toward faces, more specifically eyes, even when there are other more vibrant objects within the same composition? Indeed, the eyes are often the focal point of human connection and emotional expression, making them a natural starting point for the viewer's visual journey. Whether it's a portrait, a depiction of an animal, or even inanimate objects, our innate tendency is to gravitate toward the eyes first, seeking cues for understanding and empathy. Therefore, try to be mindful of this aspect and strategically position the eyes of your subjects to initiate the narrative unfolding within your artwork.

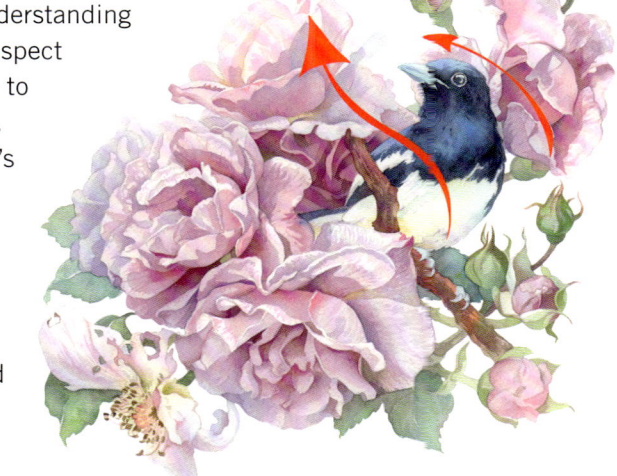

When considering the gaze of your subjects, it's essential to think about their line of sight and how it interacts with the surrounding environment. For instance, in this example, the bird is positioned on the right side of the painting, with its head turned toward the sun and the beautiful roses on the left. The juxtaposition of the bird's gaze toward the roses and the sun creates a sense of harmony and balance, emphasizing the interplay between natural elements and inviting contemplation on the cyclical rhythms of life. Note that if the bird's head were turned toward the right, away from the roses and outside the boundaries of the canvas, it would disrupt the flow of the composition and detract from the overall narrative coherence. In such a case, the viewer's gaze would follow the bird's line of sight out of the frame, resulting in a disjointed viewing experience and a missed opportunity to engage with the focal points of the artwork.

Magpie and Violet Roses

In this scenario, the positioning of the birds' heads not only influences the viewer's visual journey within the composition, but also establishes a connection between the elements within the scene. The birds' gaze serves as a visual cue, drawing attention to the roses and inviting the viewer to pause and appreciate their beauty before following the trajectory upward and toward the source of light. The eyes create a natural pathway that guides the viewers seamlessly through the artwork: starting at the bottom right and culminating with the top flower.

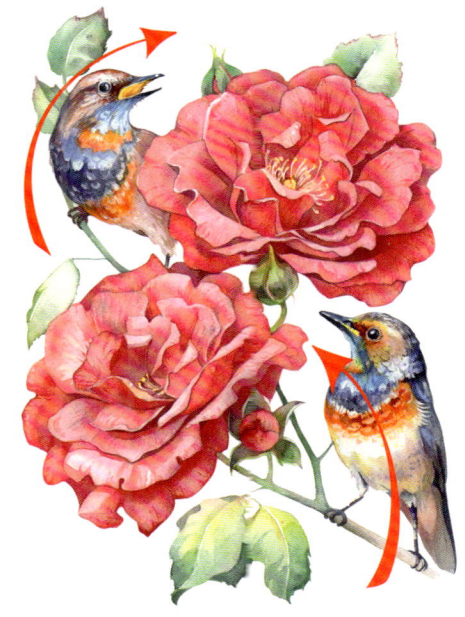

Bluethroat Birds and Red Roses

8.6 Finding Visual Rhythm

Visual rhythm, defined by the repetition or variation of elements within an artwork, is another interesting technique I often employ in my compositions. By repeating or varying elements such as shapes, colors, lines, and textures, you can add depth and interest to the composition and establish patterns that lead the viewer's eye on a journey through the painting. Similar to musical rhythm, this visual rhythm can create a sense of harmony, balance, and unity in a composition. In this section, we'll explore the concept of visual rhythm in watercolor painting and provide recommendations for incorporating it into compositions featuring landscapes, botanicals, and other natural subjects.

Examples of Visual Rhythm in Composition

- **Repetition of Motifs:** Choose a dominant motif or element from your natural subject, such as a leaf, flower, or tree, and repeat it throughout the composition. Vary the size, orientation, and placement of the motif to create visual interest. For example, in a landscape painting featuring trees, repeating the silhouette of tree branches across the composition can establish a rhythmic pattern that draws the viewer's eye from one tree to another.
- **Layering and Overlapping:** Experiment with layering and overlapping elements within the composition to create depth and complexity. Allow shapes and colors to intersect and interact with each other, creating visual harmony and movement. For instance, in a botanical painting of flowers, overlapping petals and leaves can create a sense of depth and rhythm, guiding the viewer's gaze through the intricate details of the floral arrangement.
- **Contrast and Variation:** Introduce contrast and variation into your composition to create visual tension and excitement. Play with complementary colors, contrasting textures, and varied brushwork to add interest and depth to the painting. For example, in a landscape featuring a river, contrasting the smooth, flowing lines of the water with the jagged edges of rocks or foliage along the banks can create a sense of rhythm and movement that enlivens the scene.

In a festive holiday painting, a majestic partridge bird perches gracefully amid the lush foliage of a pear tree. Here, I employed two distinct pigments to render the foliage: some leaves are delicately painted using transparent Aqua Green (Phthalo), while others are depicted with a granulating Green Apatite Genuine (mineral). The interplay of these two textures creates a mesmerizing visual rhythm that echoes throughout the composition, framing the fruits and the bird. The smooth Aqua Green leaves exude a sense of lightness and airiness, their translucent quality adding depth and dimension to the painting. In contrast, the granulating Green Apatite Genuine leaves have a rough and tactile texture, their vibrant pigments settling into the paper in a mesmerizing display of organic beauty. In addition, the viewer's eyes are drawn into a rhythmic dance of feathers on the birds neck and wings. This rhythmic interplay of light and dark marks adds visual complexity to the painting and also serves to highlight the partridge as a focal point of the composition.

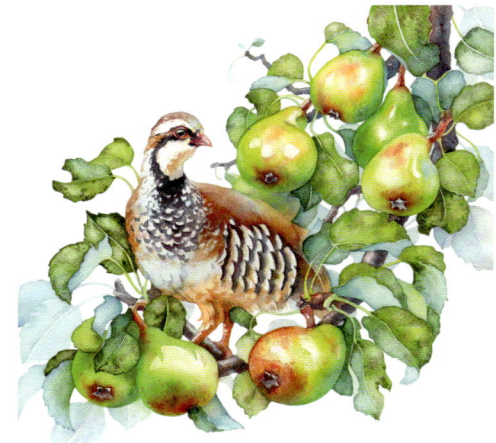

Partridge in a Pear Tree

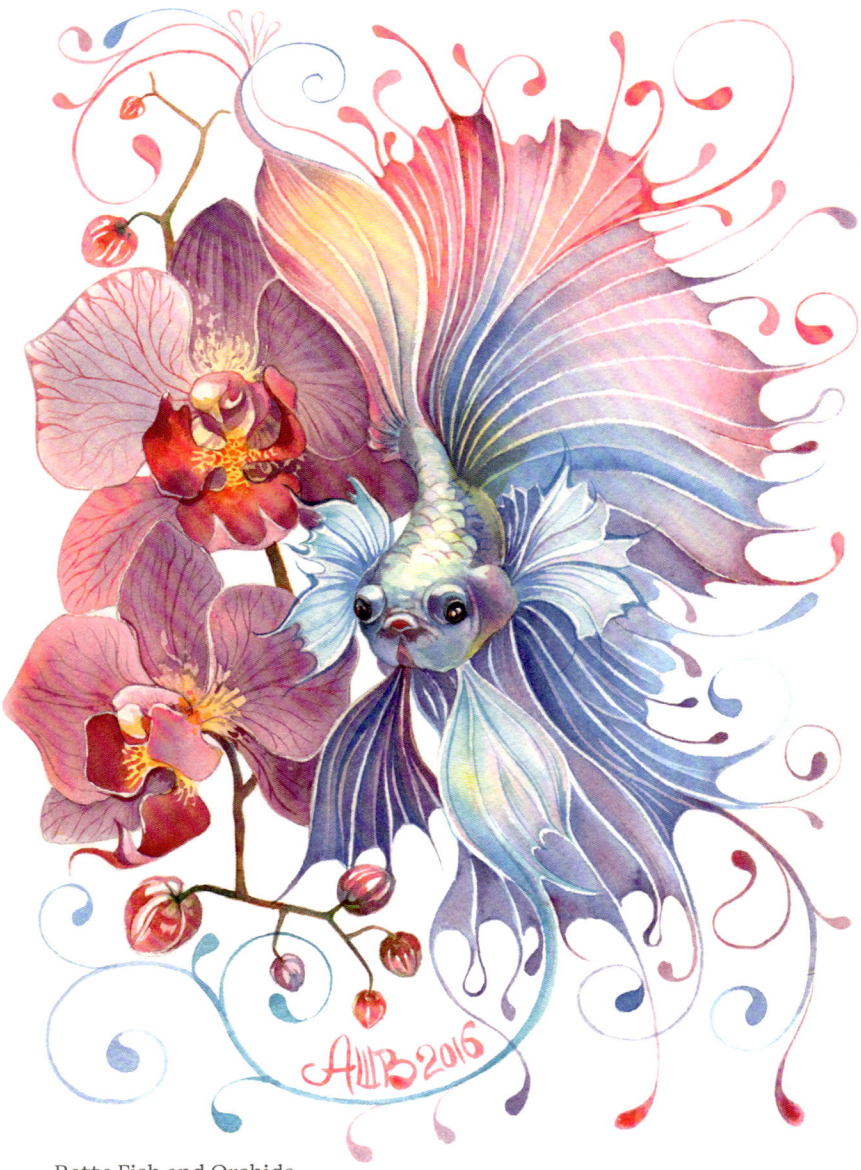

Betta Fish and Orchids

In this surreal scene, I painted a vibrant Betta fighting fish gracefully swimming alongside an elegant orchid branch. Notice how the intricate lines adorning the flowing fins echo the delicate veins of the orchid flower, establishing a rhythmic pattern that guides the viewer's eyes through the composition. As the viewer admires the fluid movement of the fish, their gaze is drawn to the intricate details of the orchid branch, where they discover a subtle yet captivating contrast in size. While the lines on the fish are bold and pronounced, mirroring the strength and agility of the creature, the lines on the orchid are delicate and refined, reflecting the fragile beauty of the flower. This juxtaposition of size and form creates a harmonious interplay between the two subjects as their shared shapes and lines intertwine to create a sense of unity and balance within the composition.

8.7 Mixing References and Matching Light

In the process of designing compositions, I often find myself exploring multiple reference images, seeking inspiration and experimenting with different combinations to achieve the desired visual impact. While this approach may seem daunting at first, it offers a wealth of opportunities for creativity and innovation. In this section, we'll delve into the process of designing compositions featuring multiple reference images, discussing the importance of testing different scenarios and matching the lighting condition to achieve a sense of realism.

Test Different Scenarios

When designing compositions with multiple reference images, it's crucial to start by testing different scenarios to explore various possibilities. Begin with a simple study, perhaps a thumbnail sketch featuring a limited number of elements, such as mushrooms in a forest setting. You can go as far as applying color and rendering some of the elements if this helps your creative process. This initial study serves as a foundation, allowing you to experiment with different arrangements and combinations before committing to a final composition.

Mix and Match Elements

As you progress, don't be afraid to mix and match elements from different reference images to create a more visually rich composition. For example, in depicting a fall forest scene, you may start with mushrooms as the focal point, but then decide to add additional organic elements, such as chestnuts or ferns, to enhance the complexity and interest of the composition. As you develop your study further, consider incorporating unexpected elements, like an animal or a bird, to add a playful and whimsical touch to the scene.

Match the Direction of Light

In the process of designing compositions with multiple reference images, one crucial aspect that often goes overlooked is the importance of light and ensuring consistency in its direction across all elements. Matching the direction of light in your references is essential for maintaining a sense of realism and coherence within the composition. If one object is illuminated from the top left, it's imperative to ensure that all additional objects are also illuminated from the same angle. Mismatched highlights and shadows can instantly disrupt the sense of realism and cohesion, detracting from the overall impact of the artwork. In some cases, achieving consistency in lighting can be as simple as flipping your reference image horizontally to match the desired angle of illumination.

Example: Fall Forest Composition Design Process

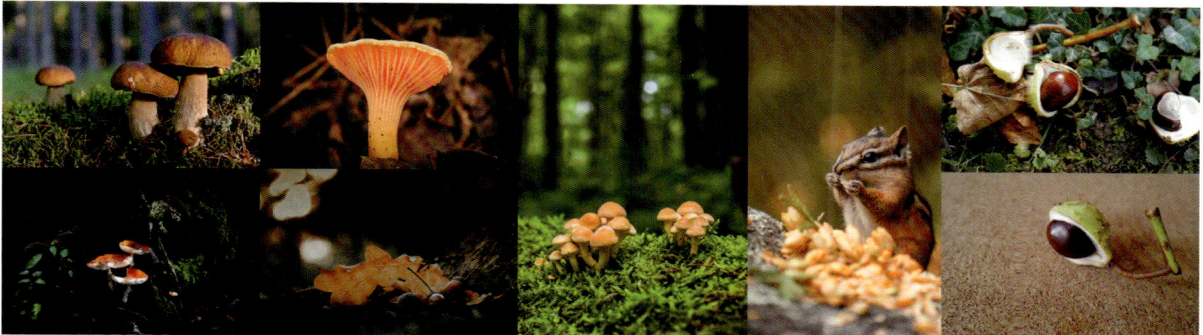

Source: Unsplash.com

In this exercise, I set out to create a magical forest composition using multiple reference images to capture the essence of the fall mood. What started as a simple watercolor study featuring a handful of mushrooms evolved into an elaborate scene with multiple plants and an animal.

I started with a sketchbook study featuring only the initial set of mushrooms that caught my eye. I also incorporated a snail—an image I've already reserved for another artwork. Although I was quite happy with the initial result, I wanted to explore the theme even further, gradually adding additional elements and drawing inspiration from different references.

In the next variation, I was able to incorporate ten different reference images, including various types of mushrooms, chestnuts, ferns, and even a chipmunk. While the process was satisfying, this composition felt somewhat complex and visually overwhelming.

In the final iteration, I opted for a square format and selected only the elements that are absolutely necessary to convey the essence of the scene: a few select mushrooms, including porcini and redcaps, strategically placed chestnuts at the bottom, and ferns that frame the background. This simplified version retains the visual richness of the forest while maintaining a better sense of balance.

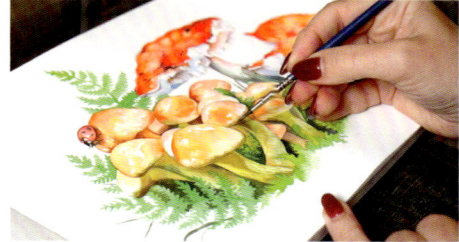

Autumn Forest (Sketchbook Exploration)

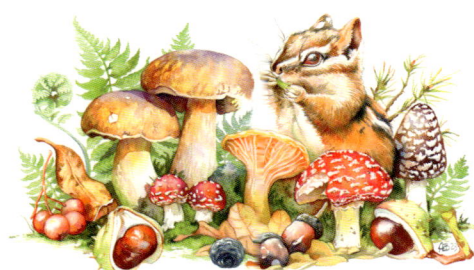

Autumn Forest (Horizontal Layout)

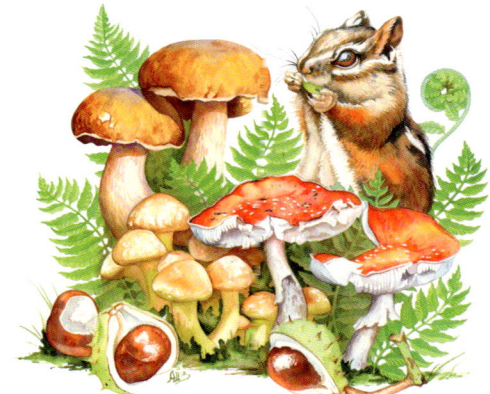

Autumn Forest (Square Layout)

8.8 Color Harmony and "Recycling" Your Palette

A cohesive palette can elevate your artwork from a collection of disparate elements to a unified masterpiece, creating visual cohesion and enhancing the overall impact of your composition. In this section, we'll delve into the importance of a cohesive palette and why recycling colors throughout your composition can be a useful tool for maintaining color continuity.

Examples of Cohesive Palettes

A cohesive palette refers to a harmonious selection of colors that work together seamlessly to create a unified visual experience. Traditional examples include:

- **Monochromatic Harmony:** A monochromatic palette utilizes variations of a single color, such as different shades of blue or green. By applying the same hue with varying levels of lightness and saturation, you can create a visually cohesive composition with a serene and unified atmosphere. While I rarely paint monochromatic compositions, these are incredibly useful as preliminary studies to help you understand the overall balance of values.
- **Analogous Color Scheme:** Analogous colors are adjacent to each other on the color wheel, such as red, orange, and yellow, or blue, green, and teal. By using different hues from within the same color family, you can achieve a harmonious palette that flows smoothly and naturally, creating a sense of unity and continuity.
- **Complementary Contrast:** Complementary colors are opposite each other on the color wheel, such as red and green, or blue and orange.

In the context of this orchid painting, the cohesive color palette guides the viewer's eye throughout the composition, allowing them to appreciate the intricate details and subtle nuances of the floral subject.

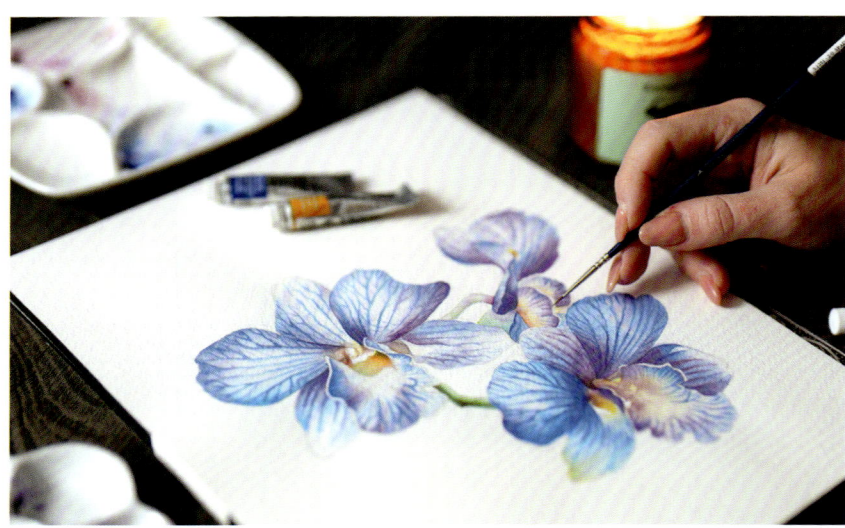

Blue Orchids Watercolor Study

I used various shades of blue, ranging from pale sky blue to vivid ultramarine, to establish the base color of the petals, while incorporating hints of purple and violet to add complexity and interest to the composition. These analogous colors blend together seamlessly, mimicking the natural variations and subtle transitions found in the petals of a real orchid.

How I "Recycle" My Palette

No matter what color palette I choose, I always try to sprinkle small accents of complementary hues throughout each composition. It's a subtle trick that goes a long way to help me create a sense of balance and establish continuity in my palette. This method of painting is particularly effective with watercolor medium because you can always glaze a thin layer of paint over multiple objects to bring them together visually. If you paint different objects by sticking to separate color schemes, the overall result can lack harmony and even look somewhat disjointed.

In this study, I recycled Quinacridone Burnt Scarlet (PR206) and Perylene Violet (PV29) by applying it on the berries and in the shadows on the bird feathers. In addition, I recycled the yellow color from the feathers to create a subtle glow on the green Monstera leaves. Repeating certain hues throughout the painting creates a harmonious rhythm that ties the elements together, fostering a more cohesive visual experience for the viewer.

In this example, I applied Quinacridone Red (PV19) on the bird in the center, then in the peony flowers on the right, and even on the tips of the green leaves sprinkled throughout the composition. A single vibrant pigment creates a visual echo that ties both sides of the composition together visually.

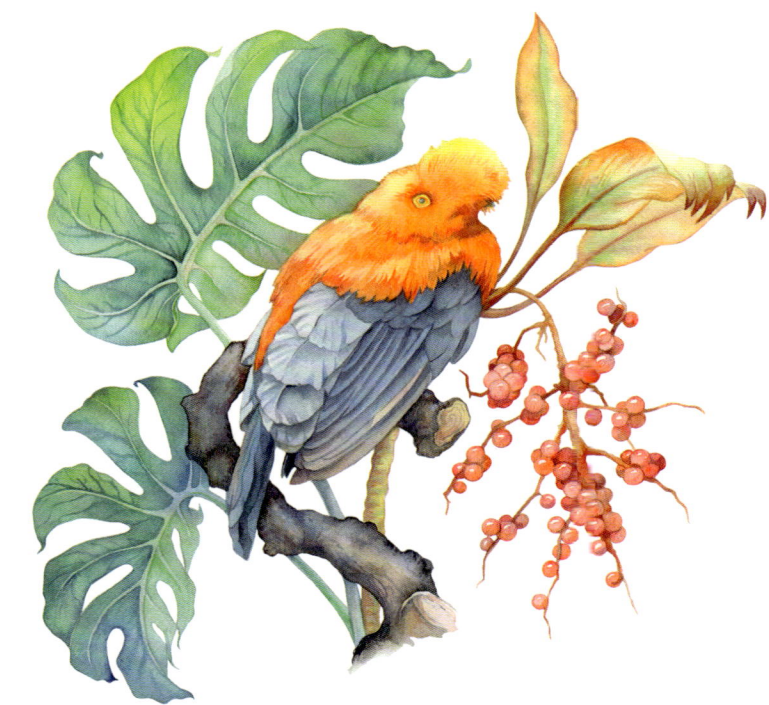

Tropical Forest

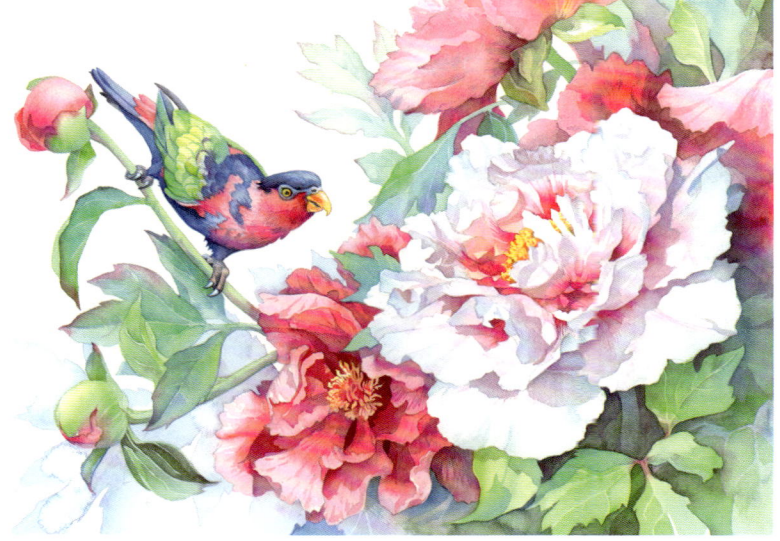

Parrot and Peony Flowers

8.9 Where to Find Composition Characters

As artists, we draw inspiration from the world around us. In this section, I'll explore various avenues for discovering reference images to fuel your creativity.

Personal Reference Photos

One of the most gratifying ways to gather reference images is by taking your own photographs. Whether it's a stunning landscape, a captivating still life, or a portrait of a loved one, your personal photos carry the authenticity and emotional connection that can elevate your artwork. I mostly take photos with my phone, organizing my subjects into distinct libraries that I can revisit at any time.

While my personal reference photos hold a special charm and authenticity, it's important to acknowledge that not every subject can be readily found in your immediate surroundings. Take, for instance, the fleeting beauty of flowers in my home country, Canada. With a short window of time between May and August when blooms are at their peak, capturing the perfect floral reference image becomes a race against time. I've learned to seize these moments, stocking up on images during this brief period to sustain my creative endeavors throughout the year.

My Favorite Sources of Copyright-Free Images

For subjects such as animals and human figures, relying solely on personal photography might not always be realistic. In such cases, I often turn to copyright-free databases to access a wider range of subjects and compositions. These resources not only provide a broader selection, but also ensure that I can explore diverse themes and styles beyond what my immediate surroundings may offer.

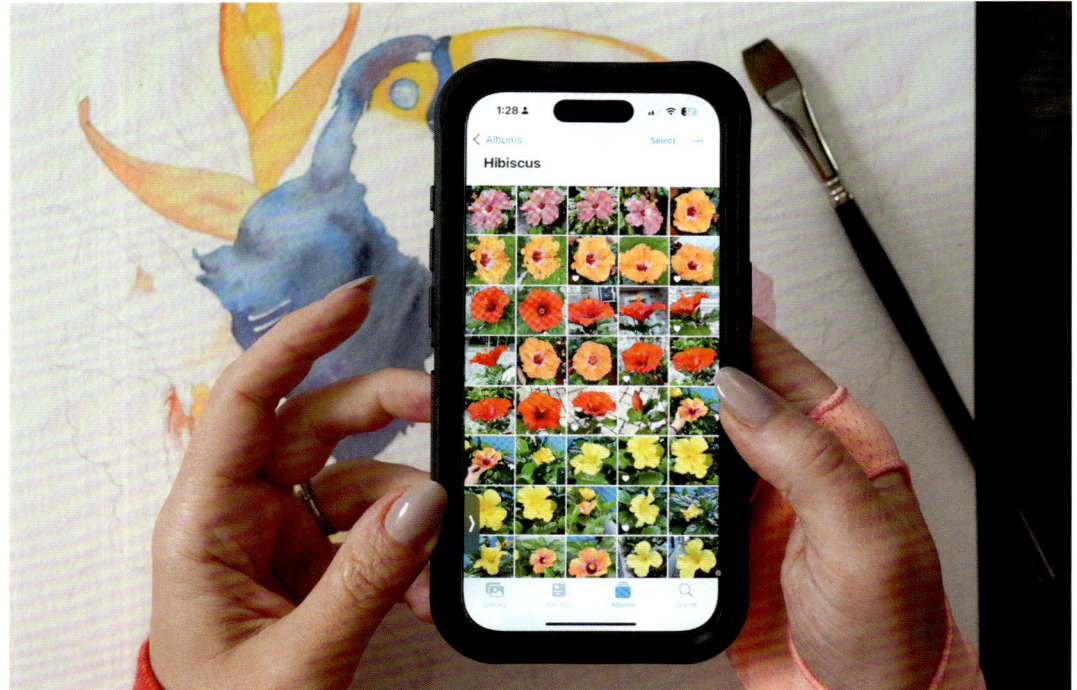

Reference Images on My Phone

- **Unsplash (https://unsplash.com/):** This website offers a vast collection of high-quality, royalty-free images across various genres, including landscapes, architecture, and portraiture.
- **Pixabay (https://pixabay.com/):** Another excellent source for royalty-free images spanning diverse categories such as nature, wildlife, and abstract compositions.
- **Wildlife Reference Photos for Artists (https://wildlifereferencephotos.com):** This family-run website offers a searchable database of affordable royalty-free wildlife photos.
- **Biodiversity Heritage Library (https://www.biodiversitylibrary.org/):** Ideal for botanical artists, this online repository boasts a rich collection of vintage botanical illustrations and scientific drawings.
- **The Metropolitan Museum of Art Open Access (https://www.metmuseum.org/):** This initiative grants free access to thousands of artworks from the Met's collection, perfect for historical references and figurative studies.
- **Wikimedia Commons (https://commons.wikimedia.org/):** A hub for freely usable media files, Wikimedia Commons houses a wide selection of images, illustrations, and diagrams suitable for artistic reference.
- **Life-Drawing Pose Reference Sites:** Websites like Line of Action (**https://line-of-action.com/**) and Quickposes (**https://quickposes.com**) offer timed gesture-drawing sessions and a variety of poses for figure studies.

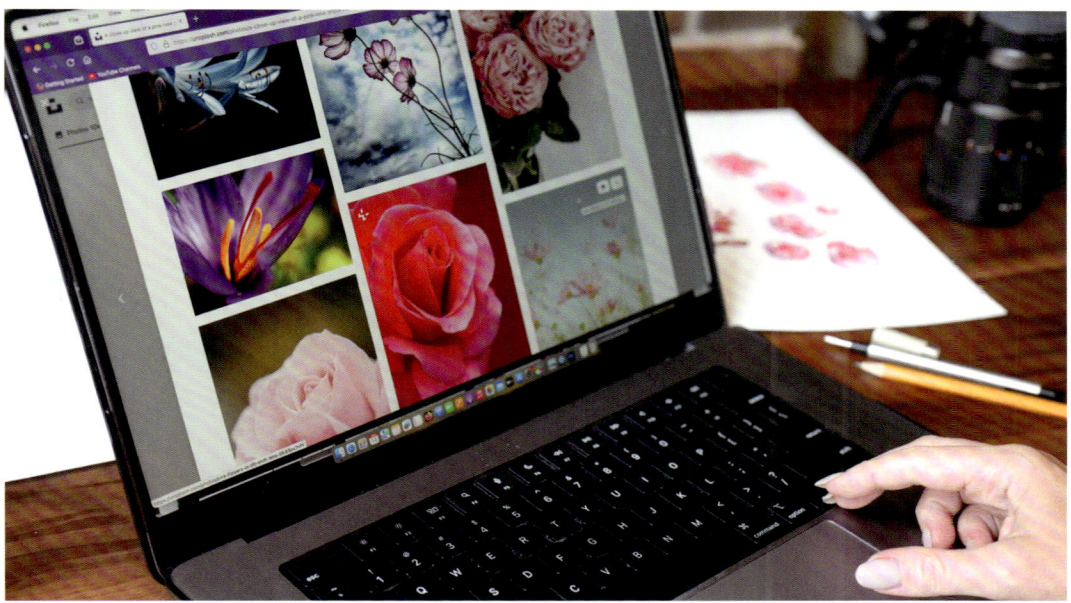

Unsplash.com is currently my favorite database for copyright-free images.

8.10 "Good" versus "Bad" References

Two of the most critical things to pay attention to when searching for watercolor references are the lighting conditions and the time of the day when the photo was taken. Whether you stage and photograph your own subjects or rely on royalty-free image sources, look for clear directional light that enhances depth and dimension. Avoid flat photos taken on a cloudy day and opt for well-lit references with clearly defined shadows because they will instantly translate into more realistic three-dimensional form on paper.

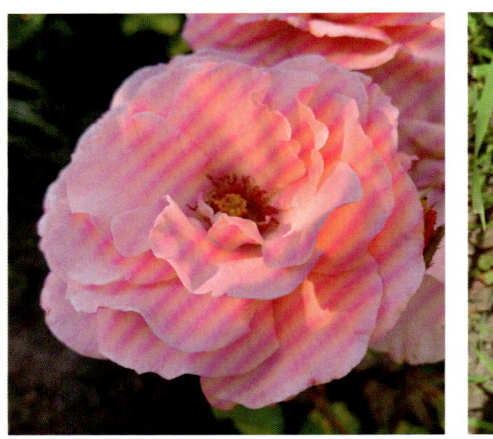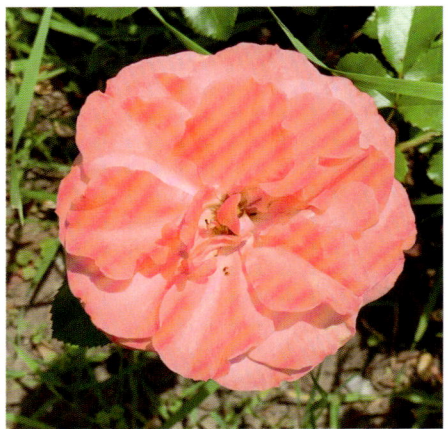

Pink rose photo taken during the golden hour versus the same flower reference taken around noon with direct light.

The Golden Hour

The "golden hour" is often considered the best time to take reference photos, especially when capturing botanical subjects, landscapes, and portraits. During this time period, which occurs shortly after sunrise or before sunset, the sun is positioned low on the horizon. Here's why this lighting condition is favorable for reference photos:

- **Soft, Directional Light:** The low shadows are more gradual and gentle, allowing for better visibility of forms and textures. The soft light also creates a more flattering effect for portraits, as it tends to minimize imperfections and produce a glowing quality on the skin.
- **Enhanced Depth and Dimension:** The long shadows cast during the golden hour add extra depth and dimension to your subject matter. They help define the contours and shapes of objects, adding interest and realism to your watercolor painting.
- **Atmospheric Effects and Color Temperature:** The warm, golden tones of the afternoon sun can add a beautiful atmospheric quality to your reference photos. They evoke a sense of warmth and tranquility, enhancing the mood and emotional impact of your artwork. This atmospheric quality is particularly effective for landscapes and outdoor scenes, where it can help convey a sense of time, place, and mood.

Direct and Diffused Light

In comparison to the golden hour, direct sunlight can create harsh shadows and stronger contrast that can obscure the details of your subject. For example, pictures taken on a sunny day right around noon tend to look overexposed, reducing the variation in hues and textures. While foggy conditions may create a soft, ethereal atmosphere, they can also obscure details and flatten the appearance of your subject matter.

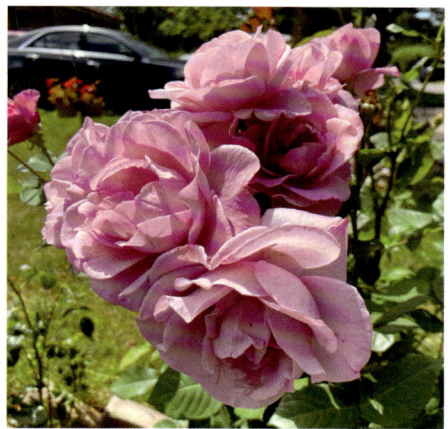 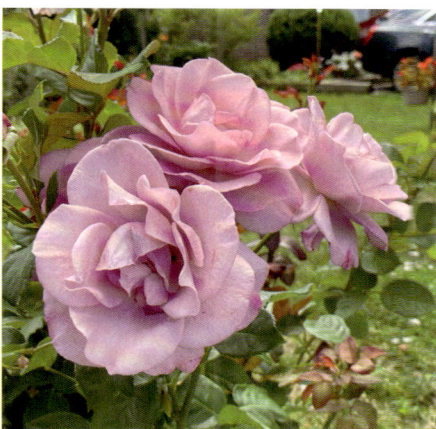

Violet roses photo taken during the golden hour versus the same flower reference taken around noon on a foggy day.

Case Study: Violet Roses

Last summer, I stumbled upon a gorgeous rose bush in my parents' neighborhood. I immediately decided to use the flowers as a complement for one of my upcoming compositions featuring a magpie bird. My first attempt at capturing the rose reference was taken in early afternoon. The clouds where covering the sun, and the light was dispersed, resulting in a more flat look that lacked strong shadows. After taking the photo with my phone and examining it closely, I realized that it would be difficult to paint the petals and decided to come back later to retake the photo. My second photo was taken during the golden hour, when strong shadows were clearly identifiable on every petal. This version was much easier to capture with watercolor by focusing on the variations in light and shadow to define each petal.

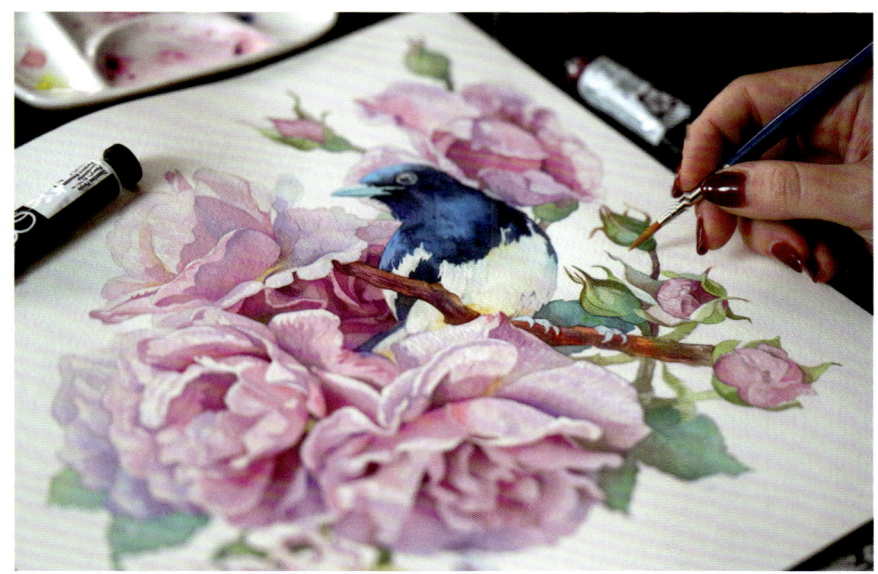

Magpie and Violet Roses in Progress

8.11 The "Host and Guest" Composition Technique

As a child, I was fortunate to have access to my grandfather's captivating library of enchanting books on Asian art and culture. Among the pages, I delved into stunning prints and illustrations, immersing myself in the intricate beauty they held. My early fascination with Asian decorative art, particularly the delicate watercolor scenes featuring birds and flowers, became a source of valuable composition lessons that I carry with me in my artistic journey. In this section, I am excited to share one of my favorite techniques: the "host and guest" approach from the Gongbi style of Chinese watercolor.

Gongbi "Host and Guest" Technique

The Gongbi style of painting traces its origins back to the Han dynasty two millennia ago. Its name, derived from "gong jin," meaning "tidy," underscores its focus on highly detailed brushstrokes that meticulously delineate organic details. At the heart of Gongbi lies the "host and guest" technique—a simple yet powerful framework for creating dynamic compositions. In this approach, a flower or plant reference serves as the static "host," providing a stable foundation for the composition. The "guest," typically in the form of a bird or animal, is then added to inject drama and narrative depth into the scene. While I primarily use this technique to combine flowers with insects and birds, its principles can be applied to any subject matter, including humans and animals.

Guiding Questions for Using "Host and Guest" Technique

- **Host Selection:** Which flower or plant would serve as the ideal "host" for your composition? Consider its shape, color, and symbolism. How will the chosen host contribute to the overall mood and theme of your artwork?
- **Guest Selection:** What type of bird or animal would make a compelling "guest" in your composition? Think about its characteristics and how it interacts with the chosen host. How will the guest enhance the narrative or story you want to convey through your artwork?
- **Composition Arrangement:** How will you position the host and guest within the composition to create visual interest and balance? Are there any natural elements, such as branches or foliage, that can further enhance the relationship between the host and guest?
- **Narrative Depth:** What story or emotion do you want your composition to evoke? How can you convey this through the interaction between the host and guest? Are there any cultural or symbolic meanings associated with the chosen elements that you can incorporate into your artwork?

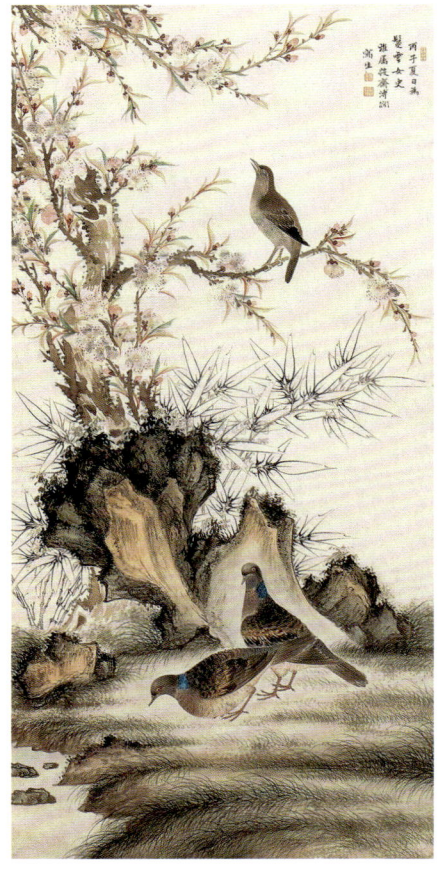

Finches and Bamboo (11th century) by Emperor Huizong of Song

Case Study: Adding a Ladybug to a Tropical Plant Painting

In one of my recent artworks, I started with a simple reference of a lush tropical plant with vibrant green leaves. While the plant itself was visually appealing, I felt it needed something extra to truly bring the composition to life. Inspired by the "host and guest" technique, I decided to introduce a ladybug perched delicately on one of the plant's stems. Despite the ladybug's small size, its presence alters the composition dynamics, adding a touch of whimsy and intrigue to the scene.

- **Sense of Movement:** I wanted to inject a sense of movement and activity into the otherwise static scene. The presence of the ladybug crawling along the stem creates a dynamic focal point that draws the viewer's eye in and adds visual interest.

- **Complementary Colors:** The vibrant red hue of the ladybug contrasts beautifully with the lush green leaves of the tropical plant. This complementary color scheme enhances the overall visual impact of the artwork.

- **Narrative Depth and Emotional Response:** By introducing the ladybug, I subtly conveyed a narrative element in the composition. The presence of the insect suggests a miniature ecosystem teeming with life, evoking a sense of delight and connection with the natural world depicted in the painting.

This subtle yet impactful addition demonstrates how even the smallest details can have a profound effect on the overall visual experience of a painting.

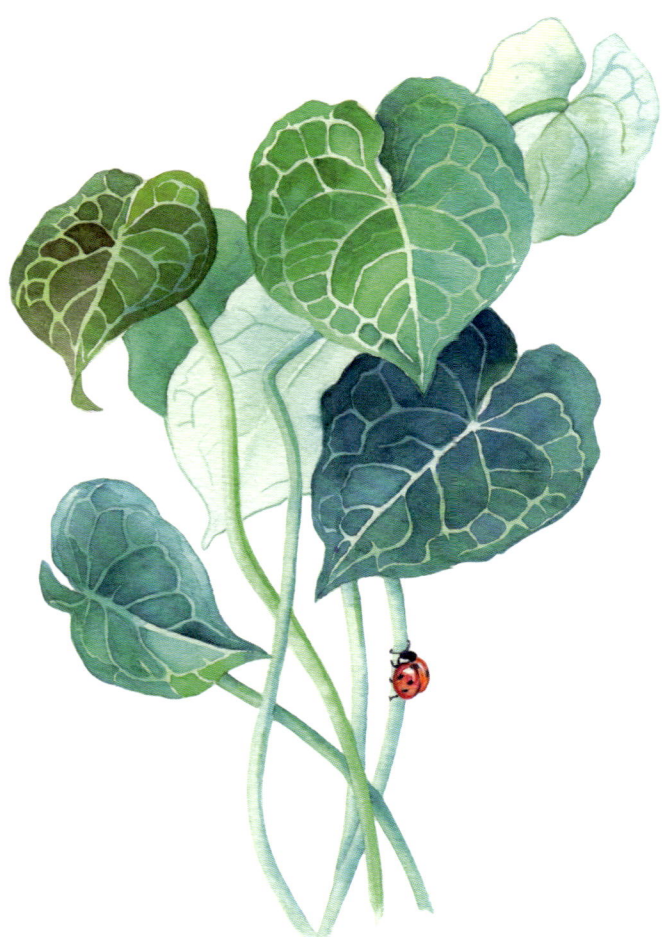

Ladybug on Tropical Plant

8.12 Folk Art Influences in Composition

Growing up in Ukraine, I was surrounded by the vibrant colors and whimsical motifs of Ukrainian folk art. As a child, I was fortunate to receive formal training in the enchanting art of of Petrykivka—an art style with a rich history where organic shapes, like birds and flowers, intertwine with decorative elements to form intricate tapestries of visual delight.

Petrykivka Palette and Composition Style

In terms of composition, Petrykivka art often features a central focal point surrounded by smaller, complementary elements. Symmetry and balance are important principles, with each element carefully arranged to create a sense of harmony and unity. Years of painting Petrykivka compositions with gouache and tempera allowed me to absorb the logic of this folk art style, mastering the art of arranging seemingly disparate elements within the confines of paper and three-dimensional objects like jewelry boxes or dinnerware.

This folk art tradition also taught me to be fearless with color. The bold color combinations inspired by Ukrainian folk art continue to infuse my watercolor artwork to this day. Whether painting botanicals or landscapes, I often find myself drawn to saturated pigments that echo the richness of Petrykivka color harmonies.

I encourage you to explore folk art in your own region, seeking out examples of composition principles embedded within your own cultural treasures. Pay attention to how elements are arranged, how colors are used, and how stories are told through imagery, and allow these insights to enrich your own artistic practice.

Guiding Questions for Folk Art Composition Explorations

- **Geometric Motifs:** What motifs commonly found in your favorite folk art can you incorporate into your composition, such as rosettes, spirals, or geometric shapes? Consider mirroring elements on either side of a central axis to achieve balance and symmetry.
- **Organic Motifs:** What types of animals, flowers, or trees commonly found in your region can you include in your composition?
- **Central Element:** How can you select a central element, such as a bird, to anchor the composition and serve as a focal point? Consider choosing a bird with symbolic significance in your folklore. How can you gradually add organic elements, such as flowers and foliage, around the central element to create a sense of depth and dimension, mimicking the process of painting a folk tapestry?
- **Color Harmony:** How can you select a color palette that reflects the vibrant hues characteristic of your favorite folk art? Consider using bold primary colors, as well as rich secondary and tertiary colors, to create a visually striking composition.
- **Narrative and Symbolism:** What narrative or symbolic elements can you incorporate into your composition to evoke themes of nature, lifecycle, or cultural identity common in folk art?

Case Study: Purple Firebird Ukrainian Petrykivka Composition

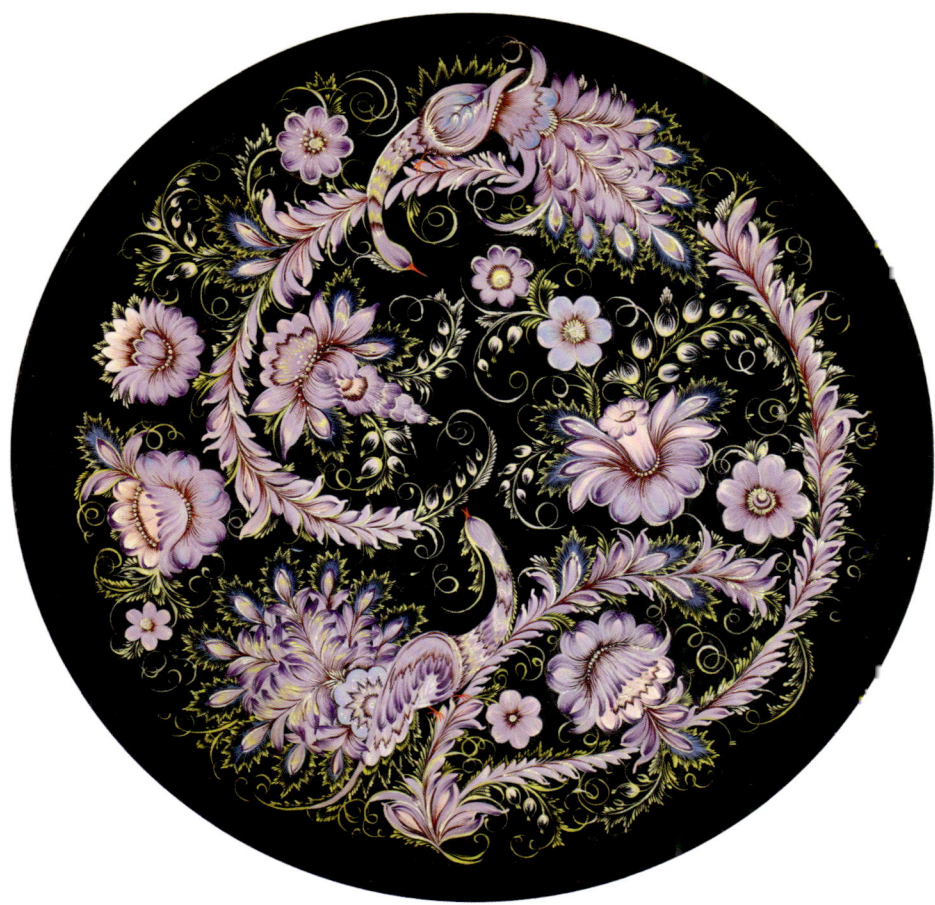

Purple Firebirds – Gouache on Wooden Panel

In this composition, painted on a wooden plate, I painted two majestic birds surrounded by an intricate arrangement of purple flowers.

- **Focal Points:** The two firebirds—legendary creatures symbolizing beauty and rebirth in Ukrainian folklore—take center stage in the composition. Their radiant plumage and dynamic poses imbue the painting with a sense of vitality and energy.
- **Symmetry and Movement:** The composition exhibits a fluid motion, with everything arranged around spiral motifs. The principles of symmetry are evident, with two birds looking at one another, mirroring the way they are perched on top and bottom. This balanced arrangement created a sense of visual equilibrium and echoed the symmetrical motifs found in traditional Ukrainian tapestries.
- **Color Harmony:** The vibrant purple hues contrast beautifully with the dark background, creating a striking color palette reminiscent of Ukrainian embroidery. The juxtaposition of warm pink and cool blue accents adds depth and dimension to the composition while enhancing its overall visual impact.

9

My Favorite
Tips & Tricks

9.1 Introduction

In this chapter, I share some of my favorite watercolor "secrets" that I've developed and refined throughout years of research, practice, and experimentation. We'll delve into techniques and approaches that have become indispensable to my personal style, and you'll gain valuable insights and practical tips to enhance your own watercolor practice.

First on our agenda is my tried-and-tested method for "sculpting" any three-dimensional subject on paper. This approach involves layering three to five washes, each with a distinct purpose, to gradually build values and achieve a sense of realism. Next, we'll dive into the art of painting shadows to sculpt three-dimensional form on paper.

Moving on, we'll tackle the challenge of handling particularly tricky color groups, including black, red, and yellow. I will also discuss special techniques for tackling value studies and painting pure-white subjects, ensuring that they shine with luminosity and vibrancy on the page.

Finally, we'll wrap up our journey by discussing how to digitize and clean up our watercolor images to remove white backgrounds and prepare them for digital sharing or reproduction. We'll explore tools and techniques for scanning, editing, and enhancing our watercolor artwork, ensuring that it looks its best in both physical and digital formats.

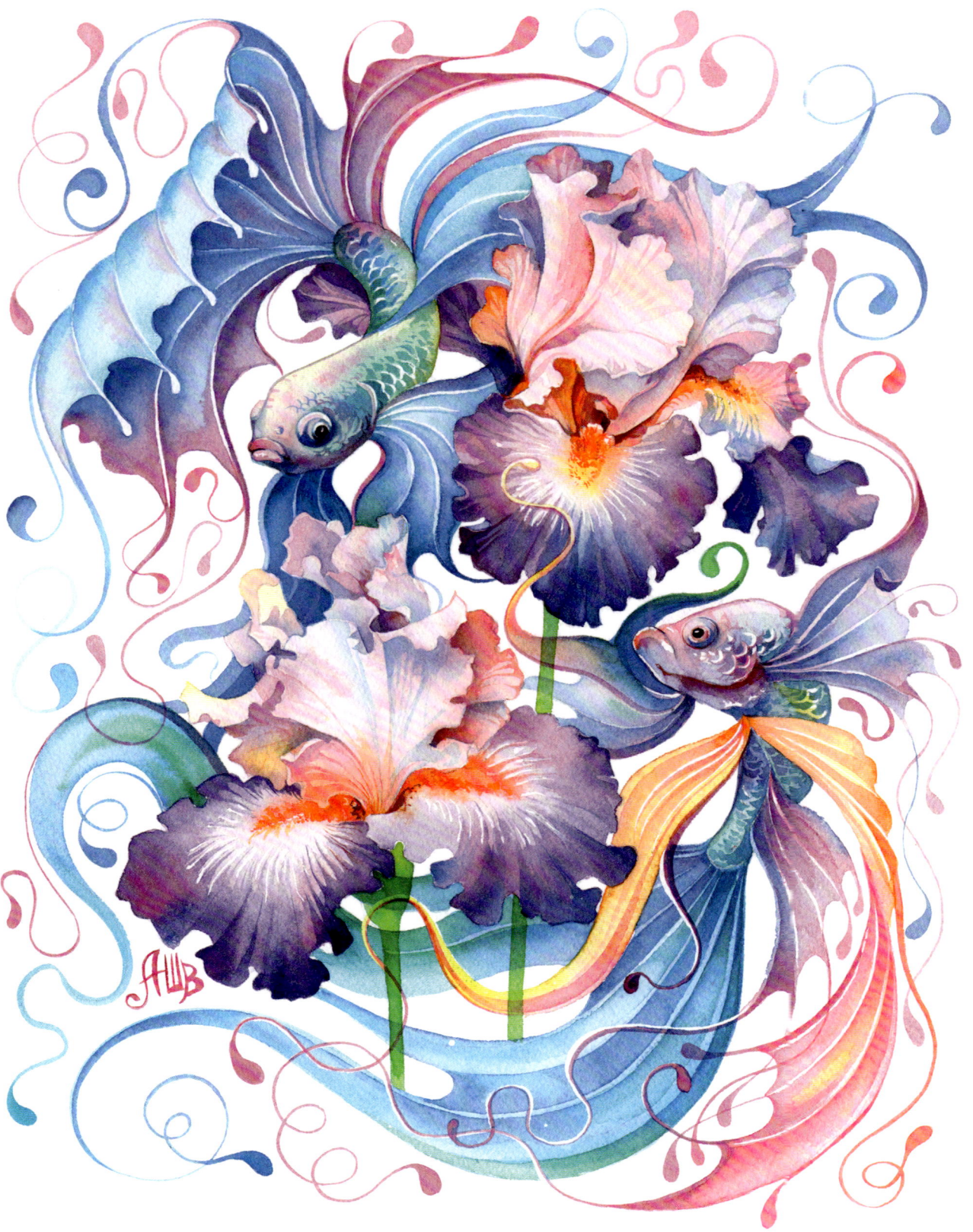

Betta Fish and Iris Flowers

9.2 My Three-Step Approach to Painting Any Subject

Over the years, I've developed a straightforward system for approaching any subject with watercolor, whether it's a single flower or a more complex composition with multiple objects and intricate details. This staged approach enables me to delve into the subtleties of each layer, starting from the initial light wash and progressing to the final dark accents. By following this method, I can avoid common watercolor challenges like messy blends or flat washes. Although this approach demands extra time and patience, I highly recommend exploring it once you feel comfortable with the basic techniques. It allows you to fully leverage the transparency of watercolor and create depth and dimension in your artwork.

My typical sequence of layers includes the following:

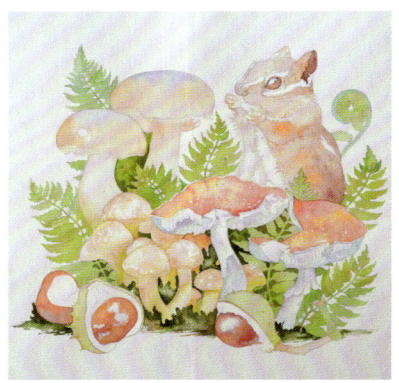

Step #1: Background Layer

The background layer acts as a roadmap for all your color variations along the way. Here, you can use multiple colors wet-on-wet, blending them directly on paper while the surface is still wet. Stick to light values, allowing yourself enough flexibility to add details and build saturation in the next two layers. In this forest scene, I applied a light wash of color all over each subject, avoiding the white segments and capturing only the main blocks of green, red, and brown color.

Step #2: Definition Layer

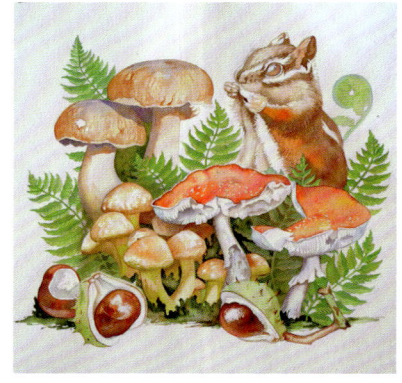

This layer is one of the more important layers, as you start glazing more saturated pigments and building a sense of three-dimensionality by amplifying darker tones. Note that by painting the first layer of shadows you are also amplifying the highlights. In this painting, I focused on adding vibrant reds and rich browns to shape the foreground chestnuts and mushrooms, while toning down the areas that are further in the distance.

Step #3: Accent Layer

The goal of the accent layer is to reassess the overall tone and adjust color balance by adding additional washes selectively. This is also the time when you can add extra detail to your work. In the final stage of the Autumn Forest, I painted fur texture on the chipmunk using thin and precise strokes of dark brown and indigo. I also added minor textural accents, like speckles of dirt on the mushrooms. Finally, I painted a glaze of Quinacridone Gold (PO48, PY150) on the mushrooms to accentuate the glowing effect. Note that I didn't touch the ferns, leaving this element with less definition to enhance visual separation between background and foreground objects.

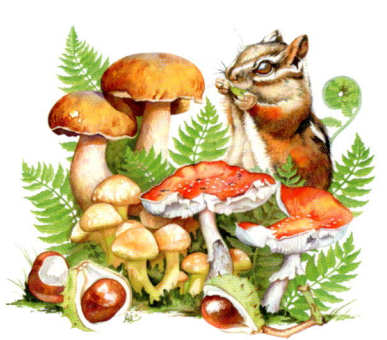

HELPFUL TIPS

Underpainting (Optional Step)

In some cases, I apply a thin wash of warm or cool color to certain sections of the painting before working on the main color blocks. This initial layer is entirely optional, but it can often influence the overall sense of light in the final artwork, adding a warm glow or accentuating cool light reflections. For more information on the use of underpainting technique, see page 118.

How Many Layers Do You Really Need?

The number of layers you glaze will depend on your artistic goals and how comfortable you are with watercolor medium. In the beginning of your watercolor journey, I recommend focusing on two layers—one to build background tones and another to add definition. Certain subjects may call for deeper tonal variations and multiple color transitions, requiring five or even more layers of transparent color for the best result. In my advanced watercolor classes, I typically show how to apply up to five washes. This allows me enough flexibility to build depth and finesse the details.

9.3 Three Ways to Paint Any Background

Painting a background is a great way to complement or even enhance your painting. In this section, I will share three of my favorite approaches, from a simple one-layer application to a more advanced layering technique that incorporates various textures, and even negative painting technique. Depending on where you are in your watercolor journey, you can apply any of these methods to make your background more interesting without overpowering the subject.

Technique #1: Loose Wash Using Wet-on-Wet Technique

This beginner-friendly technique works on practically any subject of your choice. In involves applying a loose splash of color around your subject. Simply pre-wet the surface and add a few drops of color using wet-on-wet technique. For my botanical work, I typically rely on pigments from the cooler side of the spectrum, including blues, purples, and muted greens. For this apple blossom study, I decided to use a combination of my all-time favorites: Aqua Green (Phthalo) and Dioxazine Purple (PV23). After applying the colors, I introduced a few drops of clear water to create a few abstract blooms and add some visual interest.

Technique #2: Flat Wash Using Wet-on-Dry Technique

The second technique is more controlled and includes two layers of color applied carefully to cover the entire background behind your subject. I typically introduce warm pigments (yellows and oranges) to indicate a distant source of light somewhere on top, and cool pigments (violets and blues) to accentuate the shadows at the bottom. Unlike the abstract wash techniques described above, this

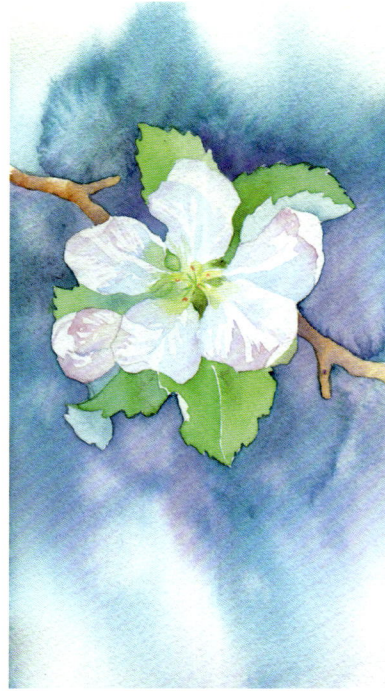

Apple Blossom: Loose Background in One Step

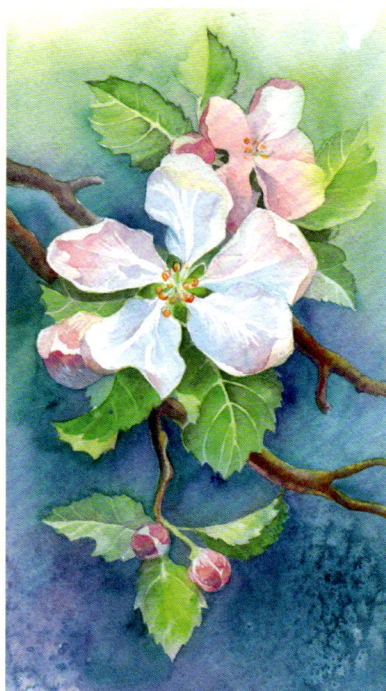

Apple blossom: Background with Texture in Two Steps

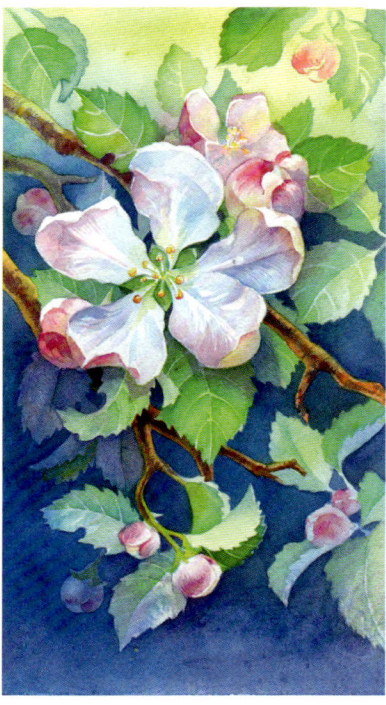

Apple blossom: Multi-Dimensional Background with Negative Painting in Three Steps

variation in color allows me to capture depth more effectively. In this example, I addec Green Gold (PY150, PY3, PG36) on top and Indanthrone Blue (PB60) at the bottom to further accentuate the nuances of light in the composition. I also sprinkled on some salt to create texture and add visual interest at the bottom of the composition.

Technique #3: Depth and Dimension with Negative Painting

The most advanced—and arguably the most striking—technique that will help you create gorgeous atmospheric effects includes negative painting. It's an absolute game changer for botanical artists, and it has been my favorite background technique for years. In this case, I will start with a solid wash around the flowers (similar to the first case technique), and then glaze thin layers of different pigments, getting progressively darker with every wash. Each time, I paint around different background objects, slowly revealing the shapes with my brush, watching the leaves emerge from the background.

Case Study: Calla Lily

In this study, I applied the same techniques to create three different background styles for the calla lily flower. I will demonstrate a breakdown of each step to help you envision the progression of layers. Note that it is essential to allow sufficient drying time between each step to avoid bleeding edges.

Technique #1: Loose Wash Using Wet-on-Wet Technique

In the first case study I used a combination of two pigments to create a simple wet-on-wet blend around the flower and leaves. I used Aqua Green (Phthalo) to subtly suggest some muted greenery in the background. Adding Perylene Violet (PV29) helped me create some visual continuity by echoing the same color within the shadows of the white flower.

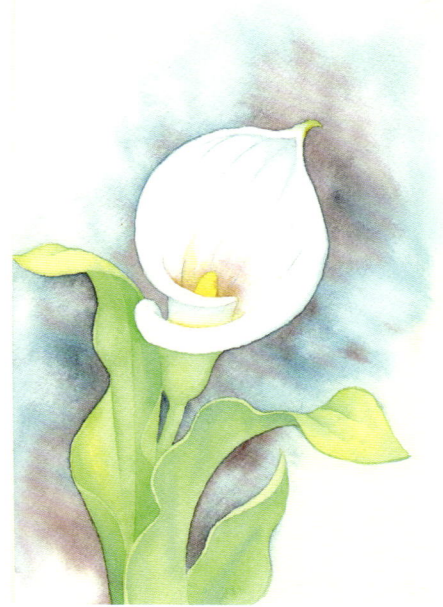

Calla Lily: Loose Background in One Step

Technique #2: Flat Wash Using Wet-on-Dry Technique

In the second study, I used wet-on-dry technique to apply three layers of color. Note that applying two layers of Aqua Green (Phthalo) instead of one helped me create a more even wash, ensuring solid and smooth coverage across the entire background. I completed the background by painting darker leaf shapes using a cooler Indanthrone Blue (PB60).

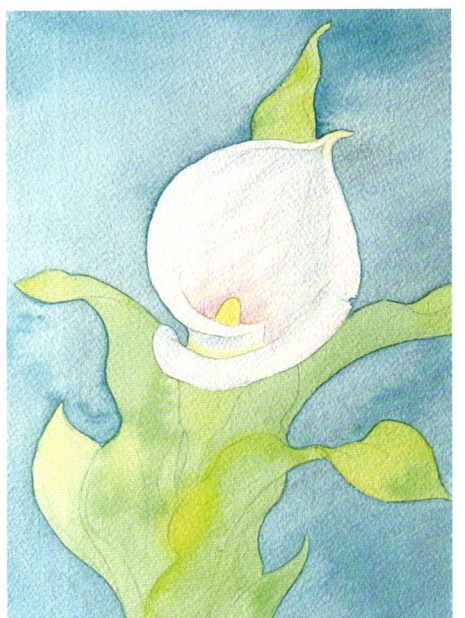
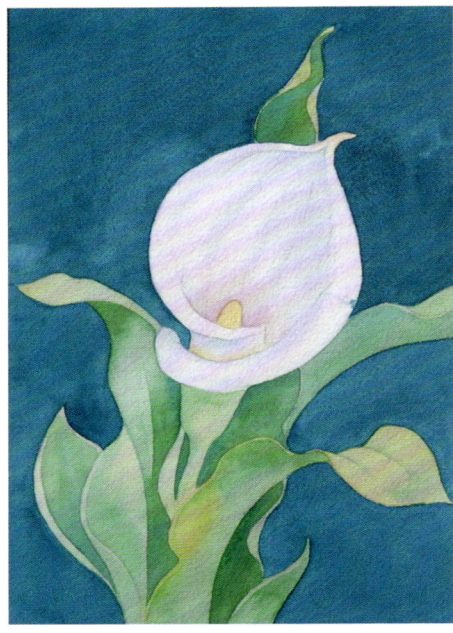

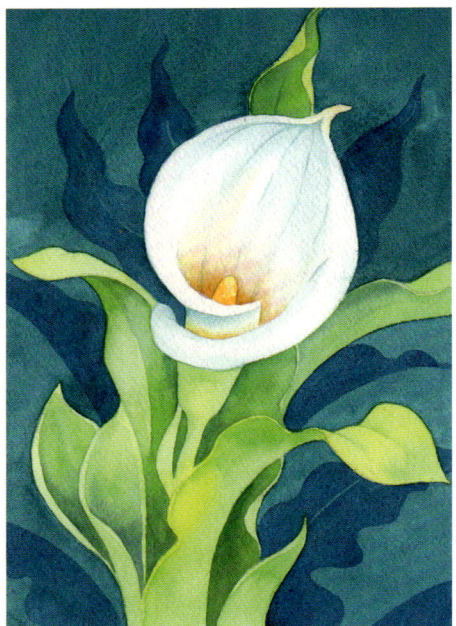

Calla Lily: Background Using Wet-on-Dry
Technique in Three Steps

Technique #3: Depth and Dimension with Negative Painting

In the last version, I applied negative painting technique to gradually build layers of depth around the flower. I started with a solid wash Green Gold (PY150, PY3, PG36), then progressed with several layers of Hooker's Green (PG36, PY3, PY150, PO48) and Aqua Green (Phthalo), painting around the leaf shapes. In my final layer, I applied extra saturated blue into my green to add depth and increase the overall contrast around the flower.

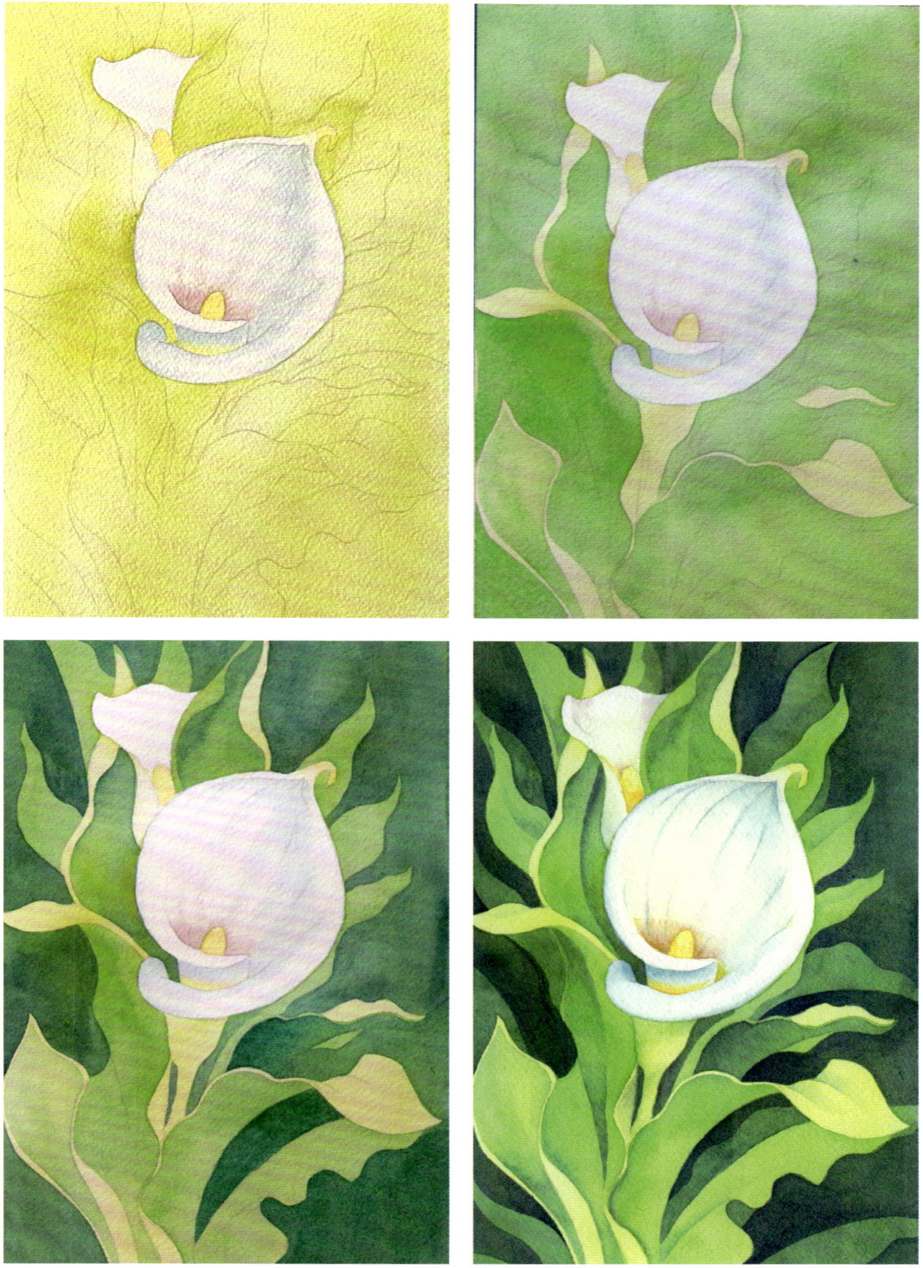

Calla Lily: Multi-Dimensional Background with Negative Painting in Four Steps

Video Available ▶ rockynook.com/watercolor-secrets

9.4 Extending My Palette

One of the most frequent questions I am asked is how I choose my pigments to create a particularly vibrant look with numerous color transitions that all seem to work in harmony. In addition to relying on Quinacridone and Phthalo pigment families that I've already discussed in the previous chapters, there is one other trick I use to achieve more striking results. I call this process my "palette extension," and it relies on color temperature to inform my color choices.

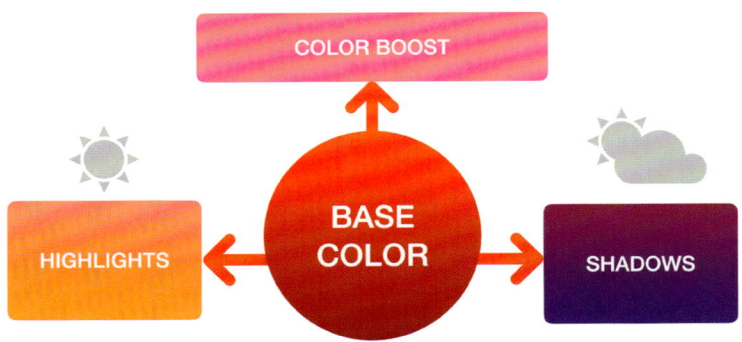

Palette Extension Diagram

I use the following method to decide on variations within any color family, always moving up and down the color spectrum to find cooler and warmer shades of my base color. By carefully observing my shapes and their position relative to light, I am able to avoid a flat, boring look and enjoy the full spectrum of pigments with confidence.

Step-by-Step

1. **Base Color:** Identify the natural color—the dominant color you see on a subject or a portion of the subject. For example, the natural color of pink hydrangea is pink, and you may choose Quinacridone Red, a.k.a. Permanent Rose (PV19) as your "base" color.
2. **Areas of Shadow:** Identify the shadow areas (more blue), and extend your base color toward the blue on the spectrum. In the hydrangea example, your shadow pinks will lean toward violet and purple. Therefore, you can explore Quinacridone Magenta (PR122) and even Quinacridone Violet (PV55) to extend your palette in those areas.
3. **Areas of Light:** Identify the areas that are facing the sun (more yellow) and extend your base color toward the yellow on the spectrum. For the warm pink petals, you can explore Quinacridone Coral (PR 209) and Scarlett Lake (PR188). The brightest highlights should, of course, remain white (use the white of your paper here).
4. **Color "Boost":** You can choose to accentuate certain colors by adding a few vibrant strokes strategically. For example, you can glaze fluorescent Opera Pink (PR122) to amplify the base pink on some of the flower petals.

Case Study: Pink Hydrangea

In this pink hydrangea study, I used Quinacridone Magenta (PR122) as the base color for the petals. For the shadows, I applied Perylene Violet (PV29), Quinacridone Violet (PV55), and Dioxazine Purple (PV37). To add warmth and accentuate the highlights on the top petals, I added splashes of Quinacridone Coral (PR209). Although Opera Pink (PR122) would have provided more vibrancy to the flower, I chose to avoid this fugitive pigment and stick to lightfast colors, as I intend to offer the piece for sale.

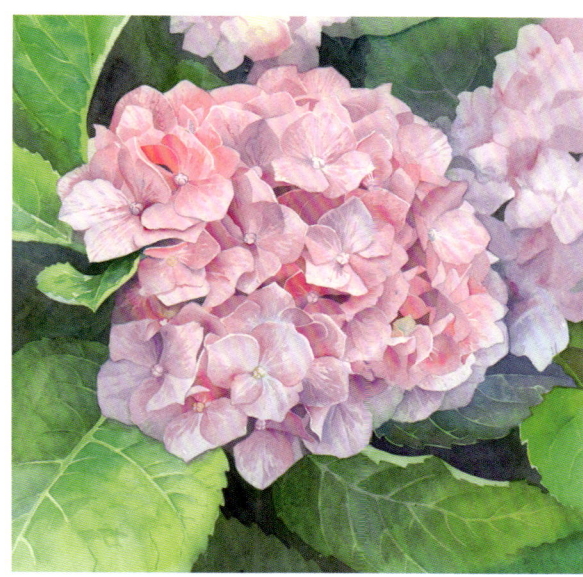

Pink Hydrangea

My Favorite Color Combos for Palette Extension

Over the years, I've discovered several effective combinations that help me boost my pigments, enhancing the overall vibrancy of my palette. For example:

- Quinacridone Violet (PV55) works as an excellent boost for Dioxazine Purple (PV23) and Perylene Violet (PV29).
- A splash of Opera Pink (PR122) does wonders to enhance both Quinacridone Red (PV19) and Magenta (PR122).
- Lastly, introducing Phthalo Blue Green Shade (PB15:3) works wonders to enhance more muted blues, including Indanthrone (PB60) and Indigo (PB60, PBk6).

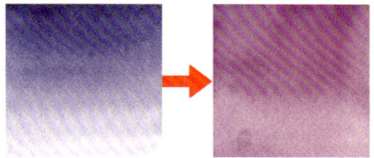

Quinacridone Violet Enhancing Dioxazine Purple

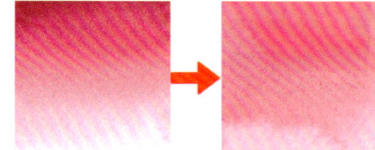

Opera Pink Enhancing Quinacridone Magenta

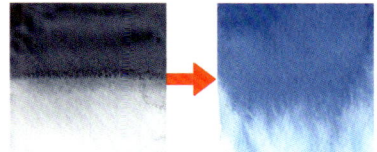

Phthalo Blue Green Shade Enhancing Indigo

Guiding Questions for Palette Extension

Think of your most recent watercolor painting and notice the areas that may look somewhat flat—perhaps lacking visual interest or a sense of depth. If you could revisit this work again, which colors would you add to your palette?

Video Available 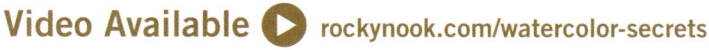 rockynook.com/watercolor-secrets

9.5 Light and Shadow Secrets

Shadows are what make our paintings look three-dimensional because they play a crucial role in creating depth and realism on a two-dimensional paper plane. Therefore, observing and capturing the interplay of light and shadow in the natural world is essential for bringing our compositions to life. I like to think of this process as framing or sculpting light on paper with your brush. There are several types of shadows that we commonly encounter in our reference images. Let's explore each type in detail, using the *White Shell* study as an example.

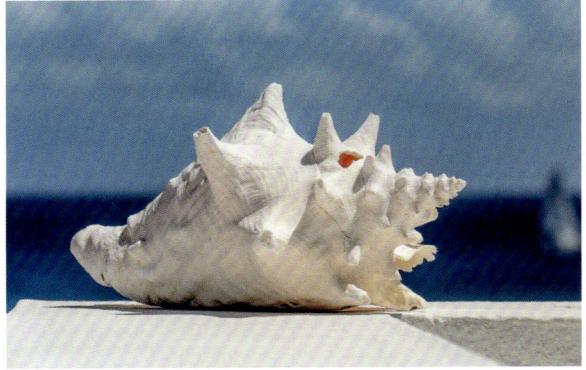

Shell Reference Photo. Credit: Steve Adams, Unsplash.com

Form Shadows

Form shadows are the areas of an object that are turned away from the primary light source, resulting in reduced illumination. These shadows define the three-dimensional form of the object and typically appear as darker areas with gradual transitions in tone. In watercolor painting, form shadows are crucial for conveying volume and depth, and they are often rendered with subtle shifts in color and value.

In this shell study, the source of light is coming from the top right, and form shadows are concentrated on the bottom-left side of each object.

Core Shadows

Core shadows represent the darkest and most defined part of the form shadows. They often appear near the edge of the form shadow, next to the adjacent light. These segments are least affected by reflected light, and I usually apply additional layers of saturated color in those areas.

Note that the **core shadows** appear as sharp transitions between light and dark within the larger form shadows on the shell, emphasizing the three-dimensional nature of the surface.

Cast Shadows

Falling shadows are cast by an object onto a surface or another object. The often vary in intensity depending on the angle of the light source. They also vary in length, depending on the distance between the light source, the object, and the surface. In watercolor painting, capturing the subtle shifts in color and value within cast shadows can enhance their believability and impact.

The main **cast shadow** can be observed on the horizontal plane the shell is resting on. Note how several cast shadows created by the shell horns are landing on the white surface. By blocking the path of sunlight, they project their silhouette onto the shell, adding drama and interest to a composition. Cast shadows created by the petal folds further define the spatial relationships and create dynamic contrast on the background flowers.

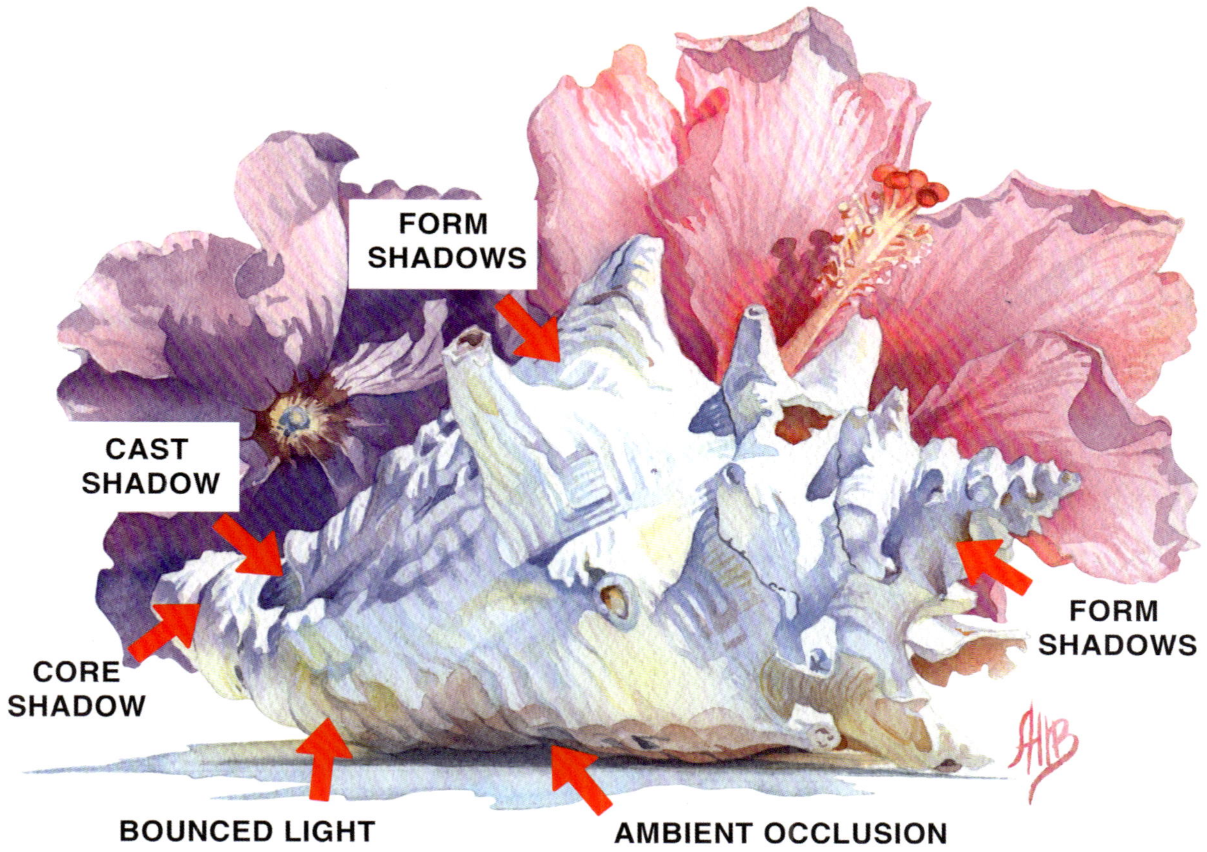

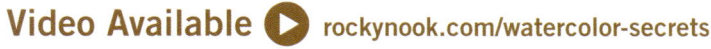

White Shell and Flowers with Large Form and Cast Shadows Identified

Occlusion Shadows

Occlusion shadows, also known as contact shadows or ambient occlusion, occur in areas where objects come into contact or overlap, blocking light almost entirely from reaching the surface. These shadows are typically the strongest, calling for the darkest most saturated color.

The **occlusion** occurs in the area immediately under the shell, where it is barely touching the ground. Another area where ambient occlusion can be observed is within the broken segment of the shell.

Shadows Receiving Reflected or Bounced Light

Shadows receiving bounced light, also known as reflected light, occur when light is reflected onto shadowed areas from nearby surfaces or objects. This phenomenon can soften the overall value of the shadow by introducing secondary illumination to darker areas.

Note how **reflected light** influences the color and intensity of the form shadows, making some of them appear lighter and warmer. Notice, too, how reflected light is affecting the cast shadow on the horizontal plane, making it significantly lighter in the area immediately behind the shell.

Video Available ▶ rockynook.com/watercolor-secrets

9.6 "Soft" or "Lost" Edges

You may be surprised to hear me say that sharp outlines between distinct objects and areas of color are not always desired. "Softening" edges or creating "lost" edges can add a touch of mystery and depth to a painting, almost like a subtle magic trick that mimics the way we perceive the hierarchy of objects in the real world. My favorite application of this technique involves gently blurring the lines between distant shapes, allowing them to blend seamlessly into the background or neighboring colors. While crisp lines ignite tension and create strong visual focus, the softened edges weave tales of tranquility or invite the viewer to explore further. In this section, I will explain my soft-edge method and provide a few additional examples to spark your creativity.

Method #1: Single Object

1. Begin by applying a wash of color to the paper.
2. Using a clean, damp brush, lightly wet the edges of the painted area that you want to soften. Gently stroke along the edges to encourage the paint to flow and diffuse onto the open surface around it.
3. To control the degree of softening, vary the dampness of your brush and adjust the pressure applied.

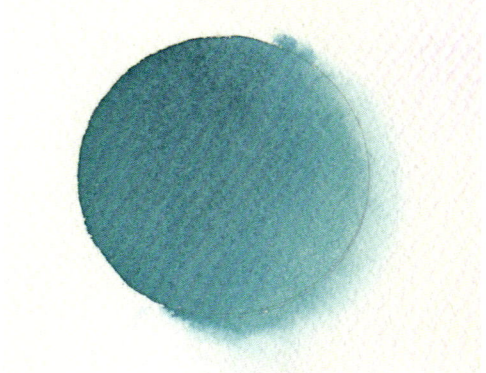

Lost Edge on a Single Object

Method #2: Multiple Shapes

1. Begin by painting the first shape with a wash of color. For the softening technique to be effective, proceed to the next shape while the first shape is still wet.
2. Apply the second color right next to the initial wash. The pigments will mix with one another on paper naturally, helping you soften the boundary between the two shapes.
3. Experiment to achieve the desired level of transition between colors or shapes. Note that a slight time delay between painting two shapes will provide a less pronounced blurring effect.

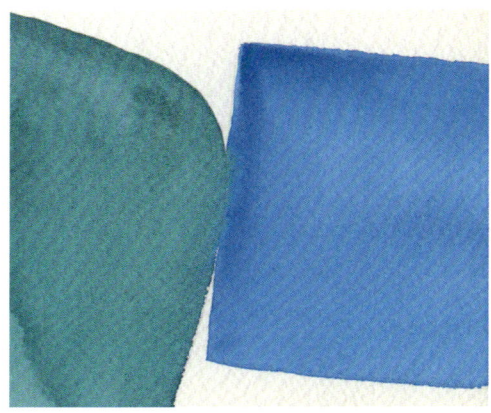

Lost Edge on Multiple Objects

Applications of Soft Edges

- **Landscapes:** Nature often provides the best examples of lost edges. Think of a misty morning where trees on the horizon blur softly into the fog, evoking a dreamlike quality. You can also look for soft edges where the waves merge with the sky, or where rooftops of distant houses meld into distant trees.
- **Botanicals:** Lost edges help create depth by suggesting elements that are receding into the background, contributing to the illusion of distance or atmospheric perspective. I often use this

technique to achieve a delicate, realistic look in my floral paintings by blending the background petals into the surrounding foliage.

- **Portraits:** Softening edges in portraits adds a gentle touch, particularly in areas like hair, clothing folds, or the transition from light to shadow on the skin.

Case Study: Summer Grapevine

In this grapevine study, I used a soft edge technique to achieve three important objectives:

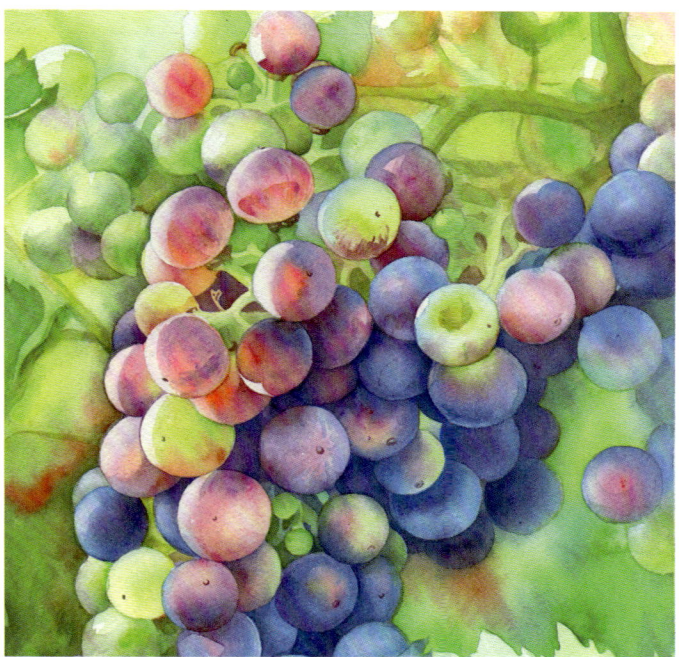

Summer Grapevine

- **Illusion of Depth:** Softening edges mimics how objects may fade or become less distinct in certain lighting conditions. Blending the background leaves and grapes allowed me to convey a sense of distance, pulling the viewer deeper into the scene and guiding their gaze through layers of atmospheric perspective.
- **Selective Focus:** By allowing certain leaves to recede into the background, I was able to bring focus onto the grapes—the focal point of the composition. Blending the distant grapes allowed me to further emphasize the sunny highlights on the foreground.
- **Emotional Impact:** Experimenting with different levels of edge softening can evoke different emotions. Notice that the edges of the blue grapes aren't confined by sharp boundaries but rather blend into the moody, dark shadows around them, teasing the viewer's imagination with hints rather than rigid definitions.

HELPFUL TIPS

- **Timing is Key:** Softening works best while the paint is still wet. Be mindful of the drying time, and work in sections to maintain control over the softening process.
- **Use a Light Touch:** Apply gentle pressure when using the damp brush to avoid lifting too much pigment during the softening process.
- **Soft Brushes:** Larger soft-bristle brushes—for example, flat squirrel brushes—are most suitable for creating soft edges.

Video Available 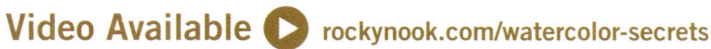 rockynook.com/watercolor-secrets

9.7 Working with Red Pigments

Painting with red pigments requires several considerations, including mixing, value balance, and drying shift. The latter can be particularly puzzling for beginners, as they may expect red to maintain its vibrancy in grayscale. In this section, I will share my favorite tips for using red watercolors while maintaining vibrant, intense, realistic hues.

Tip #1: Maintain Value Balance

The key thing that makes painting with reds tricky is value (the scale from light to dark). As we explored in chapter 7, fully saturated red can appear quite dark, similar to the value of your darkest colors. Therefore, if you start with very saturated red in your early washes, there will be no room to build additional shadows later on. In other words, you won't be able to achieve good contrast in your work because all your red segments will be too dark. Instead, I recommend starting with very diluted reds and building your shadows slowly by applying successive glazes.

Tip #2: Manage the Drying Shift

Many red pigments appear to change and even fade as they dry on the paper. This phenomenon is called a *drying shift*—a process where the color undergoes subtle changes, particularly in terms of hue and value, leading to differences between the wet and dry appearance of the paint. Even the most expensive reds from reputable brands can exhibit a strong drying shift due to their chemical composition and interaction with the paper surface. To reduce this effect, apply several successive layers of color using wet-on-dry method. To build the most intense red washes, consider pigment testing alternatives. For example, you may substitute Permanent Alizarin Crimson (PR177) for a more intense Bordeaux (PV32) or Carmine (PR176).

Tip #3: Red + Other Colors

- **Yellows:** Reds, especially those closer to violet on the color spectrum, like Quinacridone Magenta (PR122) or Quinacridone Red (PV29), don't mix very well with yellows. If you need to achieve a warm, glowing effect, I recommend doing a yellow underpainting first, before applying your red color. Alternatively, you can glaze transparent yellow using wet-on-dry method to add some warmth to your red washes.
- **Greens:** Being complementary, greens typically mix very well with reds. This aspect is particularly useful for botanical watercolors where a bit of red pigment will always give your greenery a more realistic look. For example, if you want to add some leaves around a red flower, I recommend extending your reds into your greens. You can achieve this by using either wet-on-wet technique or wet-on-dry glazing.
- **Blues:** Blue pigments mix beautifully with reds, creating a range of gorgeous purples and violets. My favorite combination is Phthalo Blue Green Shade (PB15:3) and Quinacridone Magenta (PR122), which results in a pure and vivid purple.

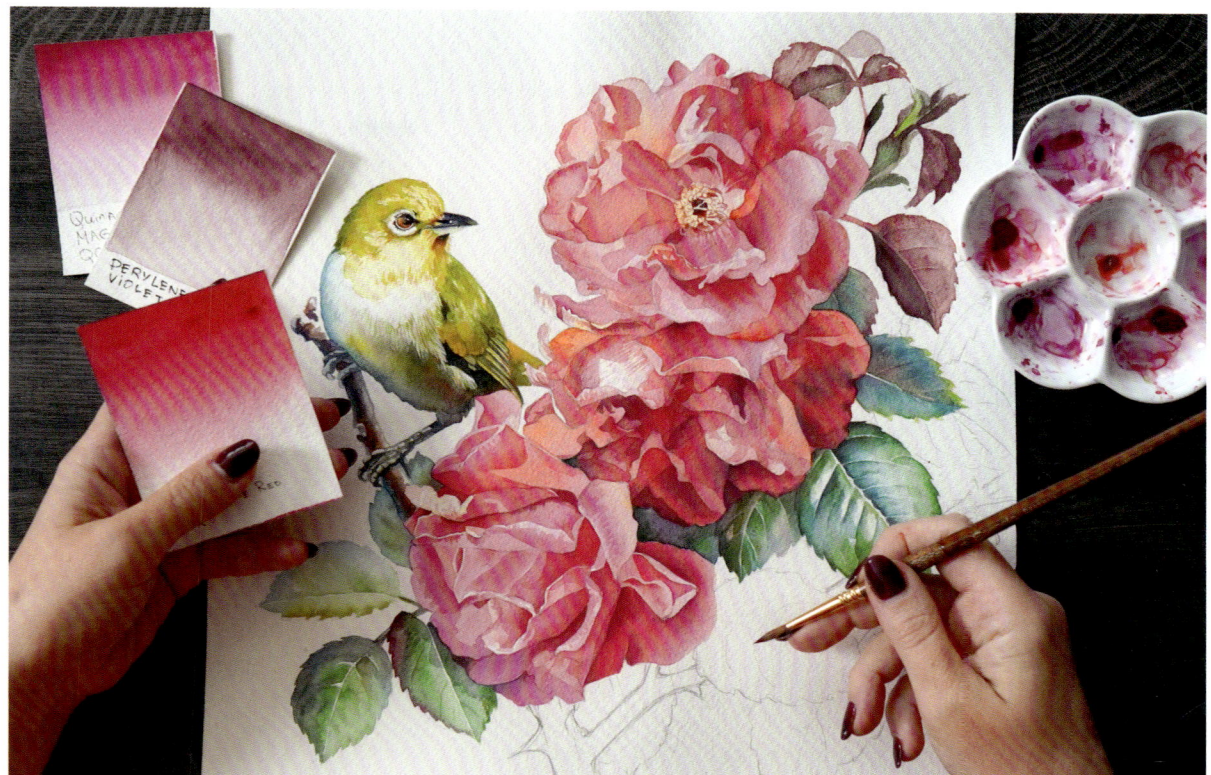
Red Rose Bush in Progress

Case Study: Red Rose Bush

In this study, I explored the full spectrum of gorgeous reds to create a visual hierarchy on the cluster of wild roses. I used Quinacridone Red (PV19) as a starting point—a base pigment for each set of petals. I then introduced variations in color temperature by applying additional pigments—everything from cool magenta to warm corals to add a sense of dimension on the petals.

- First, I applied a yellow underpainting to accentuate the warm glow on the top flower. Being closer to the sun, this set of petals receives the most sunlight. Therefore, I used my warmest reds here, including Quinacridone Coral (PR209) from Daniel Smith.
- The middle flower is pointed away from the source of light and I used a variety of darker colors here, including Permanent Alizarin Crimson (PR177) and even Perylene Maroon (PR179). Note that I also extended my green pigments onto the petal shadows to capture the nuanced shadow reflections from the leaves.
- The bottom flowers, being the furthest away from the warm glow of the sun, called for cooler Quinacridone Magenta (PR122) and Quinacridone Red (PV19).

Video Available 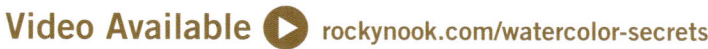 rockynook.com/watercolor-secrets

9.8 Working with Yellow Pigments

In my experience, yellow is the trickiest color family to work with due to its transparency. In this section, I will share the most effective techniques and strategies you can apply immediately to improve your results when working with yellow subjects.

Tip #1: Choose a Well-Lit Reference

Yellow pigments, unlike their red and blue counterparts, present a considerable challenge when it comes to glazing. Achieving a sense of depth and realism proves particularly difficult, as even repeated applications of translucent yellow still yield a visually flat result. Choosing a well-lit subject with strong shadows and highlights will make it easier to create definition and a sense of three-dimensional shape.

Observe the two photos of the yellow daffodil below. The flower photo on the left was taken on a cloudy day. The lack of strong shadows presents a monotonous mass of yellow petals that blend into one another. Trying to recreate it on paper will lead to a flat and lifeless painting. On the other hand, we can observe beautifully defined shadows in the flower photo on the right. This high-contrast image is much easier to paint by focusing on distinct areas of light and shadow that immediately create a sense of depth when recreated on paper.

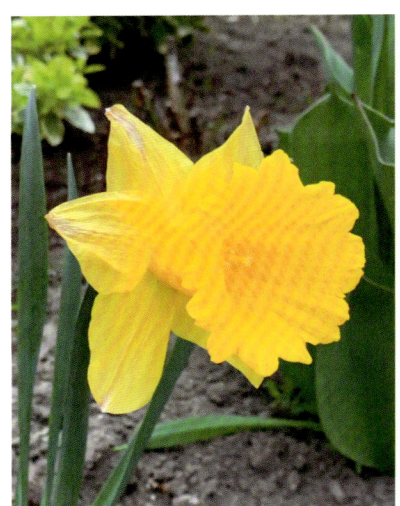 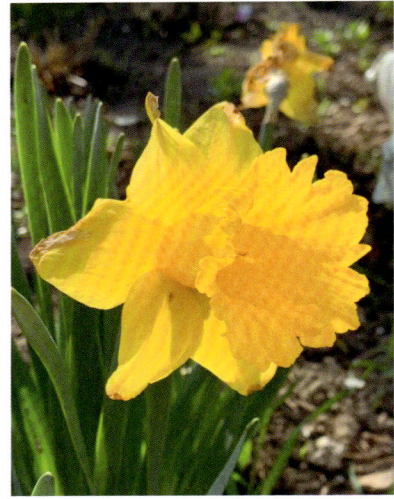

Two Yellow Daffodil References

Tip #2: Use Complementary Shadows

The natural transparency of yellow pigments creates a unique challenge when painting dark shadows. I suggest incorporating complementary colors to enrich the tonal spectrum of yellow shadows. Purples and violets, in particular, not only complement yellow aesthetically, but also amplify the perceived vibrancy of yellow tones in your artwork. While blues can harmonize effectively with yellows when juxtaposed, caution must be exercised when blending them together with wet-on-wet techniques. Such mixtures, rather than yielding natural shadows, may inadvertently produce green tones.

Tip #3: Add a Dark Background

Yellow tones often struggle to stand out against the white backdrop of our paper. To counteract this effect, I recommend incorporating a colored background to provide a visual frame for your yellow subject. Whether you choose to apply a solid, dark coverage or opt for a more loosely rendered abstract wash, introducing a background color will accentuate the yellows and imbue your artwork with a captivating sense of atmosphere and depth.

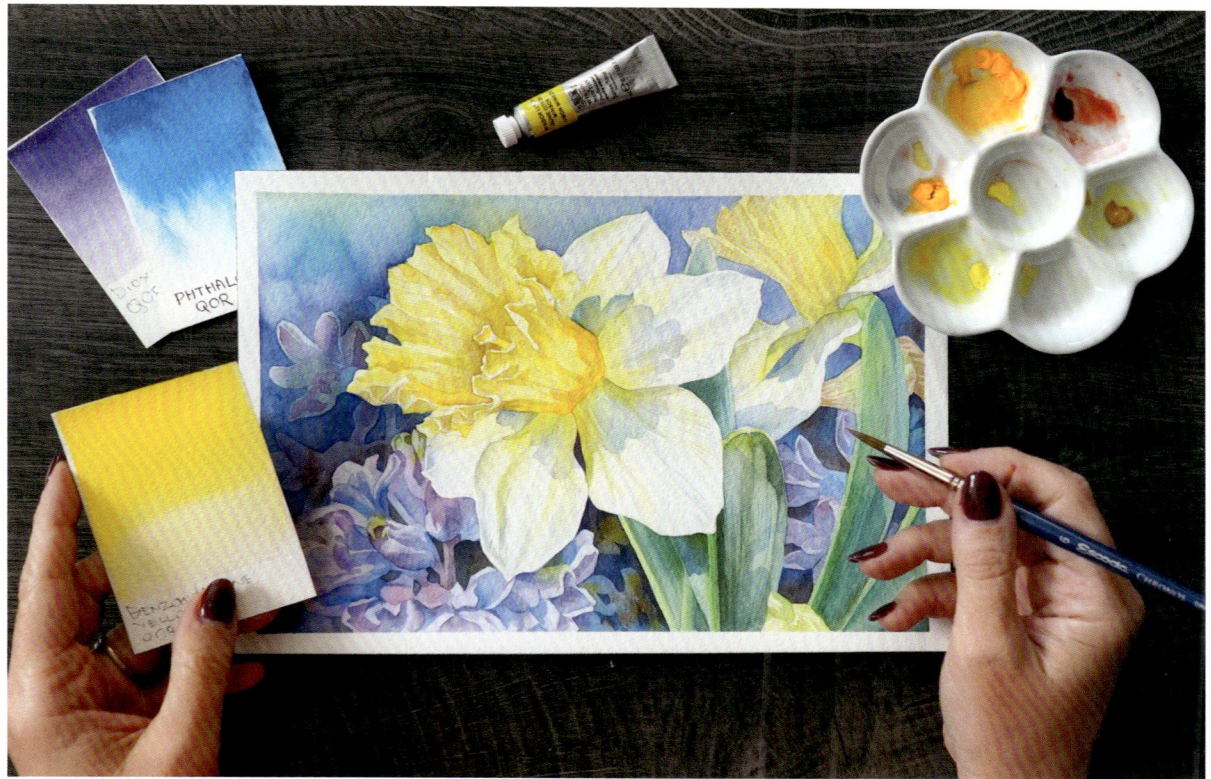

Yellow Daffodil Study in Progress

Case Study: Yellow Daffodil

In this daffodil study, I used complementary colors in three ways to accentuate the yellow petals:

- **Mixing:** I combined Dioxazine Purple (PV23) with Benzimidazolone Yellow (PY154) to create glowing shadows on the flower crown.
- **Glazing:** The petal shadows were painted with a very diluted Ultramarine Blue Violet (PB29, PV15) that I applied using wet-on-dry technique. Note that the same blue was used on the leaf shadows to maintain color continuity.
- **Background Color:** The daffodil is framed by a dark background of purple flowers and blue sky. I used several washes of Indanthrone Blue (PB60), Phthalo Blue Green Shade (PB15:3), and Perylene Maroon (PR179) to boost the vibrancy of the yellow segments. I also introduced a few minor accents of pink and violet to create visual interest on the hyacinths.

Video Available ▶ rockynook.com/watercolor-secrets

9.9 Painting Pure-Black Subjects

Pure black is not a color that can be easily found in nature. It's helpful think of it as an "absence" of color and look for opportunities to introduce additional colors into the mix when painting black subjects. After all, even the seemingly black creatures exhibit a complex interplay of colors that adds to their unique beauty and mystique. For example, some black cats may have fur that appears brownish or reddish in certain lighting conditions, especially if they have a coat with a recessive gene for a warmer hue. Note that the darkest shadows often contain reflections of their surrounding colors. This is why a black object in your room may acquire some warm undertones if your walls are covered in wood like they are in my studio. With this in mind, there are three ways to approach a very dark, almost black subject in watercolor painting.

Technique #1: Mix Primaries

The most common technique is to mix primary colors to create your own black pigment. Mixing primaries allows for a high degree of customization, allowing you to tailor the black to suit the specific needs of your composition. Some popular recipes that yield rich, dynamic blacks include Ultramarine (PB29) + Burnt Sienna (PR101) and Phthalo Blue Green Shade (PB15:3) or Red Shade (PB15:6) + Burnt Umber (PBr7).

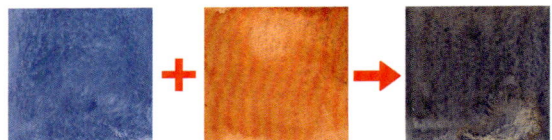

Ultramarine (PB29) + Burnt Sienna (PR101)   Phthalo (PB15:3) + Burnt Umber (PBr7)

Technique #2: Use Dark Masstones (My Favorite)

Another effective approach is to create dark tones by using highly saturated versions of other pigments. By intensifying the masstone of colors such as Indigo (PB60, PBk6), Dioxazine Purple (PV23), and Perylene Violet (PV29), you can achieve deep, rich "blacks" without sacrificing transparency or vibrancy. For example, Indigo gives out a subtle blue tint, and it blends very well with underlying layers when I water it down. While this method may not work for certain styles, particularly urban landscapes, I find it quite suitable for botanical art where subtle contrast and gentle color harmony is required.

Note that some convenience mixes contain pure black, but result in softer, more visually interesting darks. For example, Indigo from Daniel Smith is a mix of Lamp Black (PBk6) and Indanthrone Blue (PB60).

Indigo (PBk6, PB60)   Perylene Violet (PV29)   Dioxazine Purple (PV23)

Technique #3: Apply "Pure" Black

Black pigments straight from the tube offer a convenient way to achieve deep, rich tones in your paintings. Different varieties may offer slight variations in hue that allow for nuanced control over the mood and atmosphere of your artwork. For example, Ivory Black (PBk9) tends to have a warmer, slightly brownish tint, while Lamp Black (PBk6/7) leans toward a cooler, bluish tone. However, using black straight tends to flatten the painting and diminish the vibrancy of other colors. Achieving subtle transitions and maintaining transparency can also be difficult when using black in its pure form.

Ivory Black (PBk9) Lamp Black (PBk6/7)

Case Study: Black Swan

I painted this swan using Lamp Black from Winsor & Newton, applying four layers of color, including an underpainting, to achieve a greater range of tonal variation and color temperature.

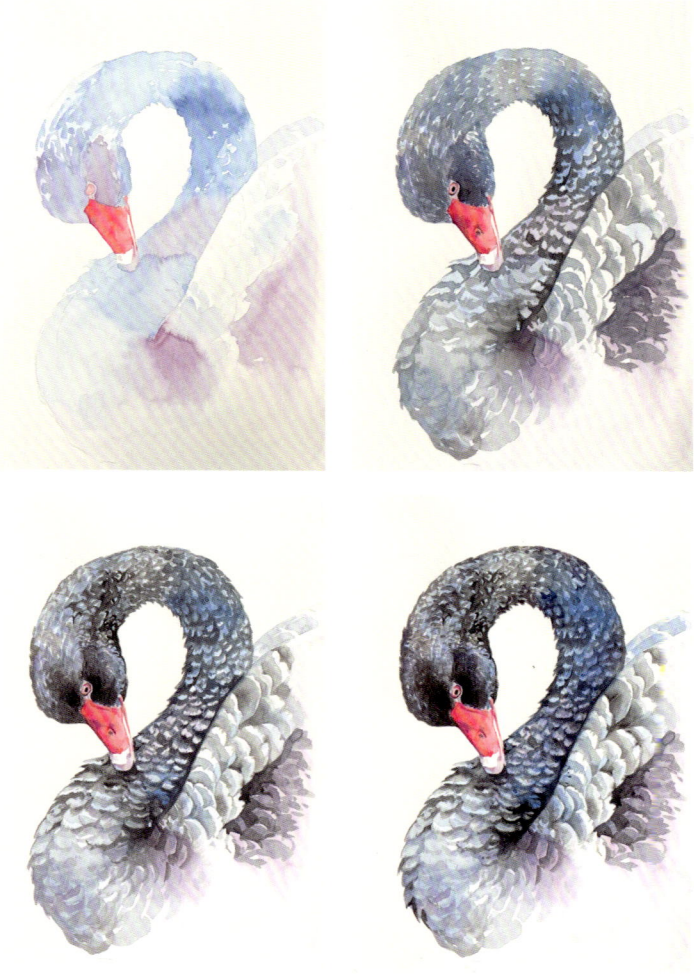

Black Swan in Four Steps

- First, I painted the beak and applied a light underpainting over the feathers, using Phthalo Blue Green Shade (PB15:3) and Dioxazine Purple (PV23). This underlying layer is important to counteract the overpowering nature of subsequent layers of pure black.
- Once the first layer was dry, I applied my first wash of Lamp Black (PBk6/7) to map out the feathers. My strokes were short and quick, to mimic the texture.
- Varying my stroke thickness, direction, and length became even more important in the next layer. I applied more saturated black, often mixing it with blue to soften the overall tone. I used longer curved strokes on the wings, leaving numerous dry spots to capture the highlights.
- To finish the painting, I introduced saturated black accents around the eye and along the neck. I also applied another glaze of blue and purple over those areas where I wanted more contrast and visual interest.

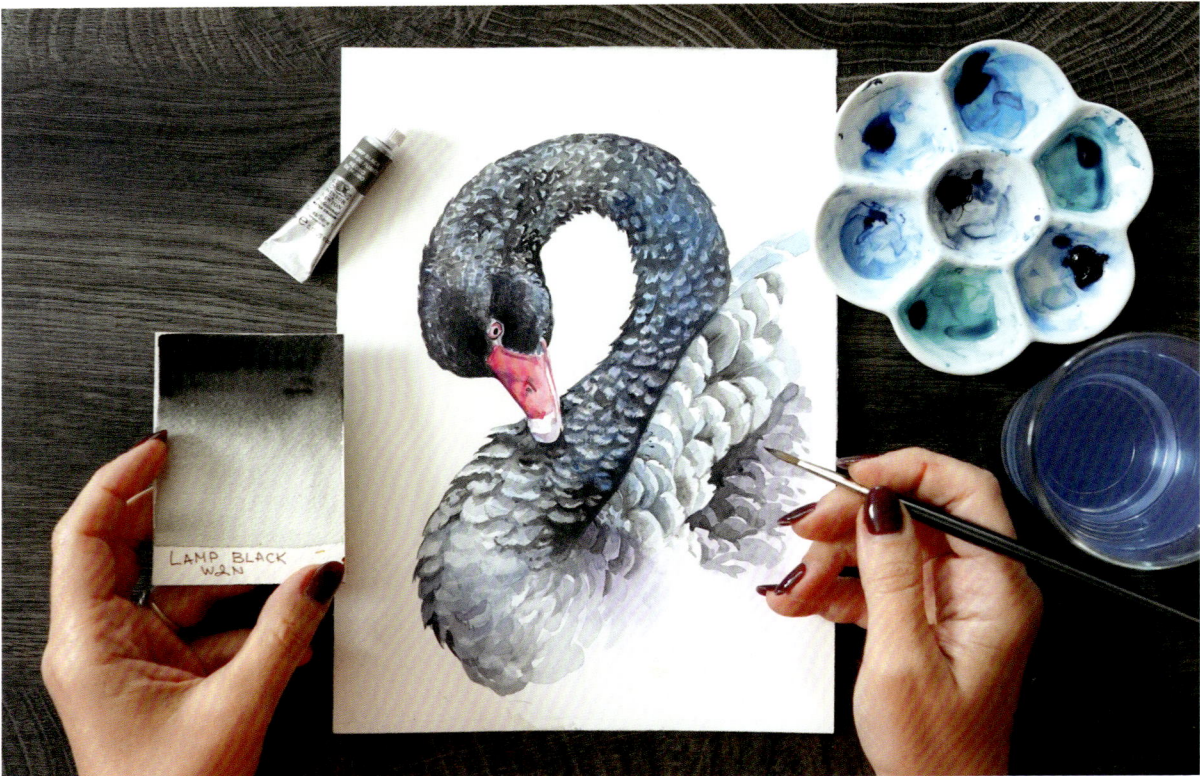

Black Swan in Progress

9.10 Painting Pure-White Subjects

How do you paint a pure-white bird or a white flower on white paper? It may seem tricky at first, especially considering that traditional watercolor techniques more or less prohibit the use of white paint. In addition, we don't have the luxury of erasing our color washes or painting over dark areas due to the natural transparency of watercolor. Luckily, there is a straightforward method that makes it a lot simpler to achieve realistic results. It involves identifying areas of light in your reference image and painting only the shadows with very diluted pigment mixtures. It may take time to get used to, but the results are so rewarding! In fact, I love the challenge of capturing white, often incorporating white flowers into my botanical compositions to accentuate the glowing nature of the watercolor medium. In this section, I will provide an overview of three of my favorite techniques for painting white subjects, using a white peony as an example.

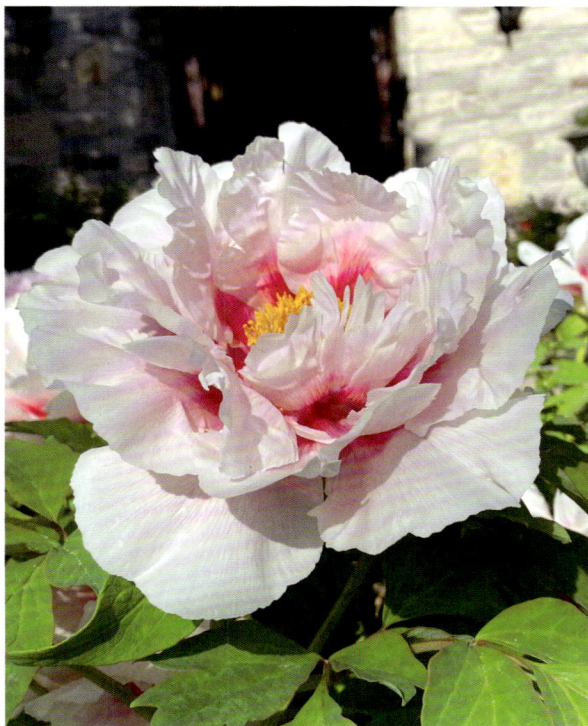

White Peony Reference Photo

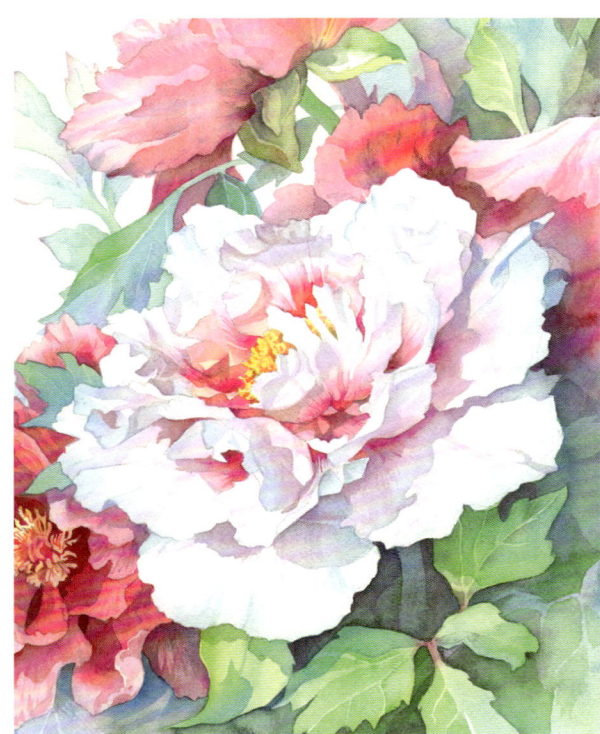

White Peony Watercolor Study

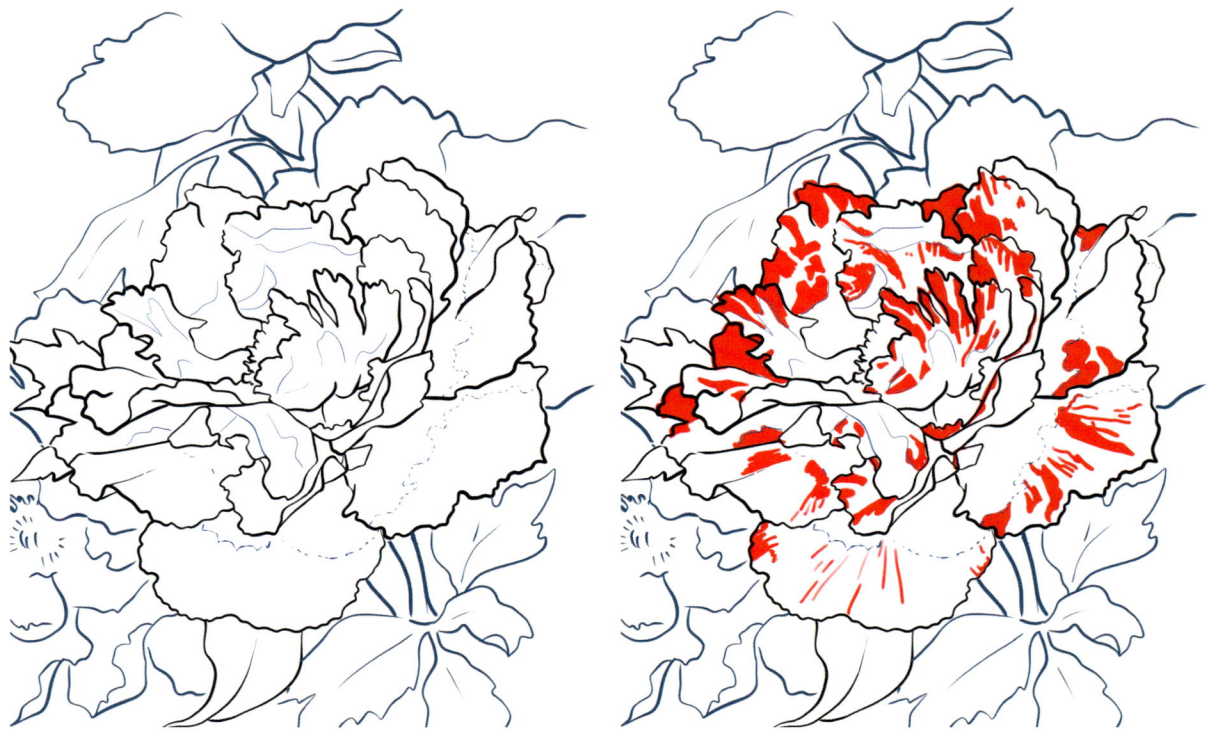

White Peony Black-and-White Outline (Major Shadows Identified in Blue)

White Peony Black-and-White Outline (Major Highlights Identified in Red)

Tip #1: Find the Shadows

The first and the most important tip is to identify the shadows and visually separate them from "true white" areas—the highlights that are positioned directly in the sun. I recommend outlining these areas in your initial sketch, so you can easily find them with your brush. In this peony study, I identified several large shadows in my sketch. I clearly marked them up so I could find and paint: 1) the larger shadows cast by the top petals on the bottom petals, and 2) some of the smaller shadow segments arising from the natural folds on the top petals. Note that the rest of the flower also has some color due to the natural translucency of the petals. These areas will be slightly darker than pure highlights (marked in red on the diagram above), but lighter compared to the true cast shadows (marked in blue on the diagram above).

Tip #2: Avoid Gray!

The second important aspect of painting white is to use realistic shadow colors instead of resorting to lifeless grays. Contrary to popular belief, shadows are not just gray; instead, they are influenced by the colors of the surrounding environment and the qualities of the light source. Shadows can vary in temperature, with cooler shadows often found in areas illuminated by natural light, and warmer shadows in areas affected by artificial light or reflected light. To capture these accurately, I typically start with cooler pigments that are closer to blue on the spectrum, and then add subtle variations in color temperature. For the *White Peony* study, I used a combination of warmer Dioxazine Purple (PV23) and Quinacridone Violet (PV55) in the center, and cooler Phthalo Blue Green Shade (PB15:3) and Aqua Green (Phthalo) around the edges.

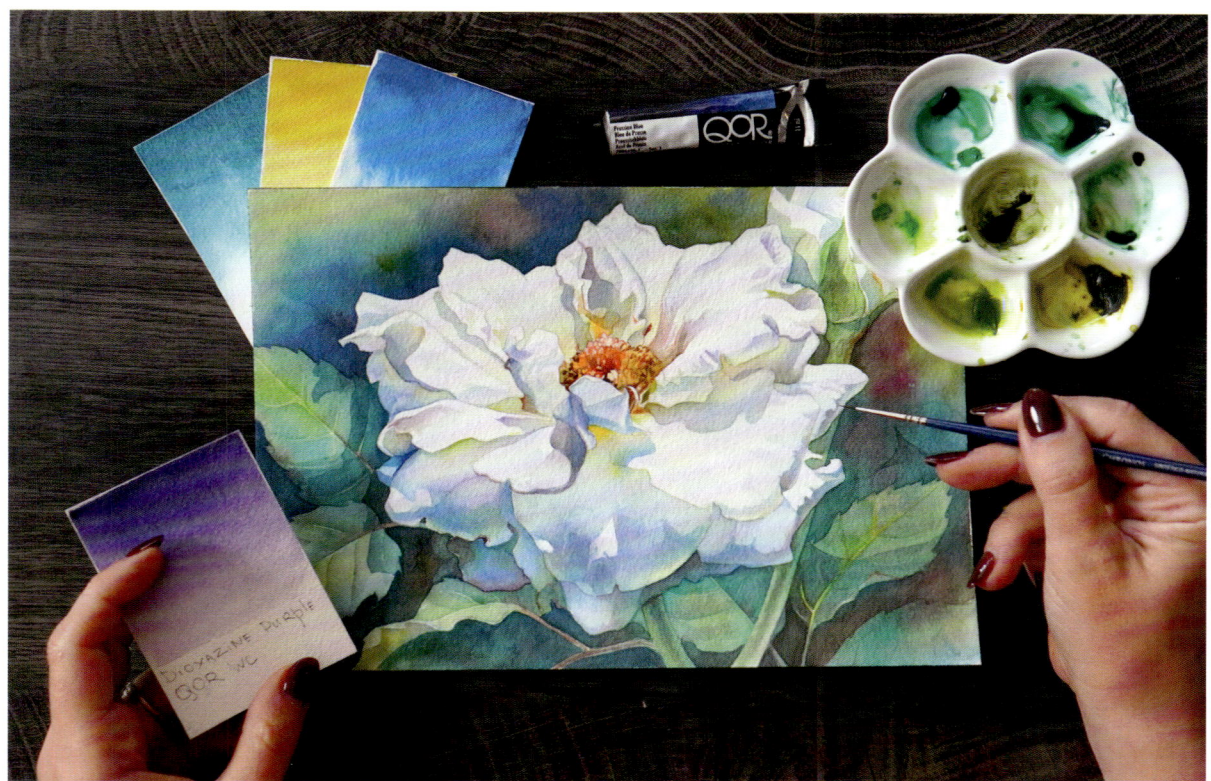

White Rose Study

Tip #3: Add a Background

The last and probably most obvious tip is to put a background behind your white subject. In my experience, this approach works better than painting an outline around the white segments by creating a more realistic sense of depth. Your background technique can include a solid wash, an abstract splash color, or a colorful object. In the White Rose case study above, the green leaves and surrounding dark background helped me frame the white petals in the center.

Video Available ▶ rockynook.com/watercolor-secrets

9.11 Why I Avoid White Pigments (and What to Do Instead)

You may have heard that the use of white pigment is generally discouraged in traditional watercolor painting. I mostly agree with this recommendation. In my experience, by adding pure white you risk creating a chalky, opaque layer that can overpower the delicate transparency of the medium. In this section, I'll explain why it's not advisable to use pure white pigments and how you can rely on the white of your paper and translucent watercolor layers to paint white objects.

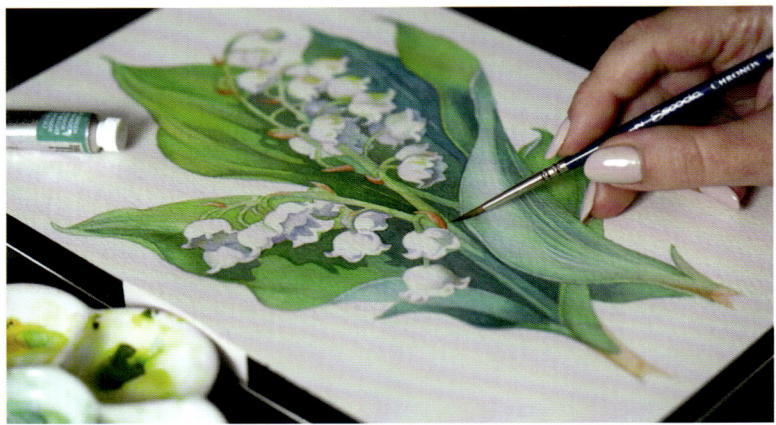

Lily of the Valley in Progress

Reasons to Skip the White

- **Loss of Transparency:** White pigment, being opaque, covers the underlying layers of paint and diminishes the inherent transparency of watercolors. This can lead to a loss of depth and luminosity by reducing the amount of light that reflects off the white paper surface.
- **Chalky Appearance:** White pigment can create a chalky or dull appearance, lacking the luminosity and freshness that are hallmarks of watercolor paintings.
- **Difficulty in Layering:** Watercolor relies heavily on layering to build up depth and complexity. The opacity of white pigment makes it challenging to layer colors effectively without muddying the painting.

Alternative Approaches

My favorite way to capture white is to use negative painting technique or masking fluid. The first method involves painting around the white areas and relying on subtle shadows to build three-dimensional form. Masking fluid can also be used to preserve particularly small details that are tricky to paint around. In both cases, I rely on the white of the paper itself to serve as the lightest value in my painting. For more information on the negative painting technique, see page 116. My favorite masking fluid and the way I apply it is shown on pages 86–87.

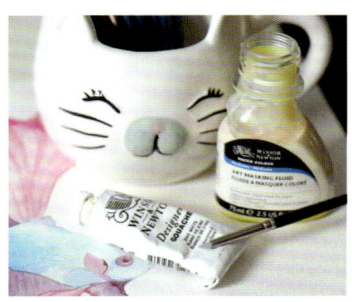

Art Masking Fluid and Zinc White Designers Gouache from Winsor & Newton

Notable Exceptions

The recommendation to avoid using pure-white pigment is based on preserving the inherent transparency and luminosity of the watercolor medium. So why do some watercolor sets include white paint? Exceptions to this rule do exist, particularly in cases where artists strategically break these conventions to achieve specific effects. For example, when painting frothy waves crashing against rocks, you may use white pigment sparingly to capture the foam, enhancing the sense of movement and energy in the scene. In addition, white color may be appropriate when making corrections, such as fixing an uneven edge or covering an accidental splash of paint.

Using White Gouache

Note that regardless of the brand, white watercolor will never look fully opaque, so it is ineffective even in these limited scenarios. Many artists prefer to use white gouache instead. Gouache is a water-soluble medium that can be easily integrated into your watercolor work. However, it is much more opaque and provides better coverage overall. My favorite white gouache is Zinc White Designer's Gouache from Winsor & Newton. Remember to always exercise restraint and use white pigment sparingly, being mindful of its potential to overpower the delicate beauty of watercolor.

Case Study: Lily of the Valley

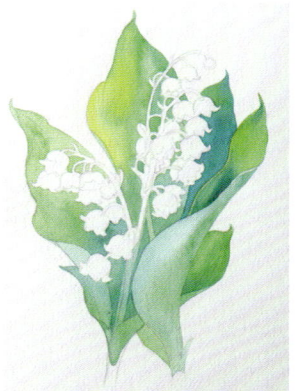 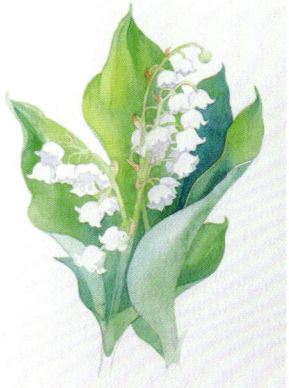 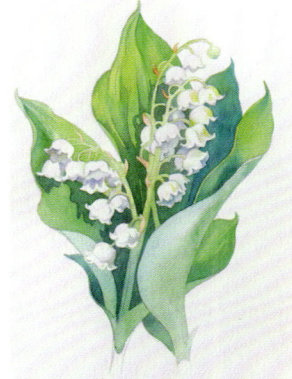 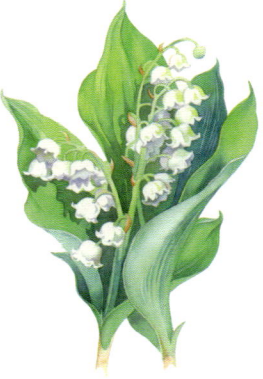

Lily of the Valley in Four Steps

Instead of using white pigment in this lily of the valley bouquet, I applied the negative painting technique. First, I painted the green leaves that surround the white flowers, carefully working around the tiny buds to leave them completely dry. My main pigment is Hooker's Green (PG36, PY3, PY150, PO48), and I used other convenience greens to add dimension by playing with color temperature. I used a cooler Aqua Green (Phthalo) from Windsor & Newton for the shadows, while a warmer Green Gold (PY150, PY3, PG36) from Daniel Smith helped me to create highlights on the leaves facing toward the light. I then applied a mix of Dioxazine Purple (PV23) and Aqua Green (Phthalo) to create subtle shadows inside each flower bud. For illustration purposes only, I applied a few strokes of white gouache to create lighter veins on the leaves. Notice that these accents look less natural and even "heavy" compared to the rest of the luminous washes.

Video Available ▶ rockynook.com/watercolor-secrets

9.12 A Simple Trick for Better Tonal Values

Creating value studies allows you to focus solely on tonal values without the distraction of color. By simplifying the scene into basic light and dark shapes, you can quickly identify areas of interest and develop a solid foundation for your final artwork. In this section, we'll explore the significance of value studies in watercolor painting and why they are essential, particularly for mastering tonal values, and especially when tackling complex subjects.

Understanding Form and Volume

Value studies help artists understand how light interacts with form and volume, allowing us to depict the three-dimensional aspects more accurately. I find this exercise particularly useful in my botanical work, where vibrant splashes of color on the petals can often obscure the overall form. By analyzing and replicating the range of light and dark values using one color, you will learn to create convincing illusions of depth and dimension in your flower studies.

Creating Depth and Atmosphere

Value studies allow artists to establish a sense of depth and atmosphere in their compositions. By manipulating values, artists can push elements forward or recede them into the background, creating a dynamic spatial relationship that enhances the overall visual impact of the painting. I find this aspect of value studies especially applicable in landscapes and still life, where capturing the hierarchy of visual planes is particularly essential.

Improving Composition

Even in the more decorative work, I find that value studies help me refine my compositions by identifying areas of contrast and focal points. By simplifying complex scenes into their basic tonal values, you will be able to better understand the underlying structure and balance of your composition, leading to more effective and impactful paintings.

Developing a Unified Palette

Lastly, value studies are very effective for developing a unified palette by removing the color "noise" often present in reference photos. I find that seeing my subjects in black and white helps me focus on the most important color groups, skip the nonessential pigments, and create more cohesive and harmonious artwork overall.

Grayscale Conversion (My Favorite Method)

A more traditional approach to value studies involves painting a quick study of your future composition using only one color, such as blue or gray. Although I enjoy this method occasionally, I also find it very time-consuming. A simpler approach involves converting the reference photo into grayscale with image-editing software. This can be done on your phone or computer to allow you to instantly visualize the tonal values present in the scene without the need for painting. As an additional practice, I often convert existing watercolor photographs into black and white to better understand the nuances of light and shadow. This allows me to analyze the tonal values present in my work and identify areas for improvement.

Case Study: Gladiolus

By comparing a grayscale image of the gladiolus flower to the original photograph, I was able to identify areas of contrast within a very complex and vibrant reference. Specifically, I was able to observe even the most subtle value shifts within the petal shadows, guiding my layering process more effectively. After I completed the first study, I converted the image to black and white again.

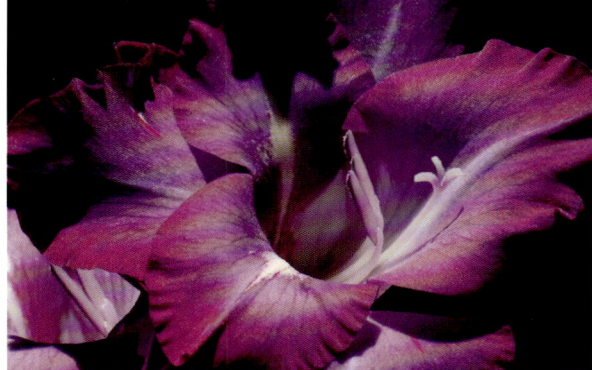

Gladiolus Reference Image (Full Color)

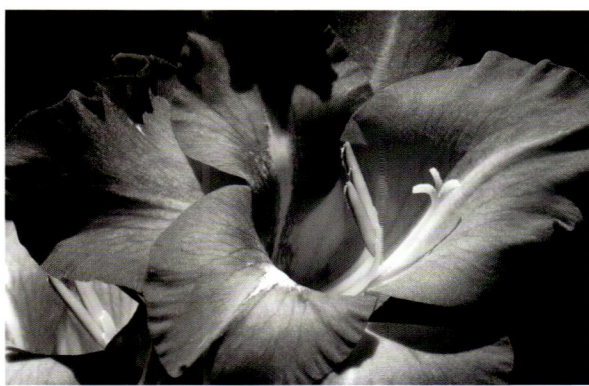

Gladiolus Reference Image (Grayscale)

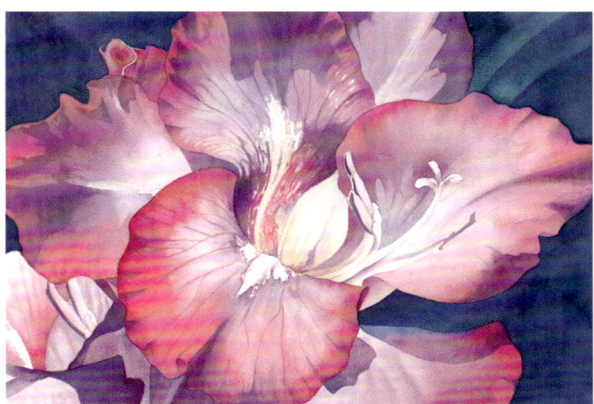

Gladiolus Watercolor – Version 1

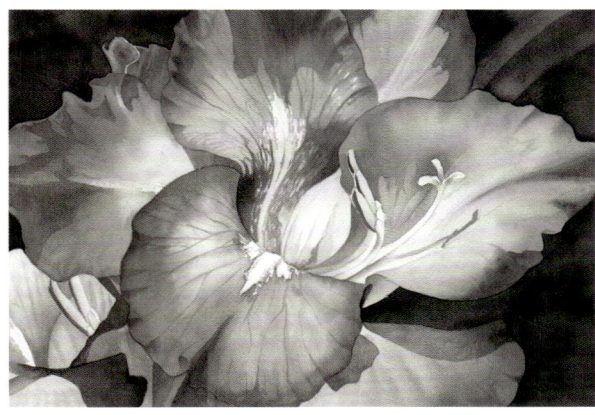

Gladiolus Watercolor – Version 1 (Grayscale)

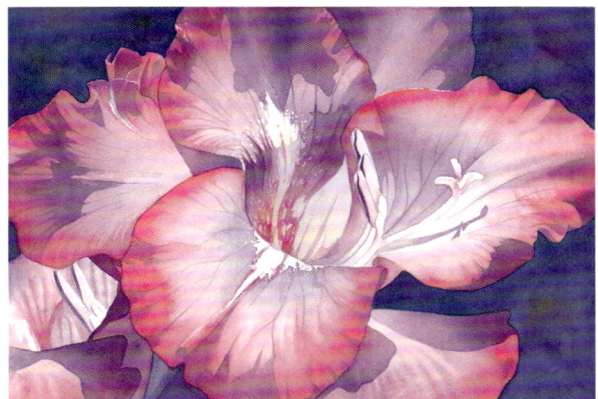

Gladiolus Watercolor – Version 2

By studying the grayscale representation of my first study, I was able to gain valuable insights into the effectiveness of my initial value choices and discover opportunities for refinement in the final artwork. Specifically, I no longer used warm reds in the second version.

9.13 Tips for Digitizing Your Watercolor Artwork

In this section, I'll guide you through the process of digitizing your watercolor artwork for display on social media and for further digital manipulation. By following these tips and techniques, you'll be able to showcase your artwork with clarity and precision, while maintaining the integrity and beauty of your original watercolor paintings.

Scanning

Before scanning your artwork, it's important to remove any speckles of dust that may be present on the surface. Choose a high-quality flatbed scanner that can provide a resolution of at least 300 DPI (dots per inch) or higher to capture fine details and colors accurately. The term DPI refers to the resolution of the scanned image, with higher DPI resulting in higher quality but larger file sizes. My favorite scanner is the Epson Perfection V550, which delivers exceptional results for watercolor artwork.

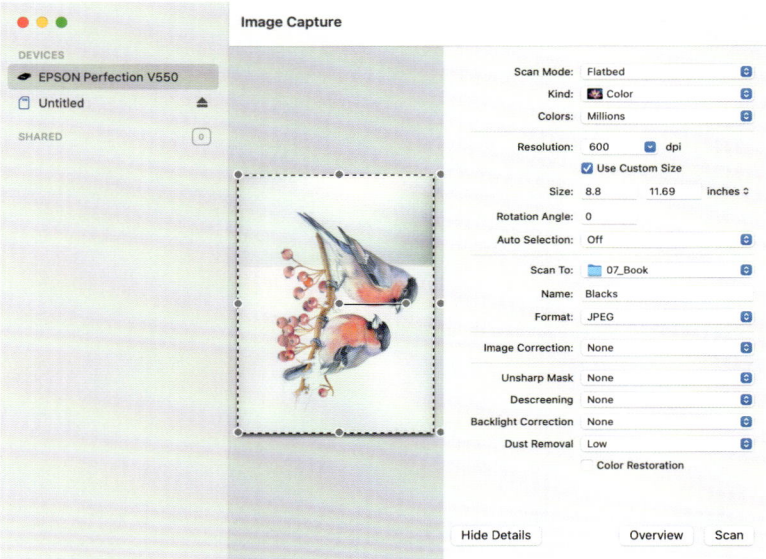

Epson Scan Window with Settings

Digitizing Extra-Large Images

For larger watercolor paintings that cannot fit on a single scanner bed, scanning in sections is the way to go. Once every section is scanned, use an application like Adobe Bridge to merge the sections seamlessly using the Photomerge function. This powerful feature automatically aligns and blends the sections together, creating a cohesive image without any visible seams. After merging, save the image as a JPG for further cleanup and manipulation. JPG, also known as JPEG, stands for Joint Photographic Experts Group. It is a widely used image format that strikes a balance between file size and image quality, making it a versatile and widely supported choice for a variety of digital imaging needs.

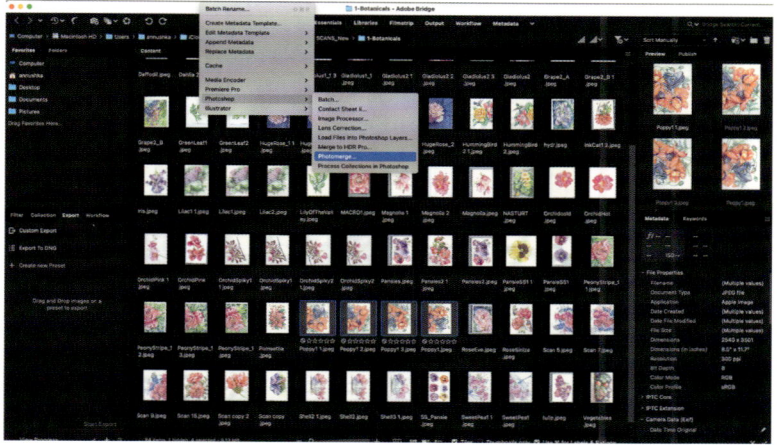

Highlight your scanned image selections in Adobe Bridge and left-click (PC) or control+click (Mac) on one of the images, then select Photoshop > Photomerge.

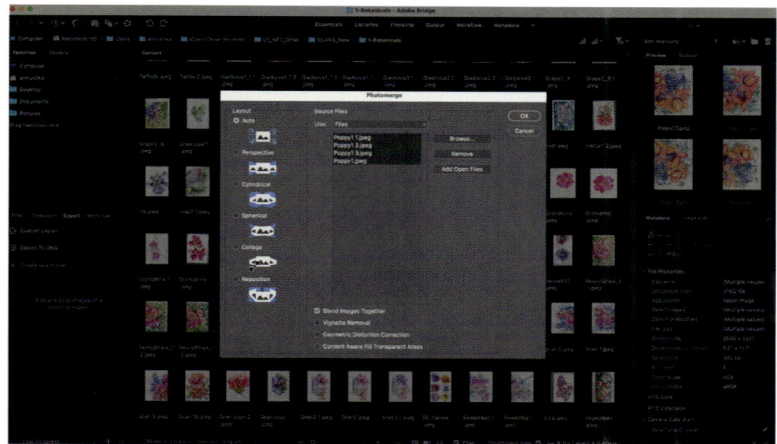

Select the "Blend Images Together" checkbox in the Photomerge window, then click OK.

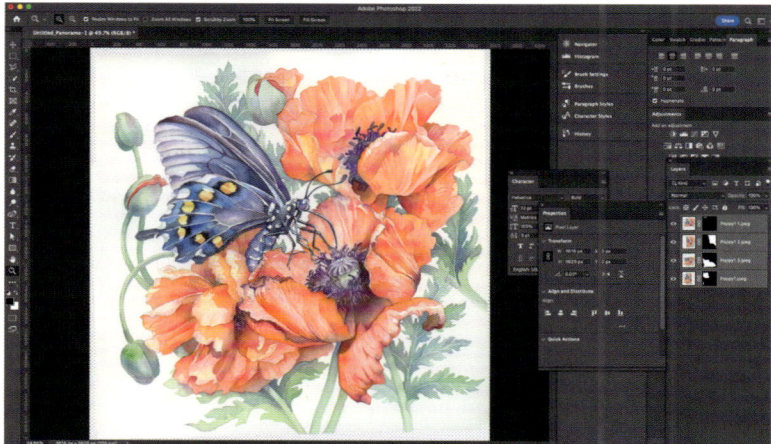

Adjust the composite image in Adobe Photoshop.

Removing the White Background

There are many methods for removing the white background from your scanned watercolor artwork, but I prefer a manual approach for the best results. Bring the JPG file into an app like Procreate and use a stylus to carefully erase the white background. This process ensures that the transparency of the watercolor paper and any textured details are preserved, resulting in a clean and polished final image. Save the edited artwork in a PNG format, which retains the transparency of the background and allows you to apply the artwork to any surface seamlessly.

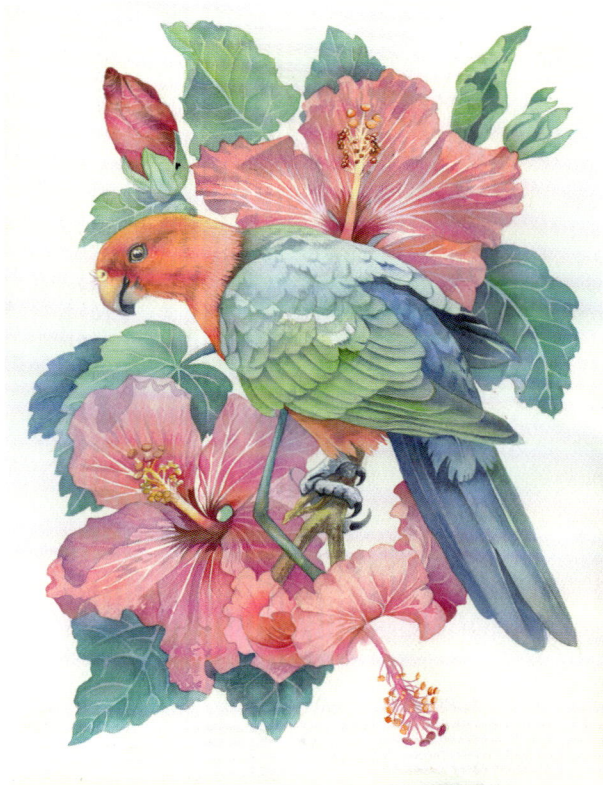

King Parrot after Scanning with Background

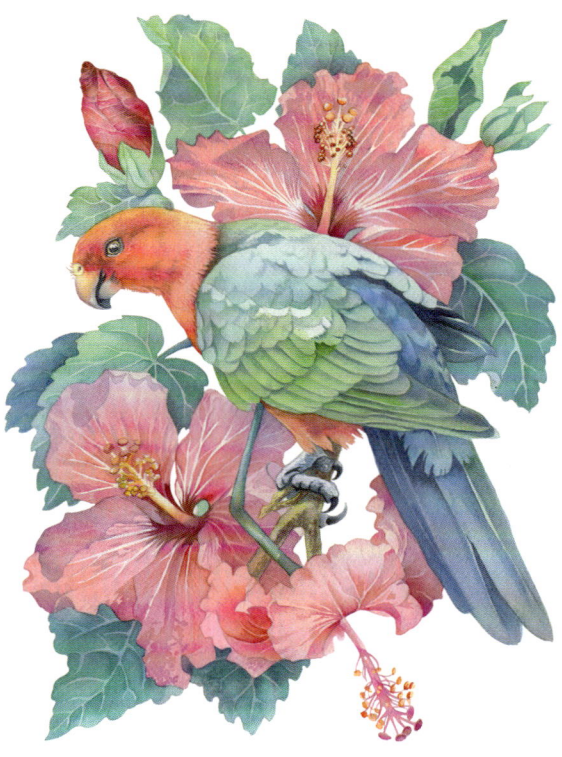

King Parrot After Scanning and Removing the Background

Color Correction

After scanning and cleaning up your artwork, the final step is to ensure that the colors are accurately represented. I use Adobe Photoshop for this purpose, employing Adjustment Layers to fine-tune the colors and enhance the overall appearance of the artwork. Adjustment Layers in Photoshop provide a nondestructive way to make these adjustments, allowing you to fine-tune the colors and appearance of the artwork while preserving the original image data.

- One of the first adjustments I make is to adjust the Levels of the image. This allows me to control the brightness, contrast, and tonal range of the artwork. By adjusting the black and white points, I can enhance the overall tonal balance and bring out the details in the painting.
- Additionally, I often use Adjustment Layers to adjust the Vibrance of the image. Vibrance controls the saturation of the less-saturated colors in the image, while protecting skin tones and preventing oversaturation. By increasing the Vibrance, I can make the colors in the artwork appear more vibrant and lively without causing any unwanted color shifts.

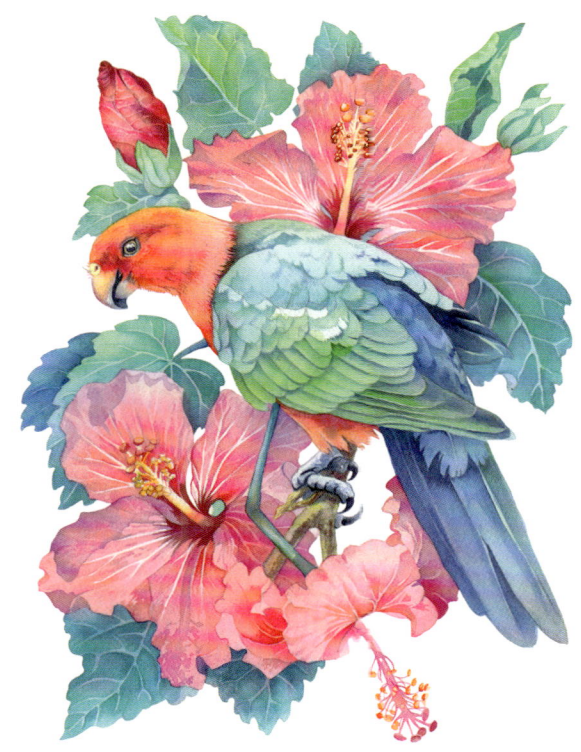

King Parrot After Color Correction

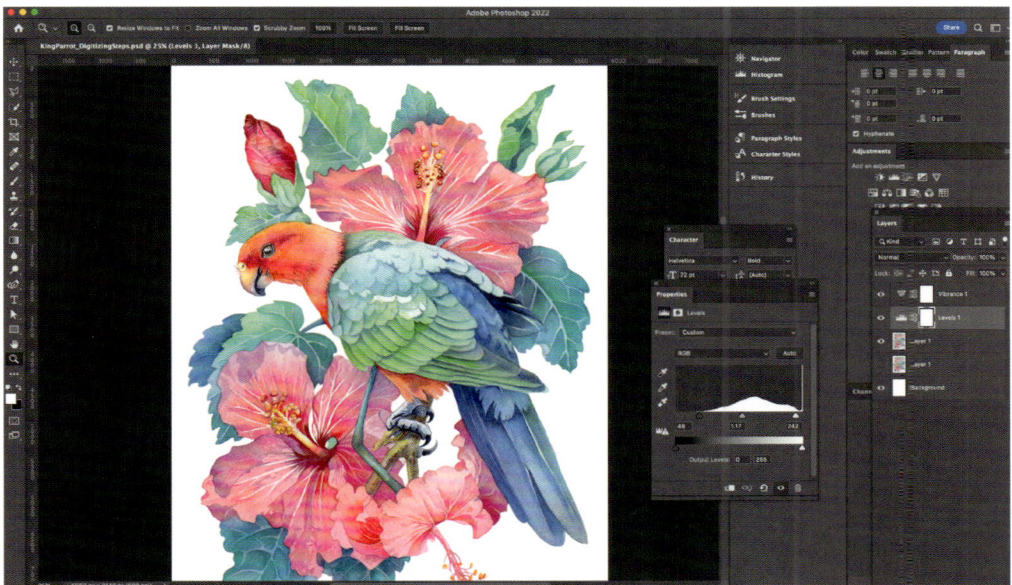

King Parrot Adjustments in Photoshop

10

Unveiling Your Potential: Strategies for Growth in Watercolor Painting

10.1 Introduction

In the final chapter of the book, I want to share with you the key strategies that have been instrumental in my growth as a watercolor artist. These tips are based on my own experiences and may not necessarily apply to everyone, but I hope they resonate with many beginners who are eager to improve and develop their skills in this beautiful medium.

Incorporating these strategies into your practice can help you unlock your full potential as a watercolor artist, allowing you to express yourself creatively and develop your unique artistic voice. Remember to paint what brings you joy, embrace the journey of growth, and never stop exploring and experimenting with this beautiful and versatile medium.

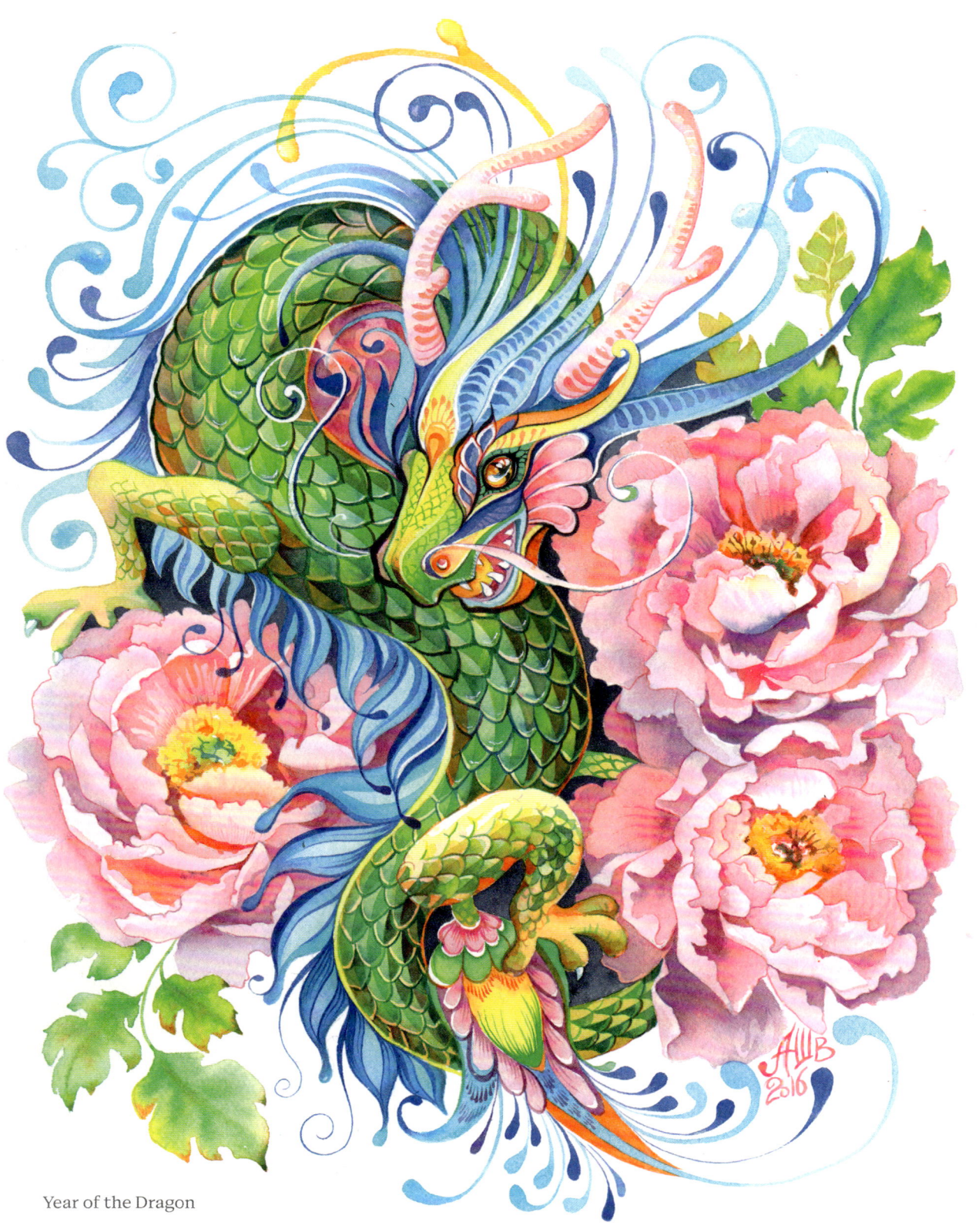

Year of the Dragon

10.2 Practice in Series

In the pursuit of mastering watercolor, consistency is key. Yet, maintaining a regular practice can be challenging, especially in the early stages when you may feel uncertain about your skills, style, or subject matter. I found that focusing on a theme, rather than producing isolated works, has significantly accelerated my progress and kept my creative flame burning bright. I highly recommend working within a series as a structured framework for your growth and discovery.

Continuous Skill Development

By committing to a series of paintings, you are compelled to confront and conquer new challenges with each piece. Whether it's refining your brushwork, experimenting with color mixing, or mastering complex techniques, each painting in the series becomes a stepping stone toward greater proficiency. Through this iterative process, you not only hone your technical skills but also cultivate a deeper understanding of the watercolor medium.

Subject-Matter Exploration

Working within a series allows for in-depth exploration of a theme, subject, or concept. Rather than flitting from one random reference to another, painting in series encourages sustained engagement with a particular motif and related techniques. Whether it's exploring the intricacies of floral subjects, capturing the essence of tropical seascapes, or depicting the beauty of everyday objects, painting in series will keep you engaged and focused on your watercolor journey.

Overcoming Creative Block

Creative block is a common hurdle that we all encounter from time to time. I found that painting in series can be a very powerful antidote to this kind of creative stagnation. By committing to a cohesive body of work, you create a sense of momentum and direction that helps to propel you forward, even when inspiration feels elusive.

Guiding Questions

- **Four Seasons:** How would you envision capturing the essence of each season through your artwork? Are there particular color palettes or motifs that you associate with each season, and how might you incorporate them into your paintings?
- **Local Birds:** Can you create a series featuring local bird species native to your region? Consider exploring their habitats, behaviors, and unique characteristics.
- **Magical Creatures:** Can you unleash your imagination and create a series of paintings featuring magical creatures such as dragons, unicorns, or fairies?
- **Historic Landmarks:** Are there iconic historic landmarks or architectural wonders in your local area or around the world that inspire you? Consider creating a series of paintings capturing the beauty and significance of these landmarks.

Case Study: The Flower Alphabet

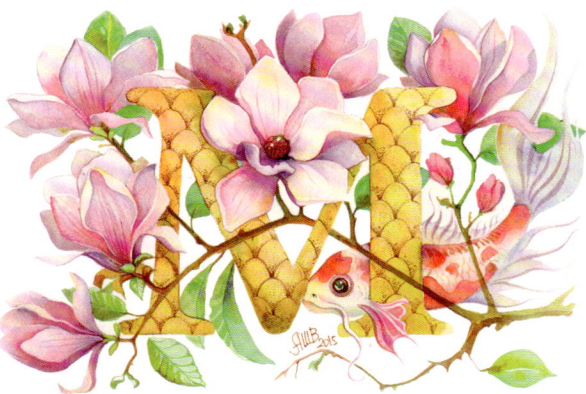

M for Magnolia

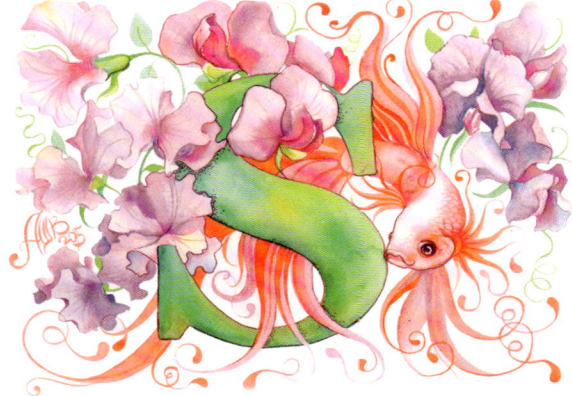

S for Sweet Peas

One of my earliest watercolor series centered around the English alphabet. Being interested in botanical art, I decided to select a flower for every letter and practice different watercolor techniques on small sheets of paper, gradually introducing new pigments as my confidence grew with each painting. The structure and discipline of working within a series provided a sense of purpose and clarity, making it easier to maintain continuous practice for months at a time. In retrospect, it's fascinating to see the evolution of my style as I progressed from basic application of watercolor and ink to more complex glazing techniques and multidimensional blooms.

Case Study: 12 Signs of the Chinese Zodiac

Next, I embarked on a more ambitious project depicting the twelve signs of the Chinese zodiac. This project presented a unique set of challenges and opportunities for experimentation, pushing me to expand my technical skills and creative boundaries. I painted on a much larger scale, tackling new subjects like animals and birds. Based on my experience painting the Flower Alphabet, I was able to delve deeper into the nuances of botanical art as well. This project spanned three years, during which I even revisited and repainted several animals, reflecting my growing confidence in my style and understanding of watercolor techniques. By the end of this series, I emerged not only with a collection of paintings, but also with a profound sense of accomplishment and growth.

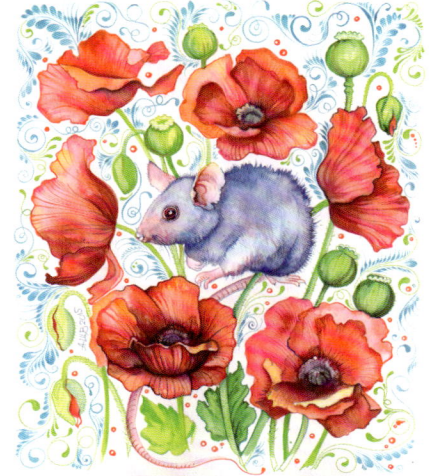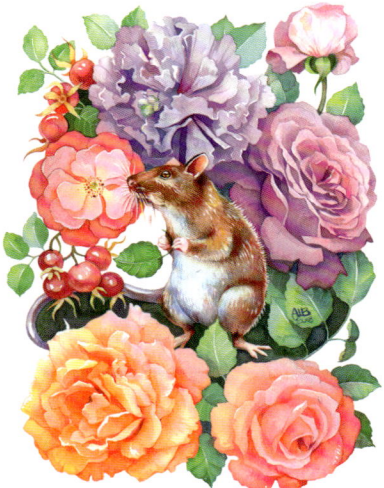

Year of the Rat painted in 2015 versus Year of the Rat painted in 2018

10.3 Paint What You Love and Be Fearless

One of the most effective strategies that has worked for me is to paint subjects that I genuinely enjoy, without worrying about whether they are conventional or expected. I am particularly drawn to organic forms and found myself combining unexpected subjects in my compositions, such as fish and flowers. While initially this approach drew some criticism and puzzled those who saw my work, I persisted because it brought me immense joy and excite-

ment. Painting surreal and unexpected scenes allows me the freedom to explore and experiment with the medium, keeping me engaged and motivated to practice consistently.

My advice to you is to embrace the subjects that spark joy and curiosity for you, regardless of whether they conform to traditional norms. By painting fearlessly and following your passions, you'll find that your skills naturally improve as you continue to explore and push the boundaries of your creativity.

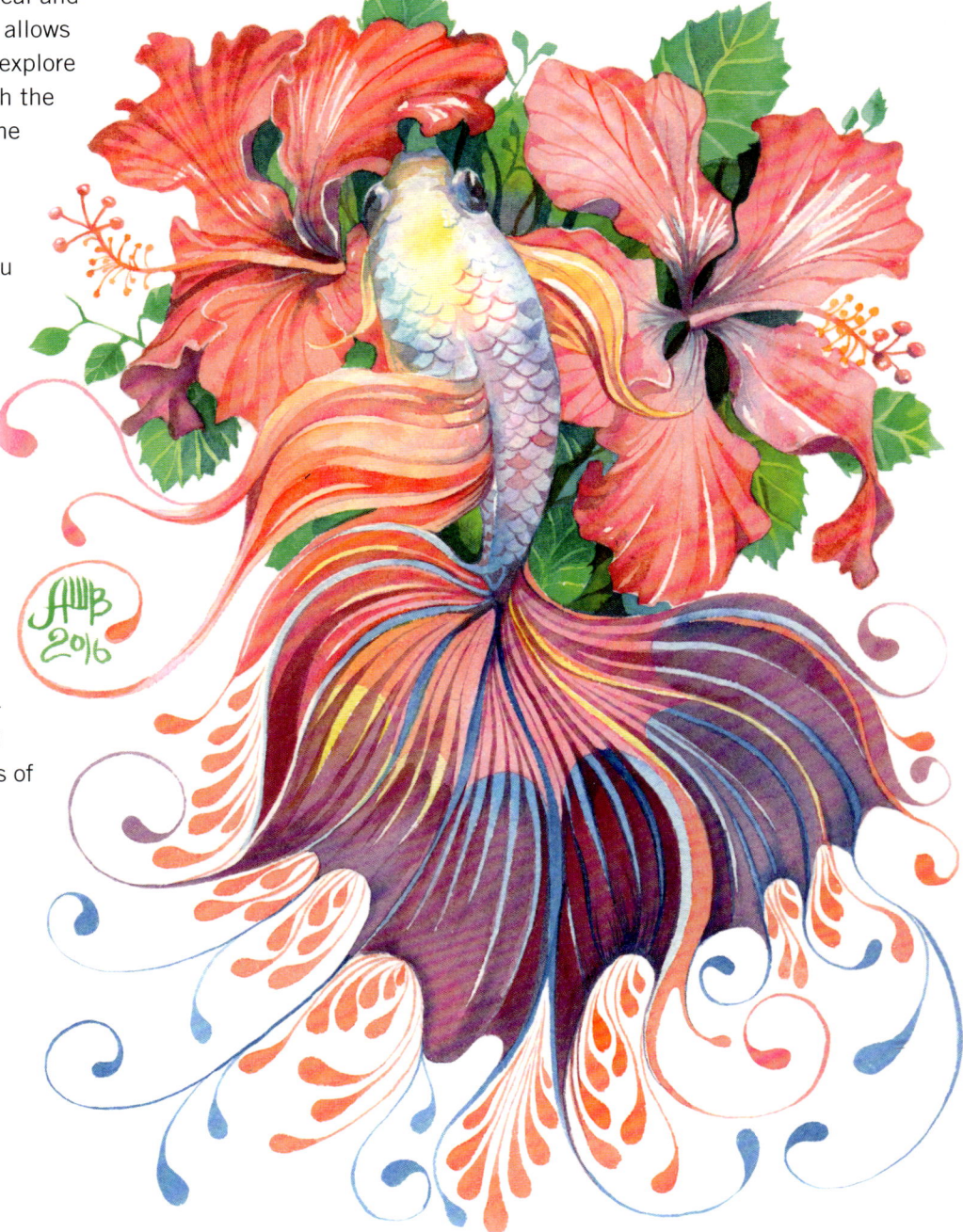

Betta Fish and Hibiscus Flowers

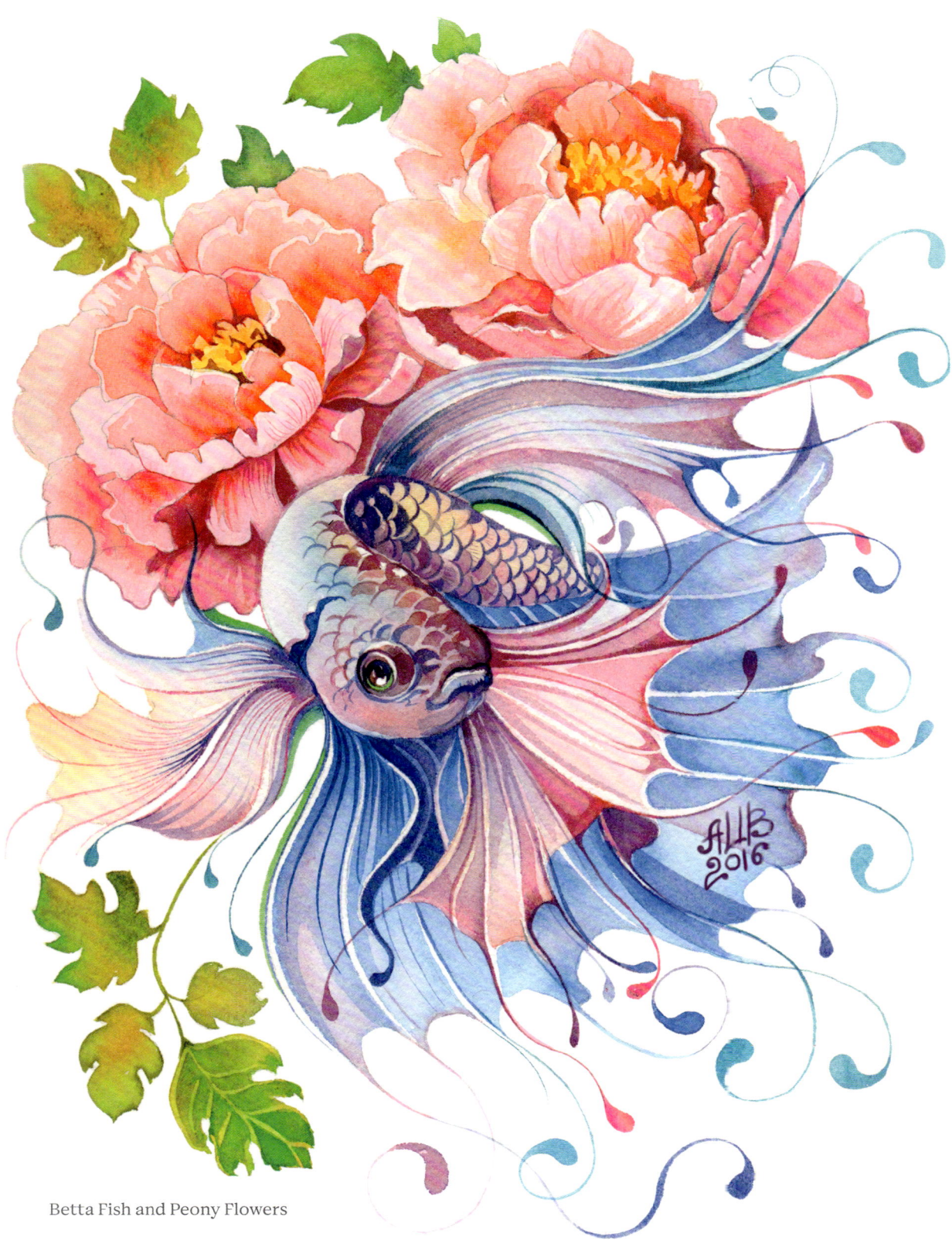

Betta Fish and Peony Flowers

10.4 Why I Paint the Same Thing Twice

Another strategy that has proved incredibly effective for my growth as a watercolor artist is to paint the same subject multiple times. The first time around is always intimidating, as I grapple with solving problems, identifying gaps in my knowledge, and navigating creative and technical challenges. During this initial phase, I allow myself the freedom to experiment, pausing to do additional research, test out new pigments and techniques, and explore different approaches. The outcome of this first attempt is not always perfect, but it serves as a valuable learning experience. The second pass is where I solidify my learnings and apply the techniques I've acquired with confidence. This repetition and patience allow the new skills to stick, and I find myself incorporating them into my regular repertoire, applying them to my next works with ease and confidence.

Case Study 1: Cockatoo and Stargazer Lilies

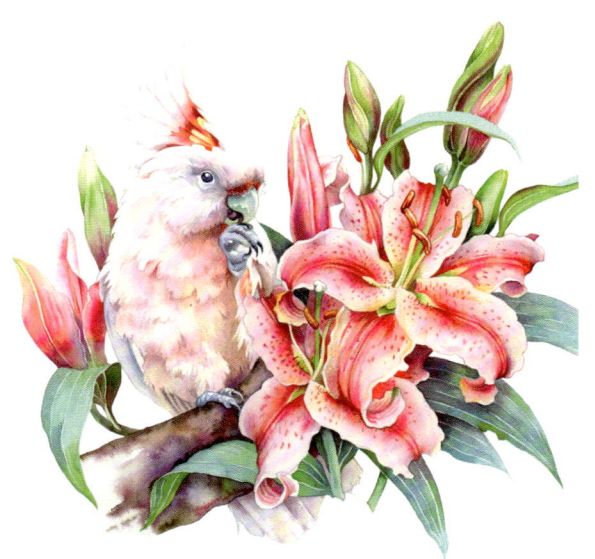 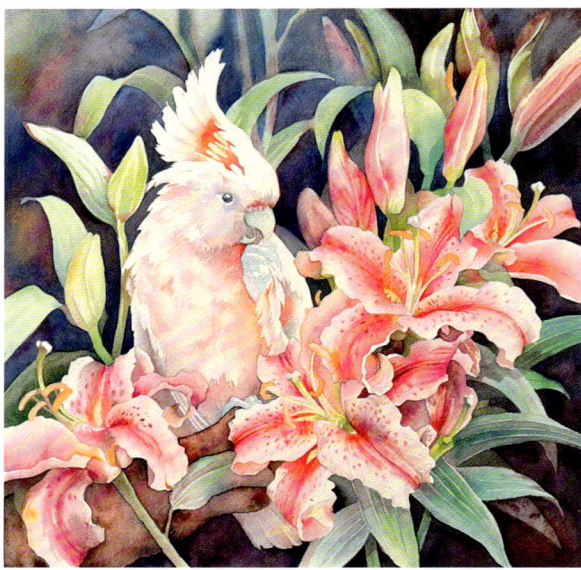

Cockatoo and Stargazer Lilies – Two Versions

- **First Iteration:** In the initial rendition of the bird, I opted for a classic composition against a clean, white background. The focus was on capturing the vibrancy of the bird and flowers. While the result was satisfactory, I felt it lacked depth.
- **Second Iteration:** Seeking to enhance contrast, I experimented with a dark-blue background in the second version. I anticipated that it would provide a striking frame for the bird, creating a visually dynamic composition. However, upon completion, I found the background to be overwhelming, overshadowing the delicate beauty of the subject. Surprisingly, I reverted to the simplicity of the first version, reaffirming the power of restraint and subtlety in watercolor painting.

Through this process, I realized the importance of restraint in composition, reaffirming the power of subtlety in watercolor painting.

Case Study 2: Mandarin Duck and Lotus Flowers

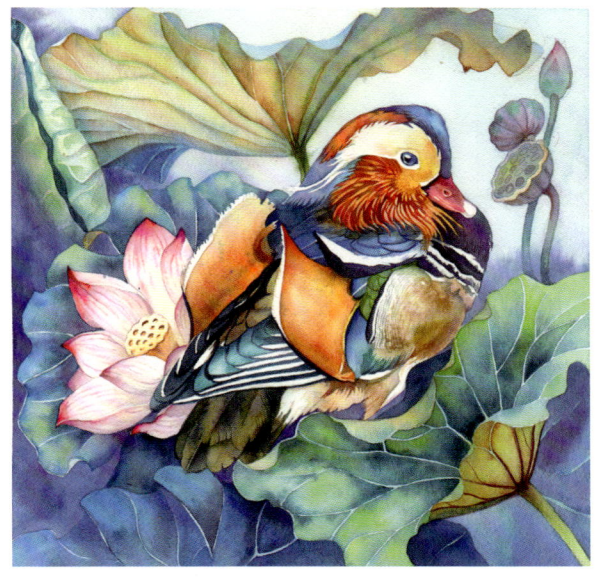 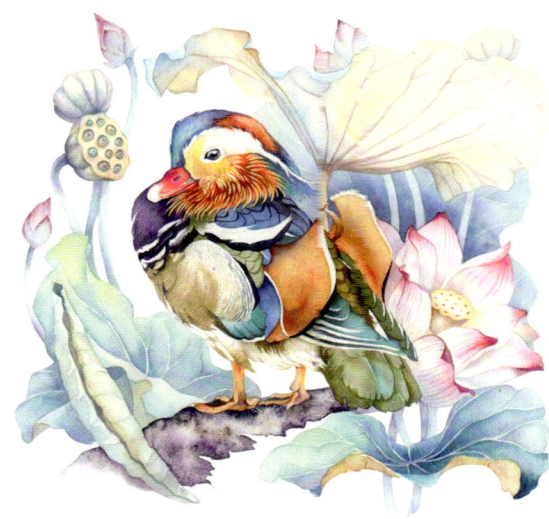

Mandarin Duck and Lotus Flower – Two Versions

- **First Iteration:** Inspired by the elegance of the Mandarin duck, I chose a dark background to accentuate its vibrant plumage.
- **Second Iteration:** In the subsequent attempt, I decided to flip the reference image, omit the background color, and adopt a softer palette for the lotus leaves. The contrast created a more dramatic focal point, highlighting the intricate details of the bird against the deep hues.

While I'm still undecided on which version I prefer, I noticed a significant improvement in painting the duck's feathers the second time around. The familiarity with the subject allowed for greater precision and confidence in execution.

HELPFUL TIP

Repetition in art isn't about producing identical copies. Instead, it's a deliberate act of exploration and refinement. You can try painting the same subject with and without the background. Or test a different arrangement of reference photos. Each iteration will offer new insights, opportunities for improvement, and avenues for creative experimentation. By painting the same subject multiple times, you deepen your understanding of its intricacies, develop technical skills, and cultivate your artistic voice.

10.5 Experiment with Your Materials

Lastly, I've found that choosing the right materials and constantly experimenting with them has been crucial for my growth as a watercolor artist. For example, upgrading to the right kind of paper, specifically 100% cotton, did wonders for my results. Cotton ensures that the techniques I apply really shine, and I no longer feel discouraged or think I'm not progressing just because I'm painting on the wrong surface. Understanding the differences between hot- and cold-pressed watercolor paper helped me improve specific techniques that worked for my style. I tend to rely on cold-pressed paper because I want to achieve smooth washes with plenty of drying time for intricate color blends. Additionally, experimenting with new pigments, especially granulating varieties, brings me tremendous joy and ensures that I'm never bored and always excited to tackle a new subject with a new set of colors. Next on my to-do list is exploring black watercolor paper and iridescent paints.

Guiding Questions

- **Paper Preferences:** Have you experimented with different types of watercolor paper, such as hot-pressed, cold-pressed, and rough? Do you know which paper texture complements your painting style best?
- **Paint Selection:** Are you familiar with the characteristics of granulating and non-granulating watercolor paints? Do you understand the difference between staining and nonstaining pigments, and how they affect layering and lifting?
- **Brush Exploration:** Do you know which brush shapes and sizes are best suited for different painting techniques? Have you tried synthetic versus natural-hair brushes, and do you have a preference based on your painting style and budget?
- **Watercolor Mediums:** Have you explored the use of masking fluid to preserve highlights in your paintings? Do you use any mediums or additives with your watercolors, such as gum arabic or ox gall, to alter their behavior on the paper?
- **Color Mixing:** Have you experimented with mixing your own colors from a limited palette to develop a deeper understanding of color theory?
- **Special Effects:** Do you incorporate salt, alcohol, or other unconventional tools into your watercolor paintings to achieve unique results?
- **Palette Organization:** Have you developed a system for organizing your watercolor palette, whether by color family, color temperature, or personal preference?
- **Mixed Media Integration:** Have you explored incorporating other media, such as ink, gouache, or colored pencil, into your watercolor paintings for added depth and complexity?

Case Study: Orchid on Hot-Pressed versus Cold-Pressed Paper

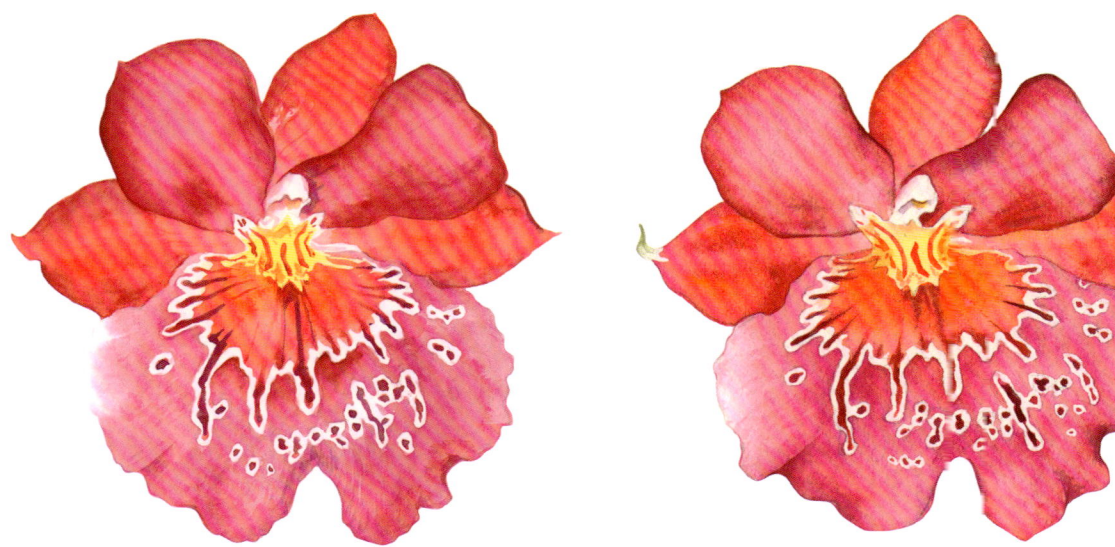

Orchid Painted on Hot-Pressed Paper   Orchid Painted on Cold-Pressed Paper

As an aspiring artist, I was eager to delve into the intricate world of watercolor painting, particularly focusing on capturing the delicate beauty of flowers. Following the common advice, I initially opted for hot-pressed paper, believing it to be the ideal surface for botanical illustration due to its smooth texture.

- **Hot-Pressed Paper Attempt:** In my first attempt at painting an orchid on hot-pressed paper, I encountered unexpected challenges. While the smooth surface allowed for precise rendering of small details, I found that the paint dried too quickly, hindering my ability to execute the multilayered techniques I desired. Despite my efforts, I struggled to achieve the depth and luminosity I envisioned for my botanical subjects.
- **Cold-Pressed Paper Experimentation:** Determined to find a solution, I decided to experiment with cold-pressed paper, despite it being less commonly recommended for botanical illustration. To my surprise, I discovered that the slight texture of the cold-pressed surface not only provided a more forgiving foundation for my wet-on-wet and glazing techniques, but also allowed the paint to remain workable for a longer duration.

Through this experimentation process, I realized that the perceived advantages of hot-pressed paper did not align with my personal artistic preferences and techniques. While hot-pressed paper may excel in capturing fine details with precision, its quick drying nature posed limitations for my style, which relied heavily on glazing. Ultimately, I made the decision to switch to cold-pressed paper for most of my water-color works, finding that it offers the perfect balance between texture and smoothness, enabling me to achieve the depth, richness, and luminosity I desire in my watercolor botanical Illustrations. This experi-ence reinforced the importance of personal experimentation and the necessity of choosing materials that align with one's artistic vision and techniques, rather than adhering strictly to conventional advice.

Index